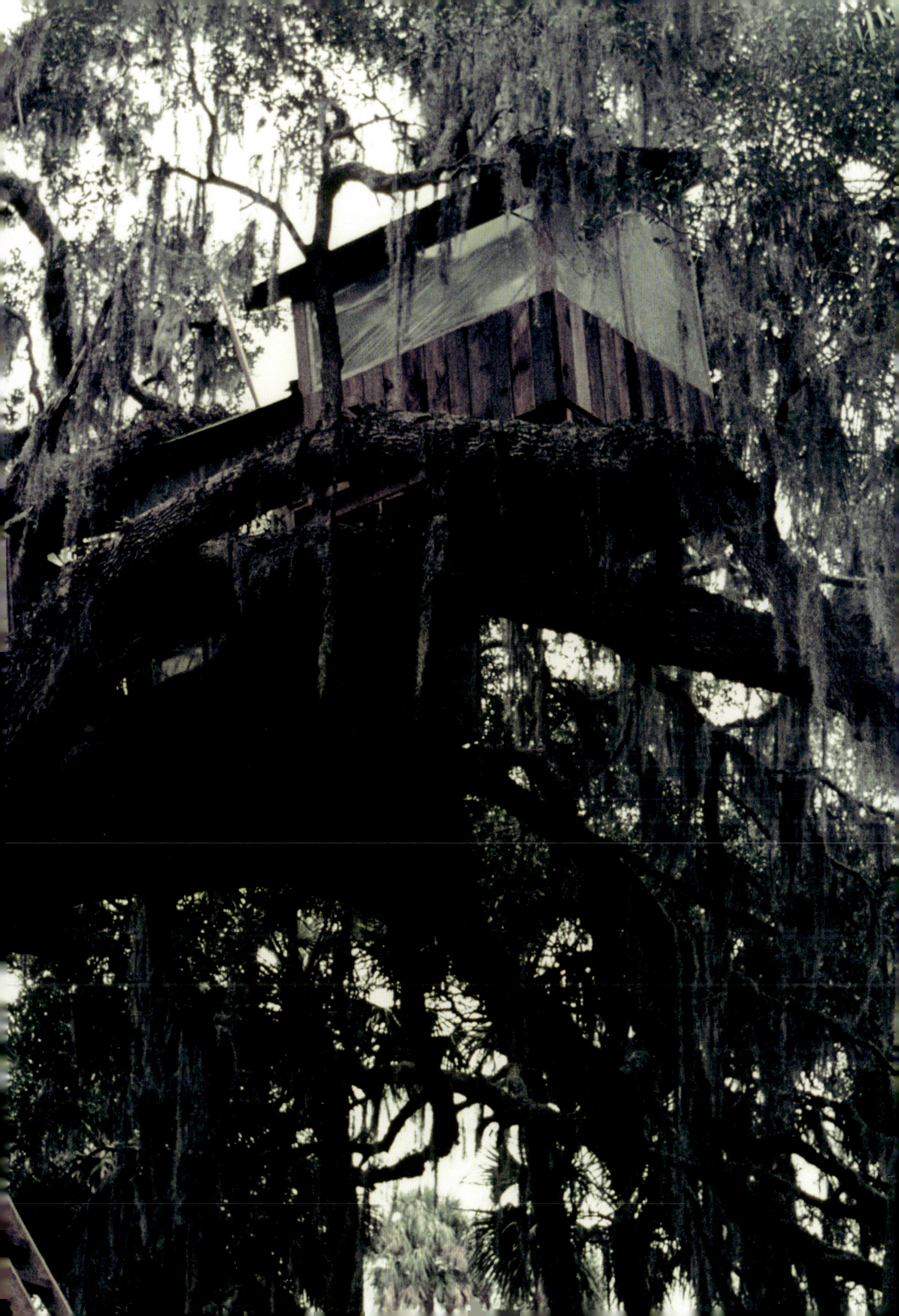

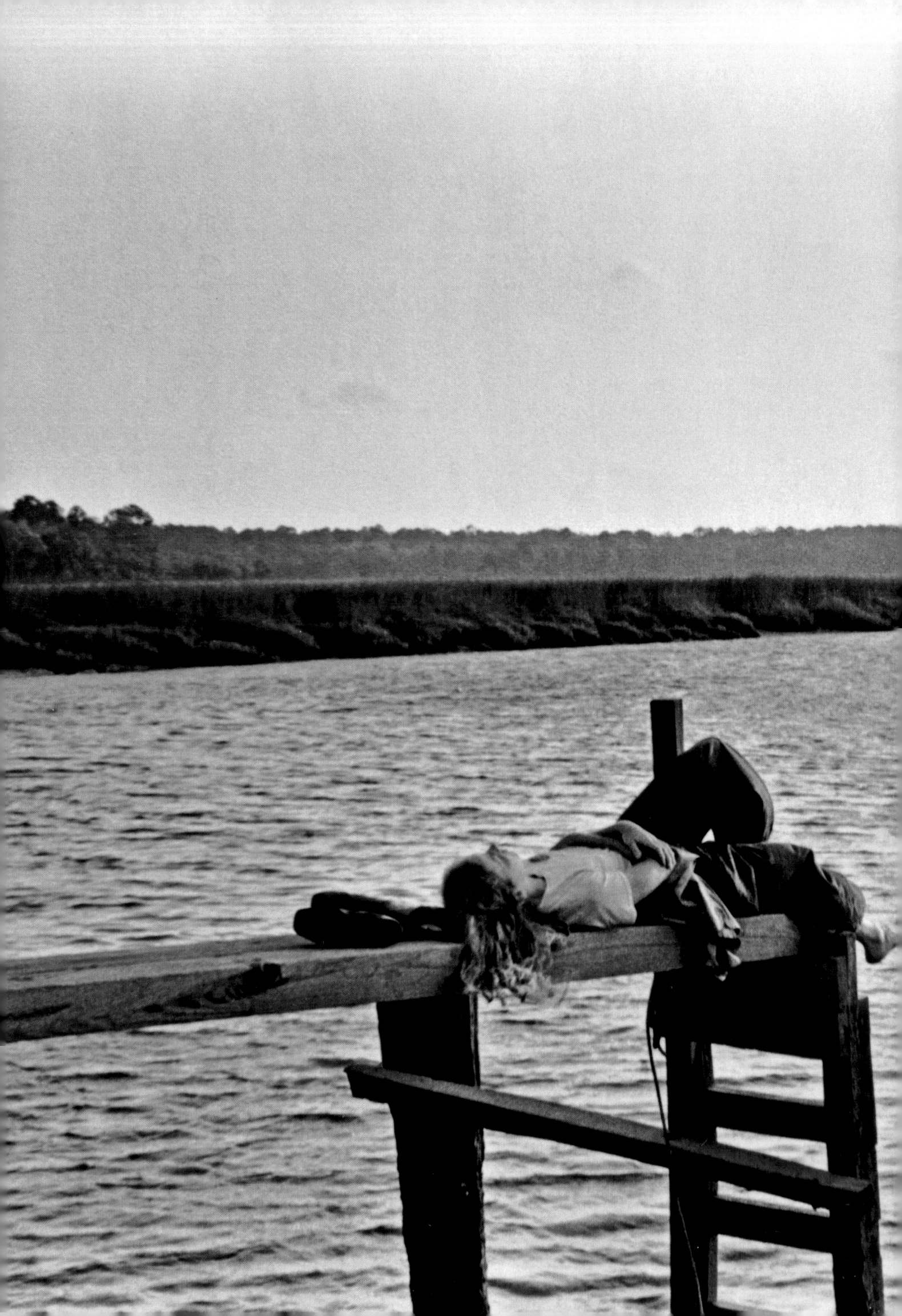

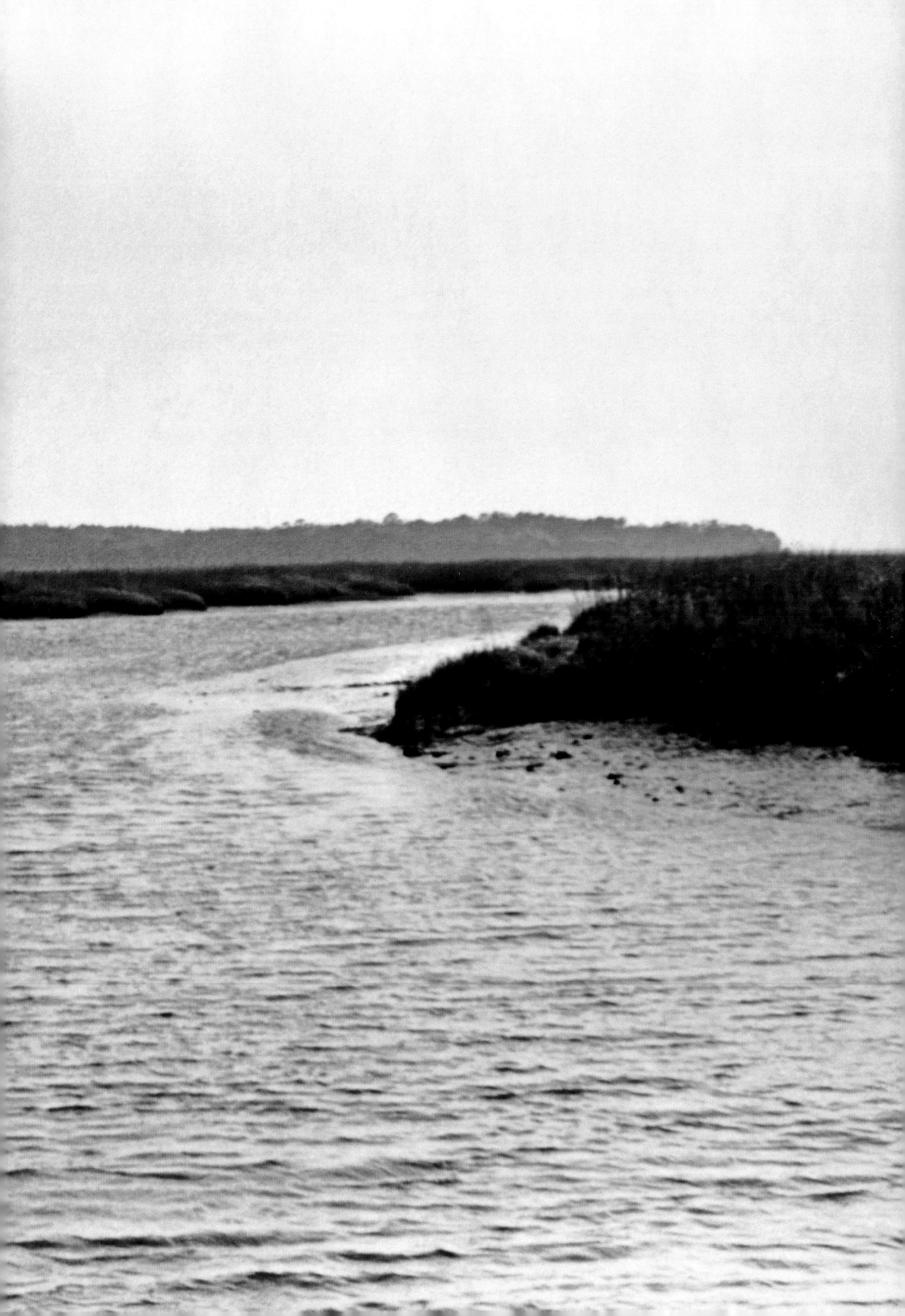

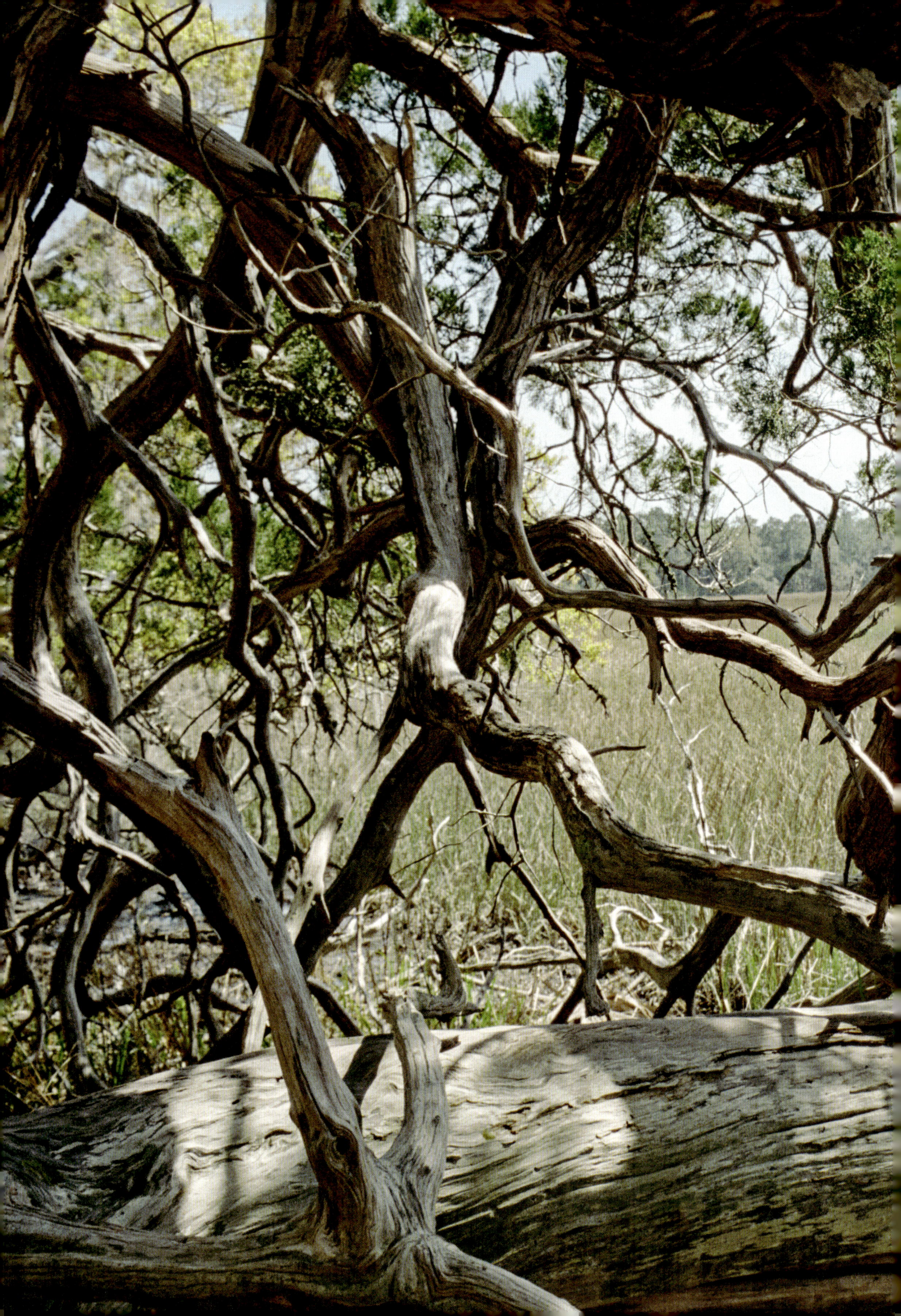

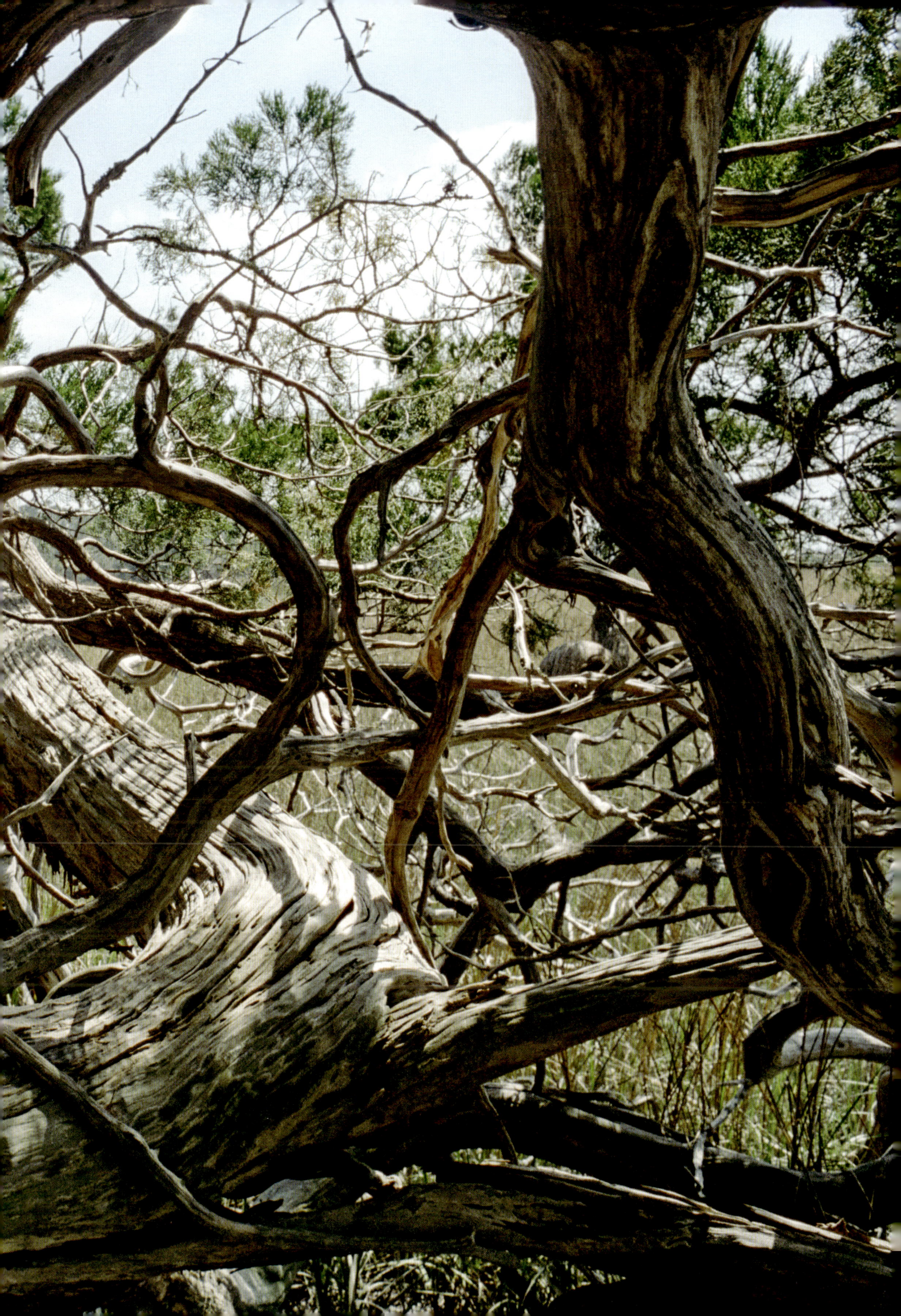

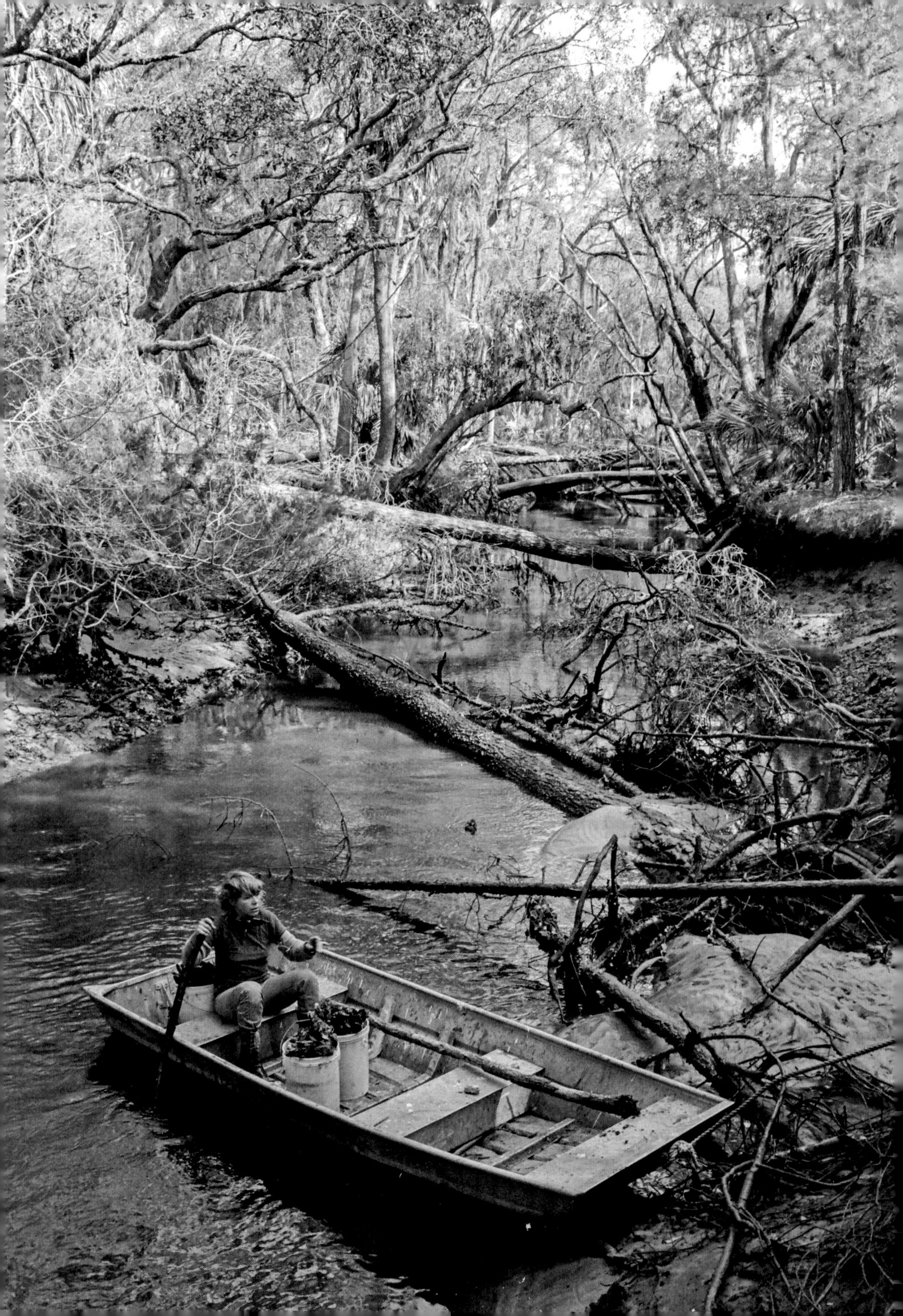

OFF THE COAST OF PARADISE

Artists and Ossabaw Island, 1961–Now

Erin Dunn & Beryl Gilothwest

Telfair Books

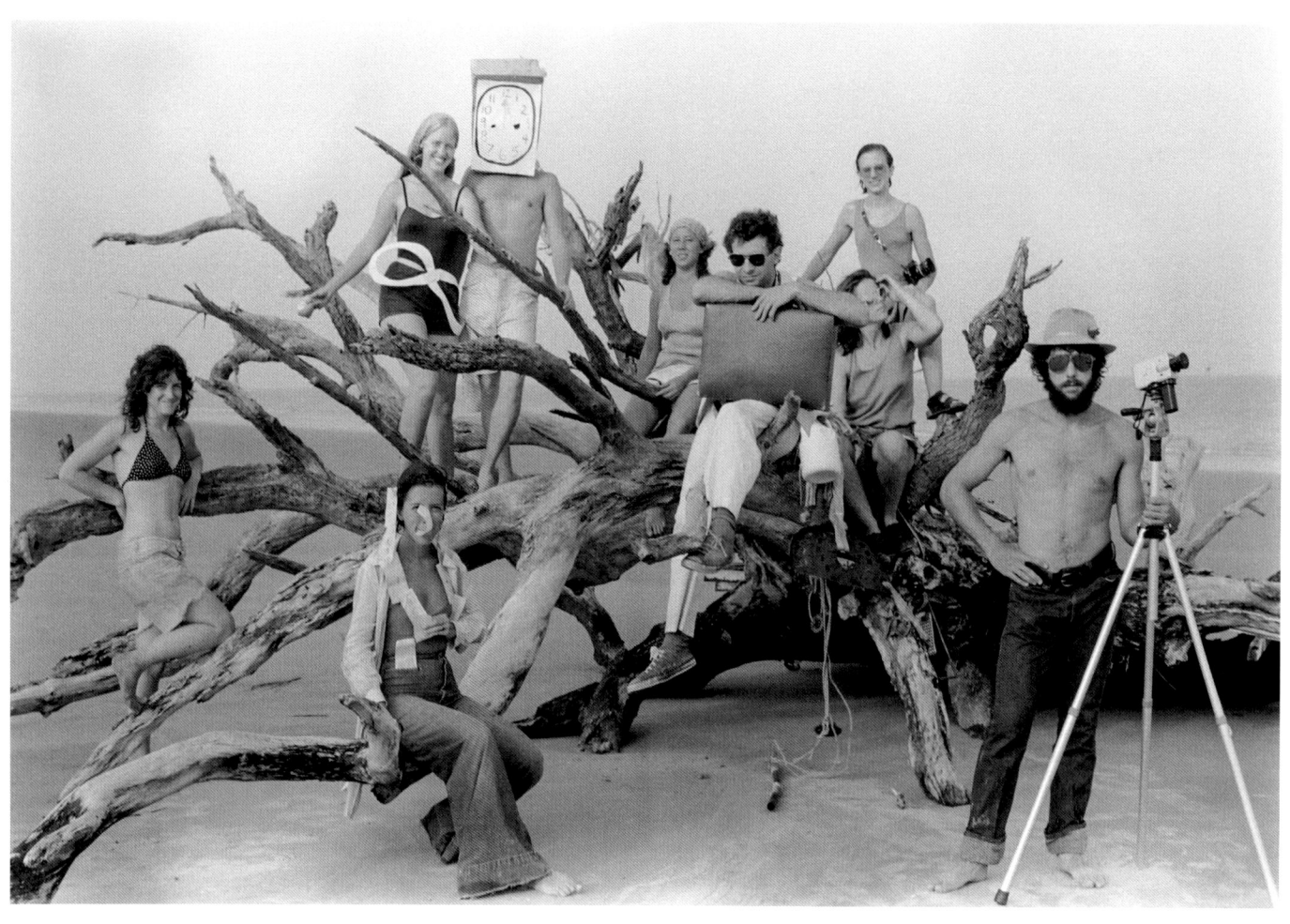

Genesis members at South End Beach, 1978. Photograph by Helen Hamada

DIRECTOR'S FOREWORD

When I moved to Savannah to accept the position of Director and CEO of Telfair Museums in the summer of 2024, I was fascinated to learn about Ossabaw, an undeveloped 26,000-acre barrier island right off the coast. In 1961, the island's former co-owner Eleanor "Sandy" Torrey West and her husband Clifford B. West founded an ambitious multidisciplinary residency program called the Ossabaw Island Project (OIP) that ran until 1982. Many of the era's most important figures spent time on Ossabaw during this richly significant yet little-known chapter in the cultural history of the Lowcountry, from the novelists Ralph Ellison and Margaret Atwood to the architects Robert Venturi and Denise Scott Brown to the scholars Roman Jakobson and Eugene P. Odum.

Over the past few years, Erin Dunn, Telfair's curator of modern and contemporary art, and Beryl Gilothwest, guest curator and the Wests' grandson, have been developing an exhibition that focuses on this history through the lens of visual art. *Off the Coast of Paradise: Artists and Ossabaw Island, 1961–Now* examines the extraordinarily complex relationships that a wide range of visual artists have developed with the island as part of the Wests' programs and in the decades since. Ossabaw manifests in the work of such artists as Harry Bertoia, Agnes Denes, Suzanne Jackson, Ellen Lanyon, Sally Mann, Michael Mazur, Ross McElwee, Betty Tompkins, and Anne Truitt in dynamic and often surprising ways. For this exhibition, Telfair Museums has commissioned a major new video work from artist Allison Janae Hamilton that showcases the ongoing significance of the island as a wellspring for the creative imagination.

The concept of bringing artists to a location of natural beauty—where they can escape the worries and tensions of the fast-paced modern world—has several precedents in the history of art. Ossabaw is one in a long line, from the artist village of Barbizon in 19th-century France to the self-sustaining Arts and Crafts colony Byrdcliffe in the Catskill Mountains at the turn of the 20th century. So, what made the Wests' programs unique? In part it is the relative isolation of the island, which can only be reached by private boat. This separation helped to preserve the natural ecosystem and required the resident artists to become somewhat self-sufficient during their time there, especially at the later, more rugged Genesis project founded in 1970. It is also perhaps due to the *genius loci* of Ossabaw, the unique, primordial spirit of the place, where ocean, land, and human history come into close contact.

In April 1962, Telfair's director, David M. Reese, wrote to Clifford West, "I feel that what you are doing there is of such importance that it is bound to succeed. If there is anything that we at the Telfair can do, please feel free to call on us." More than sixty years later, Telfair Museums is honored to mount *Off the Coast of Paradise* on the occasion of our 140th anniversary. As the first public art museum in the South, we are grateful to play a role in sharing the uniquely southern story of Ossabaw Island with the wider world.

I would like to thank Erin and Beryl for their leadership in bringing the first major exhibition on this subject to life. I would also like to thank The Ossabaw Island Foundation, particularly Elizabeth DuBose, Executive Director, and Robin Gunn, Project Coordinator, for their essential partnership. I trust that you will enjoy learning about this unique and treasured place as much as I have.

Dr. David A. Brenneman
Executive Director/CEO
Telfair Museums

FOREWORD

Ossabaw Island's history parallels that of Georgia's 100-mile coastline: Indigenous communities were displaced by colonization, pre-Civil War agricultural production was made possible by the enslavement of Black people, and the island was purchased by wealthy Northern industrialists in the early 20th century as a wintertime getaway. Ossabaw also varies little from its neighboring islands in terms of geography, climate, and ecosystem. Like most of them, it is publicly owned and protected from development, and like all but four of them, it is only accessible by boat. For all these reasons, some of the artworks on view in *Off the Coast of Paradise: Artists and Ossabaw Island, 1961–Now* might be mistaken for depicting Cumberland or Sapelo or St. Catherines. However, an exhibition like this can only be about Ossabaw, due to the island's unique 65-year history of intentional and interdisciplinary use.

This is because of two key decisions made by the Torrey and West families:

1. In 1961, Ossabaw's co-owner, Eleanor Torrey West, known as Sandy, and her second husband Clifford B. West established a multidisciplinary residency program known as the Ossabaw Island Project (OIP). The Wests intuitively understood the benefits of bringing a mix of people from myriad disciplines together to inform and inspire each other through creative and intellectual engagement. Outside of their classrooms, libraries, laboratories, and studios, OIP and later Genesis members gained new perspectives in the maritime forest, tidal creeks, salt marshes, and boneyard beach of Ossabaw Island.

2. In 1978, Sandy West and her nephews and niece donated half the island and sold the rest to the State of Georgia under the strict stipulation that future visitors could only travel to Ossabaw for the defined uses of "natural, scientific or cultural education, research or study." By intentionally omitting recreation, West and the Torreys kept important parameters on how visitors experienced the island. "Use of the island must be kept within control and limits," West wrote. "However, with the understanding of the land and with a sincere desire to share, it is possible to have people come to Ossabaw without jeopardizing that which they would like to see, to hear, and to learn."[1]

The ethos of these decisions endures in the work of The Ossabaw Island Foundation. Over the last thirty years, extensive historical research and archaeological excavations have deepened our understanding of the island. This knowledge richly informs the experiences of current island visitors, whether they are here to engage with the natural landscape, the built environment, the wildlife, or their own inner wells of creativity, bringing all of these elements into view in a new way. Allison Janae Hamilton's new film *Venus of Ossabaw*—commissioned for *Off the Coast of Paradise* and shot mostly on the island—is a prime example. In the film, Hamilton draws on Dr. Paul Pressly's research about Titus and other colonial-era Black people enslaved on Ossabaw, using her camera to introduce their histories to 21st-century audiences.

Last year, Georgia's Department of Natural Resources embarked on a major rehabilitation of the Torrey-West mansion on Ossabaw's North End, the completion of which will transform the Foundation's capabilities on the island. Sandy and Clifford West dreamed up the idea of the Ossabaw Island Project in that house and many of the artists featured in *Off the Coast of Paradise* stayed there during their time on the island. This exhibition is well timed, opening to the public exactly 100 years after the mansion was completed.

We are grateful to Telfair Museums for their partnership in telling Ossabaw's story through *Off the Coast of Paradise*. This exhibition reveals as many ways to interpret the island as there are artworks on view, manifesting the dynamic, paradoxical spirit of preservation that the forward-thinking Torrey and West families hoped to inspire. That kind of vision serves as a guiding principle for The Ossabaw Island Foundation's stewardship of this complex and magical place.

Elizabeth DuBose
Executive Director
The Ossabaw Island Foundation

1.   Ossabaw Foundation brochure, c. 1990,
     The Ossabaw Island Foundation archives.

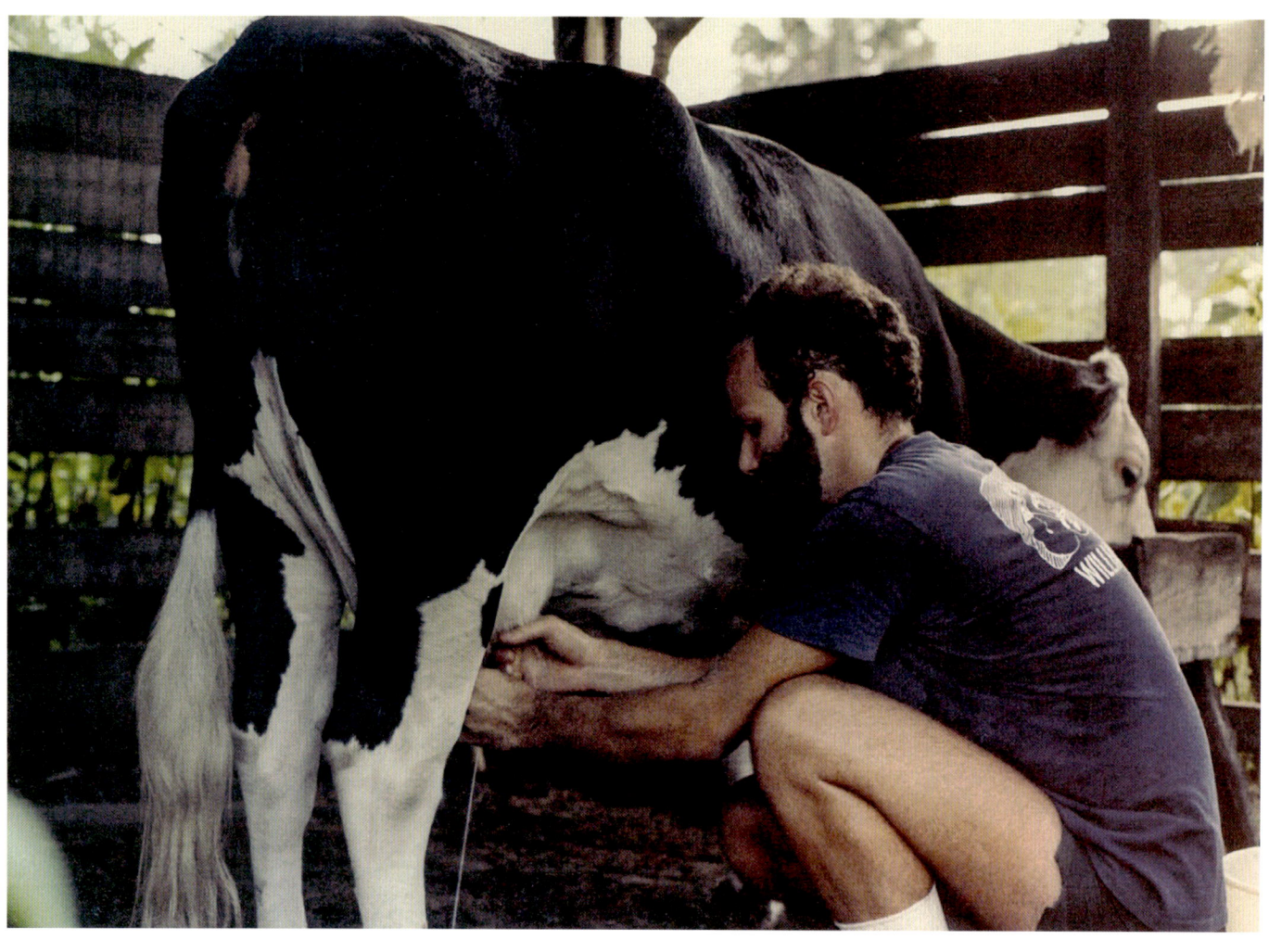

Henri Cole with Genie the cow at Middle Place, 1981

PREFACE

Landscape doesn't lie. It isn't busy with yesterday. It's in the here and now. Long ago, when I arrived at Ossabaw, I was in the here and now. This was a time of new beginnings. The boat trip across bays and inlets to the island dock still resonates for me, not with nostalgia but with mystery and hope. I was a nascent poet becoming myself. I was a skinny young man afraid of the hogs that roamed the island. Genesis (at Middle Place), where I lived, seemed to me a utopian paradise, with its tree house perched in a giant live oak, dung beetles, herons, solar shower, and Genie, the generous cow. Sometimes in a dream, I am still kneeling at her side, tugging and pressing her teats, listening to the rich milk spray into a pink bowl. Afterward, when we are finished, she does a little awkward dance in the tangled grass.

It is morning, and there are tall, statuesque, S-shaped egrets hunting in the salt marshes, amidst the cattails, frogs, and alligators. Wind shakes the palmettos. My face is chapped and I scratch a ferocious mosquito bite. Green sea water sparkles in the estuary. An animal cries in the distance. For a few hours, I revise, revise, revise at a table in the Long House, the little wood shed where I sleep with a mink family quarreling under the floorboards. I wear only shorts, tennis shoes, and the St. Christopher medal given to me by Mother. It is a lush, frugal existence on this Georgian barrier island, where humans have lived since 3000 B.C. The sun beats down on us, but the steaming Southern heat is no threat to the purity of our idealism on this heart-shaped island, where acorns and crabs are so plentiful, and enormous loggerhead sea turtles emerge from the sea to nest and lay eggs along its dark, protected shoreline.

Ossabaw—even the name sounds primordial—with its stressed/unstressed/stressed music, like *primitive* and *mythical*. Is that an alligator I see swimming up the river as I float on my back to cool off and contemplate life after weeding in the garden? Is that smoke I see coming from the oven's propane tanks, as I bake zucchini-crusted pizza from *The Moosewood Cookbook* for my Genesis comrades? Is that cattle I see ambling in my flashlight beacon on the path to the toilet in the middle of the night? Hey, let's all pile into the back of the pickup and head to the beach with Wini and Michael. The bright stars and skinny-dipping are excellent therapy for a shy young poet. Nobody watches except a lonely braying donkey.

Why do I trust my dreams of this magical place? Why do I hope one day to return, if only to discover vultures and rattlesnakes instead of humans? They say it is good to dream and process our emotions. It's romantic to say, but in my dreams of Ossabaw Island, I always speak in the throat of a strong, intelligent, loving man.

Henri Cole
Stonington, CT

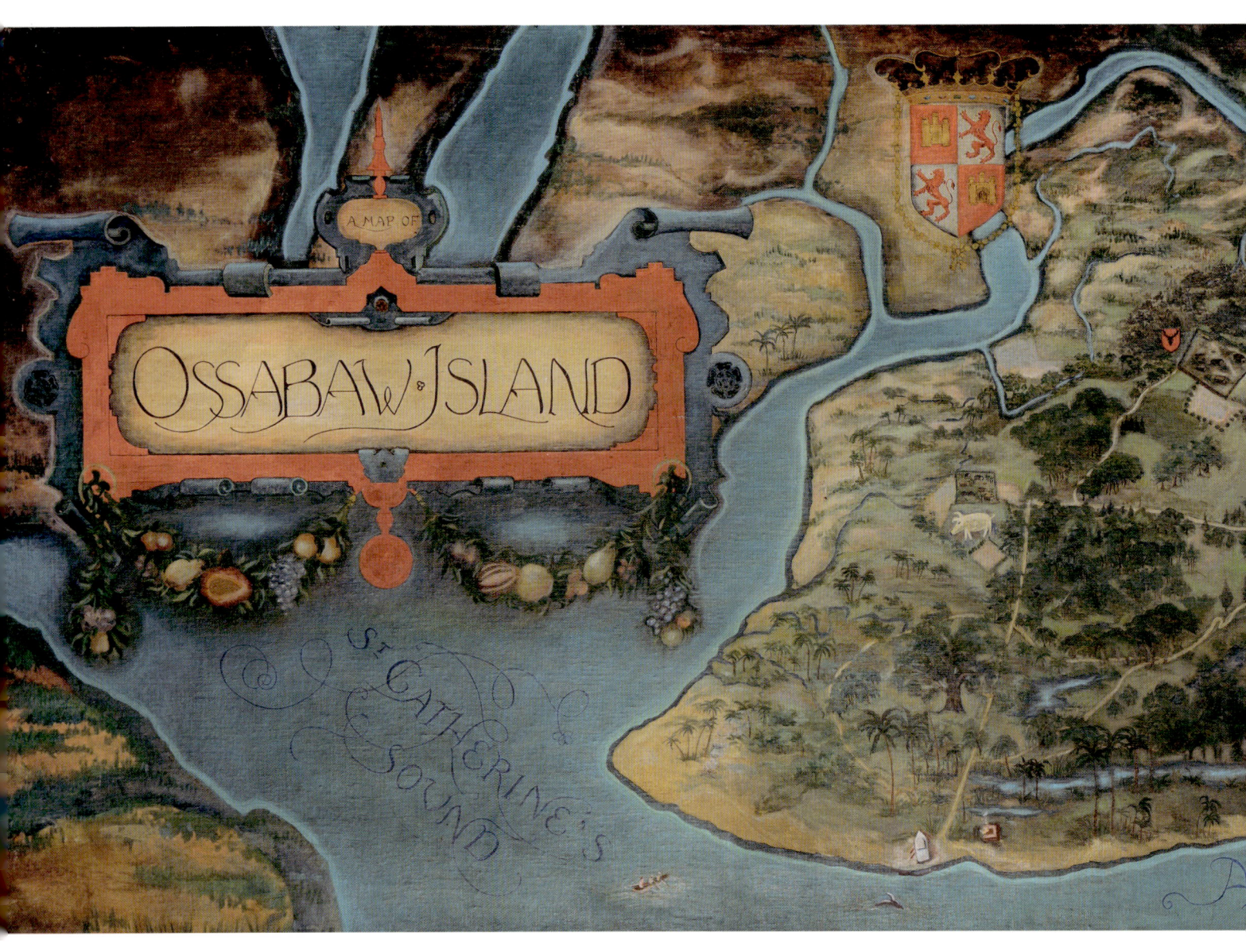

Mural of Ossabaw Island installed above the fireplace in the Main House, by an unknown artist,
c. 1926, with additions by Thomas Marker in the 1960s

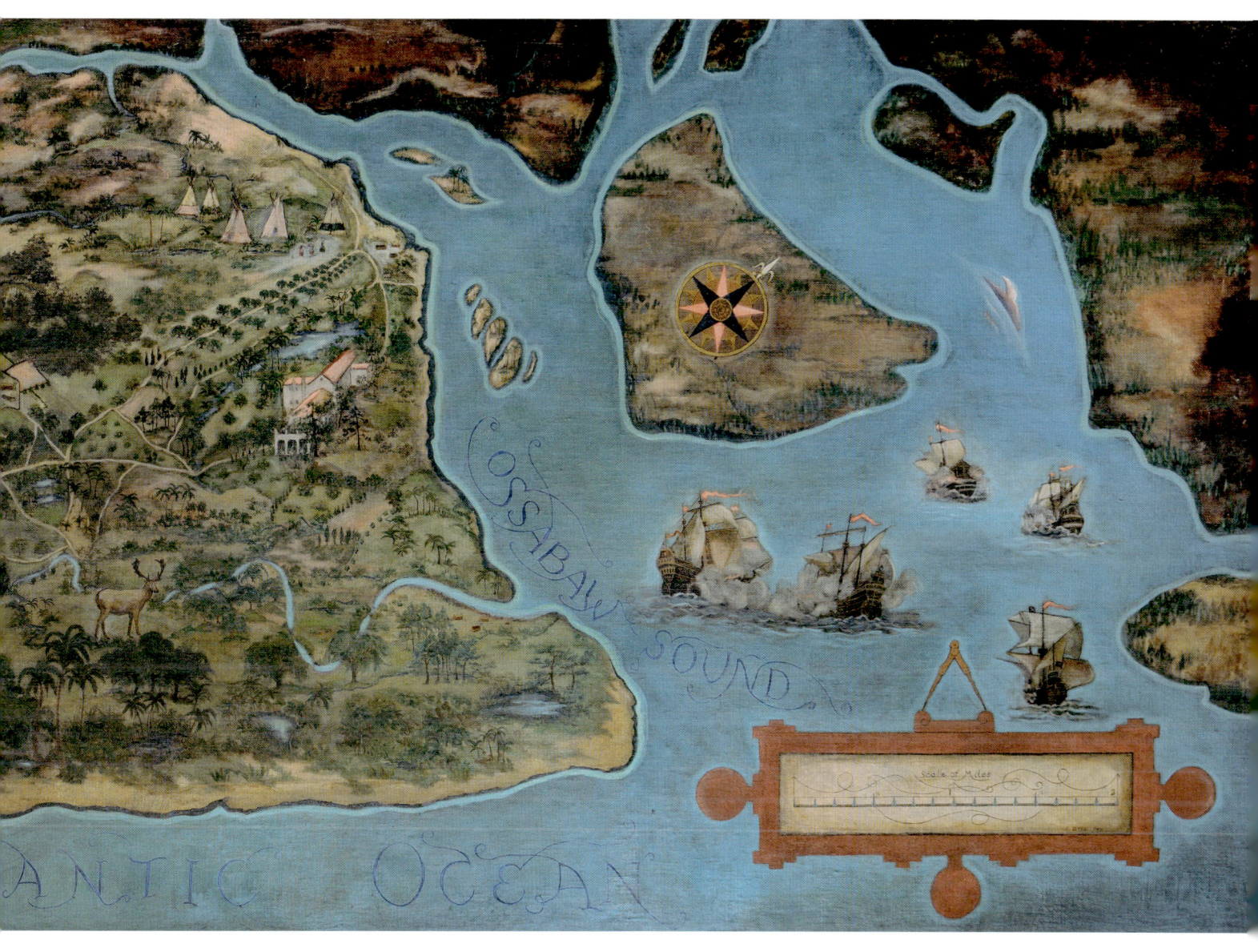

OFF THE COAST OF PARADISE

ERIN DUNN AND BERYL GILOTHWEST

During a transformative summer spent living in the wilderness of Ossabaw Island, the 25-year-old poet Henri Cole began seeing echoes of his life in the immersive environment that surrounded him. The tentative and restless nature of egrets in the marsh reminded him of the push-pull of desire, while the hungry and calculating mink crawling beneath his cabin suggested impending heartbreak. These observations come out in Cole's writing during this time, the elliptical nature of poetry acting as the perfect vessel for his experience of the island, which he describes as primordial, frugal, and lush.[1] He called one of his Ossabaw poems "Off the coast of paradise,"[2] a name that captures his mixture of fascination with the island's natural beauty and awareness of its inherent dangers. While Ossabaw has all the trappings of Eden, its darkness and its light, the island is not a parable. Ossabaw is adjacent to paradise, a very real place that is ripe for interpretation.

Ossabaw's name is thought to derive from a Muscogee word that roughly translates to "land of holly," which refers to the yaupon holly that flourishes on the island. The Muscogee people brewed its leaves to make a powerful caffeinated tea. These trees grow alongside massive live oaks, southern magnolia, and dogwood, as well as towering cabbage palms and dense thickets of sawtooth palmetto, in the maritime forest that dominates Ossabaw's 9,000 acres of uplands. The island's 17,000 acres of salt marsh produce a massive amount of food and energy, providing nursery and spawning grounds for blue crabs and several species of fish. Thirteen miles of beach run along Ossabaw's east side, the 30-foot-high dunes on Bradley Point at the north contrasting dramatically with the low-lying "bone yard" at South End, where the ocean has encroached into the forest. This part of the island is especially dynamic, shifting and changing daily. Many endangered species, including loggerhead sea turtles and wood storks, nest on Ossabaw, as well as alligators, bald eagles, and piping plovers.

North American Indigenous people began to populate Ossabaw around 5,000 years ago, establishing its first permanent villages at that time. In the 16th and 17th centuries, the Guale people were displaced from the island by Spanish settlers who instigated slave raids, spread European diseases, and forced their relocation to St. Augustine, Florida. After the Spanish withdrew from Georgia at the end of the 17th century, the

English set aside Ossabaw and neighboring barrier islands as hunting and fishing reserves for the Muscogee people. However, it wasn't long before English landowners took over the island and began cultivating it agriculturally. Over the next century, the island was timbered and farmed by enslaved Africans and their descendants, who primarily grew indigo and Sea Island cotton. In the sixty years following the Civil War, the island was stewarded by several different owners and farmed by Black sharecroppers, most of whom left Ossabaw after a series of terrible hurricanes wreaked havoc in the late 19th century. In 1924, Ossabaw was purchased as a winter retreat by Michigan-based couple Dr. Henry Norton Torrey and Nell Ford Torrey, an heiress to the Pittsburgh Plate Glass and Wyandotte Chemical Company fortunes. From 1961–1982, the island was home to a series of residency programs that brought a limited number of interdisciplinary luminaries to Ossabaw under the watchful eye of the Torreys' daughter, Eleanor "Sandy" Torrey West, among others. Since 1978, Ossabaw has been protected by the state of Georgia as its first Heritage Preserve, which stipulates that the island can only be used for "natural, scientific, and cultural study, research, and education, and environmentally sound preservation, conservation, and management of the Island's ecosystem."[3]

This brief overview barely scratches the surface as Ossabaw's histories could fill volumes, some of which exist already. However, the vast majority of the island's stories remain to be told, and countless others continue to unfold. *Off the Coast of Paradise: Artists and Ossabaw Island, 1961–Now* doesn't aim to encapsulate Ossabaw, which would be a fool's errand, but rather to show some of the ways the island, such as it is, has catalyzed creative inspiration over the last sixty-five years that artists have gone there in earnest. Ralph Ellison, who visited Ossabaw in 1971, writes, "It is worth remembering that one of the implicitly creative functions of art in the U.S.A....is the defining and correlating of diverse American experiences by bringing previously unknown patterns, details, and emotions into view along with those that are generally recognized."[4] Ossabaw—with its myriad ecologies, histories, cultures, and spirits—is the perfect vessel for this kind of inquiry.

With no bridge connecting it to the rest of Georgia, Ossabaw often feels cut off from civilization. Far from the distractions and safeguards of the mainland, artists who spend time there are forced to reckon with themselves and their environment. That kind of experience has the potential to bring out the unexpected in people, and in Ossabaw's case, it does so more often than it does not. "I want to write poems that are X-rays of the soul in moments of being and seeing," writes Henri Cole. "This includes the ghastly, the insane, and the cruel, but also beauty, Eros, and wonder."[5] The artworks in *Off the Coast of Paradise* act similarly to poetry, offering us a glimpse into the inner psyches of their makers through the lens of Ossabaw Island.

Notes

1. Henri Cole, "Preface," on p. 4 of this volume.
2. Henri Cole, "Off the coast of paradise," (Thesis, Columbia University, 1982), 20–22.
3. "Ossabaw Island: Heritage Preserve," The Ossabaw Island Foundation, accessed July 30, 2025, https://ossabawisland.org/island/heritage-preserve/.
4. Ralph Ellison, "The Little Man at Chehaw Station: The American Artist and His Audience," *The American Scholar* 47, no. 1 (1978): 31.
5. Henri Cole, *Orphic Paris* (New York: New York Review of Books, 2018), 22.

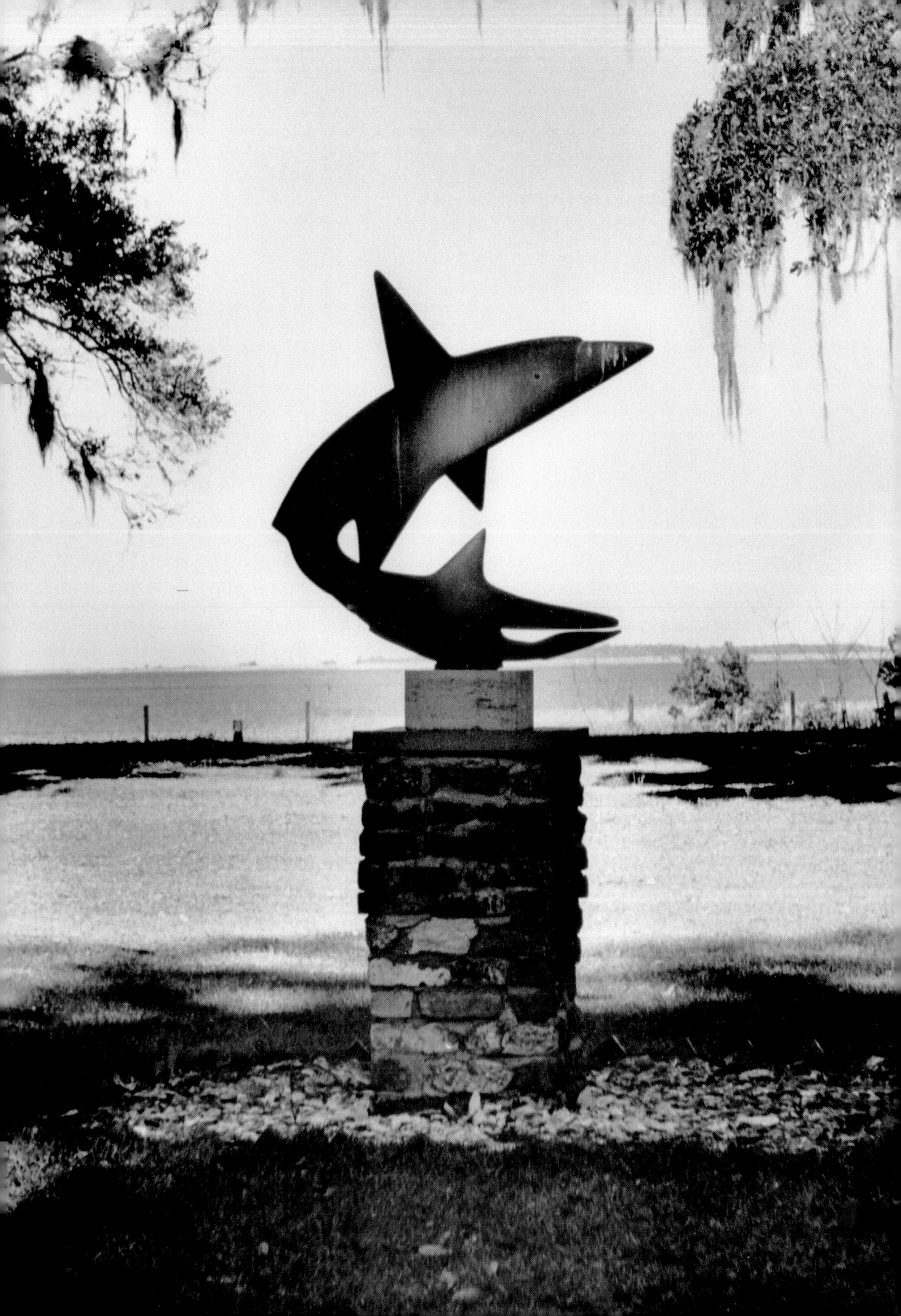

LIKE A VEIL

BERYL GILOTHWEST

Every minute my thoughts are with you—seeing you picked up at the
DeSoto Hotel—by whom? Going to the Island—how? How long was
the boat trip? And what did you see when you got there? My mind is
filled with questions—unfocused images of where you are.
—Philip Guston[1]

A pair of intertwined bronze sharks frames the view of the Ogeechee River and Wassaw
Island from the picture window of the mansion on Ossabaw Island's North End. A baby
shark hides itself beneath the tail of its mother, whose body curves gracefully skyward in
the imagined ocean depths. Created by the sculptor Berthold Tex Schiwetz and permanent-
ly installed in March 1962, *Sharks* (c. 1958) is inextricable from its place on the front lawn.
As Ossabaw's sentinel for the last sixty-four years, it symbolizes the island's rich and multi-
dimensional artistic legacy.

      Artists, writers, musicians, scientists, historians, and other intellectuals began
spending time on Ossabaw Island about a year before the sculpture was installed. In the
fall of 1961, my grandparents, Eleanor Torrey West and Clifford B. West, opened a multidisciplinary residency program known as the Ossabaw Island Project (OIP) that they
hosted out of the Main House, my grandmother's family home. Over the two decades that
the Wests' programs ran on Ossabaw and in the years since, hundreds of people have come
to the island to work on projects of their choosing.[2] The biologist I. Lehr Brisbin conducted research on the island's population of feral pigs, the then-burgeoning author Olive Ann
Burns worked on the manuscript for her classic 1984 novel *Cold Sassy Tree*, and the composers Ernst Bacon and John Edmunds collaborated on the children's ballet *Jehovah and
the Ark*, among countless other creative, scientific, and intellectual endeavors.

      The visual artists who came to Ossabaw arguably developed the most complex
relationships with the island. From the beginning, they drew from its natural majesty, isolation, and complex human history in their artistic projects. Known for his mythological-
ly inflected bronze sculptures of animals, Schiwetz was inspired by the island's wildlife
during his visits throughout the 1960s. He made a massive weather vane in the form of an

Tex Schiwetz's *Sharks*, c. 1958, in front of the Main House, c. 1962 (detail). Photograph by Clifford B. West

11

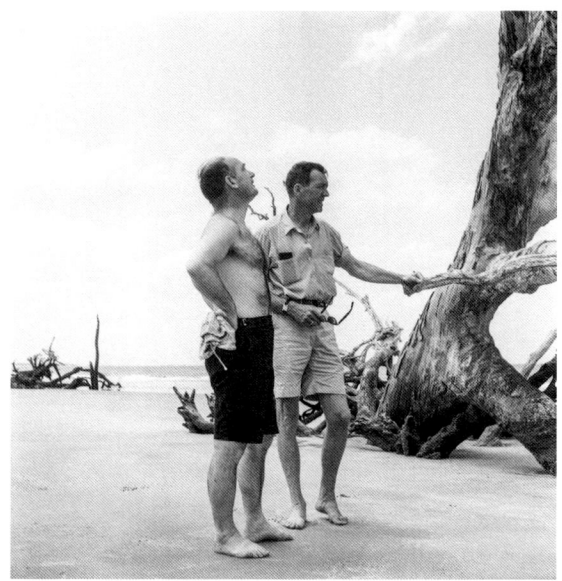

Ossabaw pelican for the island's dock and began a series of energetic, scampering shore birds inspired by the ones he witnessed on the beaches[p. 109]. For artist Agnes Denes, the entry point was more conceptual[pp. 38–41]. Ruminating on the island's shifting shadows in the bright moonlight, the constantly changing tides on its shores, and the swelling sounds of bugs in the night, Denes grounded her artistic interrogation of Ossabaw in a question: "What secret [does] the island hold?"[3] Working across painting, drawing, film, photography, textiles, ceramics, bronze casting, and other media, a diverse range of artists have come face to face with that question over the last sixty-five years.

THE CATALYST

> I take with me my paintings, stronger than before, my life, brighter than before, and my mind, richer, much richer than before.
> —a painter who attended OIP in 1976[4]

My grandmother often described Ossabaw as "a tremendous catalyst."[5] She believed that the island would speak to those who approached it with patience, flexibility, and ample time. "I always thought it would be a great idea to have a big trash can on the Vernon View dock labeled: EXPERTISE," she told a journalist in 1981. "You could come here and seem to be doing nothing at all, but that's when your imagination is really going into high gear."[6] She had witnessed many members leaving the island changed in unexpected ways. The renowned linguist Roman Jakobson claimed that he achieved an unmatched level of clarity and concentration on Ossabaw, writing that "even the peculiar ground and geographical contour of the island act as an inspiring background of our scientific theories and artistic imagination."[7] The landscape architect Diana Balmori remarked on the unprecedented combination of peacefulness and productivity that she achieved on Ossabaw, writing that her time there "will remain as a high watermark in intensity of activity and clarity of perception."[8] The textile designer Marianne Strengell created rugs, ceiling tiles, and room dividers that were directly and indirectly inspired by textures and natural formations that she came across on the island. For Jakobson, Balmori, and Strengell, among others from many different disciplines, the immersive environment of the island acted as a conduit to fresh ideas and new ways of thinking.

The unique environment of Genesis, where largely younger and less established members were given the opportunity to live in close proximity to the land, affected the work of its visual artists in surprisingly personal ways. They often directly engaged with the collective, community-minded nature of the program in their work, which can be seen in Ross McElwee's 1985 film *Sherman's March*,[9] Leslie Ferst's towering ceramic monument *The Circumnavigation* (1983)[(p. 42)], Helen Hamada's introspective self-portraits [(pp. 44–45)], and Nancy Marshall's gauzy landscapes[(p. 47)], among others. For the more established artists at the OIP, who were given access to the island's wilderness but lived and worked in comfort in the stately Main House, the island often instigated more philosophical developments in their practice.

The Pennsylvania-based sculptor, designer, and metalworker Harry Bertoia came to Ossabaw in June 1961 as part of a group of luminaries from my grandparents' extended circle who were invited to weigh in on their new idea for the Ossabaw Island Project. During a visit to South End Beach, which stretches up the island's eastern side from its southern tip, Bertoia was left with a lasting sensation of its dark, hard sand flats, which extend widely at low tide and then completely disappear when the water surges[(fig. 1)]. This dramatic change is echoed by the ongoing erosion that plagues that part of the island. "I was deeply impressed by the constant battle of the elements," Bertoia said of the experience. "The sea was taking away part of the island, eroding these huge oaks, some of them were falling, being denuded, scrubbed clean…and it was very impressive, I became aware of forces continuing."[10] A series of conversations with the biologist Colin Pittendrigh over the course of the weekend further stimulated these new lines of thinking.[11]

Not long after his trip to Ossabaw, Bertoia visited the Anaconda American Brass Company in Waterbury, Connecticut, to deepen his knowledge of the possibilities of metal casting. While he was touring the facility, several massive cauldrons of ingot mistakenly overflowed. As the artist watched rapturously, the molten metal flowed onto the floor of the plant, creating pathways of its own. "I saw the movements, I became aware of the forces internally, the way things happen inside this globe—great heat, movements," Bertoia remembered. "What we see on the surface is a volcano, eruptions. All that plus what I'd seen on Ossabaw Island came together and I knew then what I should be looking for."[12] Inspired by those experiences, Bertoia developed an entirely new form of bronze casting that he dubbed "spill-casting" for a major commission at the new Dulles International Airport in Washington, DC[(fig. 2)][13]. "This takes us back to an aspect of casting so ancient that its

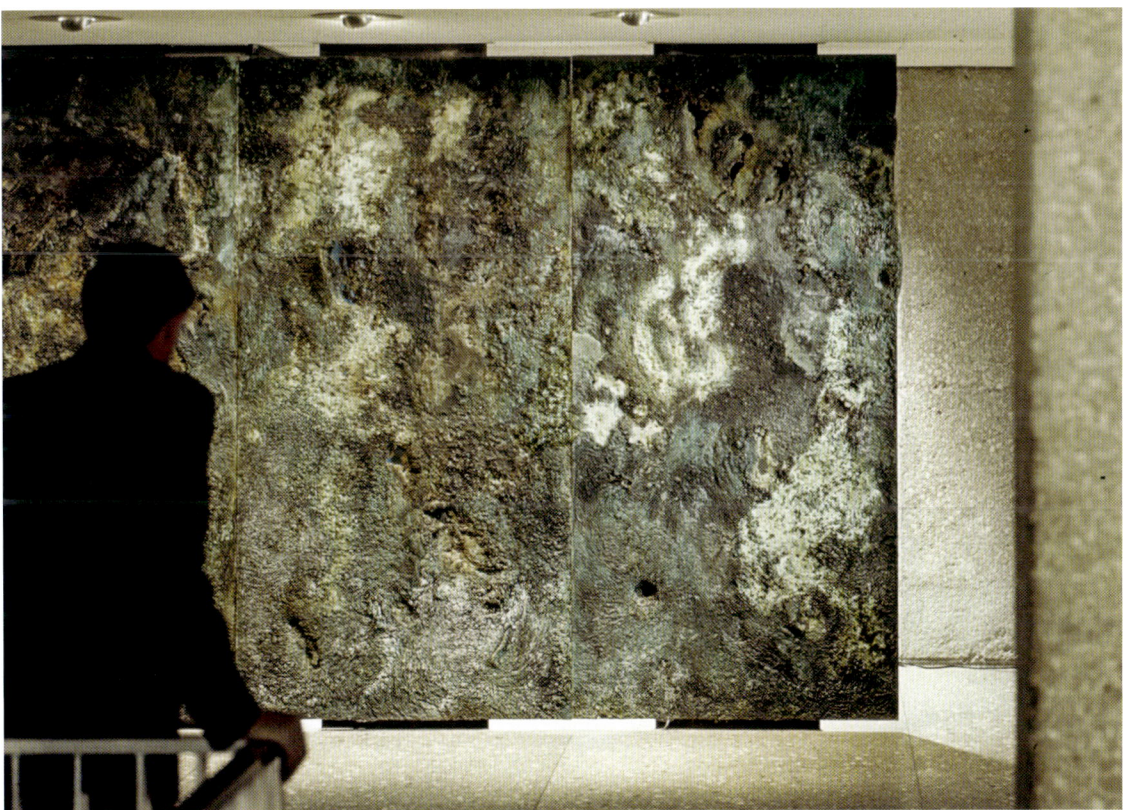

fig. 2.   Harry Bertoia's Untitled, 1962, at Dulles International Airport, Washington, DC, c. 1962. Photograph by Balthazar Korab

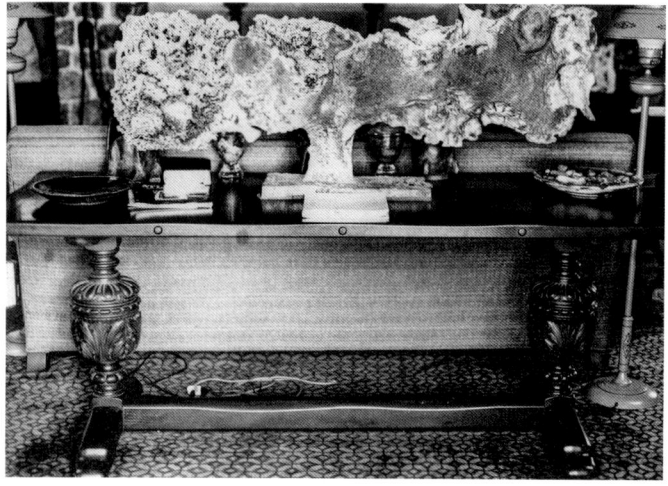

origins are unknown," wrote the critic Lawrence Campbell in 1963. "Bertoia pours his molten bronze in a shallow, concave pit, and then works on the surface of this metallic pond as it cools by scraping, cutting, punching."[14] This dangerous process was accomplished with the help of rakes, water, and even stones that he would drop into the fray.

Bertoia made several small-scale, free-standing spill-cast sculptures after the Dulles commission, including one that he gifted to the Ossabaw Island Project in 1966 [fig. 3]. In this piece, a large oblong stone juts out of the composition at the top right. The stone's smooth surface contrasts sharply with the highly textured bronze, building on the radicality of the spill-casting technique. It positioned bronze—the hallowed medium of classic statuary from antiquity to the Italian Renaissance—as a material with the potential to be as malleable as sheet metal. The sculpture stood on a table behind the couch in the living room at the Main House for many years, another emblem of Ossabaw's many possibilities.

The Washington, DC-based sculptor Anne Truitt was instantly captivated by Ossabaw when she arrived at the OIP in March 1975, writing: "Prospero rules this island. Ariel's magic airs beguile, flirt, and delight, diminishing into the dry, just barely audible touch of palmetto leaf on palmetto leaf. I am enchanted."[15] She quickly settled into the rhythm of the place, learning the names of the dirt roads that crisscross the island and going on long walks with her friend, the writer and anthropologist Tobias Schneebaum, who had been there for several weeks already. In her journal, she invoked the chemist James Lovelock's Gaia hypothesis, which argues that the earth is a self-regulating system, writing: "I almost seem to feel the island adjusting itself, balancing like a gyroscope on the point of its own purposes."[16]

After Schneebaum left a few days into her residency, Truitt dove into her work, moving organically between writing in her journal and making a series of modestly-scaled drawings. In one standalone piece, Truitt isolated two points on the paper and drew a series of lines emanating from each one [p. 59]. She filled in the gaps between these bursts of subtle but incandescent energy with varying amounts of diluted white acrylic, giving the impression of light. Though best known for her wooden towers meticulously painted with pure and exacting color, Truitt was also a painter and these drawings relate most closely to her ongoing *Arundel* series of rigorously pared down, large-scale canvases that feature graphite and white acrylic lines against a uniform white ground [fig. 4]: "In these paintings, I set forth, to see for myself how they appear, what might be called the tips of my conceptual icebergs in that I put down so little of all that they refer to."[17] This observation resonates with Truitt's drawing from Ossabaw, in which exploding lines hint at the rich experience of the island that she captured so evocatively in her journal.

As her residency continued, Truitt began to dedicate more of her time to writing. Over the last two years, she had been forced to scrutinize her trajectory as an artist and examine her past in preparation for a pair of retrospective exhibitions. "I began to see that I had used the process of art not only to contain my insecurities but also to exorcise those beyond my endurance, and must have done so with haste akin to panic,"[18] she wrote. Truitt purchased a notebook and began recording her life each morning in order to combat those feelings. By the time she arrived at Ossabaw, she had been writing in her journal regularly for more than nine months but it began to take on new significance during her time there. "I typed my notebooks and wrote seven hours straight yesterday," she wrote towards the end of her two weeks on the island. "Writing reminds me of biological dissection. The nerve is picked up, lost, found again, and finally exposed very slowly and with skillful patience."[19] In between transcribing existing journal entries on her typewriter, she started writing about everything from an artistic epiphany at the Solomon R. Guggenheim Museum in 1961 to the births of her three children, weaving observations about being an artist, a mother, and a person into a multilayered portrayal of her life.

"At Ossabaw Island I began to realize—I might be writing a book...The more I typed, the more I thought to myself, well, good god, this is interesting," Truitt later remembered. "I mean, the fact that it might be a book, that it might have this shape. I decided I would be faithful to it because that's my policy with my work."[20] Seven years after Truitt left the island, Pantheon Books published *Daybook: The Journal of an Artist* [fig. 5].

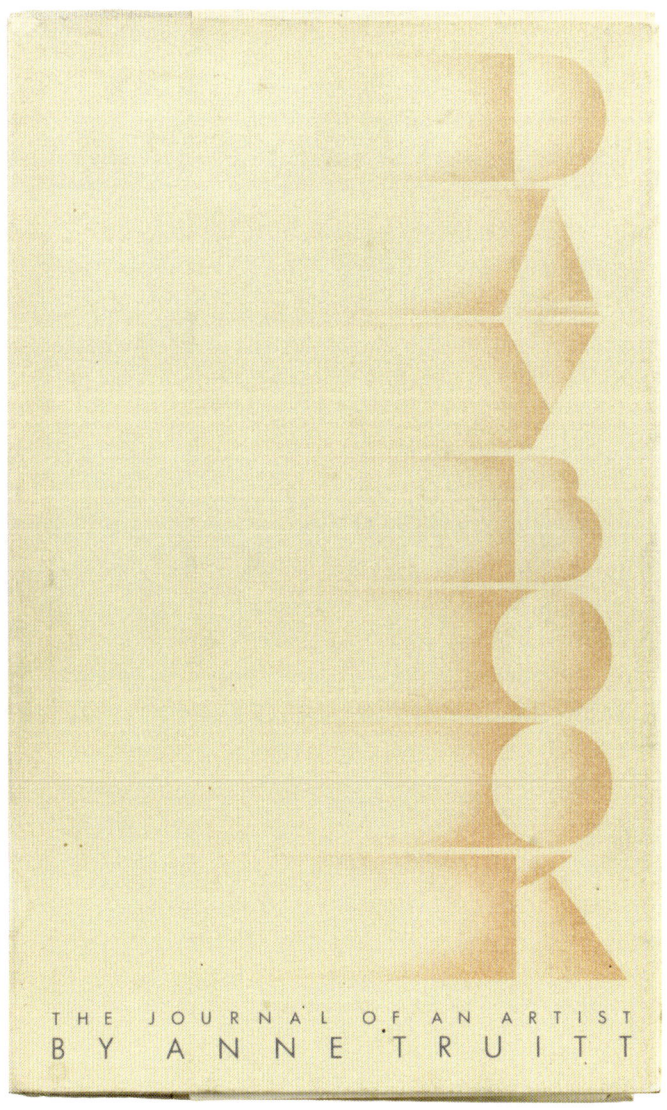

fig. 5.   Anne Truitt, *Daybook: The Journal of an Artist* (Pantheon Books, 1982)

Its thoughtful observations, incisive commentary, and especially its complex and unvarnished look at the realities of being an artist, led to numerous reprintings and three additional volumes published in 1986, 1996, and posthumously in 2022. While the entries about Ossabaw are virtuosic in their conjuring of its unique majesty, the island's lasting significance in *Daybook*'s creation is the time, space, and solitude that activated Truitt's understanding of herself as an author. Neither *Daybook* nor Harry Bertoia's spill-cast sculptures telegraph an obvious connection to Ossabaw. Rather, the island exists as a catalyst in the fabric of their creation.

THE TERRAIN

> Sun slants through feathery gray hanging moss and echoes in the hot,
> secret hearts of the unseen lethal snakes.
> —Anne Truitt[21]

Ossabaw pulsates with rustling branches and the slow, steady thrum of frogs calling out from shallow water. The salty decay of its many marshes mixes with the scent of layer upon layer of oak leaves decomposing in the maritime forest—an aromatic cocktail. The thick trunks of the ancient oaks hold up masses of tendril-like branches that rise in peaks and cascade into valleys, grazing the ground like spider legs. The moss that hangs from them in bouquets gives the forest an impenetrable density, such that the shafts of sunlight that *do* break through feel like shimmering spotlights. With its muted palette—the rich greens of the forest and marsh range from hunter to veridian, but never malachite—the beauty of the landscape isn't always obvious. The island also isn't as welcoming as its subtle splendor may suggest. Highlighting Ossabaw's miles of forest, venomous snakes, alligators, and feral pigs, the painter and OIP member Jean Zaleski cautioned, "Ossabaw is not for everyone; certainly not for the timid...It is imperative for safety reasons that one's whereabouts are always known."[22]

The contradictory nature of Ossabaw's terrain, eluding straightforward interpretation, makes it catnip for visual artists. The Boston-based painter Michael Mazur came to the OIP in January 1975 with the specific aim of conjuring the island's landscape in a new body of work. The United States Department of the Interior had invited him to participate in a traveling exhibition they were organizing in honor of the country's bicentennial. Forty-five artists were sent around the country to engage with resources under the department's purview, which included "the remains of American wilderness."[23] While the commission was a departure for Mazur, who did not consider himself to be a landscape painter, he was immediately drawn to the density of Ossabaw's maritime forest that extended out from his studio in the retrofitted garage where my great-grandmother used to park her Packard.

Mazur started working through how best to capture Ossabaw's forest on the picture plane, but initially resisted working outside. Slowly, he began bringing his materials into the woods and scrutinizing the surrounding environment more closely:

> The arbor or canopy of Georgia Pine is the higher tree with the live
> coastal oaks providing the actual curves making up the natural canopy.
> The cabbage palm is slightly lower providing the foliage variation and
> "Spikey" [*sic*] pattern and distinguishing the landscape as Southern or
> semi-tropical. I must study the palm growth better. The floor is oak
> leaf (small elliptical leaves) and grass—short from grazing wild cattle
> and deer + pigs.[24]

The palmettos soon became the primary focus of the oil paintings, charcoal and pastel drawings, and monoprints that Mazur made on Ossabaw and over the next year back home in Boston. The most striking of these works are monumental, immersive drawings,

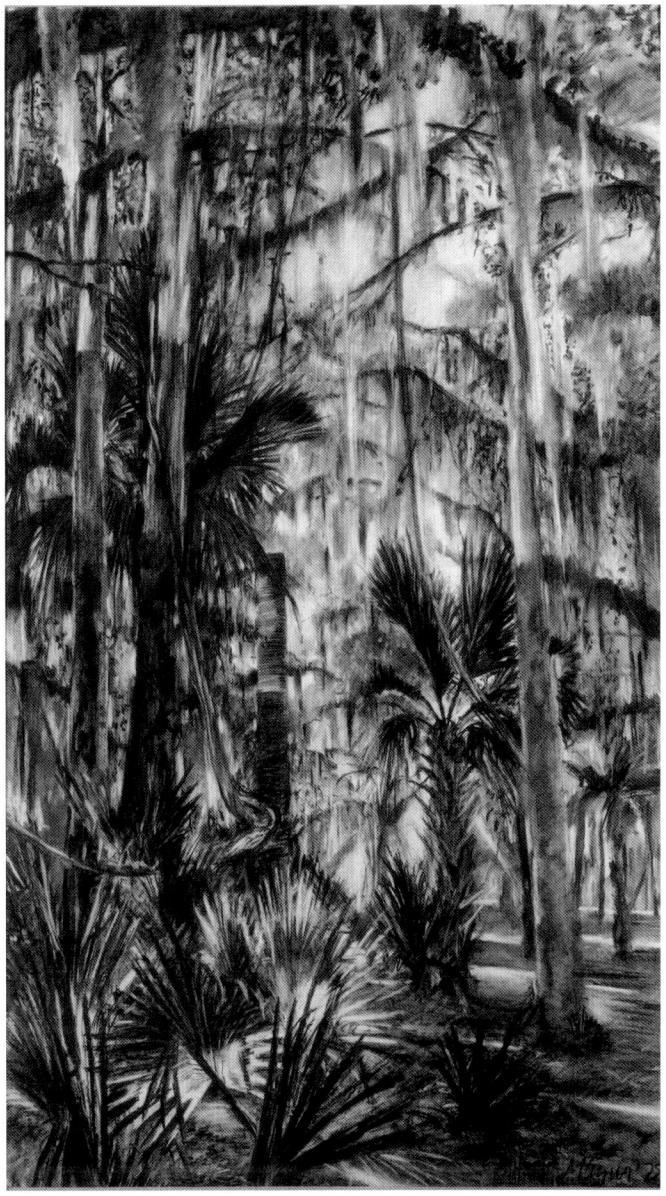

fig. 6.   Michael Mazur. *Landscape-Ossabaw*, 1975. Charcoal with smudging and erasing on
ivory wove paper, 71 ½ × 41 in. Art Institute of Chicago

including *Landscape–Ossabaw* (1975) [fig. 6], in which Mazur contrasts a trio of angular palmettos with a blanket of dripping Spanish moss brought masterfully to life using an eraser.
In *Palmetto* (1975) [p. 105], which is nearly 6 × 8 feet, Mazur examines the central section of
forest, obscuring the ground and the sky. The titular trees dominate the composition in a
claustrophobic cacophony of branches and fronds rendered in every shade of green, from
neon to nearly black. Mazur complicates this *horror vacui* by capturing each frond with an
acute specificity and personality. The striking contrasts in these drawings lend them a fore-
boding quality, evoking the multilayered reality of Ossabaw's forests.

     The critic Robert Taylor drew a connection between Mazur's Ossabaw works
and a series of macabre etchings that the artist made of a psychiatric hospital in the early
1960s, writing that the density of his drawings "imply without the narrative and literary connotations of the closed wards, the fragility, danger and exuberance of the natural
order."[25] Mazur continued to engage these contradictions and work outside the studio
when he returned to Boston, where he began to explore the relationship between plants
and architecture in the greenhouses at Wellesley College [fig. 7]. From the wildness of
Ossabaw to the fight against human intervention in Wellesley, Mazur sought to reveal the
overwhelming power of nature.

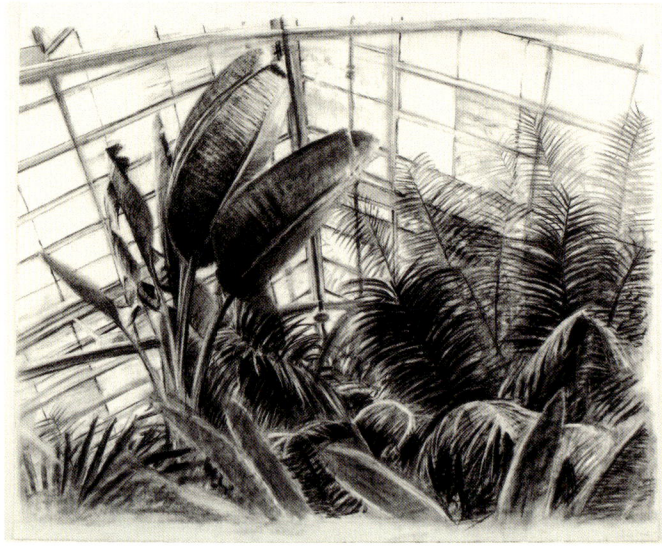

The painter Ellen Lanyon arrived at the OIP in March 1976 in the wake of a transformative visit to the Everglades courtesy of *America 1976*, the same exhibition that Mazur participated in. A lifelong city dweller, Lanyon's trip to Florida was both a shock to the system and a galvanizing experience that left her wanting more. Beginning several years earlier, the artist started to include animals in her uncanny still lives, which often incorporated unlikely pairings that toyed with perceptions of reality. However, Lanyon's connection to her new subject matter took on a fresh significance in the wake of her meaningful experiences of wilderness and wildlife in the Everglades and then on Ossabaw.

Lanyon described Ossabaw as "remote...heavy with humidity & a sense of danger in the tangle of jungle forest...the threat of snakes & insects—but all so fanciful—& containing the thrill of discovery. The balance of nature at hand."[26] Her characterization of the island at the crux of beauty and danger is palpable in *Ossabaw Storm Warning* (1975) [p. 95], which showcases how the particular light cast by ominous gray storm clouds brings out the lush greens of the marsh. A dainty Chinese box fluttering in the wind disrupts the intensity of the natural phenomenon at play, juxtaposing the real and the imagined.

This contrast also plays out in *The Egret* (1976) [fig. 8], one of four paintings that Lanyon began during her residency at the OIP. The regal, snowy white, titular bird lords over the left side of the composition, standing in shallow water before a dense thicket of palmettos and marsh grass. Reminiscent of the decorative ceramics that adorned the Main House's dining room table at the time, two porcelain birds stand below its long, thin, black beak, gazing at each other coquettishly.[27] By pairing the austere living egret with its flirtatious decorative counterparts, Lanyon comments on loosening norms around sex during the 1970s. "Who is the reality?" she wrote in her journal. "The live egret......askance at the porcelain lovers—being honest in himself in courtship plumage—or the phony pair?"[28] In asking these questions, the artist asserted her curiosity and uncertainty around evolving social conventions. "Lanyon's creatures were trying to escape from their surfaces," writes Lucy Lippard. "In an identifiable metaphor for liberation, they began quite literally to venture out of their confines."[29]

Lanyon not only came to understand the humanity of the egret while on Ossabaw, but also the potential peril that the bird faced in an increasingly industrialized world. "It was what I had looked for all along," she later explained, "the substitution of creatures domestic and wild for the dramatization of the human condition."[30] Both Lanyon and Mazur—as well as many other artists who came to Ossabaw before and after them—were left awestruck by the island's terrain. However, while its endless expanse of maritime forest, salt-water marsh, and wide beaches certainly captured their imaginations, the island's simultaneously frightening, quiet, powerful, and fragile ecosystem is what stayed with them long after they left it behind, continuing to reveal its potential for metaphor.

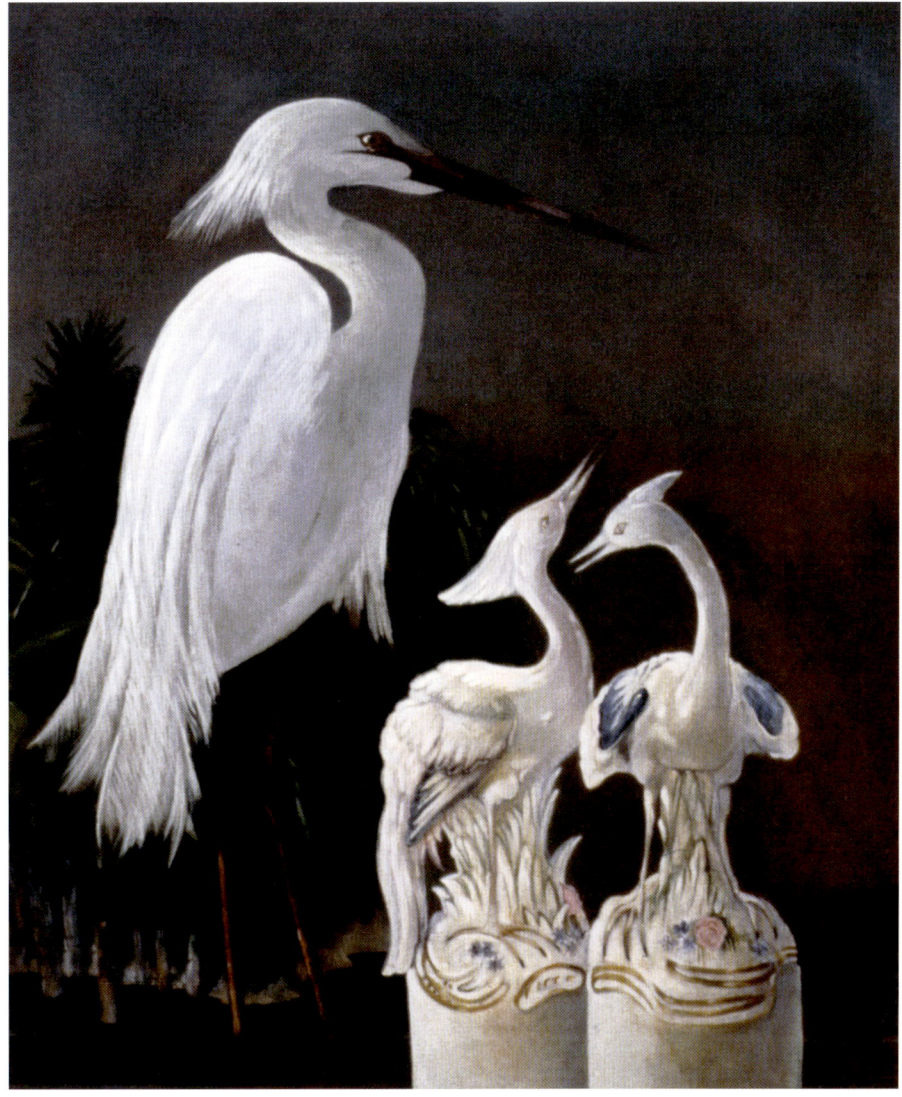

fig. 8.   Ellen Lanyon. *The Egret*, 1976. Acrylic on canvas

THE PARADOX

See, if I was on the other side, and I wanted meat over there? Or fish?
If I was on the other side, I'd have to buy whatever I wanted. But not
over here. Over here it's free. On an island, everything's free.
—Cyrus Martin Sr.[31]

When the artists Agnes Denes and Tyrone Mitchell attended the OIP in 1981, they were separately struck by the fact that many of the African American staff members on the island lived in the tabby cabins that housed enslaved workers during the pre-Civil War era.[32] "I found that an interesting contrast," Denes wrote. "Paradox is my baby."[33] Queenie Mae Williams, a Black woman born and raised in Savannah, lived in the last of the three tabbies and worked in the kitchen at the Main House for decades and throughout the OIP and Genesis years. Williams was a beloved figure on Ossabaw and she appeared often in the writings, memories, and artwork of members from the two programs. The photographer John Earl took portraits of her over many years [p. 133], the author Ralph Ellison kept a slip of paper with her address and phone number on it [fig. 9], and the sculptor Anne Truitt's last memory of the island was of Williams, who told her to "take safety with [you]."[34]

    Williams did not consider herself an artist and never officially participated in the OIP or Genesis, but she nonetheless engaged with those communities in a distinctly

fig. 9.   Queenie Williams's home address and phone number on a slip of paper that she gave to Ralph Ellison, March 1971

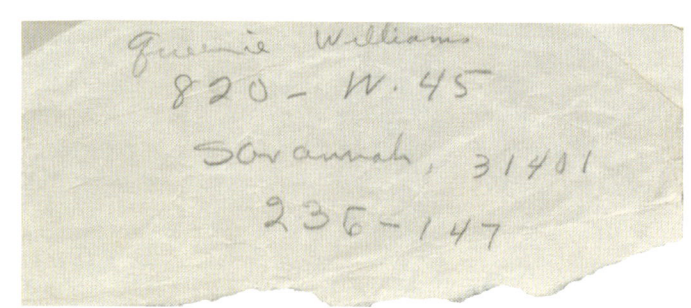

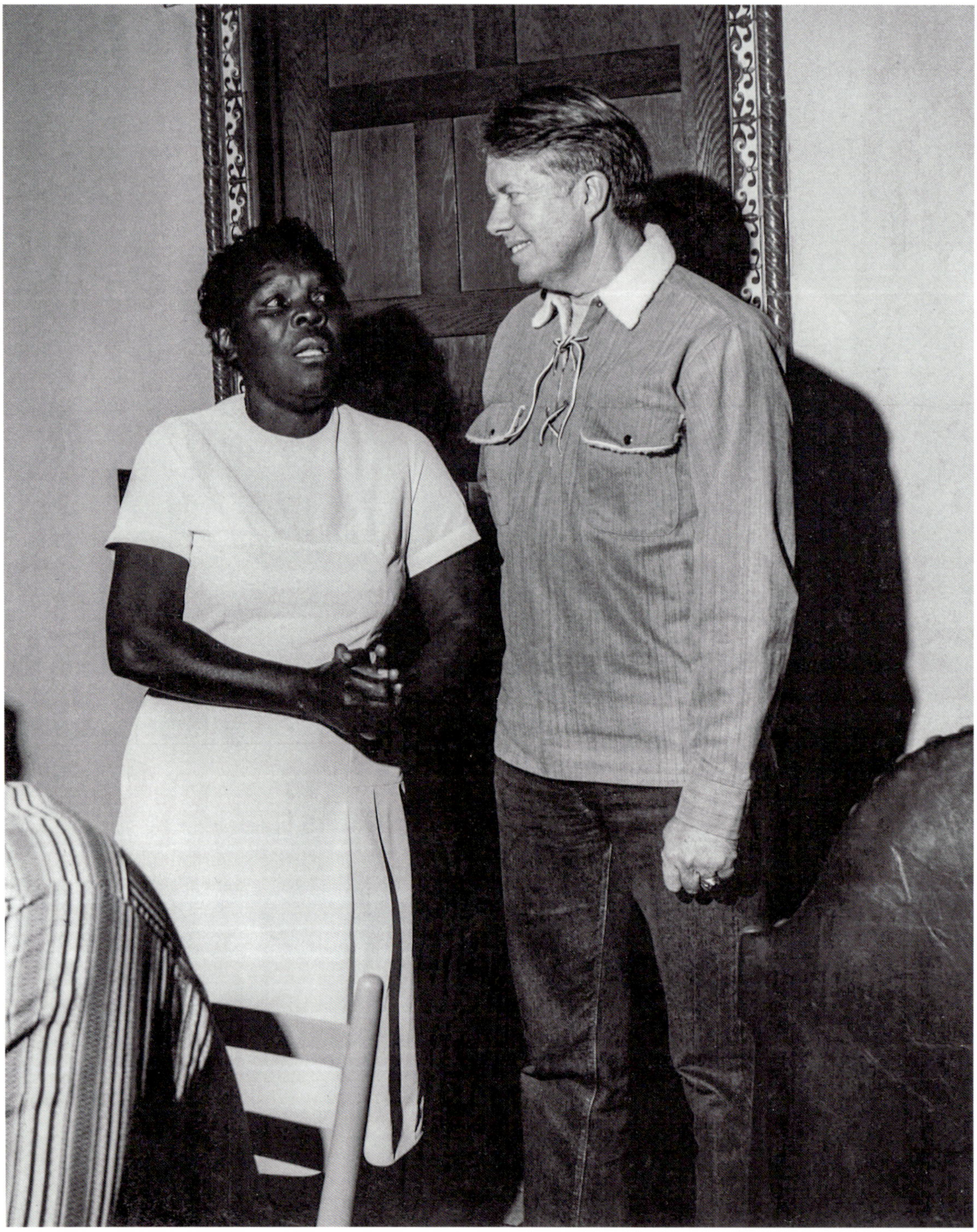

fig. 10. Queenie Williams singing for Georgia Governor Jimmy Carter in the Main House dining room, December 1972

artistic capacity. On some evenings, she would come into the dining room after dinner and start singing spirituals, walking around the table as she performed and grasping the hands of those in her audience [fig. 10]. Many former members and journalists have commented on the power of these performances. "When I felt enwrapped [*sic*] in Queenie's voice and eyes, and the touch of her hand, I recognized the change that has occurred in me since I came here," wrote the painter Julia Hough. "I have a whole new way of seeing, of thinking."[35] The paradox lies in Williams's official role in all of this, which diverges from the invited guests assembled around the table. She was there in a service capacity and was almost certainly the only person of color in the room.[36]

Denes's use of the word "paradox" speaks to the enduring tension of Ossabaw's complex human history, which is essential to fully understanding the island's sense of place. Guale, Muscogee, English, Spanish, West and Central African, and Gullah Geechee[37] peoples are among those who have lived on Ossabaw over the last 5,000 years, a multicultural legacy that is rooted in both cultural heritage and tradition and a violent history of displacement and enslavement. I have personally felt proprietary over Ossabaw for my entire life, grounded in the knowledge that my ancestors legally owned the island and reaped the financial and philanthropic benefits of its sale. But where does that leave the descendants of Indigenous tribes who were forced off the island by European settlers or the enslaved Africans who were held captive there? Many artists have tackled these questions in their art, especially in the last thirty years as systemic racism has come to the forefront of American consciousness.

Tyrone Mitchell, a New York-based sculptor, applied to the OIP specifically because of the island's significance in African American history.[38] He was immersed in Gullah Geechee culture while growing up in the Black communities around Savannah and was eager to explore its roots on Ossabaw when he arrived in October 1981. During extensive wanderings around the island throughout his residency, Mitchell began to feel the presence of the enslaved people and freedmen who had lived there before.[39] While a pair of brutal hurricanes forced Ossabaw's dwindling Black community off the island at the turn of the century, Gullah Geechee culture endured there through figures such as Cyrus Martin. Born on nearby Skidaway Island in 1900, Martin spent most of his life living and working on Ossabaw. Mitchell was drawn to Martin's stories of his experiences with spirits on the island, specifically one that he often told about a ghost known as Par Tank that attacked him in the middle of the night in the form of a disembodied hand.[40] Mitchell started collecting branches, vines, and other objects related to his experiences on the island that felt significant if not easily explained, paying close attention to everything that happened around him.

Back in New York City after leaving Ossabaw, Mitchell began to consider how the found objects he collected might figure into his sculpture, working through ideas during a residency at the Studio Museum in Harlem from 1981–82. The focal point of *Buzzard's Vine* (1983) [p. 141] is a thickly braided vine that Mitchell took from the island and then sanded down and varnished. It extends downward from an aluminum pyramidal form until it is chopped off cleanly after seventeen inches. The sculpture's title refers to a humorous moment that took place on one of Mitchell's walks around the island. When he stopped to scrutinize a clump of intertwined vines hanging from a tree, a buzzard flew over and released some droppings on his head to voice its displeasure: "The sculpture came out of a first impression," he later said.[41] In her memoir, the Geechee griot Cornelia Walker Bailey from nearby Sapelo Island writes about the "Buzzard Lope," a popular dance that her father and his friends often performed during celebrations known as shouts. Bailey explains that the dance refers to the way buzzards circled around an enslaved man who was worked to death in the oppressive August heat.[42] The *Buzzard's Vine*'s titular vine metaphorically anchors the work to the island, creating a powerful site-specificity grounded in the ancestral spirits that he perceived on Ossabaw. In doing so, Mitchell evokes a complex combination of humor, joy, violence, and suffering, all of which is inherent to Black history on the island and in the United States more broadly.

fig. 11. Rashod Taylor. *Tabby Houses, Ossabaw Island, GA*, 2024. Tintype, 7 15/16 × 9 15/16 in.
Nelson-Atkins Museum of Art

The photographer Rashod Taylor came to Ossabaw in 2024 to capture the island as part of his *My America* series. Using wet plate tintype photography, which was developed during the pre-Civil War era, the artist explores what it means to live as a Black man in the United States today in this ongoing project. On Ossabaw, Taylor photographed the marsh, the main road that bisects the island, and the three tabby cabins (fig. 11, pp. 144–145) on the North End. Each one-of-a-kind tintype acts like a living memory, evoking the atrocities that his ancestors endured in places like Ossabaw and their continued relevance today.

Taylor's photographs echo the work of Sally Mann, who spent the day on Ossabaw in March 1996 during a weeklong trip to Savannah on commission for the High Museum of Art in Atlanta. A native Southerner who has spent her whole life living in Lexington, Virginia, Mann had the specific ambition of complicating the romanticized Southern landscape in a new body of work. In many ways, Ossabaw's history made it a perfect subject. In addition to its history of enslavement, the island holds the memory of such events as the burning of a Guale village called Azapo on its south end by Spanish settlers in 1579, among many others. Mann aimed to capture the tension of such histories in her photographs of the American South.

Mann arrived in Savannah armed with 19th-century barrel lenses and long-expired orthochromatic film, which she had never used before.[43] "I struck out with ... an entirely new aesthetic ambition," she said, "wanting to do something so radically different than what I had been doing."[44] Her choice of materials was inspired by the solarization and flared edges in a series of glass negatives in her personal collection that were taken by a Civil War veteran around Lexington. Over the course of her day on Ossabaw, Mann photographed the island's horses, its tabby cabins, and a dilapidated shed near the dock at the North End. Covered in peeling white paint and leaning over to the side as if on the brink of collapse, the shed is diminutive amid the surrounding arching oaks and dripping moss in Mann's photograph[p. 139]. The building's tenuousness functions as a metaphor for the myth of the Confederate south. "These photographs are about memory and time and the still point at which they intersect," Mann later said of her *Mother Land* series, which included Ossabaw. "I noted the ways we compose history's beautiful lie."[45]

Mann's most indelible subject on Ossabaw proved to be the mottled pink stucco walls that act as gate posts at the entrance to the Main House grounds. Covered in moss, overtaken by vines, and flanked by two empty planters, they telegraph a palpable sense of my family's faded Roaring Twenties wealth and privilege. In Mann's *Georgia, Untitled (Ossabaw Gates)* (1996)[p. 138], that feeling is exacerbated by the blemishes and discolorations of the orthochromatic film. Anchored in the center of the photograph, the walls extend past the left and right edges of the composition—acting as a barrier to entry. A dirt road emerging from the bottom right corner guides the eye through the wide open doors of the gate, leading the viewer into the wilderness. In the words of Hilton Als, "Mann does not rearrange the fact of the earth in her work, but she doesn't turn away from the death that lies in it, either."[46] By portraying the crumbling shed and tarnished gates as the scars of human intervention in nature, Mann evokes the violence imbued in the Southern landscape as an intrinsic element of its extraordinary beauty.

The paradox of Ossabaw's landscape remains relevant for artists working there today. In her new film *Venus of Ossabaw* (2026), the multidisciplinary artist Allison Janae Hamilton engages with the history of enslavement on the island through the lens of *marronage*.[47] When Hamilton's protagonist, Venus, escapes from a plantation on Ossabaw and makes her way down Georgia's coast to Spanish Florida, she faces a choice in terms of her freedom. Hamilton emphasizes Venus's agency in the situation by focusing on her decision to either join the Catholic church in Saint Augustine or remain with the maroons. Along with Mitchell, Taylor, Mann, and others, including the painters Suzanne Jackson, and Marcy Hermansader, Hamilton looks beyond the preserved natural splendor of Ossabaw Island to consider its human history as a microcosm of the American experience.

LIKE A VEIL

In the mid-1960s, my grandparents asked their friends and recurring OIP members, architect Olav Hammarstrom and textile designer Marianne Strengell, to design an Ossabaw museum built from island materials on the Main House grounds[fig. 12]. It was to comprise three buildings, one dedicated to the island's natural resources, another to its human history, and a third to the work of OIP members.[48] While the museum was never realized, today artworks with ties to Ossabaw abound in museums, private homes, universities, and other venues all over the United States. The diversity of this body of work is remarkable, from point of view to medium of expression to engagement with the island's

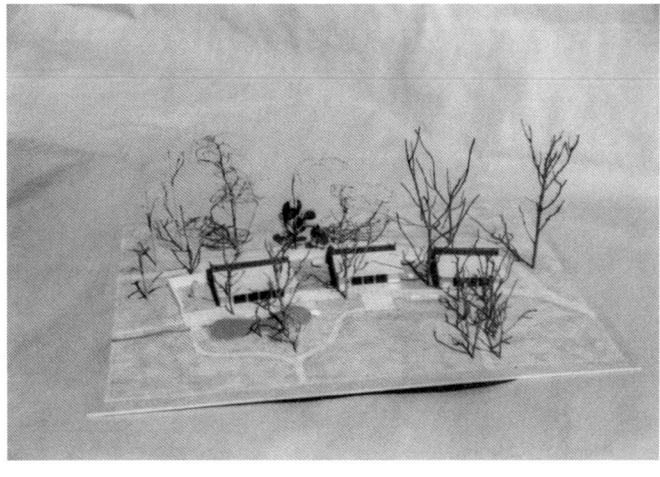

fig. 12.   Olav Hammarstrom's model for the Ossabaw
           museum, March 1969

multi-layered reality. Notably, many of these works also diverge from the traditional style and *modus operandi* of their makers.

As my grandmother said, the level and type of expertise one brings to Ossabaw is beside the point. Rather, the island proposes something new to the artists who spend time there. The expanse of self-contained wilderness might catalyze a richer understanding of the dense maritime forest or a sense of ancestral spirits or even a renewed clarity of intention. The combination of solitude, unhampered nature, immense beauty, and rich historical and cultural significance yield limitless possibilities. In the end though, it is the indescribable quality of Ossabaw—which draws from each of those elements but extends far beyond them—that has and will continue to resonate most powerfully with creative minds. "I was taken with a subtle feeling of nostalgia, a bit of sadness mixed with an invisible cause," Agnes Denes wrote of her time on the island. "Hard to describe, like a veil, you know it's there but can't see it."[49] Ossabaw, like art, cannot be quantified.

Notes

1. Philip Guston quoted in Musa Mayer, *Night Studio: A Memoir of Philip Guston*, 4th ed. (Zürich: Hauser & Wirth Publishers, 2023), 168. This quote is drawn from an undated letter to Guston's wife, the poet Musa McKim, who attended OIP from February 18–March 4, 1974. OIP members were instructed to meet the program's director(s) at the Hotel DeSoto Hilton in downtown Savannah upon their arrival. They were then transported to Ossabaw via private boat from the Vernon View neighborhood of Burnside Island.

2. Eleanor Torrey West and Clifford West's programming on Ossabaw included Genesis, Public Use and Education, and Professional Research. Please refer to Erin Dunn's essay on p. 60 of this volume for more details on the structure of the OIP and Genesis.

3. Agnes Denes, *Thoughts of Ossabaw*, unpublished manuscript, undated, courtesy of the artist.

4. A letter to Mrs. West that was signed "Carol" (the painter's identity is unknown), November 15, 1976, West family archives.

5. *Ossabaw Island, Georgia*, directed by Justin P. West (Northampton, MA: Fine Arts Video, 1990), film. Sandy West is quoted at 8:32.

6. Michael Blumenthal, "Ossabaw island—haven for both Man and animals," *Smithsonian* 12, no. 7 (October 1981): 131.

7. Roman Jakobson quoted in Clifford West and Eleanor West, *Ossabaw* (Ossabaw Island Project Foundation, 1973), 26.

8. Margaret Ann Keister, "The Ossabaw Island Project, a Program Fostering Creative Production and Experience," (PhD diss., University of Georgia, 1992), 255.

9. See Wini Wood's text on p. 120 of this volume for additional background on *Sherman's March* and its legacy, as well as a firsthand look at how the film was made.

10. "Tape-recorded interview with Harry Bertoia" by Paul Cummings, Archives of American Art Oral History Program, June 20, 1972, transcript, 21.

11. Eleanor Torrey West's notes from the symposium to launch the Ossabaw Island Project, June 24, 1961, West family archives.

12. "Tape-recorded interview with Harry Bertoia," transcript, 21

13. Bertoia was commissioned by Eero Saarinen, whom he knew from the Cranbrook Academy of Art, to make a large-scale public artwork for Dulles. The resulting work, which Bertoia completed in 1962 for Kevin Roche following Saarinen's untimely death, is made up of nine spill-cast panels that are collectively 36 feet long and eight feet tall. It remains on view at the airport to this day.

14. Lawrence Campbell, "Creative Casting," *craft horizons* XXIII, no. 6 (November/December 1963).

15. Anne Truitt, *Daybook: The Journal of an Artist* (New York: Pantheon Books, 1982), 145.

16. Corrected typescript of *Daybook* by Anne Truitt, n.d., BMC.M109, box 4, folder 1, Anne Truitt Papers, Bryn Mawr College, 184.

17. Anne Truitt, *Daybook*, 99.

18. Anne Truitt, *Daybook*, 4.

19. Corrected typescript, Anne Truitt Papers, 198.

20. Audio recording of Anne Truitt, spring 1998, transcript, Anne Truitt Estate.

21. Anne Truitt, *Daybook*, 145.

22. Jean Zaleski, "Getting Away From It All: Isolation as Inspiration," *Women Artists News* 7, no. 1 (April-May 1981): 6.

23. Robert Rosenblum, "Painting America First," *America 1976* (United States Department of the Interior, 1976), 8. Mazur's official subject was the adjacent Wassaw Island, a large portion of which was managed by the federal government as a National Wildlife Refuge. He took a day trip there during his first week at OIP, but Ossabaw is the primary subject of this body of work.

24. Journal, 1974–75, January 7, 1975, box 11, folder 27, Michael Mazur papers, c. 1936–2016, Archives of American Art, Smithsonian Institution, Washington, DC.

25. Robert Taylor, "Visual perception as subject," *Boston Evening Globe*, October 21, 1976, 43.

26. Journal, 1974–1980, box 24, folder 17, Ellen Lanyon papers, c. 1880–

2015, bulk 1926-2013, Archives of American Art, Smithsonian Institution, Washington, DC.

27. Lanyon explored every nook and cranny of the Main House, including the attic, during her residency and included many of the objects that she discovered in her drawings and paintings. One example is an antique Chinese chair in the living room that is the subject of Lanyon's colored pencil drawing *Ossabaw Chair* (1976).

28. Journal, 1974-1980, Ellen Lanyon papers.

29. Lucy Lippard, "Under the Wing of Survival: Ellen Lanyon," *Ellen Lanyon* (Chicago: N.A.M.E. Gallery, 1983), 3.

30. Ellen Lanyon quoted in Lucy Lippard, "Under the Wing of Survival," 4.

31. Cyrus Martin Sr., quoted in Fred Powledge, "Island Fever" *Esquire*, March 1977, 114.

32. The cabins on Ossabaw's North End were built by enslaved workers in the first half of the 19th century. They are built of tabby, a cement material made by mixing lime from burned oyster shells, sand and water. This method of vernacular architecture is seen in buildings from the time across the Southeast.

33. Agnes Denes, Email to author, June 8, 2024.

34. Corrected typescript, Anne Truitt Papers, 202.

35. Julia Hough to Eleanor West, December 17, 1975, West family archives.

36. While members of the OIP and Genesis came from all over the world and from many different cultural backgrounds, the vast majority of them were white.

37. The historian Emory Campbell describes Gullah culture as "a system of beliefs, customs, artforms, foodways, and language practiced among descendants of West Africans who settled along the coasts of North Carolina, South Carolina, Georgia and Florida from (the) slavery period to the present." Geechee, which refers more specifically to enslaved West Africans who arrived in the region through the Ogeechee River in southeastern Georgia, is also commonly used, so the collective term Gullah Geechee will be used here unless specified otherwise. See Emory Campbell, *Gullah Cultural Legacies*, 3rd ed. (Hilton Head Island, SC: Gullah Heritage Consulting Services, 2008), 5.

38. Mitchell is one of many African American artists who were drawn to the Georgia and South Carolina Sea Islands during this time (as well as before and after) due to the land's historic significance for the African diaspora. Please see Thomas Lax's essay on p. 148 of this volume for an in-depth exploration of this topic.

39. After two centuries of slavery on Ossabaw, several families remained on the island after its abolishment in 1865. They received tracts of land under Special Field Order No. 15, which reserved coastal land for the settlement of freedmen. The order was revoked by President Andrew Johnson less than a year later and the land was restored to its Confederate owners. Many freedman stayed on Ossabaw as sharecroppers, which was a very difficult life. See Allison Dorsey, "'The great cry of our people is land!' Black Settlement and Community Development on Ossabaw Island, Georgia, 1865-1900" in *African American Life in the Georgia Lowcountry: The Atlantic World and the Gullah Geechee*, ed. Phillip Morgan (Athens and London: University of Georgia Press, 2010).

40. See Vaughnette Goode-Walker's text on p. 160 of this volume for more information and background on Martin and this story.

41. Tyrone Mitchell, Phone call with the author, October 27, 2023.

42. Cornelia Walker Bailey with Christina Bledsoe, *God, Dr. Buzzard, and the Bolito Man* (New York: Anchor Books, 2000), 178-182. Bailey describes a shout as "a celebration, an organized celebration, done in a circle, to the beat of a stick, a broomstick."

43. An early form of black-and-white film, orthochromatic photography is described by Mann as a "graphic arts film characterized by extremely high contrast." She chose to use this film because it could mimic the more complex wet collodion process that she was interested in but didn't feel ready for. Sally Mann, *Hold Still: A Memoir with Photographs* (New York: Back Bay Books, 2015), 221.

44. Sally Mann interviewed in "Picturing the South: Sally Mann," posted November 5, 2021, by High Museum of Art, YouTube, 5:04, https://youtu.be/8nh2eOiWaoO. At the time, Mann had recently completed her renowned and controversial *Immediate Family* series. The technical precision of those photographs is in sharp contrast to the messiness of the *Mother Land* images.

45. Sally Mann quoted in "Sally Mann," *Picturing the South: 25 Years, High Museum of Art*, accessed May 6, 2025, https://link.picturingthesouth.high.org/essay/sally-mann/

46. Hilton Als, "The Color of Humanity in Sally Mann's South," *The New Yorker*, February 28, 2018, accessed July 28, 2025, https://www.newyorker.com/culture/photo-booth/the-color-of-humanity-in-sally-manns-south.

47. See Allison Janae Hamilton's text on p. 164 of this volume for more information on *Venus of Ossabaw*. For additional background on how Black Georgians sought freedom in coastal Florida in the late 18th and early 19th centuries, see Paul M. Pressly, *A Southern Underground Railroad: Black Georgians and the Promise of Spanish Florida and Indian Country* (Athens and London: The University of Georgia Press, 2024).

48. "Ossabaw Newsletter," c.1975, box 92, folder 5, Ralph Ellison papers, Library of Congress.

49. Agnes Denes, *Thoughts of Ossabaw*.

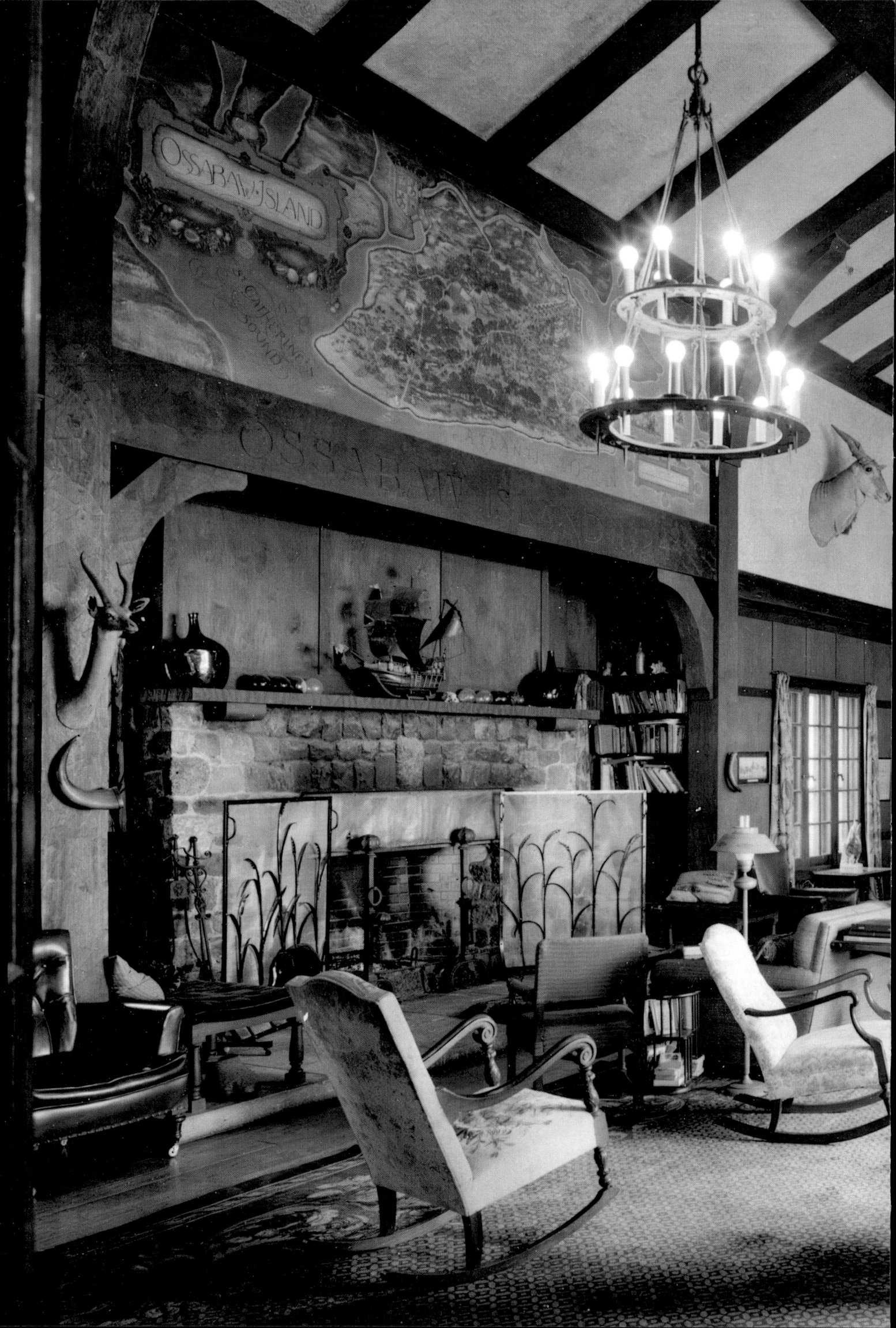

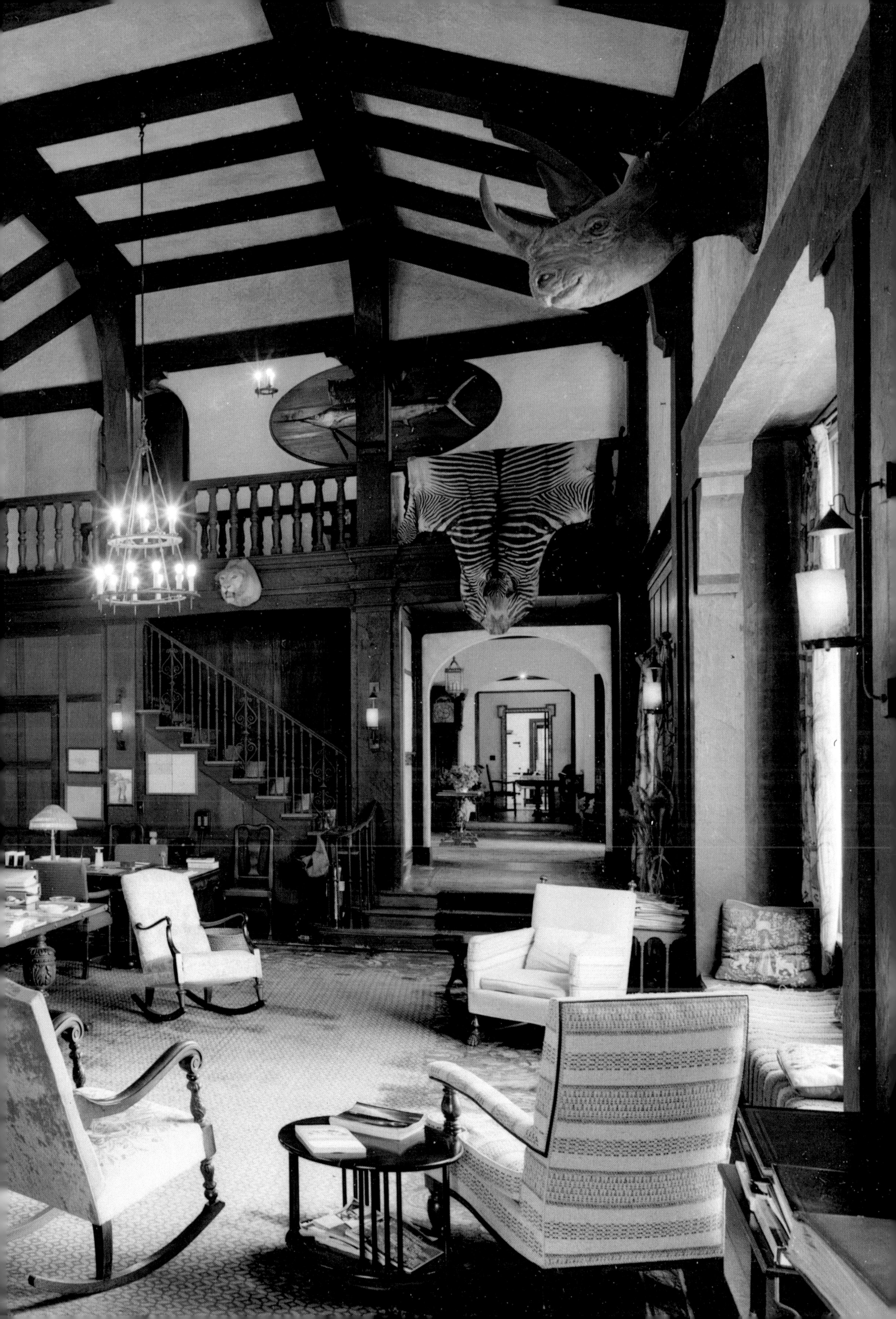

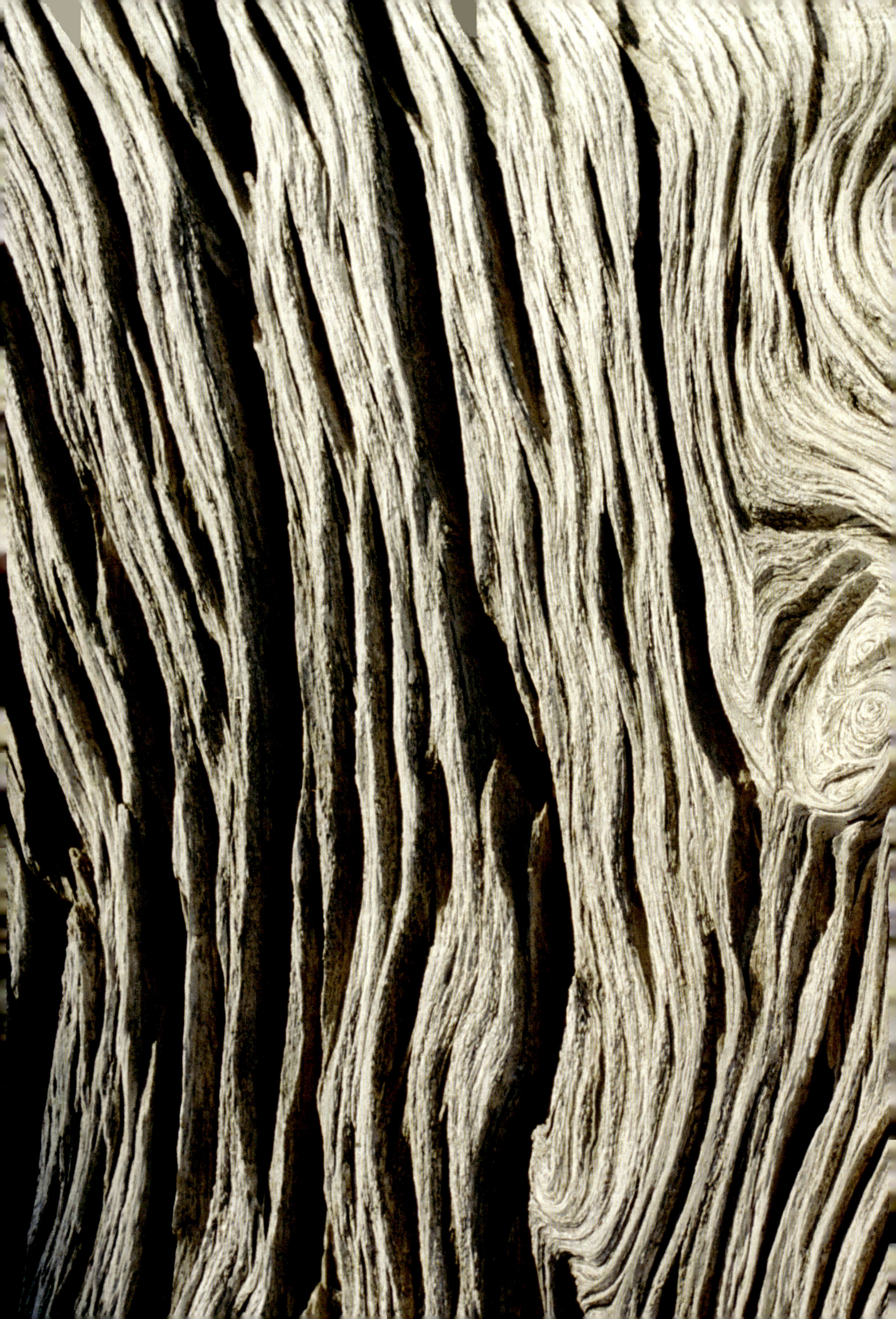

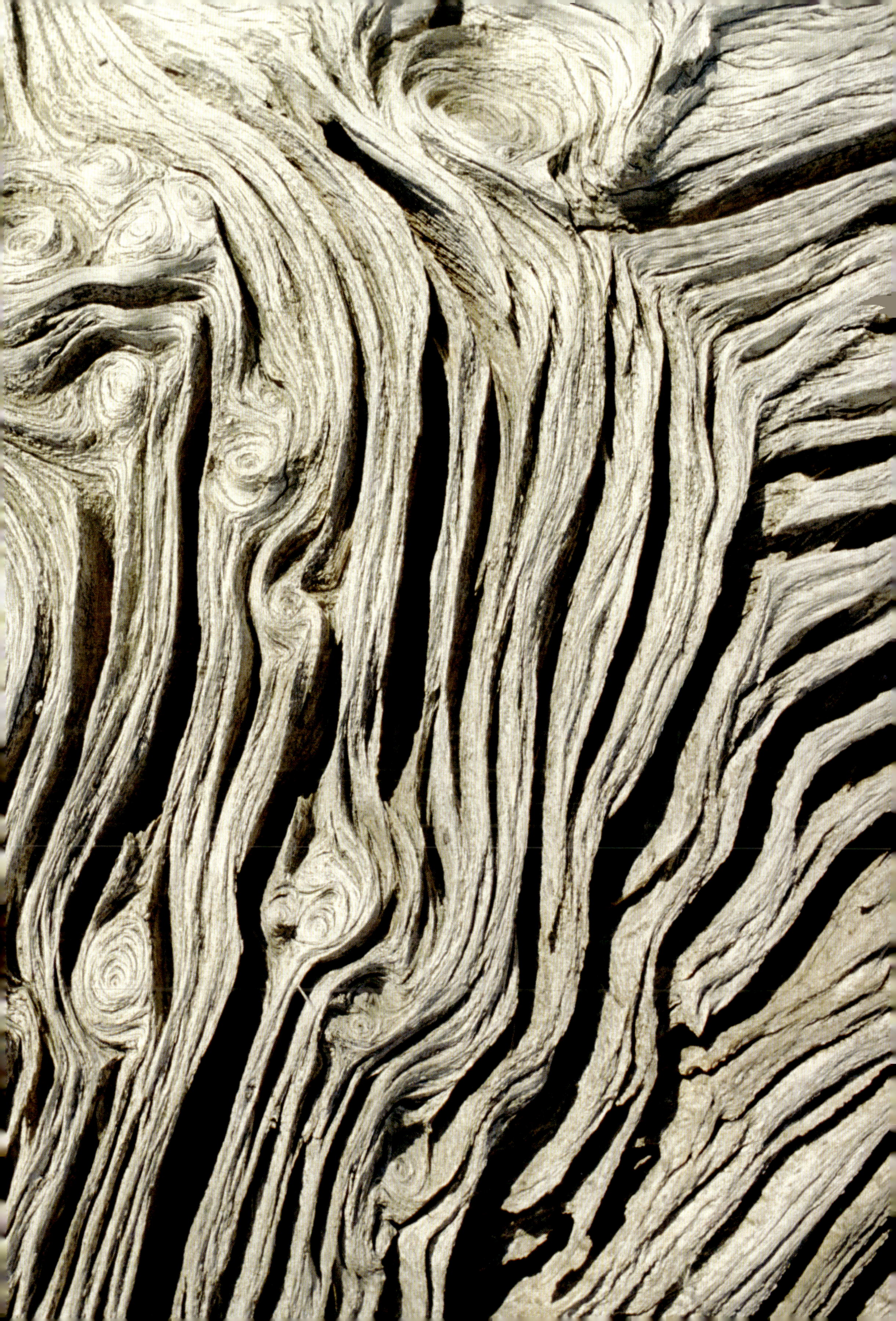

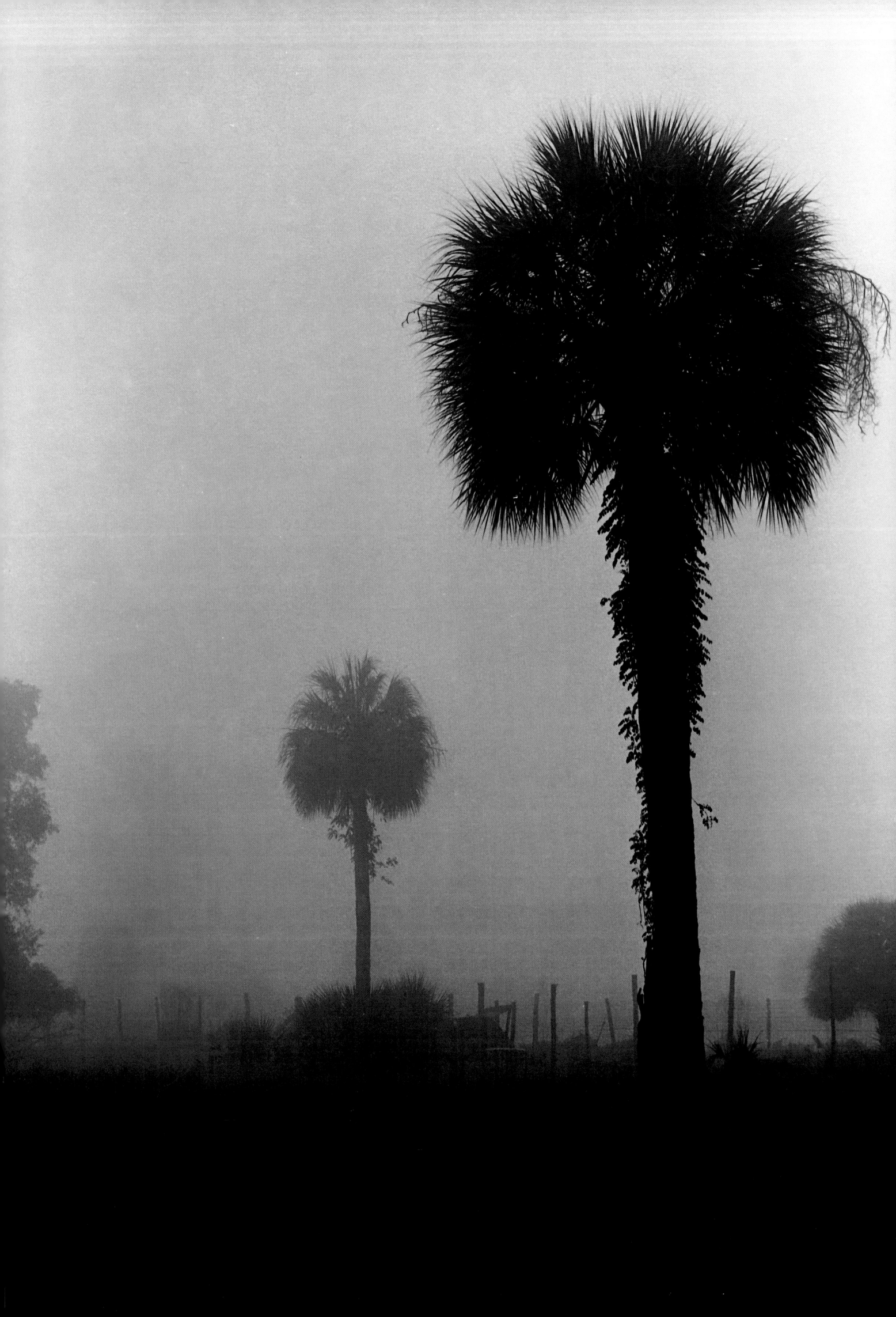

THE CATALYST

OIP and Genesis co-founder Eleanor Torrey West often described Ossabaw as "a catalyst." She believed that the island would speak to those who approached it with patience, flexibility, and ample time. For visual artists, the immersive environment of Ossabaw frequently acts as a conduit to fresh ideas and new ways of thinking.

HARRY BERTOIA (1915–1978)

The Italian-born Harry Bertoia was an American sculptor, print-maker, and metalworker best-known for his Sonambient sculptures, monumental public commissions, artist jewelry, and the iconic Diamond and Side chairs that he designed for Knoll. Bertoia studied at the Detroit Society of Arts and Crafts and later at the Cranbrook Academy of Art, where he developed a passion for metalworking. Following the success of his work at Knoll in the early 1950s, Bertoia gained the freedom to dedicate more time to sculpture. He was commissioned to make public works for buildings by such architects as Eero Saarinen and Roche & Dinkeloo. Bertoia began introducing sound into his art in the early 1960s, releasing a series of LPs of taped recordings of his Sonambient sculptures installed in a barn on his property in Barto, Pennsylvania. An old friend of Clifford West from Cranbrook, Bertoia visited Ossabaw Island in June 1961 as an advisor to the nascent Ossabaw Island Project, a role that he maintained until his death in 1978. The "almost primeval" landscape that Bertoia witnessed on the island's beaches in 1961 was part of the inspiration for his unique bronze spill-casting technique.

pp. 34–36

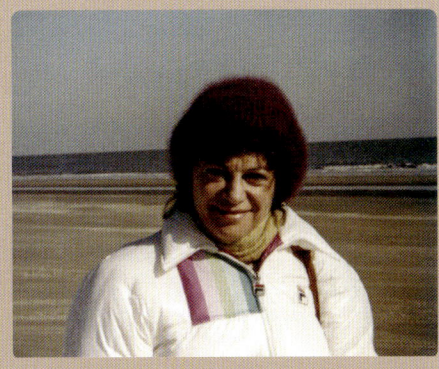

AGNES DENES (B. 1931)

Agnes Denes is one of the most prominent artists and environmental activists of the contemporary age and is recognized as a pioneer of the Land Art movement. Denes's most famous works are often created on a monumental scale and imbued with sacred geometry in alignment with the Earth; including the planting of a forest in an elliptical shape down a mountain, a grove of trees planted in what resembles a thumbprint, and her most famous installation, *Wheatfield—A Confrontation*, which was planted in Manhattan in summer 1982. Denes employs the concept of "Eco-Logic," a term she coined in the 1960s that refers to the two pillars of her work: ecology and logic. In addition to her ecological installations, Denes is known for her innovative use of nontraditional materials immersed in science, philosophy, and mathematics to explore geometric designs as a narrative for human evolution. Her body of work *Future City* imagines a new world where "philosophy and introspections are the dominant methodologies for navigating the future." Denes attended the Ossabaw Island Project from January 9–26, 1981. She photographed patterns carved into the sand by the changing tides on Ossabaw, her images of these natural fractals emulating the esoteric patterns for which her art is known.

pp. 38–41

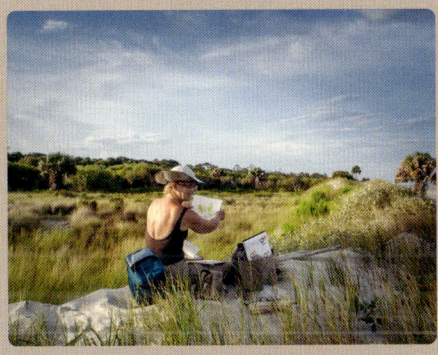

BETSY CAIN (B. 1949)

Betsy Cain's multimedia practice is rooted in the vernacular of the Georgia Lowcountry. Themes of the human body and the Coastal Southeast manifest in her figurative and abstracted images of spartina grass, live oaks, and other natural elements. Cain studied at Auburn University in Alabama, and the Instituto Allende in San Miguel de Allende, Mexico, before receiving her BFA in 1972 and MFA in 1976 from the University of Alabama, Tuscaloosa. She was an artist in residence at the Roswell Museum and Art Center in New Mexico from 1980–81 before moving to Savannah, where she has lived as a working artist for the last four decades. While she first visited Ossabaw in the early 1990s, Cain began spending more time on the island as a participant and informal organizer of The Ossabaw Island Foundation's Visiting Artists Program in the late 2000s and early 2010s. During that time, she developed a close friendship with Eleanor Torrey West and became one of West's caregivers during her last years on the island.

pp. 37, 89

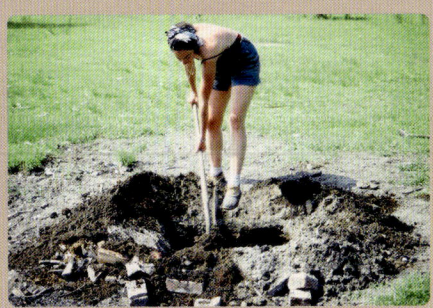

LESLIE FERST (B. 1954)

Leslie Ferst has been working as a studio artist and educator for nearly fifty years. She received a BA in the history of art from Skidmore College in 1976 and an MFA in ceramics from Boston University in 1984. She was a Genesis member on Ossabaw Island several times during those early years, experiences that became the foundation for her artistic practice and continue to shape the content and vision of her work to this day. In between stints at Genesis, Leslie studied the extensive collection of Mimbres bowls at Harvard's Peabody Museum. She understood these bowls to be symbolic metaphors for the natural world, where humans and animals were intertwined in a symbolic interplay of multiple universes—an idea that resonated with the folklore of Ossabaw and what she experienced on the island. Later, Ferst began to understand Ossabaw as a living metaphorical grotto while researching garden grottoes at the Winterthur Museum in Delaware. In tandem with her career as an artist, Ferst has taught ceramics full- and part-time at many institutions, including nineteen years in the art department at Skidmore College.

pp. 42-43

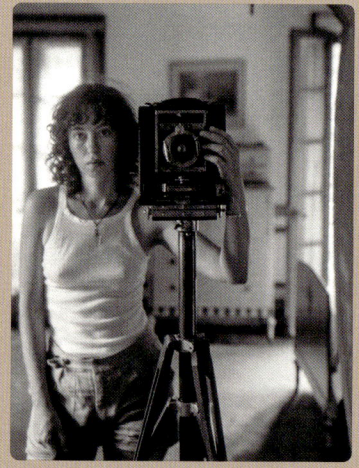

NANCY MARSHALL (B. 1946)

Nancy Marshall's photography focuses on the southern landscape, influenced by the history of photography and antiquarian techniques of platinum, palladium, and albumen printing. Her career began with a year-long internship in the photography department for Governor Jimmy Carter before moving to Georgia Public Television. After participating in a workshop hosted by Mary Ellen Mark at the Apeiron Workshop, Marshall joined Nexus, a cooperative photo gallery in Atlanta that later became the Atlanta Contemporary Art Center. Marshall was a Genesis member in 1979 and 1980, having been inspired to apply by an exhibition held in Savannah of Helen Hamada's photographs of Ossabaw, and has returned often in the years since. "The main point was the exploration and effort," she once explained. "This was the gift of Genesis."

pp. 47-49

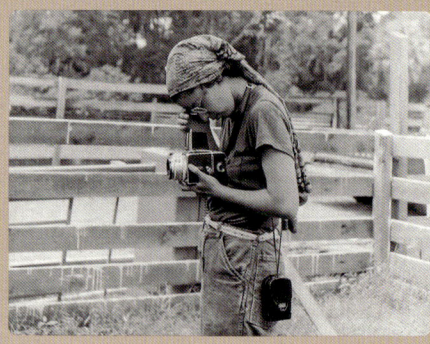

HELEN HAMADA (B. 1951)

Helen Hamada is a photographer and filmmaker based in Stanfordville, New York. She graduated from Penn State University in 1973 with a BA in art/photography and was a Genesis member from February to June 1974, later returning to co-direct Genesis from 1976–1980. During those years, she created a large body of photographs of herself, the landscape, the wildlife, and the activities of both Genesis and the OIP, and has continued photographing while pursuing various personal and professional careers. In 1980, she moved to Millerton, New York, to work at Apeiron Workshops, a premier photographic workshop center, until 1982. In 2003, Hamada filmed and produced a video about an aikido instructor who had his lower leg amputated. In 2015, she completed a multi-year oral history video series of Genesis for The Ossabaw Island Foundation. In 2023, she produced a film about a family of Armenian descent who migrated from Turkey during the 1915 genocide to Lebanon and later to the US. From 2012–24, she and her partner offered a small-scale, international artist-in-residence program from June to September annually out of their home in upstate New York. Currently, Hamada is working on a book of photographs of Ossabaw Island trees and a film about the worldwide family of aikido.

pp. 44-46

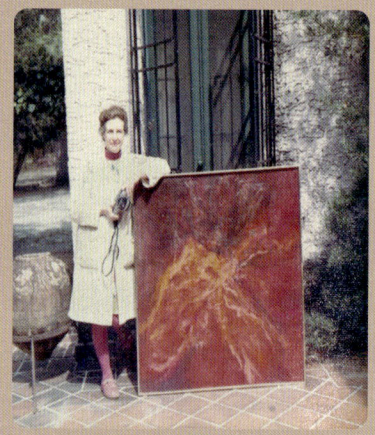

LORRAINE MCCARTY (1920–2004)

Lorraine McCarty was a prominent painter in Michigan who focused on abstracted landscapes (skies in particular) in her oil and acrylic paintings. She lived in Michigan most of her life, studying painting at Wayne State University in Detroit, and the Cranbrook Academy of Art in Bloomfield Hills, as well as Stephens College in Columbia, Missouri. McCarty taught art at numerous venues in the Detroit area, including the Flint Institute of Arts. She designed her own home in Royal Oak, which was featured in *Better Homes and Gardens*. In 1962, McCarty obtained her pilot's license and flew in the All Women Transcontinental Air Race, known as the Powder Puff Derby, where she won first place in 1964. She was a member of the Ninety-Nines, an international organization for female pilots. McCarty painted Ossabaw during her first residency at the OIP from October 21–November 5, 1965, choosing in one painting to render the intensity of the island's pervasive green in its complementary color, a rich, bloody red. She returned twice more, from December 1–21, 1966, and from March 24–April 8, 1973.

p. 51

ROSS MCELWEE (B. 1947)

Ross McElwee is one of the most esteemed documentary filmmakers working today. He started producing and directing documentaries in 1976, and his body of work includes ten feature-length documentaries and several shorts, most of them shot in his homeland of the American South. In three of his films, *Backyard* (1984), *Sherman's March* (1986), and *Time Indefinite* (1993), McElwee experimented with an autobiographical approach, working as a one-person film crew and weaving into the final non-fiction film a highly subjective narration along with personal experiences. Born in North Carolina, McElwee received a BA from Brown University in 1971 and an MS in 1977 from the Massachusetts Institute of Technology, where he studied in a program headed by documentarian Richard Leacock. He attended the Ossabaw Island Project from February 2–March 2, 1981, followed by a stint at Genesis, and shot a significant portion of *Sherman's March* during his time on the island.

pp. 120–24

IRENE O'GARDEN (B. 1951)

Irene O'Garden is an acclaimed poet, essayist, and playwright based in Garrison, New York. She has written many plays and books, including two memoirs, a collection of poetry, a collection of essays, three children's books, and the off-Broadway play *Women on Fire*, which was nominated for a Lucille Lortel Award. O'Garden came to Ossabaw Island as a Genesis member in 1981 with a focus on the visual arts. Using a quill she made on the island, she created a series of loose ink drawings that chronicle the unique nature of Easter Sunday at the semi-sustainable community, showcasing her singular voice as a storyteller.

pp. 52–53

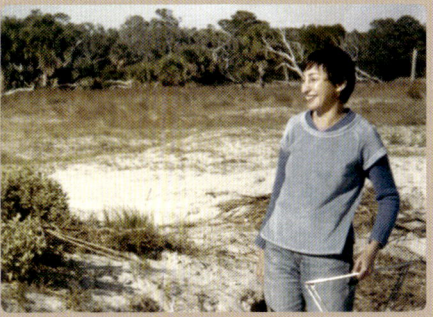

ATHENA TACHA (B. 1936)

Athena Tacha is a visual artist whose work exists at the intersection of art, science, and technology. She works across many media, including sculpture, conceptual art, photography, film, and artist books. Tacha was one of the first artists to develop environmental site-specific sculpture in the early 1970s and won over forty public art commissions from Alaska to Florida. Tacha holds an MFA from the School of Fine Arts in Athens, Greece; an MA in art history from Oberlin College in Ohio; and a PhD in aesthetics from the Sorbonne in Paris. From 1963 until 1998, when she moved to Washington, DC, Tacha was affiliated with Oberlin, first as Curator of Modern Art at the Allen Memorial Art Museum and then as Professor of Sculpture. Tacha first came to the Ossabaw Island Project as a guest of her close friend Ellen H. Johnson in the fall of 1979 before returning as an OIP member from October 31–November 21, 1980. Captivated by the repeating patterns carved by wind and water in the sand on Ossabaw, she took photographs of sand waves on the island's beaches and created a series of reliefs cast directly from them.

pp. 56–57

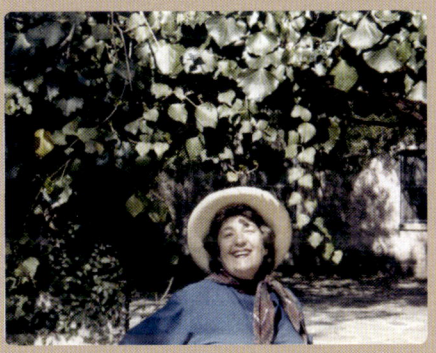

MIRIAM SCHAPIRO (1923–2015)

Miriam Schapiro's practice, which included paintings, sculptures, prints, and multimedia collages, addressed and challenged the gendered division between fine art and craft. Schapiro's work considered women's histories and experiences and she established her signature "femmages" or collages that feature "feminine" materials such as lace and aprons. After earning a BFA and an MFA from the University of Iowa, she moved to New York City in 1952 and became the first woman to have a solo exhibition at André Emmerich Gallery in 1958. In the early 1960s, she began incorporating decorative elements into her work. In 1967, she moved to San Diego with her husband, painter Paul Brach, to lecture at the University of California. While there, she founded the Feminist Art Program at the California Institute of the Arts alongside Judy Chicago. Returning to New York City in 1974, Schapiro became a trailblazer for the Pattern and Decoration movement through engagement with the art world's trivialization of forms considered domestic, feminine, or ornamental. Throughout the 1970s and 1980s, Schapiro continued her opulent "femmages" on large canvases, including *Ossabaw Heart* (1982), which connected to her residency at the OIP from February 5–March 5, 1982.

p. 55

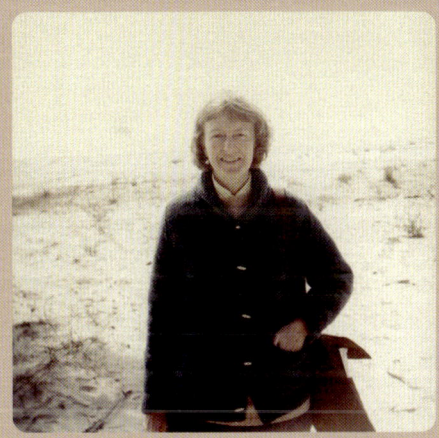

ANNE TRUITT (1921–2004)

Anne Truitt was a major figure in American art for more than forty years, best known for her large-scale, meticulously painted wood sculptures. Abstract yet rich with feeling, her work is grounded in memories and sensations accumulated over a lifetime. This referentiality is in stark contrast to the literalness of Minimalism, a movement with which her work is sometimes associated. For Truitt, abstraction provided a syntax for her impressions—of people, places, ideas, and events. She wielded color and form as metaphors for thought, developing a visual grammar that remains unique in the history of art. As she explained, "What is important to me is not geometrical shape per se, or color per se, but to make a relationship between shape and color which feels to me like my experience. To make what feels to me like reality." She is also renowned for her four books—*Daybook* (1982), *Turn* (1986), *Prospect* (1996), and *Yield* (2022)—which distilled years of journal entries into a vivid account of her life as an artist. Truitt was an OIP member from March 17–31, 1975, during which time she realized that her journals might constitute the beginnings of a manuscript.

p. 59

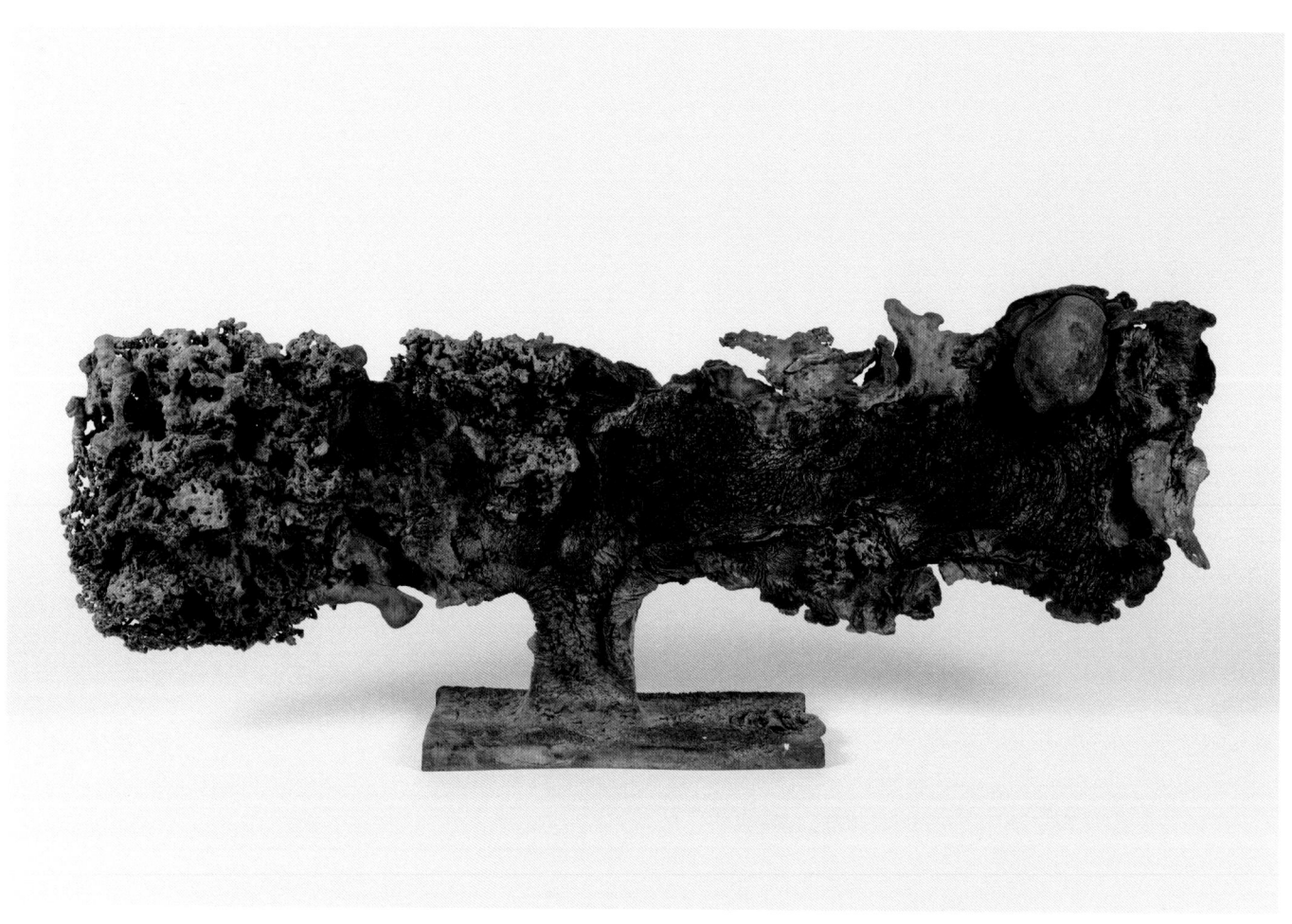

Harry Bertoia (1915–1978)
Untitled, 1966
Bronze and stone
24 × 58 × 9 ½ in.
The Ossabaw Island Foundation

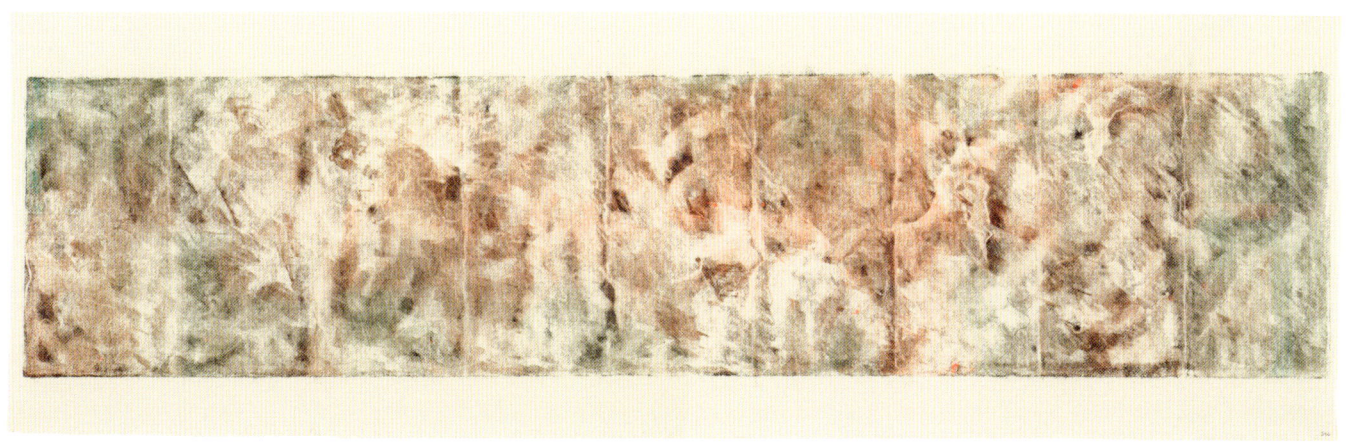

Harry Bertoia (1915–1978)
Untitled, 1962
Monotype on laid rice paper
12 ¼ × 39 in.
Allentown Art Museum, SOTA Print Fund, 1992.5.9

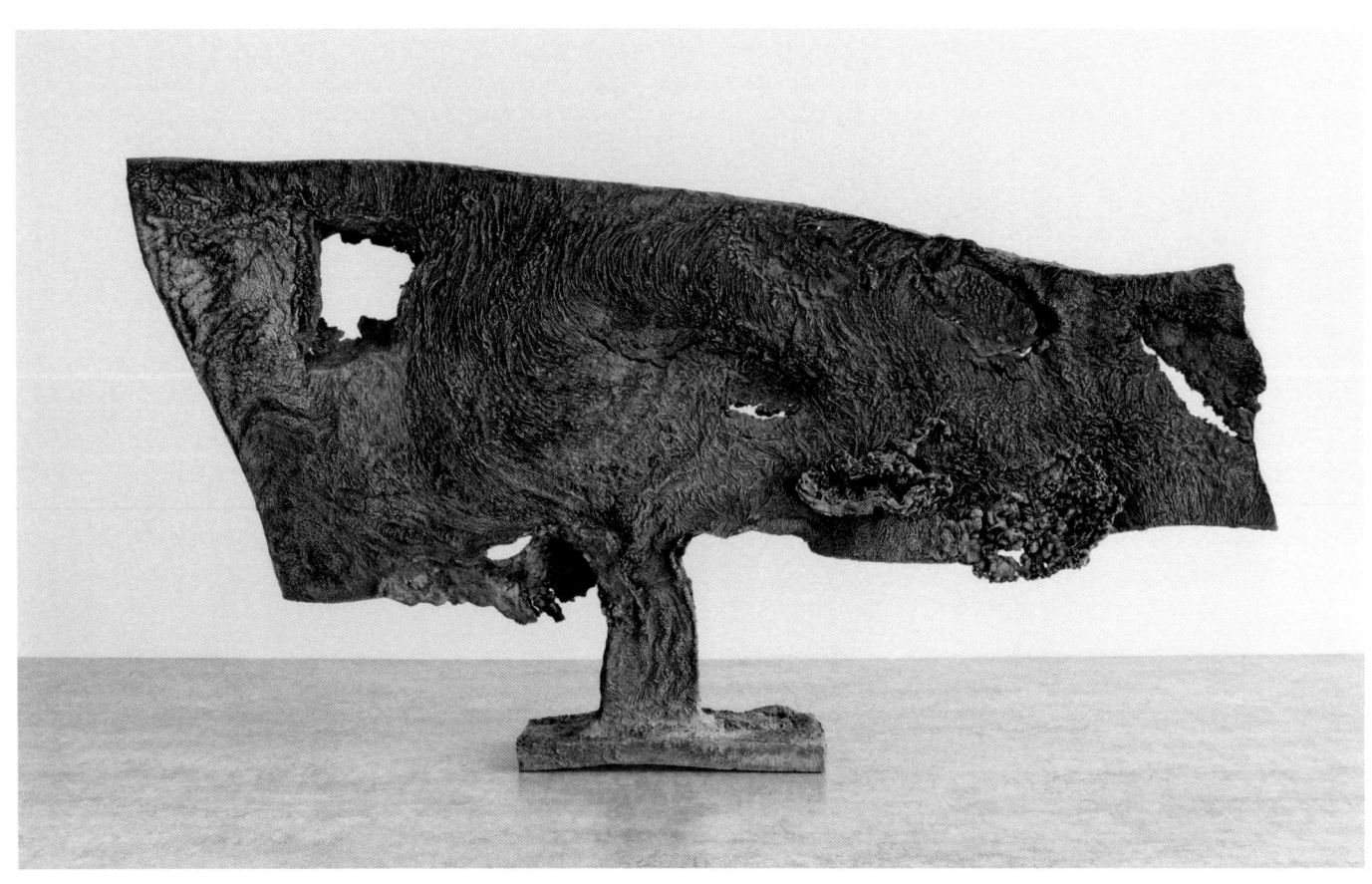

Harry Bertoia (1915–1978)
Untitled (Spill Cast), c. 1962
Bronze
25 ½ × 51 × 6 ½ in.
Courtesy of Michael Rosenfeld
Gallery, LLC, New York, NY

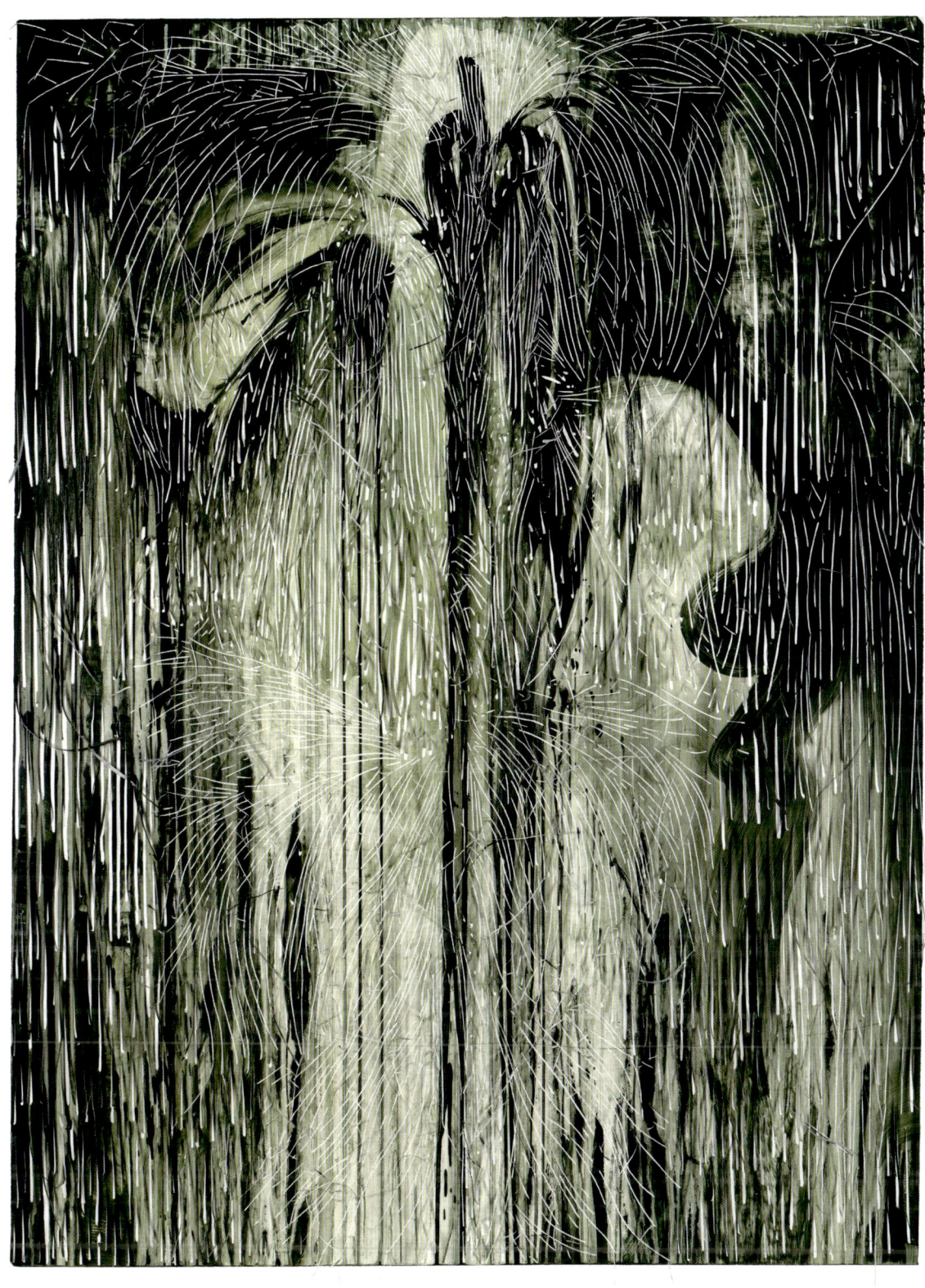

Betsy Cain (b. 1949)
Fire Tree, 2010
Oil on Yupo paper
56 × 40 in.
Private collection

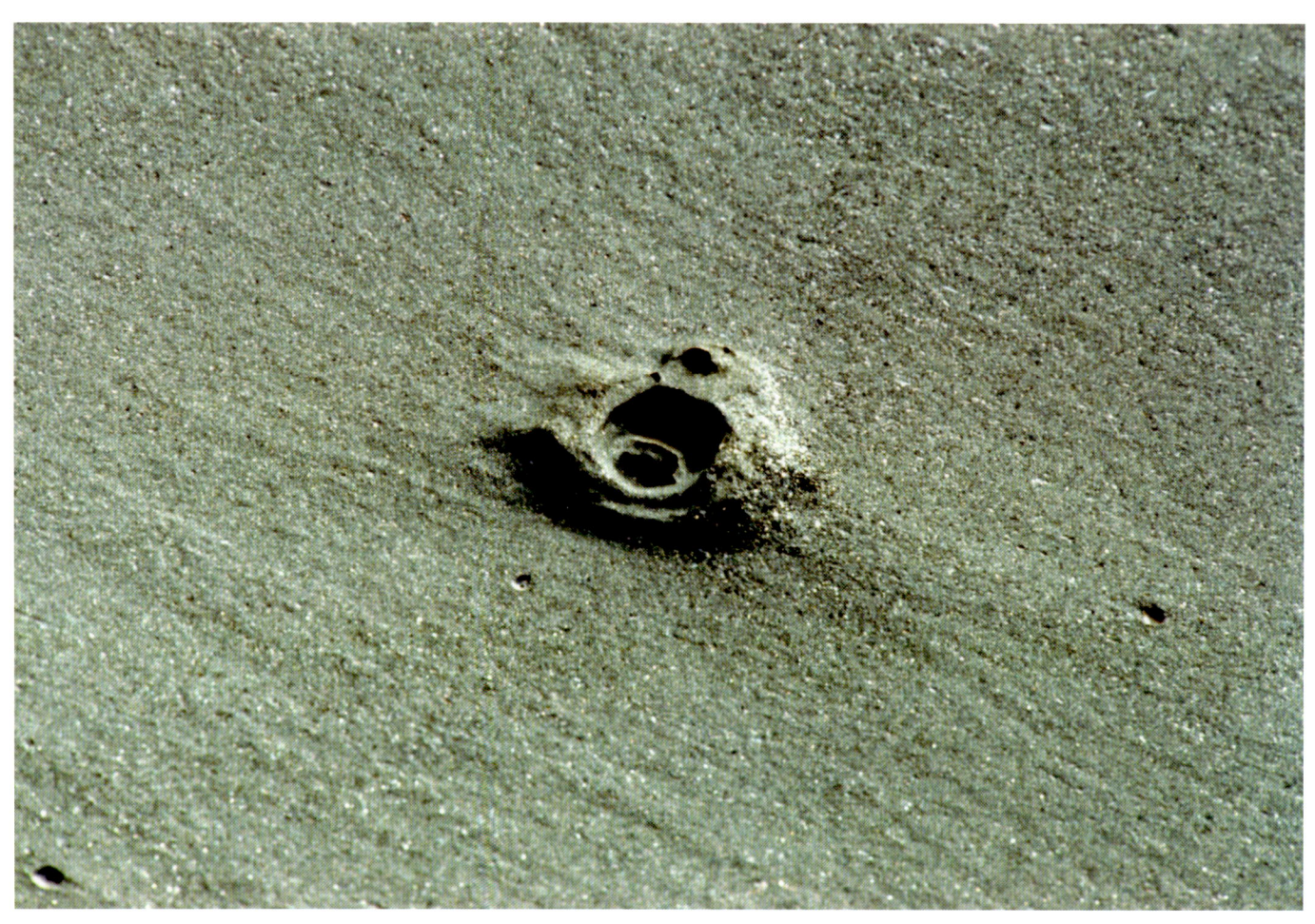

Agnes Denes (b. 1931)
Life Beneath the Surface, 1981
Archival pigment print
12 × 18 in.
Collection of the artist

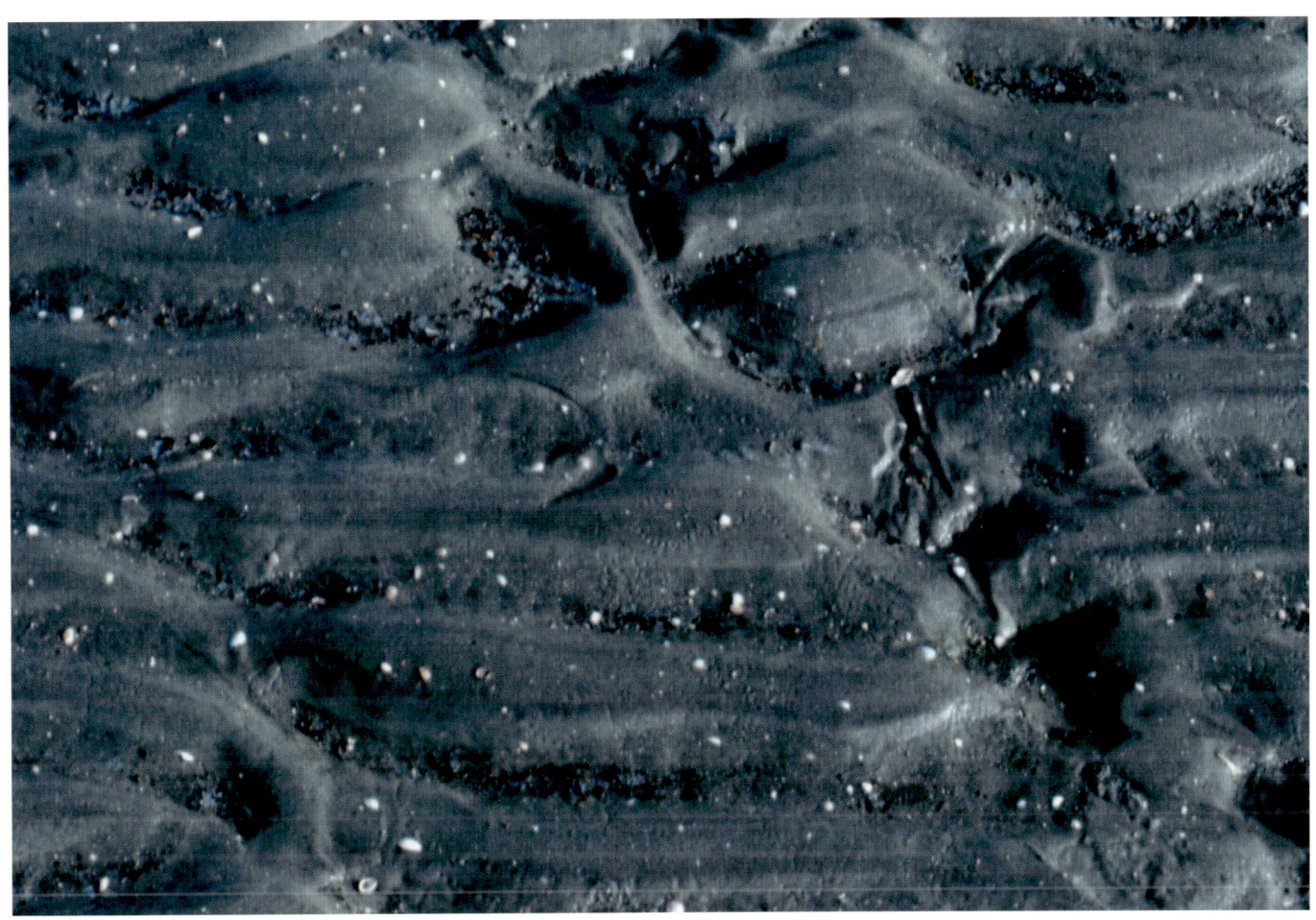

Agnes Denes (b. 1931)
Silver Shores, 1981
Archival pigment print
12 × 18 in.
Collection of the artist

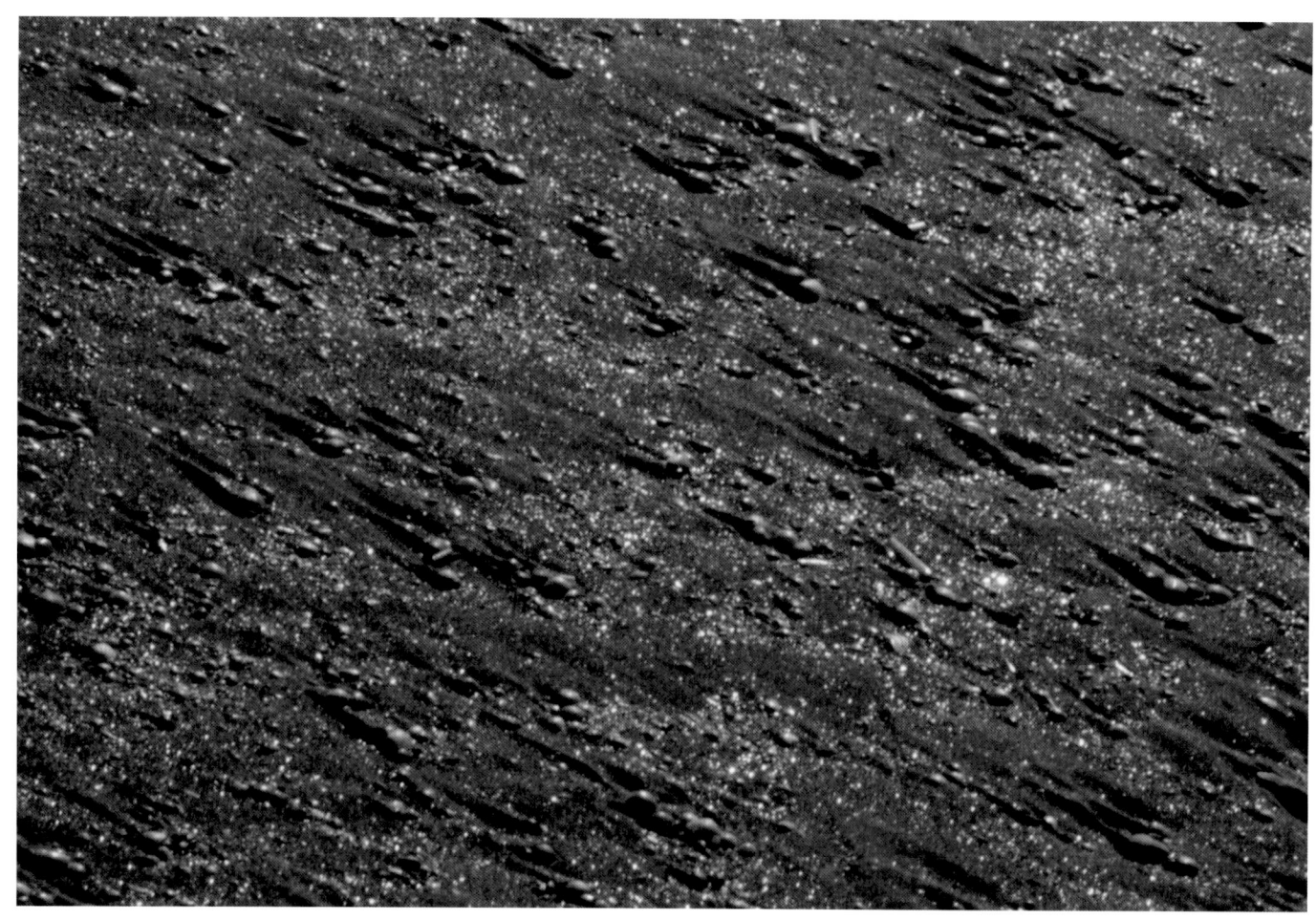

Agnes Denes (b. 1931)
Patterns in Motion, 1981
Archival pigment print
12 × 18 in.
Collection of the artist

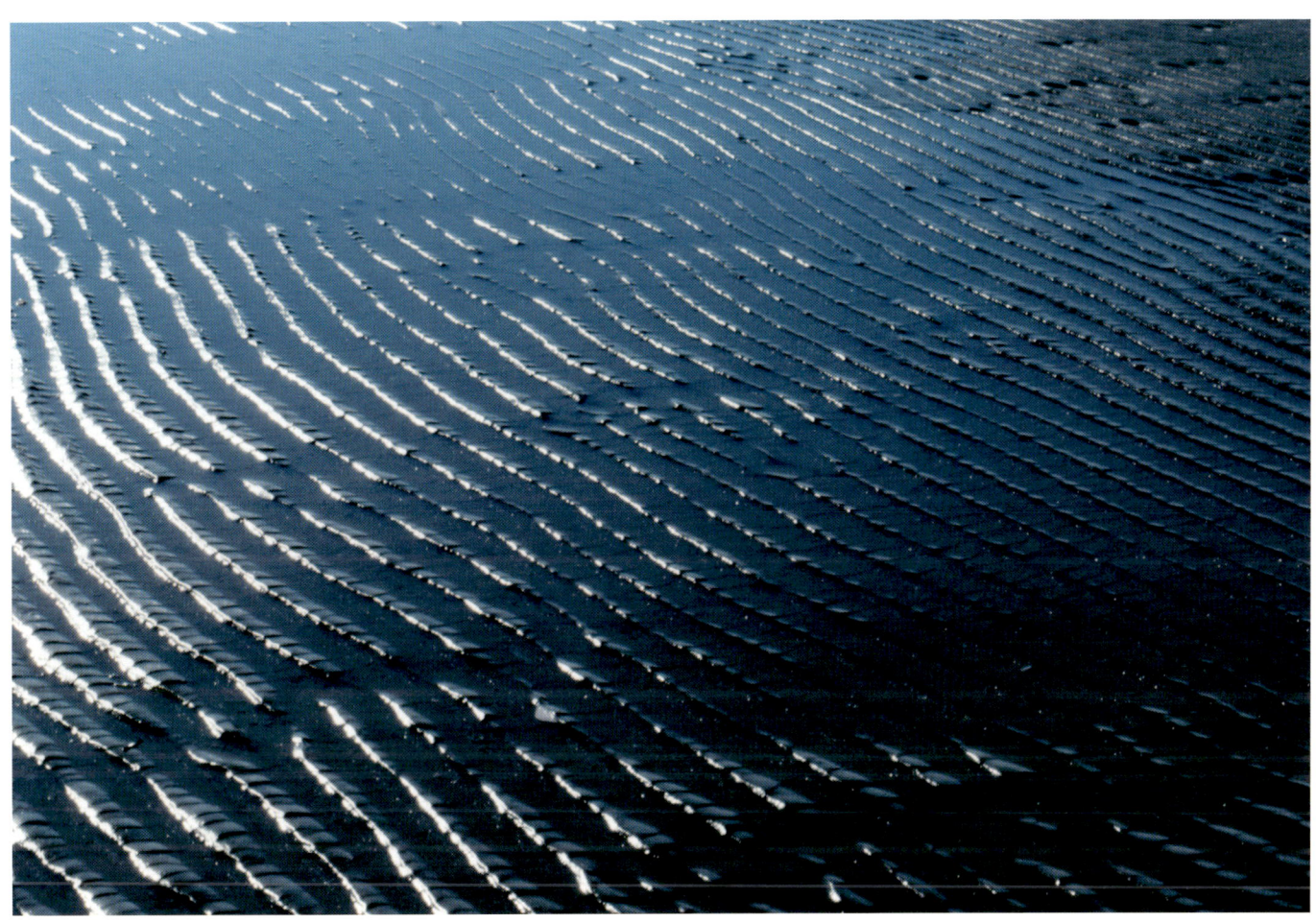

Agnes Denes (b. 1931)
Sun's Reflection on Wet Sand, 1981
Archival pigment print
12 × 18 in.
Collection of the artist

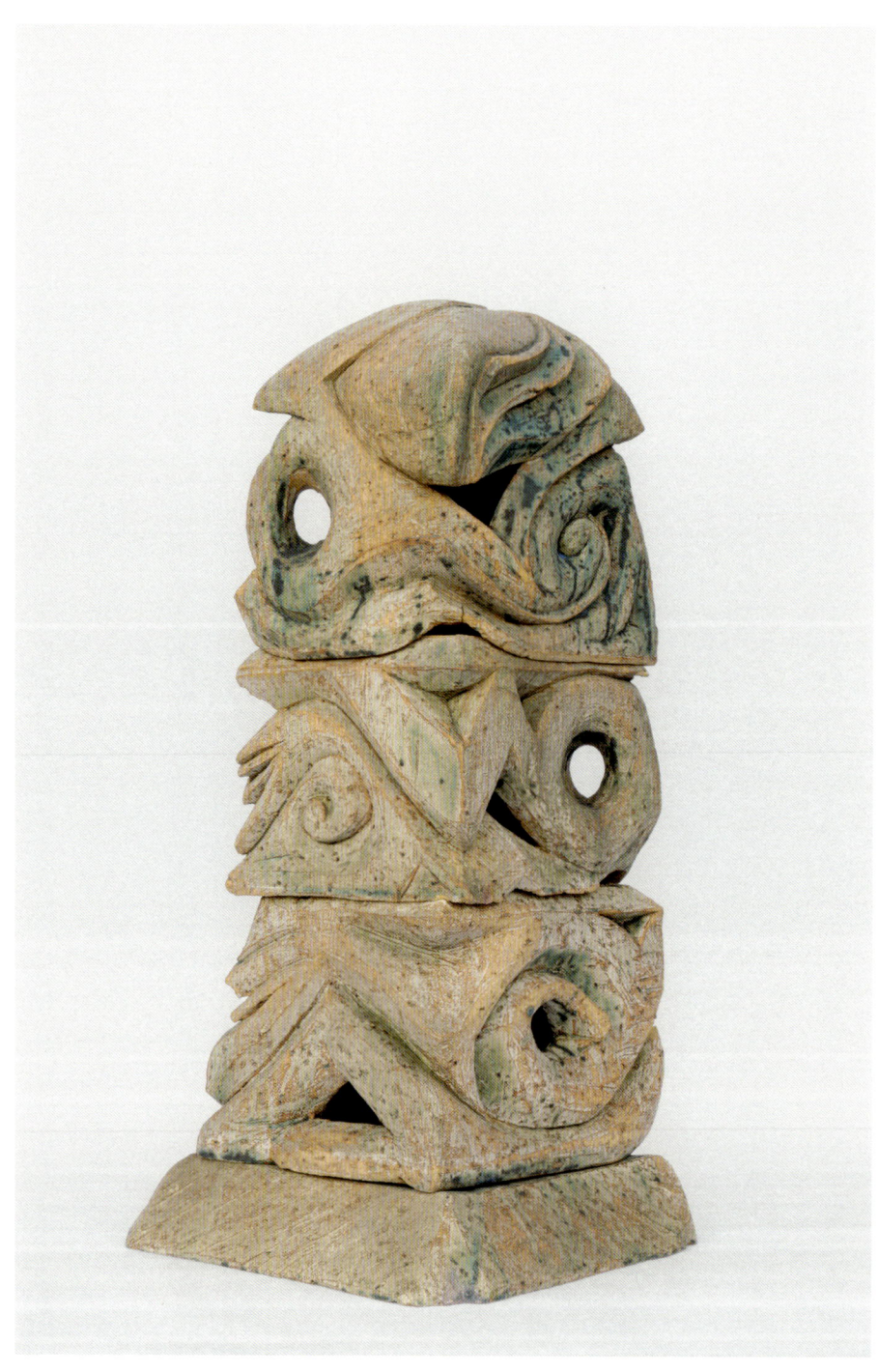

Leslie Ferst (b. 1954)
The Circumnavigation, 1983
Clay and glaze
36 × 18 × 18 in.
Private collection

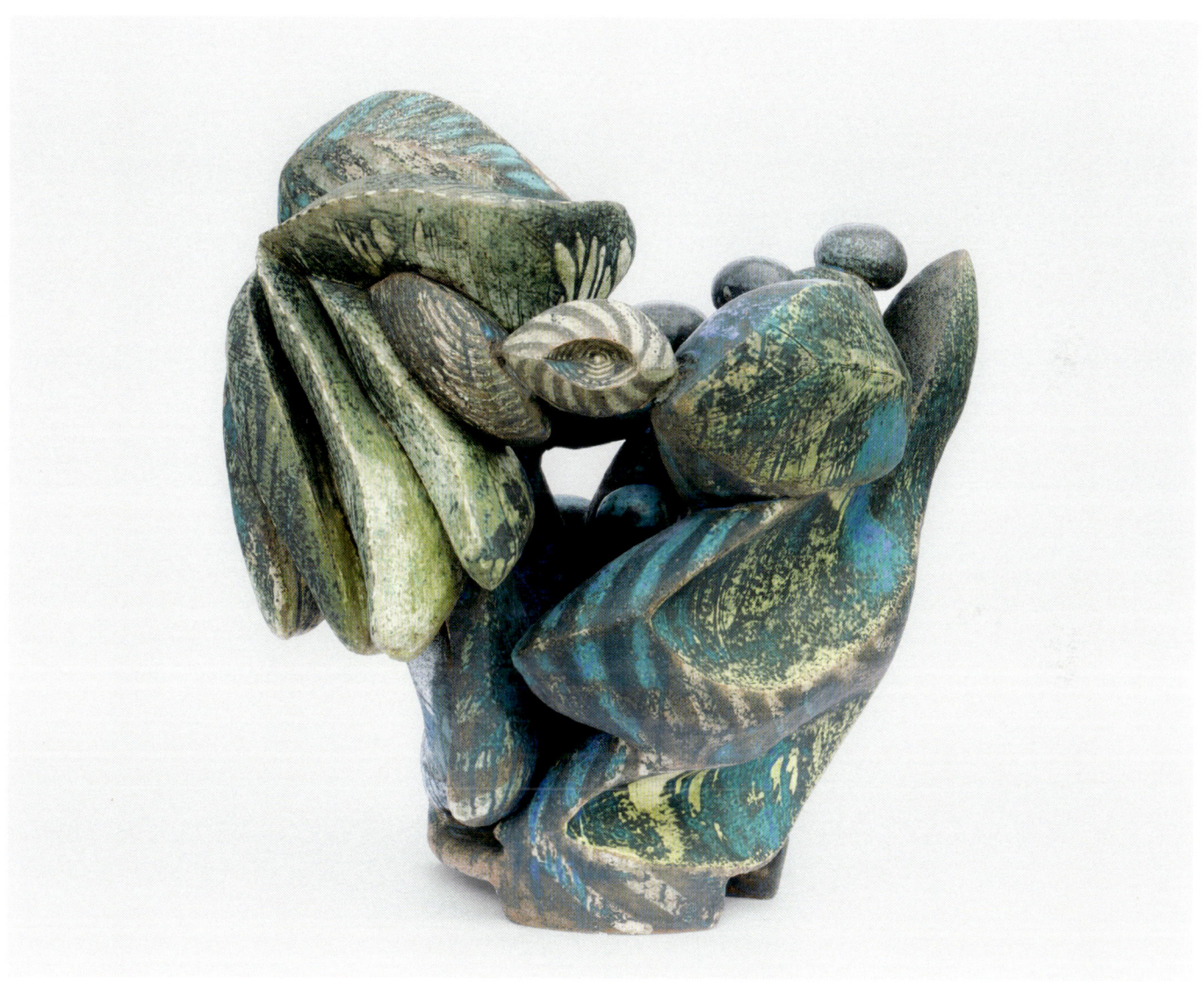

Leslie Ferst (b. 1954)
Grotto, 2002
Clay and glaze
30 × 25 × 25 in.
Private collection

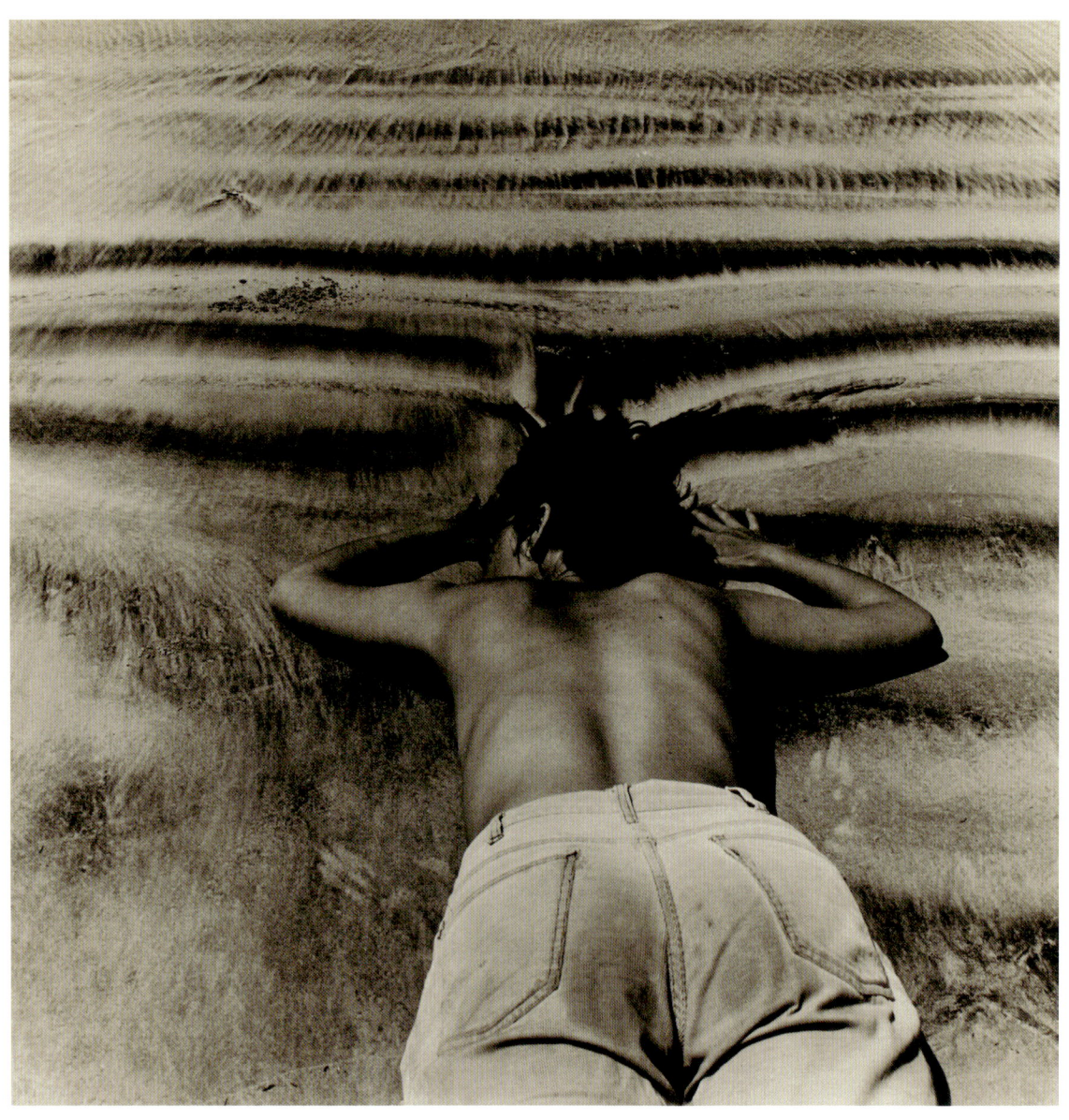

Helen Hamada (b. 1951)
Ossabaw Island, 1974
Gelatin silver print
6 ½ × 6 ½ in.
The Ossabaw Island Foundation

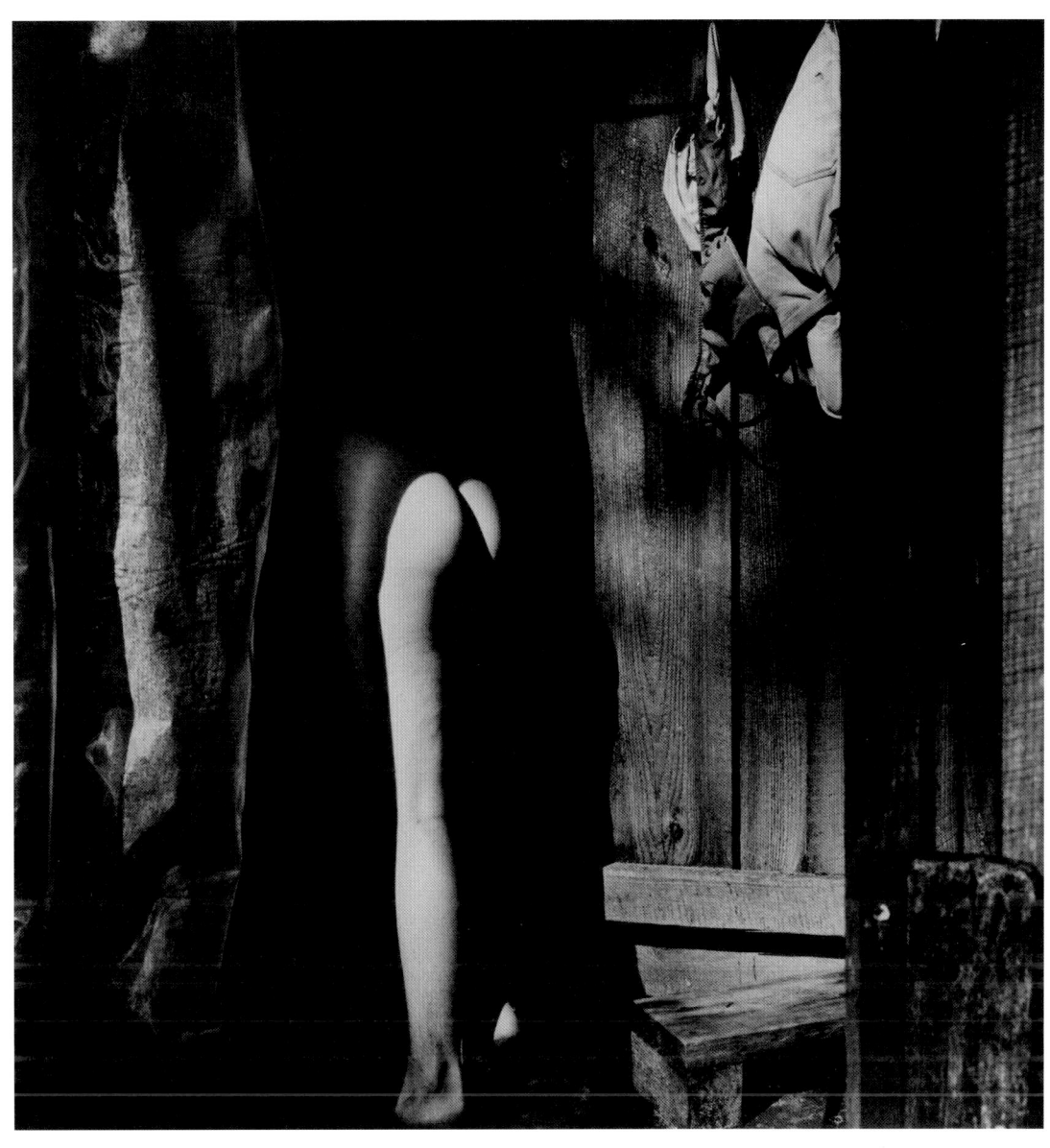

Helen Hamada (b. 1951)
Ossabaw Island, 1974
Gelatin silver print
6 9/16 × 6 1/4 in.
The Ossabaw Island Foundation

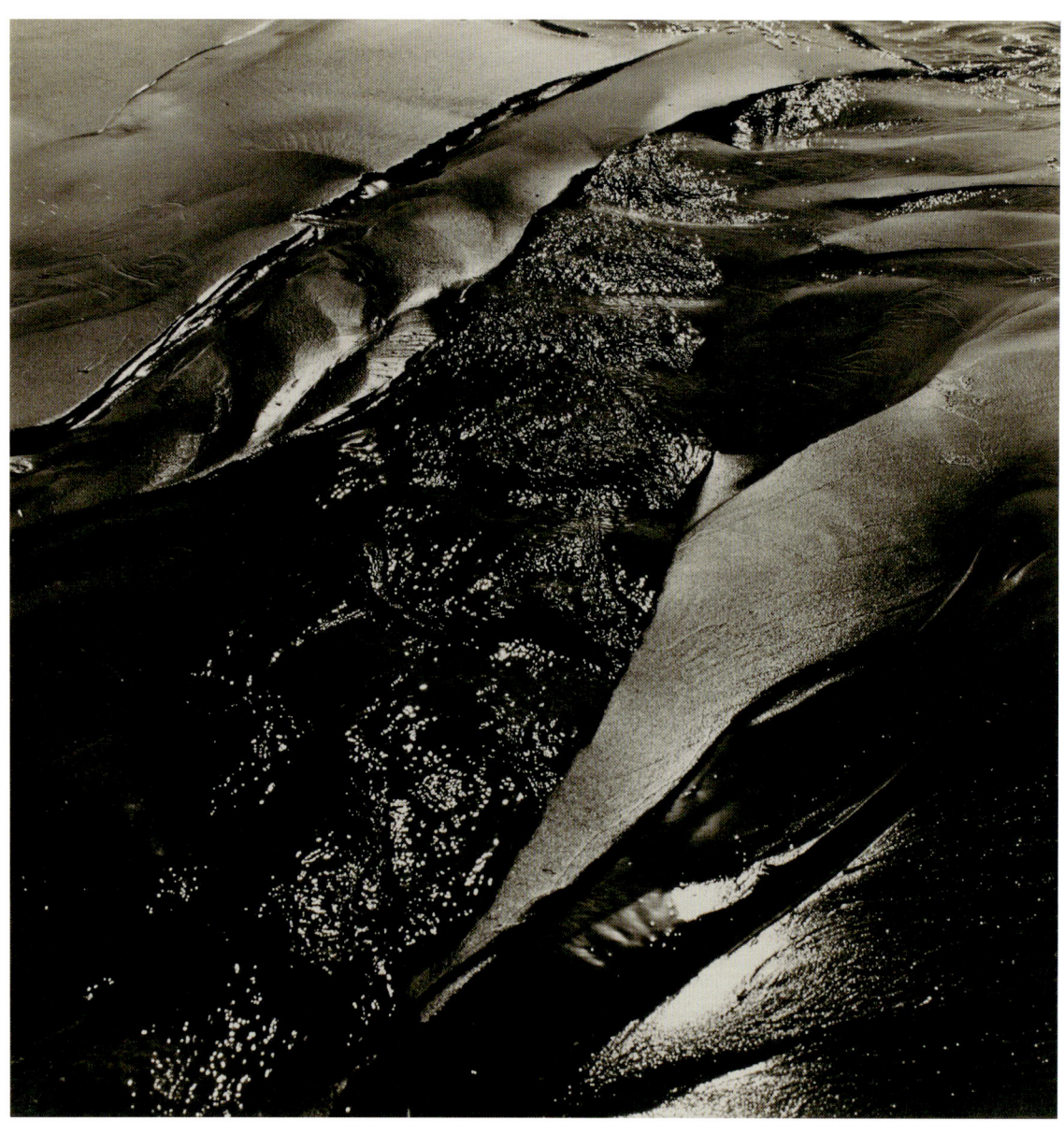

Helen Hamada (b. 1951)
Bradley Beach, 1974
Gelatin silver print
6 ½ × 6 ½ in.
The Ossabaw Island Foundation

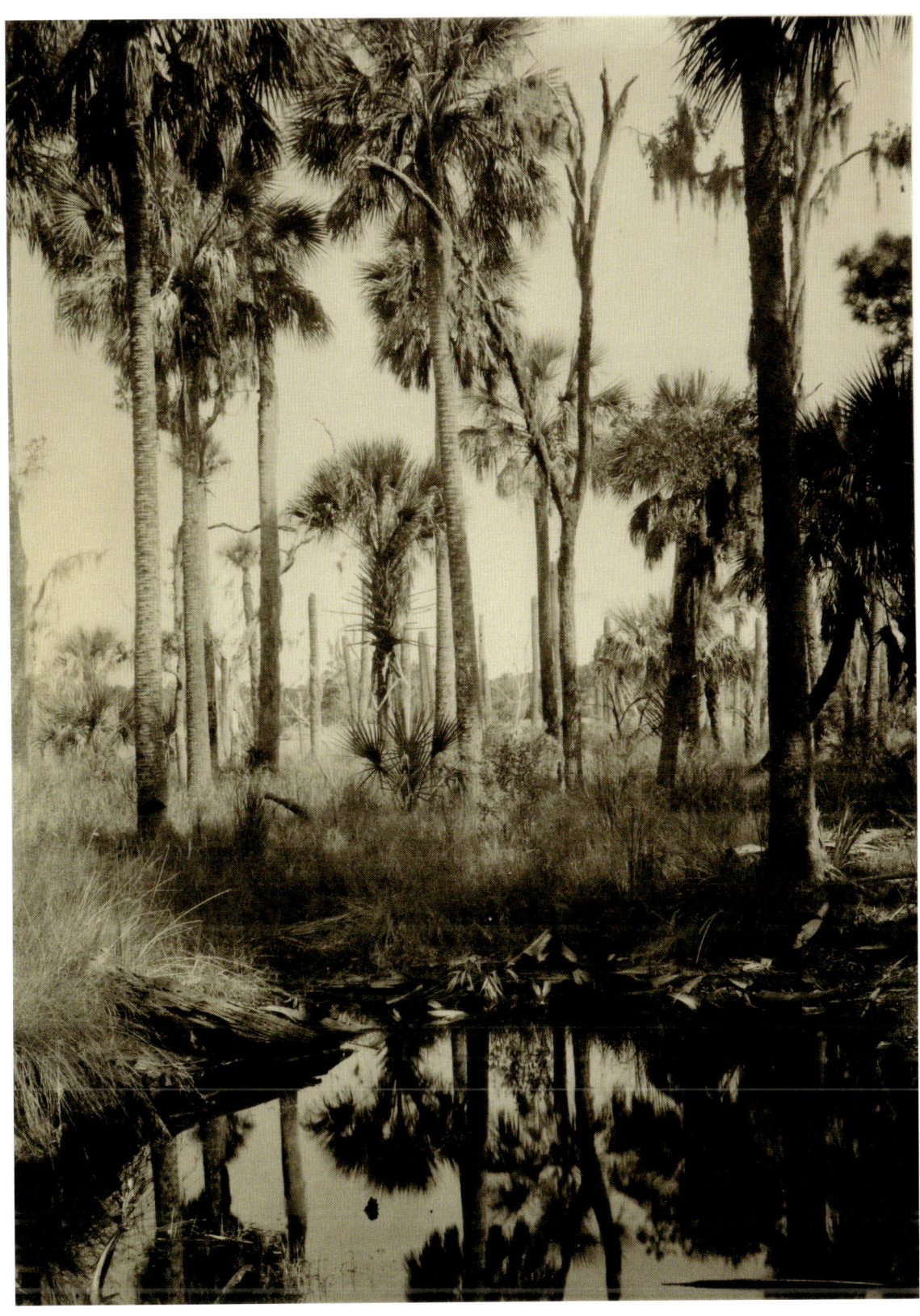

Nancy Marshall (b. 1946)
Untitled, c. 1979
Palladium print
7 × 5 in.
High Museum of Art, Atlanta; Gift of
Ann and Ben Johnson, 2000.280

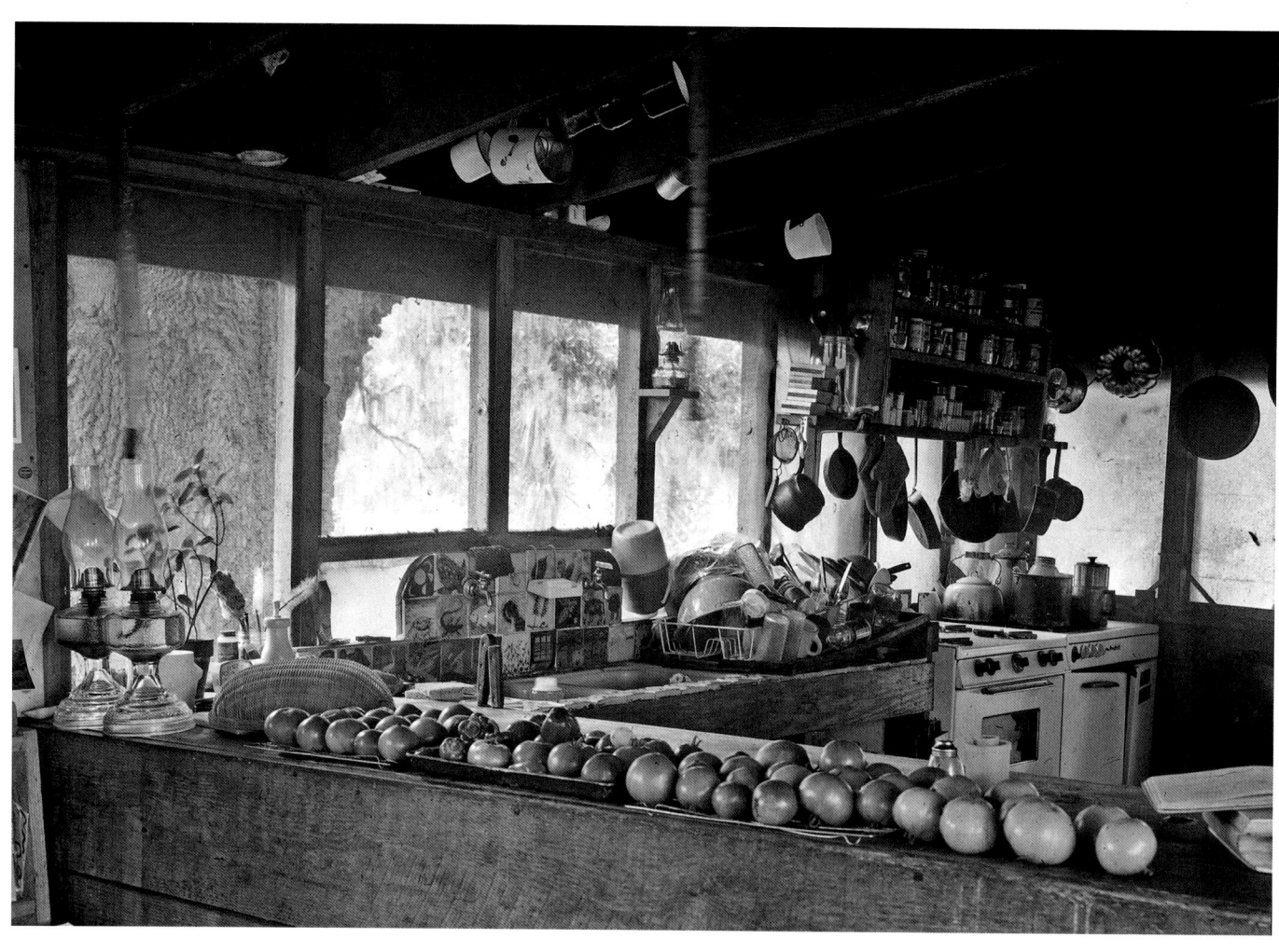

Nancy Marshall (b. 1946)
Cookshack, 1979
Platinum palladium print
5 × 7 in.
Collection of the artist

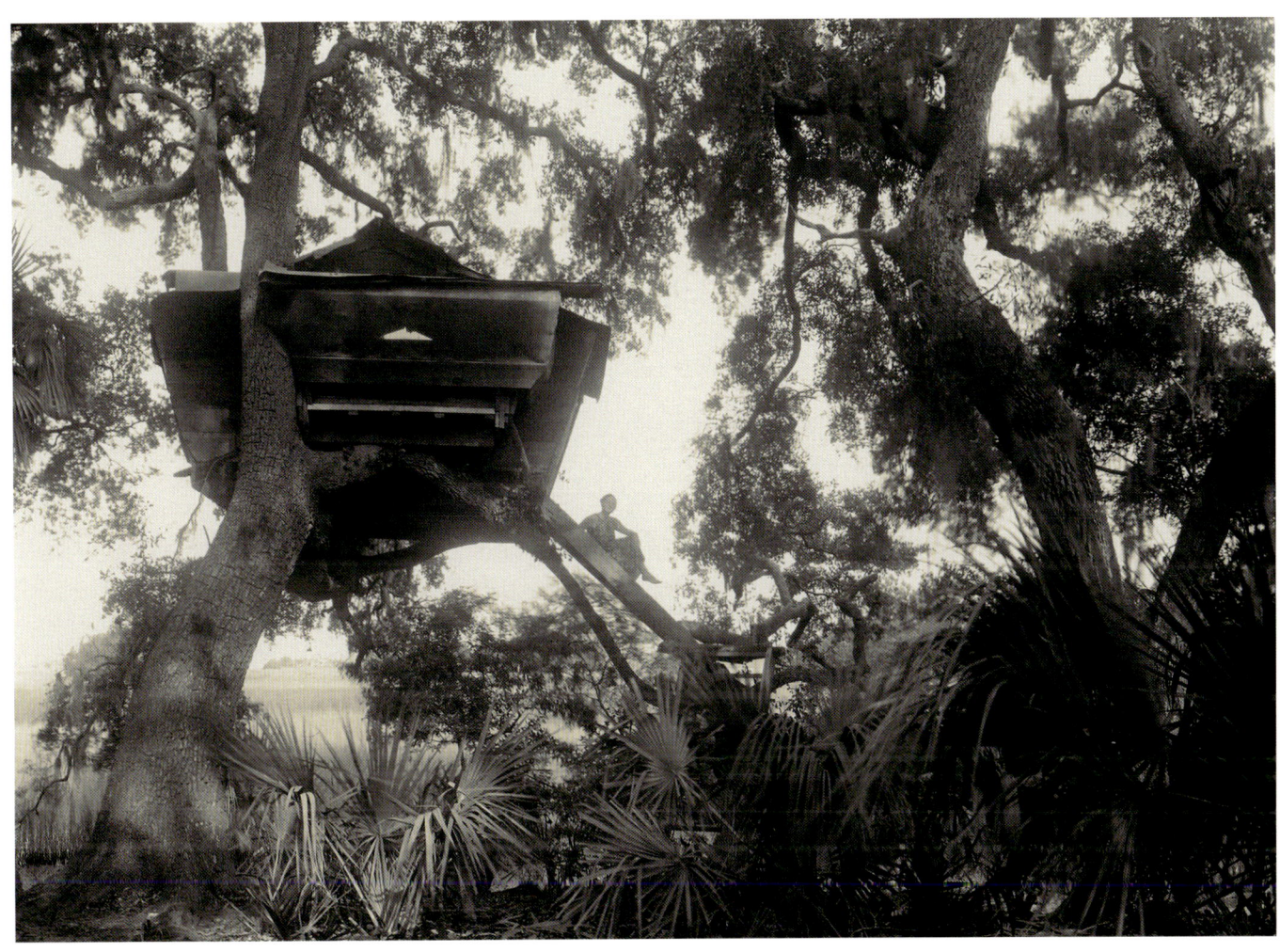

Nancy Marshall (b. 1946)
*The Treehouse, Middle Place, Ossabaw Island (Portrait
of Deborah Shepherd, Genesis Project Member)*, 1979
Platinum palladium print
4 ⅞ × 6 ⅞ in.
Collection of the artist

Lorraine McCarty (1920–2004)
Untitled, 1965
Oil on canvas
49 ¼ × 47 ⅛ in.
The Ossabaw Island Foundation

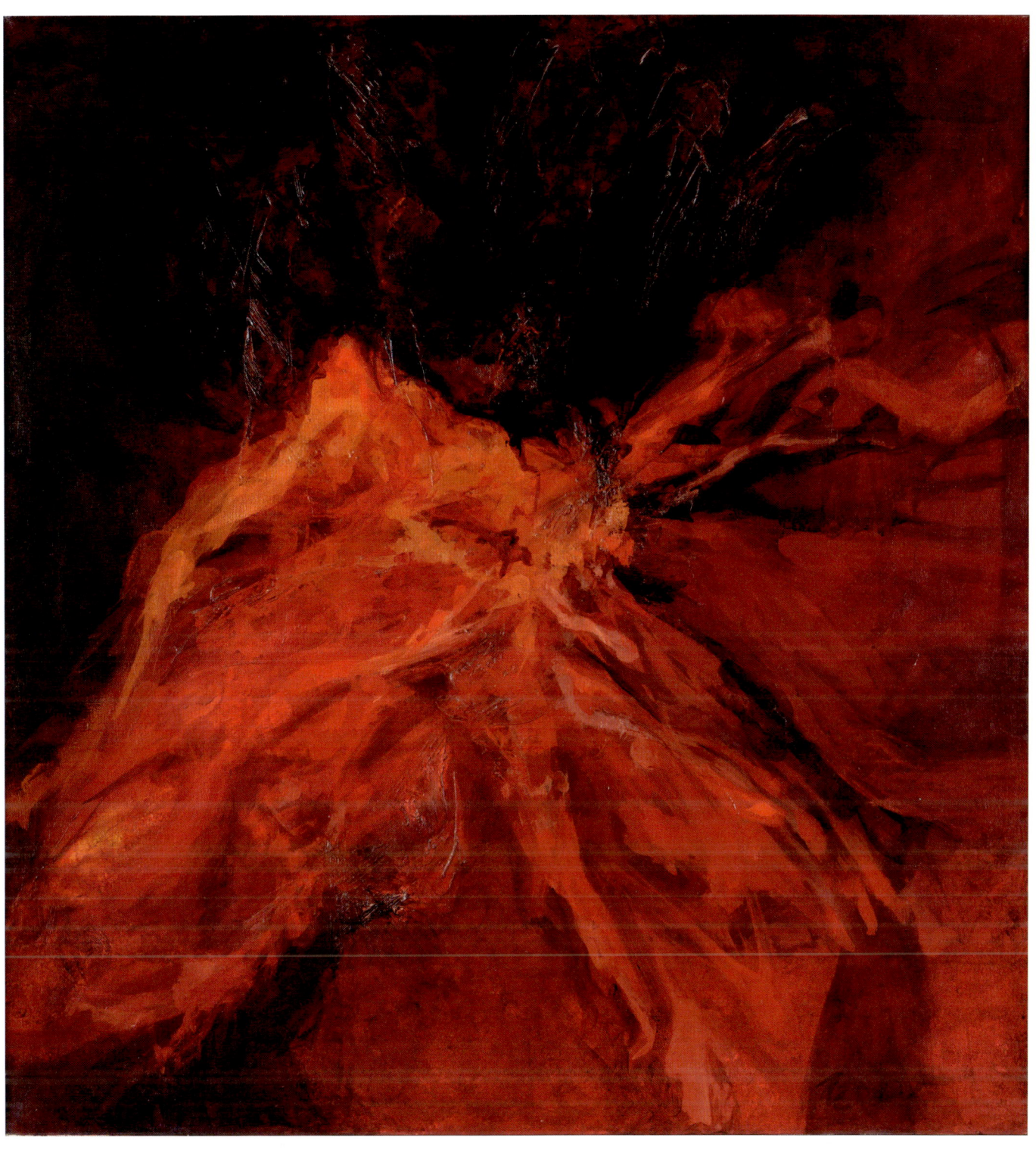

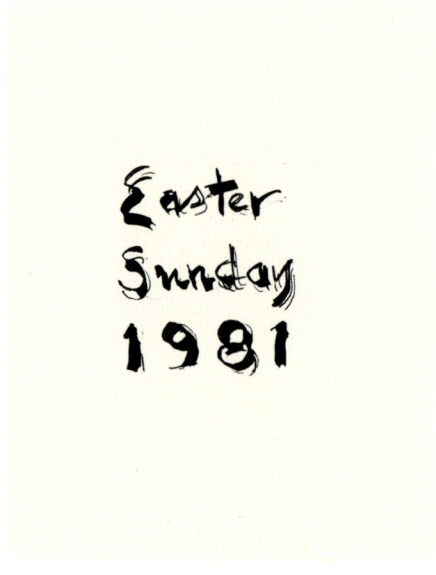

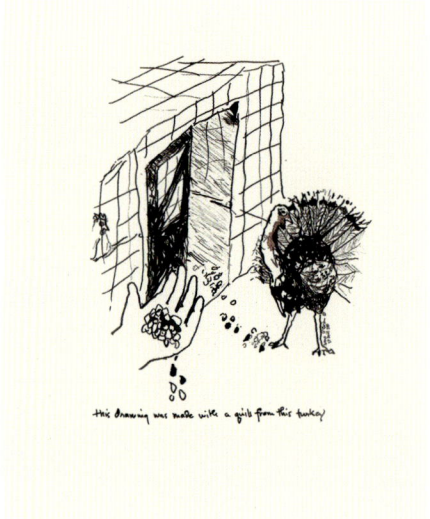

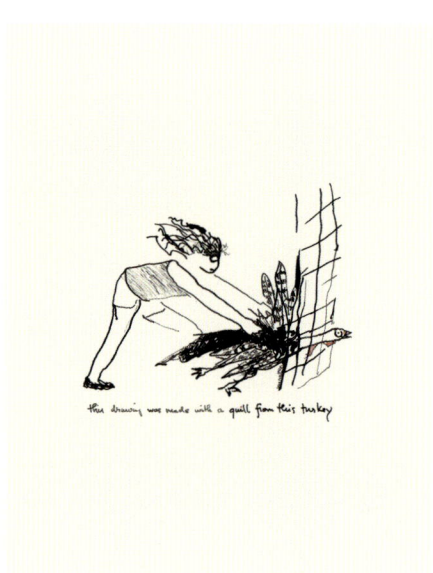

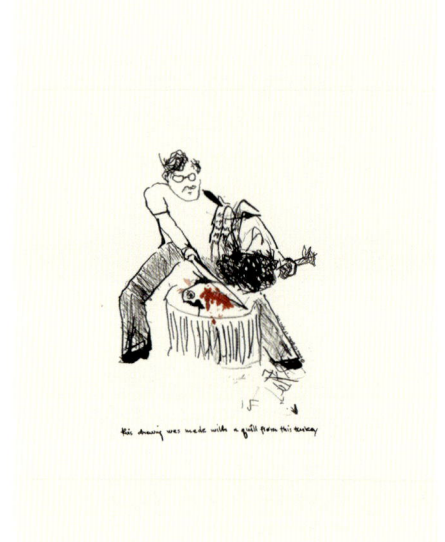

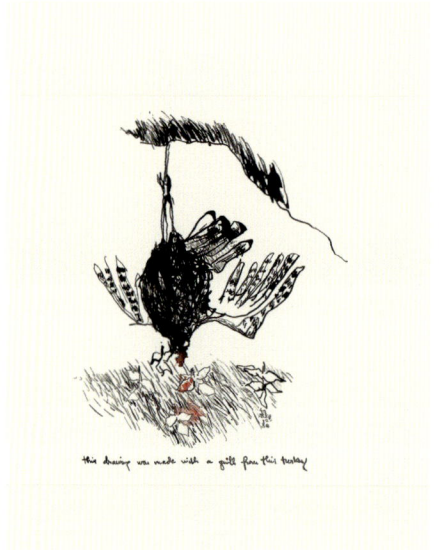

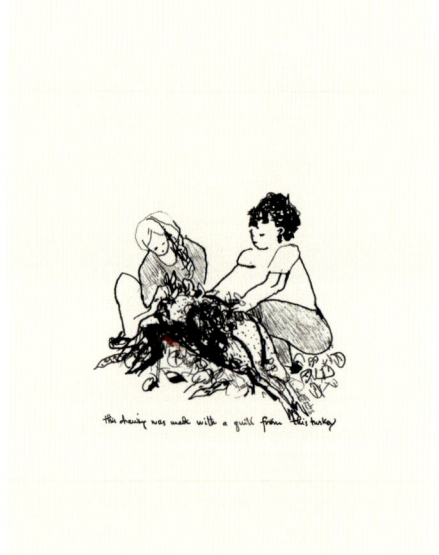

Irene O'Garden (b. 1951)
Easter Sunday, 1981
Higgins India ink on Bristol paper
11 × 8 ½ in. each
Collection of the artist

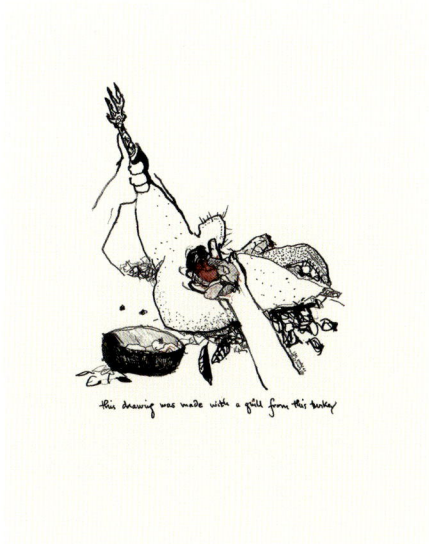

this drawing was made with a quill from this turkey

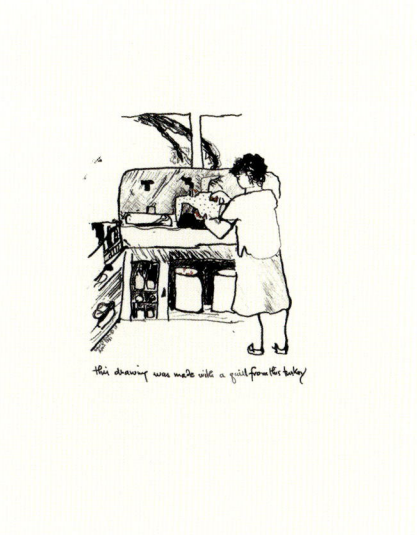

this drawing was made with a quill from this turkey

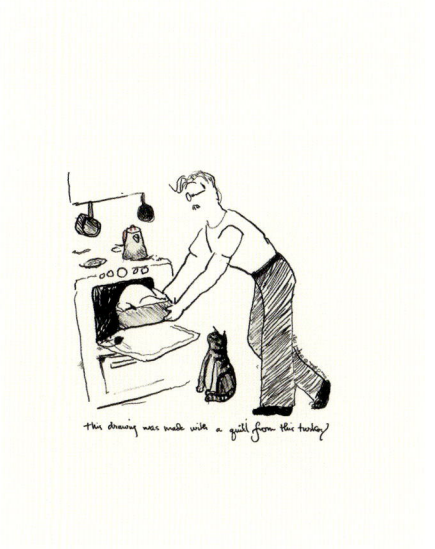

this drawing was made with a quill from this turkey

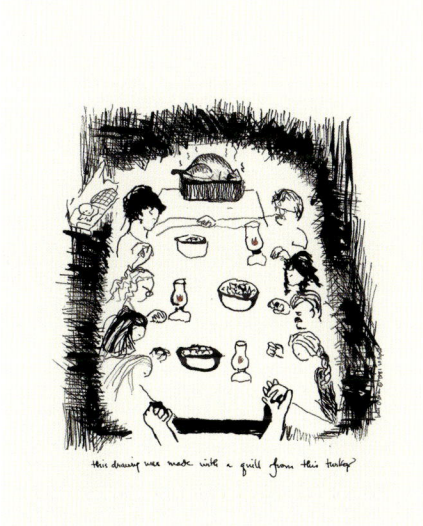

this drawing was made with a quill from this turkey

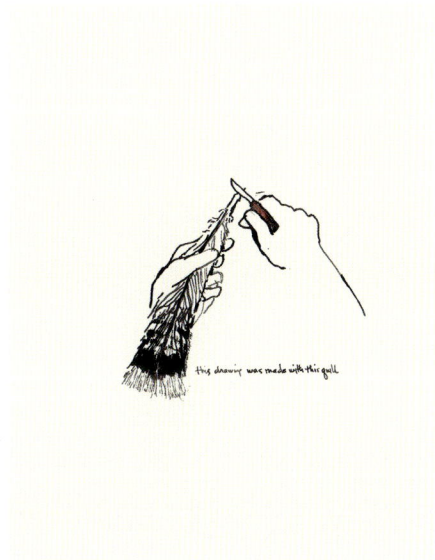

this drawing was made with this quill

Miriam Schapiro (1923–2015)
Ossabaw Heart, 1982
Acrylic and fabric on paper
31 × 32 in.
Estate of Miriam Schapiro, courtesy
of Eric Firestone Gallery

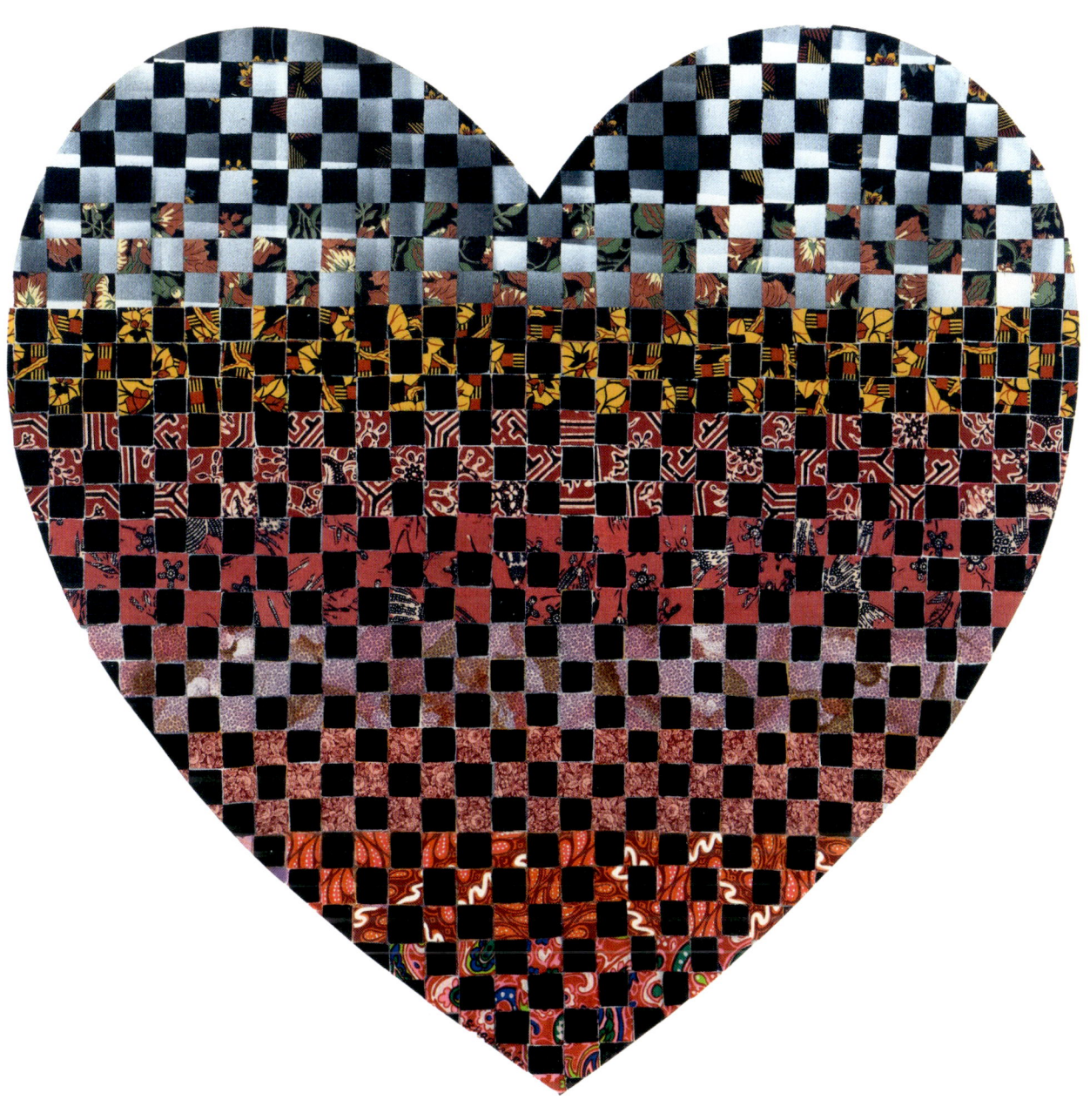

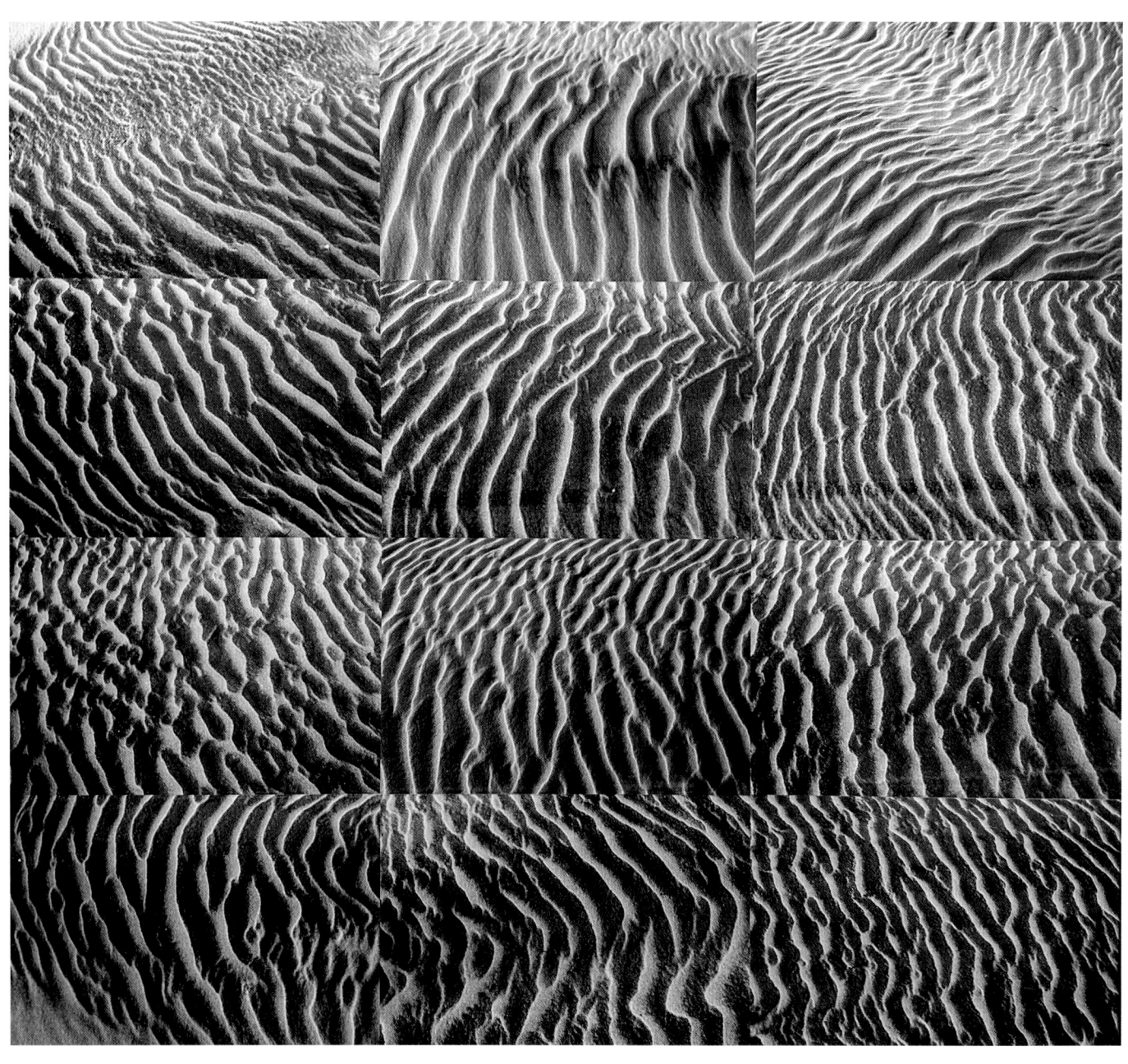

Athena Tacha (b. 1936)
Windtracks (Ossabaw), 1980/2005
12 chromogenic digital prints on metallic photo
paper cold mounted with UV protective film
37 ½ × 42 in.
Collection of Ingleside at Rock Creek,
Washington, DC

Athena Tacha (b. 1936)
Tide Beach, 1980–81
Rag paper pulp relief
24 × 28 ½ in.
Collection of the artist

Athena Tacha (b. 1936)
Tide Beach, 1980–81
Rag paper pulp relief
23 ⅞ × 29 ½ in.
Collection of the artist

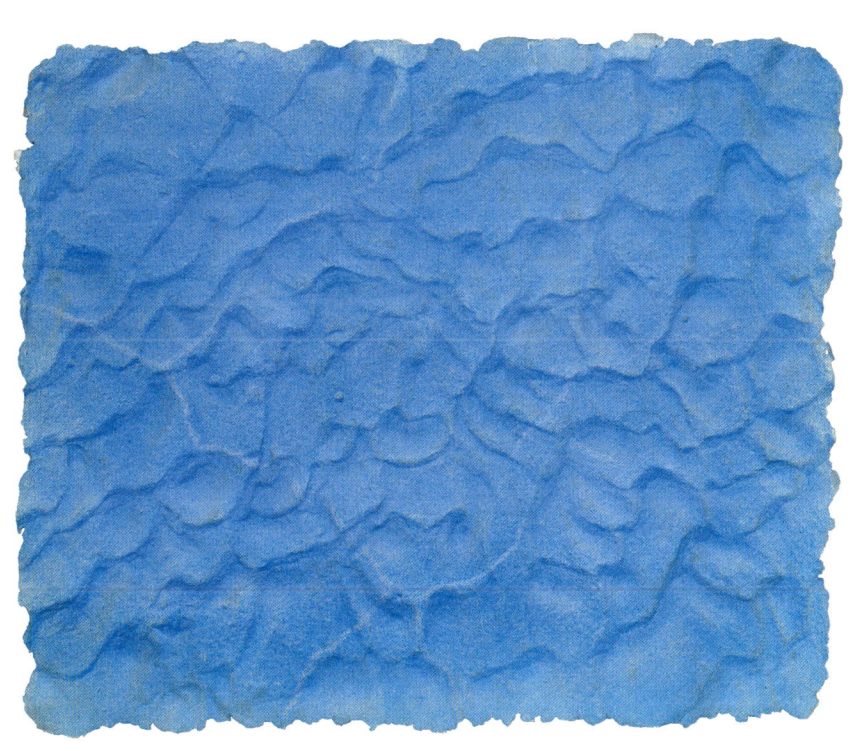

Anne Truitt (1921–2004)
Ossabaw Island, 25 March '75, 1975
Graphite and acrylic on paper
9 × 5 ¼ in.
Estate of Anne Truitt, courtesy
Matthew Marks Gallery

AT 25MARCH '75

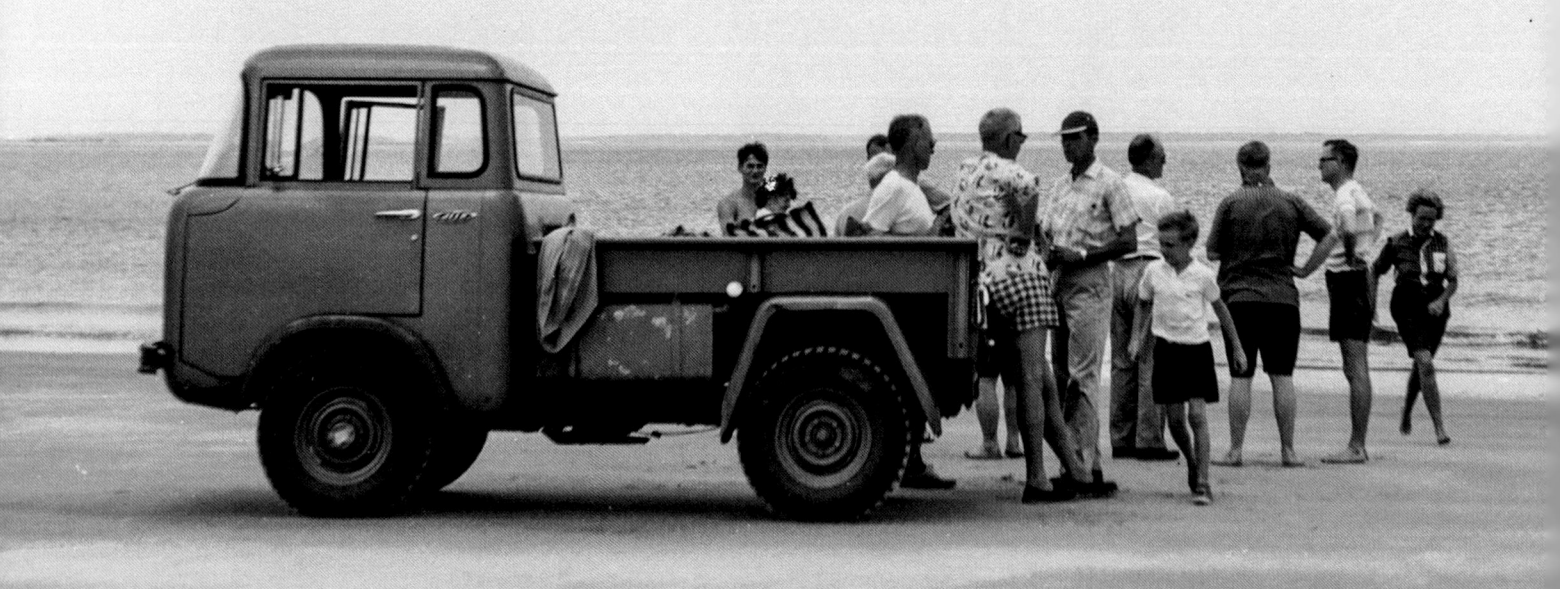

'THE CENTER OF ALL CREATION': THE OSSABAW ISLAND PROJECT AND GENESIS

ERIN DUNN

Like a magician or lover, / Ossabaw threatens, surprises, / chastens, enchants. Surely / everyone here, looking beyond / the golden salt marshes / to those other islands / hovering above the blue bay— / surely everyone learns, / at the last, / how this air supports miracles.
—Carol Burdick, "Island," 1977[1]

OSSABAW ISLAND PROJECT (1961–1982)

Despite feeling "apprehensive" as the agreed upon date drew near, Ossabaw Island's co-owner Eleanor "Sandy" Torrey West busied herself with preparations in advance of a pivotal meeting on June 22, 1961. She and her husband, painter and educator Clifford B. West, had invited a group of esteemed individuals of all backgrounds and careers for a weekend on the massive, undeveloped barrier island off the coast of Savannah. The Wests wanted them to be the first to hear their big idea: "Can we open Ossabaw to the thinkers and doers in all the disciplines from all over the world and let them come down here and work?"[2] From his own experiences at the Cranbrook Academy of Art in Michigan, and through his connections with prominent artists, such as designer and sculptor Harry Bertoia, Clifford understood that uninterrupted time and space were essential priorities for creative work, yet difficult to come by in the hustle and bustle of the modern age. Sandy and Clifford saw an opportunity to share the magnificence of Ossabaw outside of their family without destroying its wilderness through boundless recreation. In her diary describing the 1961 meeting, Sandy bore witness to the genuine reactions of their visitors to Ossabaw's astonishing environment, writing, "They are winded by the beauty and wildness."[3] After positive reinforcement and counsel from the group, the program opened in October of that year as the Ossabaw Island Project (OIP).

Beach trip during the conference to form the Ossabaw Island Project, June 1961 (detail). Photograph by Clifford B. West

From the beginning, an impulsive "let's try it and see what sticks" energy dominated the planning. Although there were certainly models, such as Yaddo in Saratoga Springs, New York, and The MacDowell Colony in Peterborough, New Hampshire, the OIP differed in a few fundamental ways. Firstly, the landscape was isolated and unfamiliar to most of the participants, which often served to be transformational (and occasionally overwhelming). Sandy and Clifford quickly realized how "the unusual atmosphere of this island stimulates people and projects, increases awareness and intensifies concentration through quiet and isolation," a sensation amplified by the sheer physical separation from society.[4] Secondly, the residency was truly interdisciplinary in nature, mixing together artists, writers, theorists, linguists, scientists, mathematicians, businesspeople, religious leaders, ecologists, and architects, among others. They believed that the power of informal exchanges across disciplines would lead to more interesting results, an inclination that bore fruit down the road. Thirdly, members were given the prerogative to spend their time on the island as they wished. Magic was bound to happen when, as Sandy remembered, you "get the right kind of people and then leave them completely alone."[5] Composer Samuel Barber, who was an OIP advisor, supported this decision to avoid pressure when he commented, "I know from a musician's point of view that maybe three years later they'll remember what the marsh grass sounded like."[6] Just as OIP member Julius Rutzky found beauty by photographing a dried palm frond up close(fig. 1), the discovery and tactile experience of Ossabaw's site specificity and its reverberating effects far outweighed any expectations of an immediate outcome.

The residencies established in the early to mid-20th century in the United States had the same central belief at their core: that talented people needed opportunity, time, and space to think through their creative work and that the greater world might ultimately benefit in some future way from that experience. In an article explaining her reasons for co-founding the OIP, Sandy derided the "man-made noise" of everyday life that resulted in a lack of quiet spaces within the environment as well as over communication that seemingly replaced true personal connection.[7] At the time, Sandy mentioned these issues to bolster her argument for the necessary role of the OIP to be that place of "natural quiet" for creative individuals of all disciplines. She used her own husband as a prime example, noting, "We ourselves have not been untouched by the Ossabaw Island Project. My husband, who is a painter and a teacher, has felt during his years of teaching a need for films from the point of view of art with emphasis on form, material and orientation."[8] In *Time Form Color* (1962), Clifford West's camera guides the viewer's eye across the dead trees on Ossabaw's beach in an impressionistic fashion, emulating the gaze of an artist rather than a documentarian. Stimulated by this new direction in his practice, his later artistic films about the Italian Renaissance were shown in museum settings across the U.S., including the Telfair Academy of Arts and Sciences (now Telfair Museums) in 1972.

Most of the better known artist colonies that influenced the OIP were established in the Northeast through wealthy patronage and continue to be viewed as the

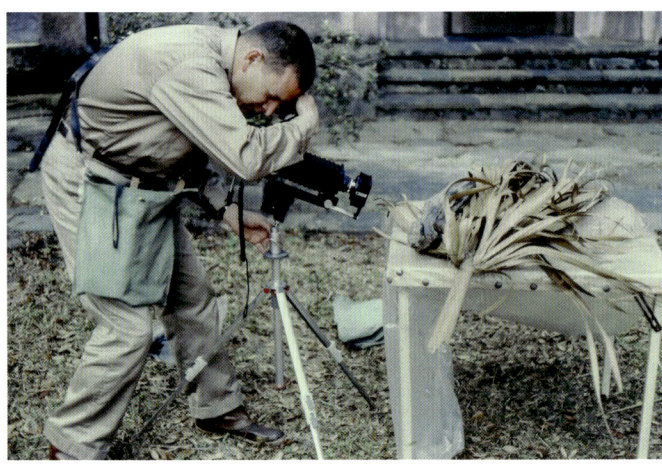

fig. 1.   Julius Rutzky photographing outside
the Main House, 1963. Photograph by
Thomas Marker

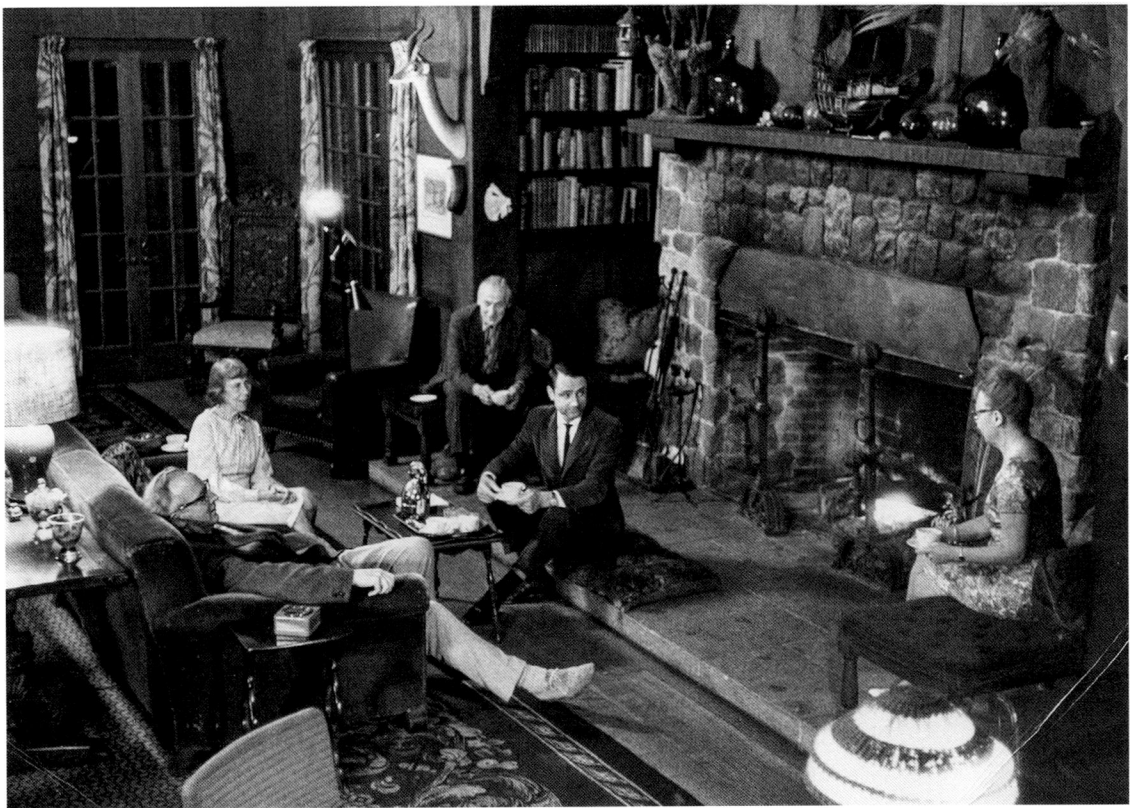

fig. 2.　William Vandivert, Georgina Klitgaard, Thomas Marker, Nick Rusakis, and Rita Vandivert in the Main House living room, 1966. Photograph by William Vandivert

preeminent residency programs in the United States. The Southeast wasn't lauded for avant-garde art programs, with a few notable exceptions, such as Black Mountain College in Asheville, North Carolina.[9] The OIP's history in coastal Georgia remains a more obscure entity, perhaps because of its truncated existence from 1961 until 1982, but also likely due to its isolated location in the southeastern landscape and its lack of advertising. Maintaining an air of mystery and perhaps exclusivity, the OIP didn't advertise but rather relied on the word of mouth and recommendation of past participants, friends, and advisors, which at various points throughout its history included Samuel Barber, Harry Bertoia, composer Aaron Copland, writer Annie Dillard, writer Ralph Ellison, linguist Roman Jakobson, art historian H. W. Janson, and architect Robert Venturi, among others.

Founded in idea and corporation in 1900 on a 400-acre estate in upstate New York by Spencer and Katrina Trask, Yaddo continues to foster the talents of writers, painters, composers, and other individuals in creative fields. In 1926, the residency officially opened and was hailed by *The New York Times* as "a new and unique experiment which has no exact parallel in the world of the fine arts."[10] Yaddo's successful history can count James Baldwin, Sylvia Plath, and Langston Hughes as just a few of its illustrious participants who have offered undeniable contributions to American art and culture. In comparison to the OIP, Yaddo's structure was stricter and lacked the interdisciplinary component. In an interview, Sandy remembered that when she and Clifford began brainstorming the OIP, she called Elizabeth Ames, executive director of Yaddo, who warned her that no one with a reputation in the arts would want to come and talk with anybody from the Ford Motor Company.[11] One historian noted, "The culture at Yaddo certainly cannot be described as officially promoting interdisciplinary practices or formally advocating cross-fertilization of the various arts. On the contrary, the pattern of life at Yaddo frequently encourages concentrated and isolated work—residents are forbidden to interrupt one another's periods of concentrated activity."[12] Yaddo enacted quiet hours from 9 a.m. until 4 p.m. every day. Because individuals were hosted in a 55-room mansion on a grand estate, Yaddo fought with an elitist perception. Ossabaw's legacy was equally tied to the philanthropic traditions of the Gilded Age and the wealth of the industrialists. Like Yaddo, it was housed in a large manor with well-appointed spaces, as evidenced by the post-dinner salons in the stately living room[fig. 2]. Founded 61 years after Yaddo, the OIP embodied a similar spirit of individual philanthropy and a desire to share the wealth in some form. Sandy remarked, "I fell heir to this island.... All I wanted to do is give people a place that had no demands on them and where they would be with other interested people in different fields. I didn't care what they did here. I cared what the island did to them."[13]

MacDowell opened in 1907 as an artist residency situated on 400 acres in southern New Hampshire, developed by musicians Marian and Edward MacDowell at their summer home. Still in operation today, the retreat continues to thrive, currently offering 32 studios free of charge and set apart from one another in the woods. Similarly to Yaddo, residents are discouraged from interrupting their fellow creatives during the day. Writer Hermann Hagedorn clarified that "Petersborough exists for the purpose of giving the artist that solitude for mental clarification which the average American can find scarcely anywhere else."[14] Perhaps unsurprisingly, individuals often attended two or more residencies and there was an informal network between the administrators at the OIP, Yaddo, and MacDowell to share correspondence back and forth about their behavior and working patterns and how they might fit in with the different cultures (or not).

While the OIP made strides to improve its infrastructure—at various points throughout the project's history, facilities included two pianos, a darkroom for photography, a pottery wheel and a kiln, movie and slide projectors, a four-harness 6½-foot loom[fig. 3], a bronze casting foundry, and a library—Yaddo and MacDowell undoubtedly offered more equipment and better studio spaces.[15] Ossabaw's physical location restricted options because everything had to arrive on a boat with limited capacity. However, comparing her time at MacDowell and Ossabaw, the writer Perdita Buchan wrote to Sandy in 1980, "Right now I am at the MacDowell Colony for a month trying to finish the novel I began on Ossabaw. This is a nice place, but nothing is quite like Ossabaw."[16] Buchan is likely referring to the island's inimitable atmosphere, something neither Yaddo nor MacDowell could claim.

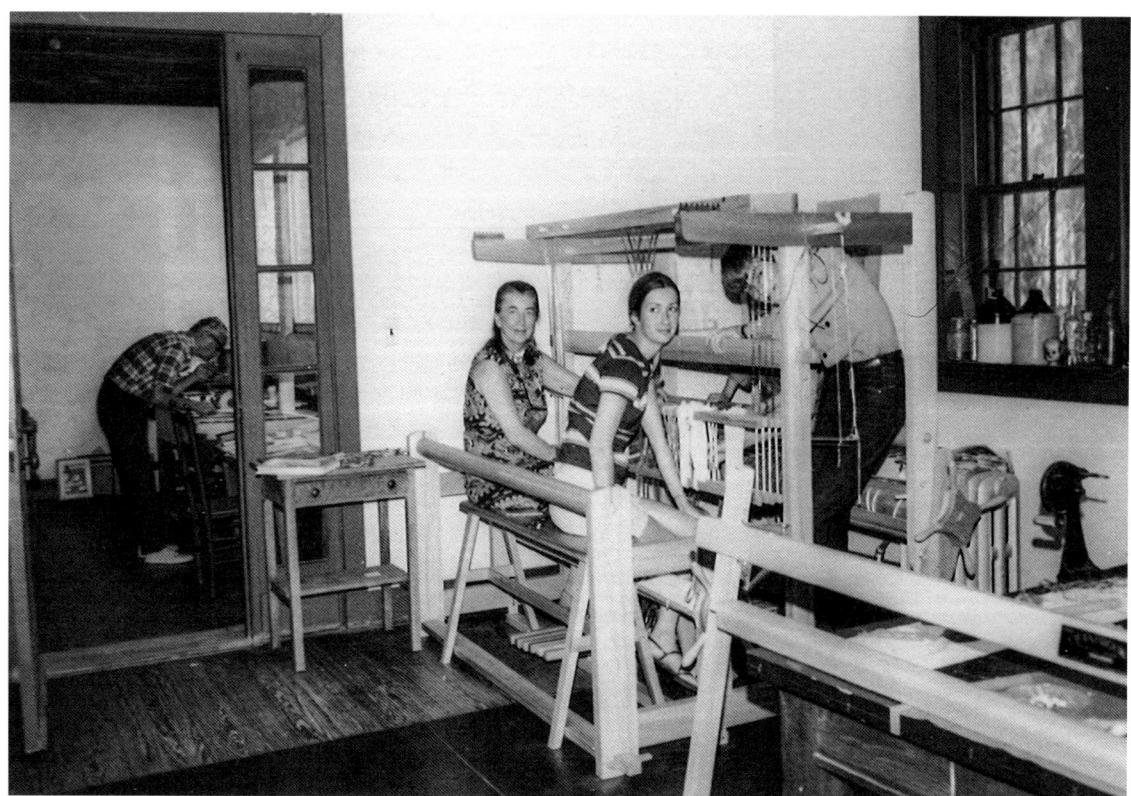

fig. 3.   Advisor Marianne Strengell showing Gilian Wohlauer and Justin West how to use the four harness loom she donated to the OIP in the Main House, c. 1969

fig. 4.   Sign for Ossabaw Island Project members'
bedrooms at the Main House

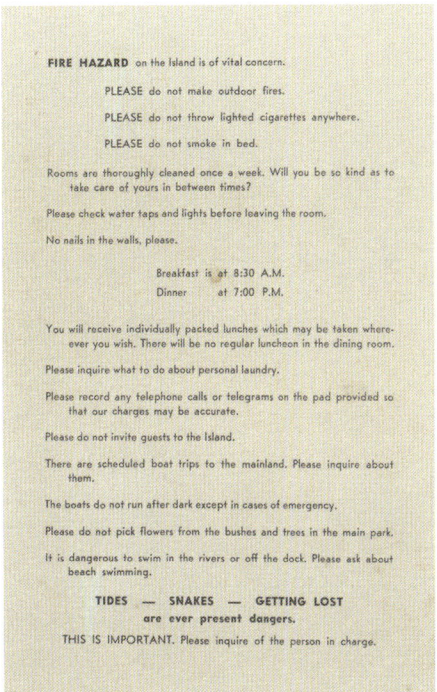

FIRE HAZARD on the Island is of vital concern.

PLEASE do not make outdoor fires.

PLEASE do not throw lighted cigarettes anywhere.

PLEASE do not smoke in bed.

Rooms are thoroughly cleaned once a week. Will you be so kind as to take care of yours in between times?

Please check water taps and lights before leaving the room.

No nails in the walls, please.

Breakfast is at 8:30 A.M.
Dinner   at 7:00 P.M.

You will receive individually packed lunches which may be taken wherever you wish. There will be no regular luncheon in the dining room.

Please inquire what to do about personal laundry.

Please record any telephone calls or telegrams on the pad provided so that our charges may be accurate.

Please do not invite guests to the Island.

There are scheduled boat trips to the mainland. Please inquire about them.

The boats do not run after dark except in cases of emergency.

Please do not pick flowers from the bushes and trees in the main park.

It is dangerous to swim in the rivers or off the dock. Please ask about beach swimming.

TIDES   —   SNAKES   —   GETTING LOST
are ever present dangers.
THIS IS IMPORTANT. Please inquire of the person in charge.

At landlocked residencies, there wasn't the same sense of isolation that came from being on an island with no physical connection to the mainland, surrounded by only a handful of other people. There was a sense that Ossabaw was different, almost other-worldly in its separation from the real world. Writer Olive Ann Burns came to understand that the world out there didn't matter because "Ossabaw IS the world when you're on it."[17] The lack of connection to the mainland offered a firm severance described by one participant as "a demarcation, a boundary, a place where a transition takes place."[18] Sheer scale was also an obvious difference; both Yaddo and MacDowell operated on 400 acres of cultivated land, whereas Ossabaw boasted 26,000 untamed acres of maritime forests, marshscapes, and beach. Artist Jean Zaleski compared her experiences at several residencies, including MacDowell, the Virginia Center for the Creative Arts, the Montalvo Center for the Arts, and the OIP, in a 1981 essay for *Women Artists News*. She touched on what made Ossabaw so unique, noting it as her most "unusual and inspiring experience" because of the wild environment, intense isolation, and likely encounters with wild animals.[19] Indeed, members had to abide by a strict set of rules for their safety, the most important one being that they had to sign out if they intended to leave the Main House, where danger potentially lurked around every bend. A sign on their closet doors warned: "TIDES — SNAKES — GETTING LOST are ever present dangers. THIS IS IMPORTANT."[(fig. 4)]

One friend cautioned sculptor Anne Truitt about the cottonmouth snakes she might encounter, writing, "Please be very, very careful. You can be sitting perfectly calmly, by yourself, minding your own quiet, contemplative business, when, from out of nowhere – BANG!"[20] There was a concerted effort through the recommendation and application process to ensure that participants understood the perils of the environment. There would be no hospitals, no stores, and no way to leave quickly.

The administration of the OIP was relatively simple and informal. The formative group from June 1961 was the foundation of an Advisory Board. Board members, and later, previous Project members, proposed distinguished men and women from various creative fields, who were then encouraged to apply for periods ranging from one week to two months. The administrative positions fell to trusted family and friends. Detroit artist Thomas Marker served as the first executive director until 1967, followed by Clifford's sister and brother-in-law, Anne and Chuck Wood.[21] Marker was the only fine artist in the position during the 21-year history of the OIP and was known for his steadying and

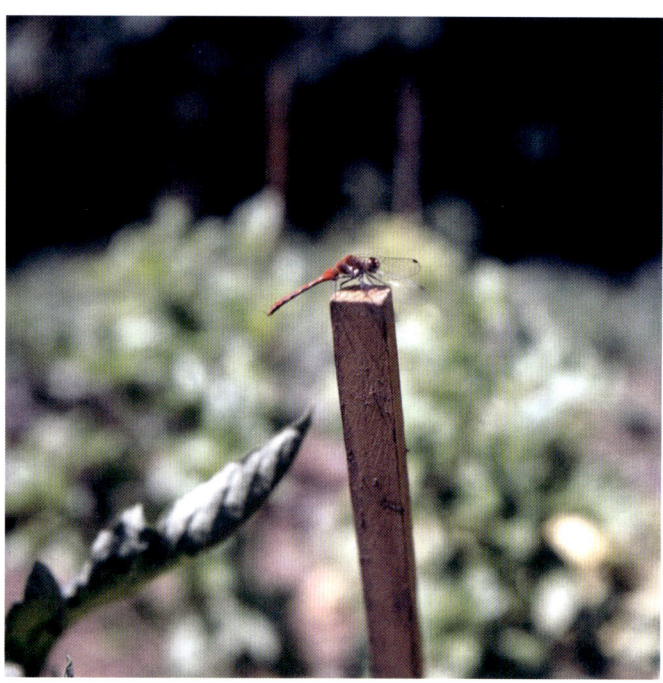

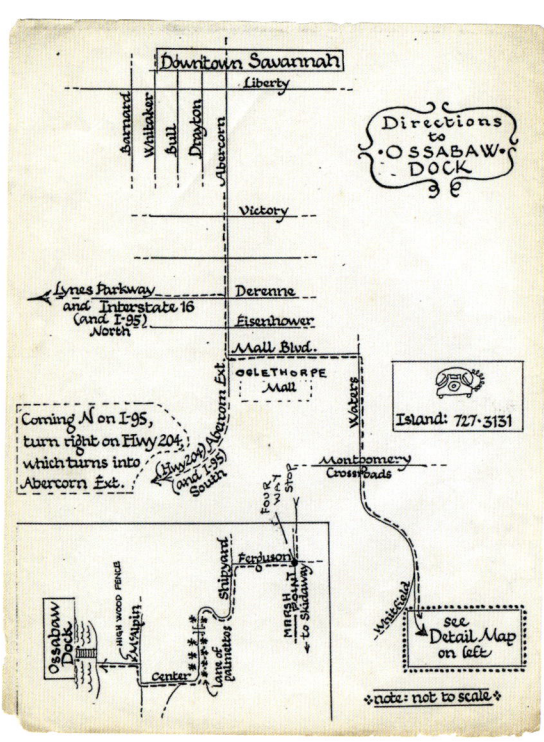

fig. 5.   Insect on Osssabaw, c. 1963.
           Photograph by Thomas Marker

fig. 6.   Hand-drawn map by Wendy Hunter of downtown
           Savannah to the dock on Burnside Island,
           where incoming members would catch the
           boat over to Ossabaw Island, c. 1970s

responsible presence. Famed linguist Roman Jakobson, who stayed on Ossabaw several times throughout the 1960s and 1970s, described Marker as the "chief magician" in a letter from 1965.[22] Marker not only worked in an official capacity, but kept an active practice on the island, often photographing and painting descriptive scenes with watercolors. His charming painting *Things on Ossabaw* (1961) [(p. 102)], made during the first year of the OIP, offers an insight into the wide variety of wildlife, big and small, that he came across on the island, both outside in the wilderness and crawling along his bedroom windows at night [(fig. 5)]. The work gives a sense of being surrounded by creatures, bringing them vividly to life while annotating precise, almost scientific details in pencil.

If accepted, members faced few stipulations to attend. In the early days, the Project asked for a nominal fee of $25 per week (increased to $75 per week in later years), which was waived if the cost proved a hardship. The expenses for the program were largely subsidized by the Wests' personal fortune. An oft-repeated quote from Sandy noted that the money was sort of beside the point as it "wouldn't even pay for the lemon in their tea," but it did help with the basic administrative costs of running the program.[23] The Project generally operated from October 1 to June 1 of every year, closing due to the brutally hot and humid coastal Georgia summers and to provide some respite for the Wests and their staff.

Upon arrival in Savannah, members were picked up from the Hotel DeSoto Hilton downtown and driven to the dock on Burnside Island to take a boat over to Ossabaw [(fig. 6)]. Members were offered a private bedroom in the Main House or in nearby buildings on the property such as the Little House, a home built for Sandy's brother when he lived on the island. Fed three meals a day, the participants partook of a hearty breakfast and lunch was self-serve, leaving members to their own devices until they dressed up for dinner at 7 p.m. around the dining table. After dinner, a salon of sorts took place in the great living room in the Main House, where members could share what they were working on. Many participants remember watching Clifford West's films, which were frequently screened. There were opportunities to head to the mainland every Friday. While the participants weren't waited on hand and foot, there was a dedicated staff that helped to ensure everyone's comfort, including James Brownlee and Queenie Williams, Cyrus Martin, Arthur, Agnes, Eugene, and Liz Graves, Mable Daniels, and Roger, Sarah, Stanfield, and Mary Parker.

Most of the fine artists who attended the OIP had an established practice and came highly recommended by their peers. In that way, Ossabaw's influence often organically overlaid ideas and directions that were already in progress. Although Ossabaw's environment could feel antithetical to ideas of domesticity, both Miriam Schapiro and Daga Ramsey found the island the perfect complement to their exploration of femininity within the landscape. Working in a collaging technique dubbed "femmage," feminist artist Schapiro produced the work *Ossabaw Heart* in 1982 [p. 55], shortly after her visit to the island with her husband, the painter Paul Brach. The island's shape has often been compared to a heart and in a notebook documenting her visit, Schapiro described Ossabaw as "nature at her romantic best."[24] Her fabric and acrylic collage, in the shape of the traditional symbol of love, may have symbolized a yearning to return.

Swedish American artist Daga Ramsey, best known as a printmaker, visited the OIP in 1969 and 1971 [fig. 7]. After completing a series of drawings, Ramsey noted in her application an intention to make a Scandinavian wool rya rug with a long pile, based on her previous sketches. Using skeins of colorful yarn that she brought with her to Ossabaw, Ramsey constructed an abstraction of *Queen Bess Creek*, a small inlet on the northwest side of the island. The tactical textile reframed the dense environment into a soft aerial study of color, shape, and form [p. 107].

In addition to artists, the OIP welcomed minds from the fields of science, industry, education, and religion. Interaction between different disciplines proved invaluable. Sandy often touted the exchange of ideas between people of all careers and backgrounds as why the OIP stood out from other residencies. Writer Lin Root suffered from writer's block on Ossabaw and began weaving instead after learning the skill from another member. When she turned her attention back to writing, she found that her fingers and mind moved with ease.[25] After active journalist Olive Ann Burns began writing the beginnings of a story based in the fictional Georgia town of Cold Sassy, she shared the first

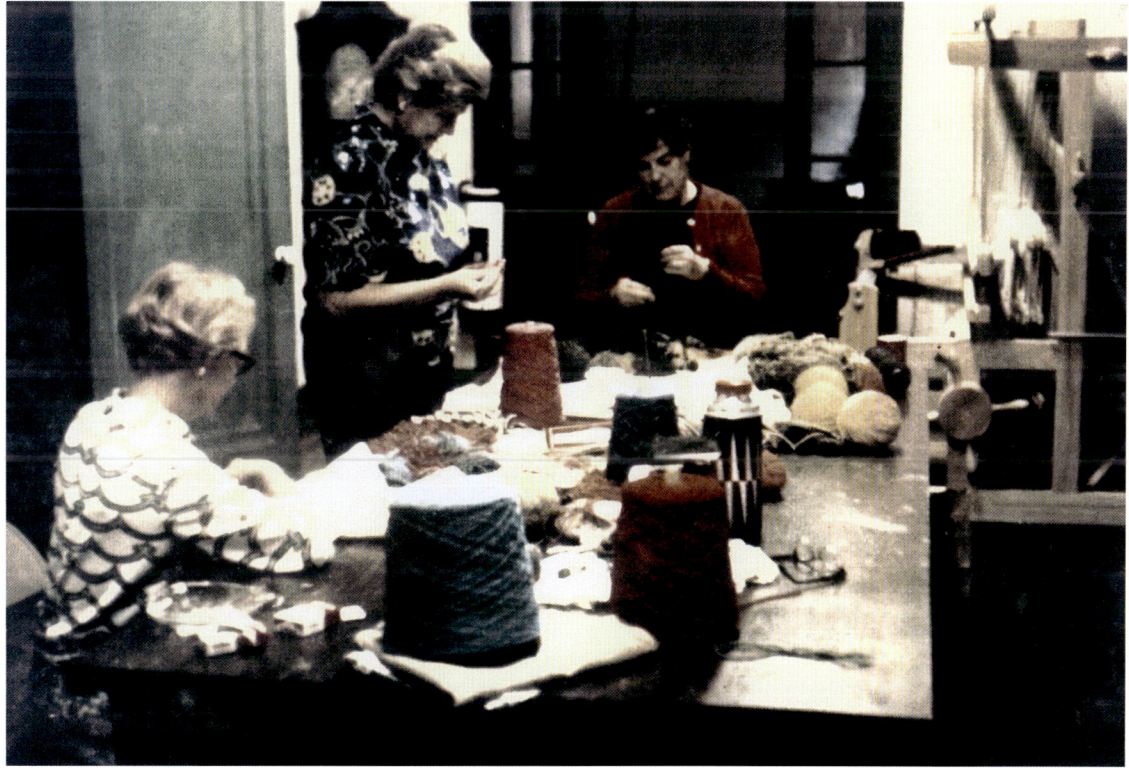

fig. 7.   Co-director of the OIP Anne Wood, printmaker Daga Ramsey, and painter Margueritte
Kimball in the Main House's loom room, November 1969

fig. 8.   Olive Ann Burns writing in the Little
           House, 1980. Photograph by Helen Hamada

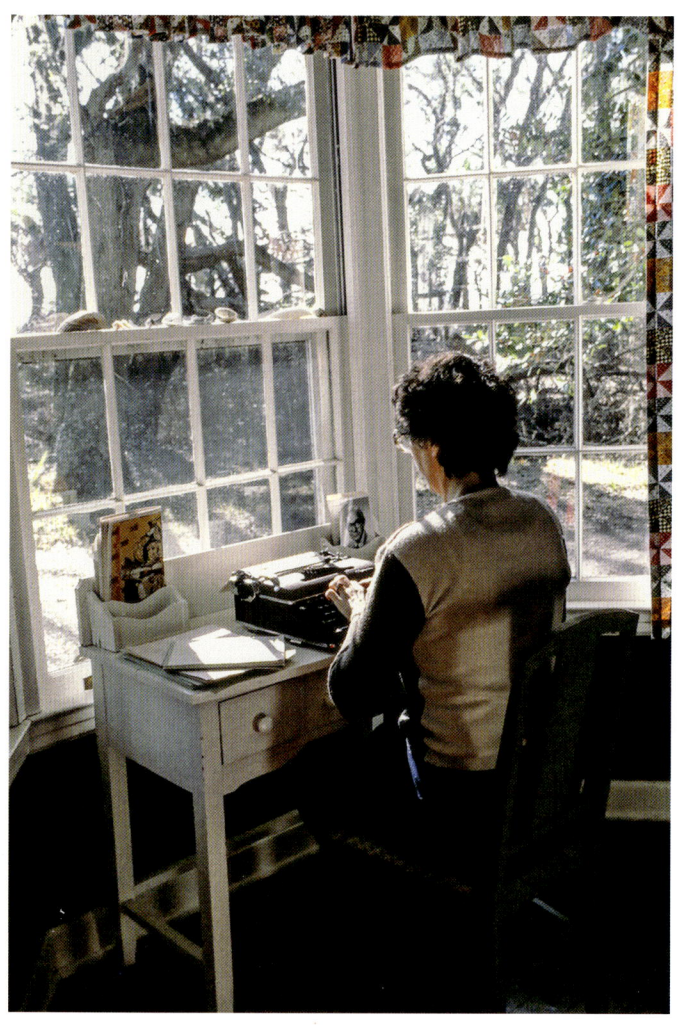

few chapters with Israeli literary theorist Menakhem Perry, her new friend and a fellow Project member at the time [fig. 8]. While Burns did not consider herself to be a novelist, Perry unequivocally convinced her to see the book through. Her beloved novel *Cold Sassy Tree* was published a few years later in 1984. There are also many anecdotes from visual artists about how they were inspired by or learned to think about their art differently after speaking with another member working in a different discipline. For instance, conversations between Harry Bertoia and biologist Colin Pittendrigh led the artist to think about his sculpture in a new way.[26]

During one of his many residencies at the OIP, nature photographer John Earl became life-long friends with translator Willard Trask, whom Earl noted inspired him "as much as another photographer would have done. Maybe more so."[27] Earl even asked Trask to serve as best man at his wedding to Susan Tinkelman, whom he met at the OIP in 1977. Although he originally studied to be a musician, Earl changed course and began photographing under the tutelage of James Valentine, an OIP member in 1969. They collaborated on photography for the environmental publication *Guale, the Golden Coast of Georgia* (1974), which included writings by OIP member Robert Hanie and an introduction by OIP advisor and "father of modern ecology" Eugene P. Odum. Some of the most incredible vistas in the book were Earl's depictions of Ossabaw in its most primordial form, and his photographs decorated the walls of the Main House and other buildings on the island for many years [pp. 90-91]. A frequent member of the OIP and Genesis, he also served as an official board member and an unofficial advisor in later years. A professor of photography at the Savannah College of Art and Design (SCAD), Earl brought his students to the island many times, teaching them to love the land as he did. Indeed, Ossabaw Island left a lasting impression on most of its visitors and influenced a great number of artworks and concepts, proving that Sandy and Clifford's "big idea" was worth it after all.

While the OIP operated successfully, several stakeholders felt there lacked an opportunity for young people to engage with Ossabaw and focus on its unique environment in a more sustained way. The island was like an outdoor laboratory with a thriving ecological environment largely untouched by human intervention. In the summer of 1970, Genesis, described as "An Experiment of Man and Nature in Harmonious Co-existence," opened to students. Apropos of the name, participants had unfiltered access to the land, which proved impactful and almost spiritual for many. Many years post-Genesis in 1990, artist Marcy Hermansader got to the heart of the matter when she wrote, "Being on Ossabaw was for me like being at the center of all creation. It was a place where life was so abundant and varied it was like a living textbook of ecological connections."[28] Genesis members resided at Middle Place, located on Buckhead Creek, approximately three miles south of the dock at the North End. Based on archeological evidence, the Guale were indigenous to that area before 1568. Prior to the Civil War, enslaved Africans labored on a plantation there that harvested Sea Island cotton. After the South's defeat, freed African Americans likely established a small settlement, most eventually leaving for the Pin Point community on the mainland after a series of deadly hurricanes. In the 20th century, a lumber mill occupied the site, a commercial activity that left behind a mound of sawdust still in existence today. Although there was no running water or electricity, there was an abundance of natural resources and abandoned rudimentary structures that members restored as living spaces, and new lodgings were built with available materials like island timber, resulting in constructions such as the Tower House, the A-frame, and three treehouses. Genesis participant Nancy Marshall's photograph of fellow member Deborah Shepherd from 1979 shows one of the treehouses nestled amongst the towering live oaks, light filtering through the branches [p. 49].

Initially structured as a program for Georgia-based college and graduate students, Genesis soon expanded to include universities from around the country. Students from multiple disciplines were eligible to earn school credit, and the intention of the program gradually broadened to allow participants outside of a formal degree-seeking program to experience a form of alternative living off the land. Like the OIP, the application process was uncomplicated, but it was less dependent on an established network. Applicants were required to have a proposed project, but no outcome was required, also similar to the OIP. In the late 1970s, the program began to operate year-round, which added to the diversity of ages, skill sets, and backgrounds. Although no age limit was formally imposed, the program primarily attracted younger participants in part due to the physically demanding nature of the site. Genesis members learned how to develop a community based around sustainable practices and, as one member noted, "Genesis could be called a training ground for environmental awareness. While becoming sensitive to nature, each person learns from every other, sharing new discoveries, information gleaned from successes and failures of the projects, ideas born of silent, starry nights or solitary strolls through the woods."[29]

Members contributed five hours a week to communal chores and one day a week to cook for the entire group. There was a well for fresh water, a food garden, and a cook shack. Participants had access to fresh meat, often wild boar, fresh eggs and chickens, and milk from the beloved cows Daisy and Genie. Participants often remembered the strong sense of community and camaraderie instilled by the shared workload, which ensured the success of the program. Despite its primitive nature, Genesis had a few tethers to the world beyond. Trucks were available for the members' use if needed, and a weekly grocery run to Savannah provided requested food and supplies. Frequent cross-pollination occurred between Genesis and the OIP members. For instance, Genesis members often came up to the Main House for talks and film screenings, and the OIP members often stopped by Genesis during their visits.[30] Artist Jean Zaleski, an OIP member, found a favorite subject in the daily milking of Genie, one of the Genesis cows [fig. 9]. This fruitful

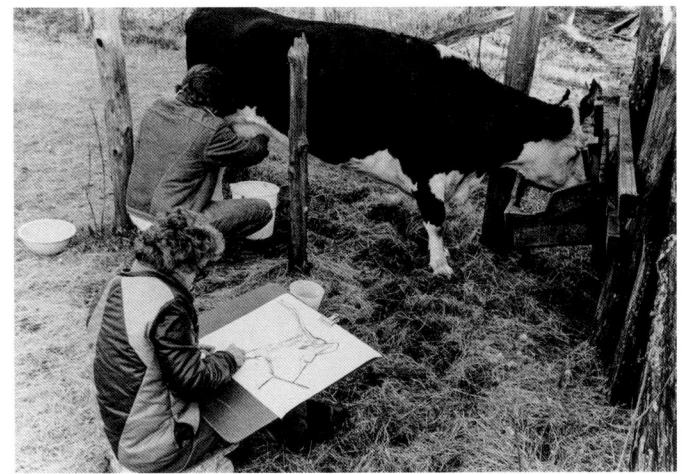

fig. 9.   Genesis co-director Michael Billa milks
Genie the cow while OIP member Jean
Zaleski sketches her at Middle Place, c.
1981. Photograph by Helen Hamada

intermingling between disciplines, age groups, life experiences, and interests remains one of the most distinct features of the residency programs on Ossabaw Island.

Engaging directly with the environment tended to viscerally impact Genesis participants and their work. When Helen Hamada arrived in February 1974, she noted that her life changed completely: "I tell people I was born on Ossabaw. When I went there, that's when my life began."[31] On the island, Hamada photographed in black and white with a Hasselblad 2 ¼ × 2 ¼ camera; her images often showed bodies intertwined with the landscape—imitating it, touching it, blending in with it. Her work evokes the elemental feeling that so many participants describe of being intimately connected with the land in a way that seemed impossible anywhere else. In an interview with Hamada in 2015, Wini Wood stated her most distinct memory was the sensation of being naked in the sunshine and how there was seemingly no division between the body and the rest of the universe on Ossabaw.[32] Hamada's self-portrait from 1974 (p. 44)—in which she lies topless and facedown on the sand, her arms raised to her face level—conjures this awareness. Her wild, dark curls spring up in the wind as sand blows above her head. Her bare back reveals her ribs, which echo the natural formation of the sandy ripples she lies upon.

Other artists incorporated the environment into their work more literally. Returning to his hometown of Savannah, the painter T. J. Reddy attended Genesis in 1981. In letters to his wife Vicky in Charlotte, North Carolina, Reddy wrote of Ossabaw, "It's quiet, spacious, lots of light and water and sky and mystery, wild animals everywhere... No painting yet. I want to and have been collecting materials from the island, moss, weeds, grasses, quills from the turkeys, that I will use to paint with."[33] Reddy noted that he used sawdust from the towering pile left behind by the defunct lumber mill, which was adjacent to his accommodations (fig. 10), in his painting *From the Window of the Tower House, Middle Place, Ossabaw Island, GA* (1981) (p. 142). Not only did the heap serve as a vantage point to watch spectacular sunsets, but it was also the only place for radio reception between Middle Place and the Main House. The granular texture of the sawdust modulated the color of Reddy's paintings, especially the blue, which, in his mind, stood for "the sky and water meeting in the minds of my ancestors that transcended into a spiritual experience resulting in music now known as the blues."[34]

The artist Marcy Hermansader lived at Genesis for six weeks in 1982. Coming from the Northeast, nothing prepared her for the surreal landscape she encountered. She brought a portfolio of paper and colored pencils, but soon discovered that the high levels of atmospheric humidity had rendered many of the sheets unusable. One of her drawings from her time on the island, *The Magic Hoe* (1982) (p. 134), was made on light-colored paper that she imbued with the soil of Ossabaw. Featuring elements such as a shovel, an ax, a handsaw, a bow saw, a pitchfork, a rake, and a hoe, the work reveals her interest in the agricultural history of the island. The title references an African American folk story about Bruh Rabbit stealing Bruh Wolf's magic hoe that would weed a field by itself through the magic command "Swish." However, Bruh Rabbit doesn't know how to stop the hoe, resulting in the destruction of the entire crop.[35] The composition is populated with figures and depictions of the tabby cabins that formerly housed enslaved workers on the island. These buildings continued to be used as housing for the island staff, as well as Genesis members. The environment weaves in and around the tools of industry and narratives of labor, a history that remains inseparable from the land. In the hanging Spanish moss at the top of the composition, Hermansader collaged some found mosquito netting—a technique she continues to use in her work today.

As early as 1964, Sandy West began considering how Ossabaw could be preserved in the long term. In September 1970, the quest gained more urgency when Chatham County reassessed the island's property taxes, resulting in a 607% increase. Through persistence, ingenuity, and a series of private donations, grants, and her own funding, the island resisted development until the right owner could be identified. West ultimately had three priorities: "The first was to save the island. The second was the welfare of the people who live on the island....The third thing was my own work, and, of course, behind it all was this idea that you can preserve a piece of land and use it at the same time."[36] Partly convinced by her conversations with former Governor Jimmy Carter, Sandy and her family decided to sell the island to the state of Georgia for $8 million in 1978, donating half of its appraised value of $16 million. One of the main stipulations ensured that the island became a protected Heritage Preserve site. The Heritage Trust Act, established in Georgia in 1975, preserved certain properties with unique natural characteristics, historical or recreational value. Ossabaw's particular agreement determined its appropriate use for "natural, scientific and cultural study, research and education, and for environmentally sound preservation, conservation and management of the island's ecosystem." Sandy reinvested her half of the money back into running the programs for another four years. However, they shuttered completely in 1982. As West remembered in a 2000 interview with Georgia Public Broadcasting, her dwindling fortune wasn't due to frivolous spending, but rather her investment in the OIP and Genesis:

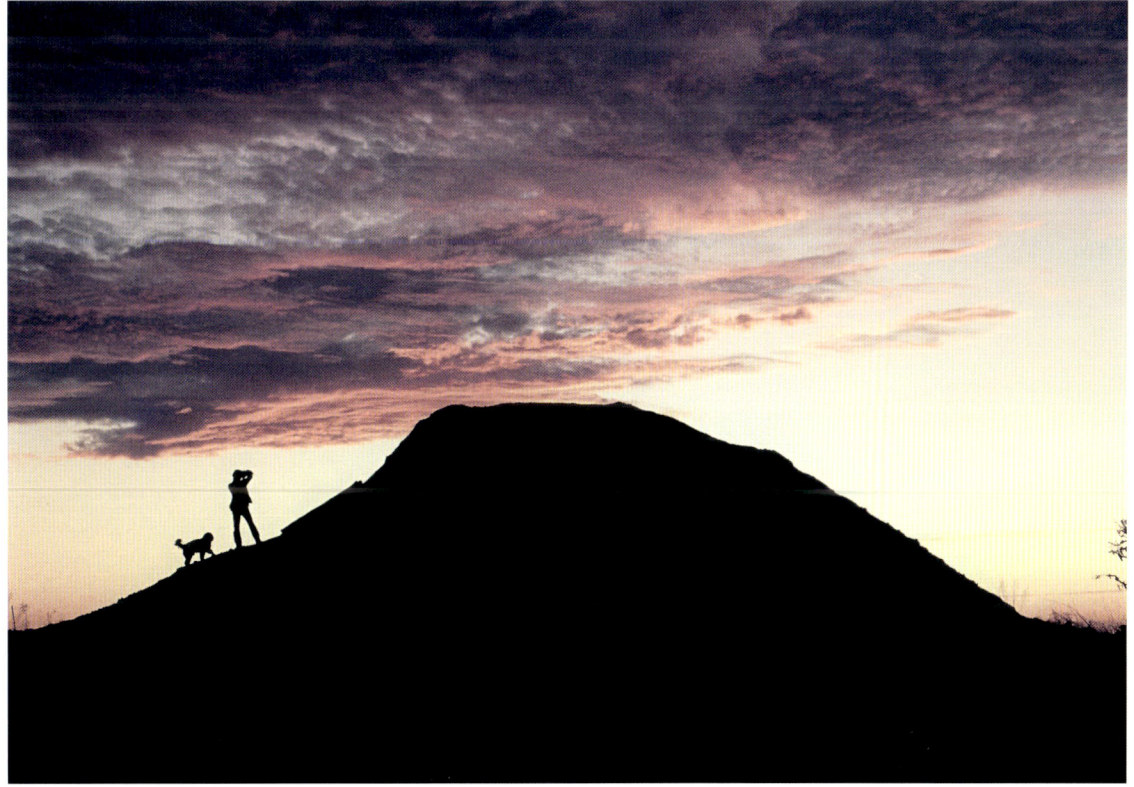

fig. 10.   Genesis member and dog on the sawdust pile at Middle Place, 1974.
Photograph by Stephen Schoenholtz

"I spent it on something I believed in, because I was encouraging the biggest thinkers and doers in the country to get together and to inspire themselves and ideas coming out of it... at the same time, I was preserving this piece of land."[37]

Sandy and Clifford's son Justin got to the heart of the matter when he discussed the sale of the island, the loss of Sandy's fortune, and the shuttering of the programs: "Was it a good investment? I'd probably say no...On the other hand, was the money worth a *Cold Sassy Tree* or a piece of music? Could it have all been done smarter? Probably. Could it have been done better? I don't think so."[38] Both a testament to the ideas and ideals of residencies, the location and time spent there had lasting impacts on artists, scientists, conservations, naturalists, and more who continue to advocate for the protection of Ossabaw. Like Yaddo and MacDowell served to inspire aspects of the OIP, the Project went on to serve that purpose for myriad others. In just a few examples, painter Judy Barber used expertise gleaned during her time in the OIP to bolster another Georgia residency. She was named executive director of the Hambidge Center in Rabun County in 1990, a position she held for more than a decade. Another OIP member, Dennis Elliott, went on to found the International Studio & Curatorial Program (ISCP) in New York City in 1994. OIP co-director and poet Carol Burdick established a writers' retreat called Summer Place at Alfred University in Alfred, New York, which she directed for around 20 years.

Efforts to preserve the legacy of the OIP and Genesis continue to this day. From 2006 until 2011, The Ossabaw Island Foundation offered free access to the island for dozens of local artists, including Suzanne Jackson and Betsy Cain, in exchange for the donation of selected works to an annual fundraiser. Today, the foundation continues to facilitate trips to the island for those who have creative, research, or other specific purposes. The state of Georgia recently allocated funds in its budget to rehabilitate the Main House, meaning that the building may once again be used to host large groups on the island and possibly another artist residency through the efforts of local nonprofits.[39] Although the Ossabaw Island Project and Genesis ended over 40 years ago, the island retains its edenic pull, calling out to old and new from its shores, its generative atmosphere remaining at the center of it all.

Notes

1. "Island Verses" (1977 and 1979), AAA.johnelle, box 7, Ellen Hulda Johnson Papers, 1872-2018, Archives of American Art, Smithsonian Institution, Washington, DC. Carol "CB" Burdick (1929-2008) was a poet and writer who served as co-director of the OIP with Albert Bradford from 1979-1982, the final years of the program.
2. Margaret Ann Keister, "The Ossabaw Island Project, a Program Fostering Creative Production and Experience," (PhD diss., University of Georgia, 1992), 92.
3. Sandy West's notes from the first meetings about the Ossabaw Island Project in a notebook labeled "Mrs. Clifford B. West; Ossabaw Island; June 22, 1961," West family archives.
4. Clifford B. and Eleanor West, *Ossabaw* (Ossabaw Island Project Foundation, 1973), 2.
5. Keister, 85.
6. Jane Brown Gillette, "Enchanted Isle," *Historic Preservation*, November/December 1995, 5.
7. Eleanor Torrey West, "Climate: For Contemplation, Communication and Work," *Dobbs Alumnae Bulletin*, November 1964, 17.
8. Eleanor Torrey West, 17.
9. An interdisciplinary, experimental liberal arts college in operation from 1933 until 1957. Many notable figures taught there including Josef and Anni Albers, John Cage, and Robert Rauschenberg, among others. For a more in-depth focus on this institution, refer to *Leap Before You Look: Black Mountain College 1933-1957*, ed. Helen Molesworth (New Haven: Yale University Press, 2015).
10. Micki McGee, "Creative Power," in *Yaddo: Making American Culture*, ed. Micki McGee (New York: Columbia University Press 2008), 1. Yaddo Timeline, 126.
11. Keister, 90.
12. Karl Emil Willers, "In Good Company," in *Yaddo: Making American Culture*, 53.
13. Charles Rippin, "Ossabaw," *Coastal Quarterly* (Spring 1977), 38.

14. Hermann Hagedorn, "The Peterborough Colony: 'A Workshop, with a wonderland thrown in,' for creative workers in the seven arts", *The Outlook: An Illustrated Weekly Journey of Current Life* 129 (Sept–Dec. 1921) Google Books.

15. Allison Wade and Kathryn Wade, "One More Ecosystem on Death Row?" *Catalyst For Environmental Equality* II, no. 4 (1972), 17.

16. Perdita Buchan to Sandy West, July 18, 1980, West family archives.

17. Olive Ann Burns, "Ossabaw: An Atlanta writer working on her first novel discovers an unreal world of natural and intellectual wonders on this island by the sea," *Atlanta Weekly*, May 11, 1980, 16.

18. Fred Powledge, "Island Fever," *Esquire*, March 1977, 91.

19. Jean Zaleski, "Getting Away from it all: Isolation as Inspiration," *Women Artist News*, April 1, 1981, 5-6. Founded as the Women Artists Newsletter in 1975, this publication served as a space for information exchange and communication for a community of women artists. One of its most fervent contributors was Miriam Schapiro, who was a member of the OIP in 1982.

20. Letter to Anne Truitt, March 5, 1975, BMC.M109, box 55, folder 10, Anne Truitt Papers, Bryn Mawr College.

21. For a complete listing of project directors, refer to the chronology on p. 166.

22. Ossabaw Island Correspondence, 1957-70, Letter from Roman Jakobson to Thomas Marker, February 16, 1965, MC 72, box 6, folder 3, Roman O. Jakobson papers, MIT Distinctive Collections, Massachusetts Institute of Technology, Boston.

23. Ann Hardie, "Isle on the edge," *Atlanta Journal-Constitution*, January 30, 2000, B1.

24. Ossobow [*sic*] Residency, Recipe, Women's Culture, Feminism, Quotes, Collage, 1982, MC 1411, box 103, folder 130, Miriam Schapiro Papers, Special Collections and University Archives, Rutgers University Libraries, New Brunswick, NJ.

25. Louis Chapin, "Georgia Island Becomes Teacher," *Tallahassee Democrat*, August 1, 1973, 6.

26. Keister, 65, 84, 92. Refer to Beryl Gilothwest's essay "Like a veil" on p. 10 of this volume for a more in-depth understanding of Bertoia's new direction in sculpture.

27. Keister, 71.

28. Rachel Rosenfield Lafo, *Belief in the Underground: The Art of Marcy Hermansader* (Lincoln, MA: DeCordova Museum and Sculpture Park, 1990), 3.

29. Clifford B. and Eleanor West, *Ossabaw*, 11.

30. This intersection between OIP and Genesis members is discussed in the essay "Ross, Me and *Sherman's March*" by Wini Wood on p. 120.

31. Interview with Helen Hamada conducted by Anna Robertson, July 20, 2021.

32. Video interview of Wini Wood by Helen Hamada, 2015.

33. Letter from T. J. Reddy to his wife Vicky, June 28, 1981, T. J. Reddy Papers MS0079, box 4.36.1, Special Collections and University Archives, J. Murrey Atkins Library, University of North Carolina, Charlotte.

34. Letter from T. J. Reddy to his wife Vicky.

35. *Drums and Shadows: Survival Studies Among The Georgia Coastal Negroes* (Athens, GA: University of Georgia Press, 1940), 110-11.

36. Henry Eason, "Ossabaw Purchase Arranged by State," *The Atlanta Constitution*, April 8, 1977, 1A, 18A.

37. GPB, 2000.

38. Ann Hardie, "The Old Lady of Ossabaw," *Atlanta Magazine*, March 1, 2011, accessed March 9, 2024, https://www.atlantamagazine.com/great-reads/ossabaw-sandy-west/.

39. See the Ossabaw Island Artist Residency: https://artssoutheast.org/ossabaw.

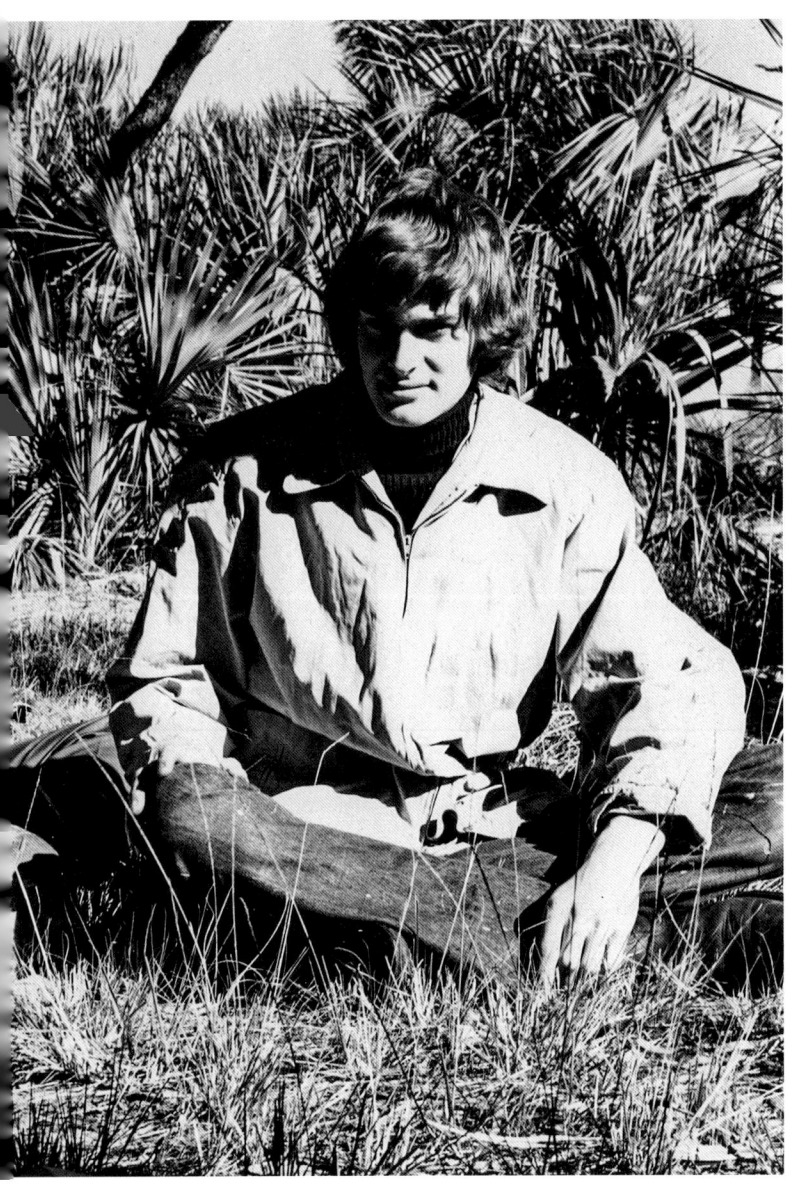

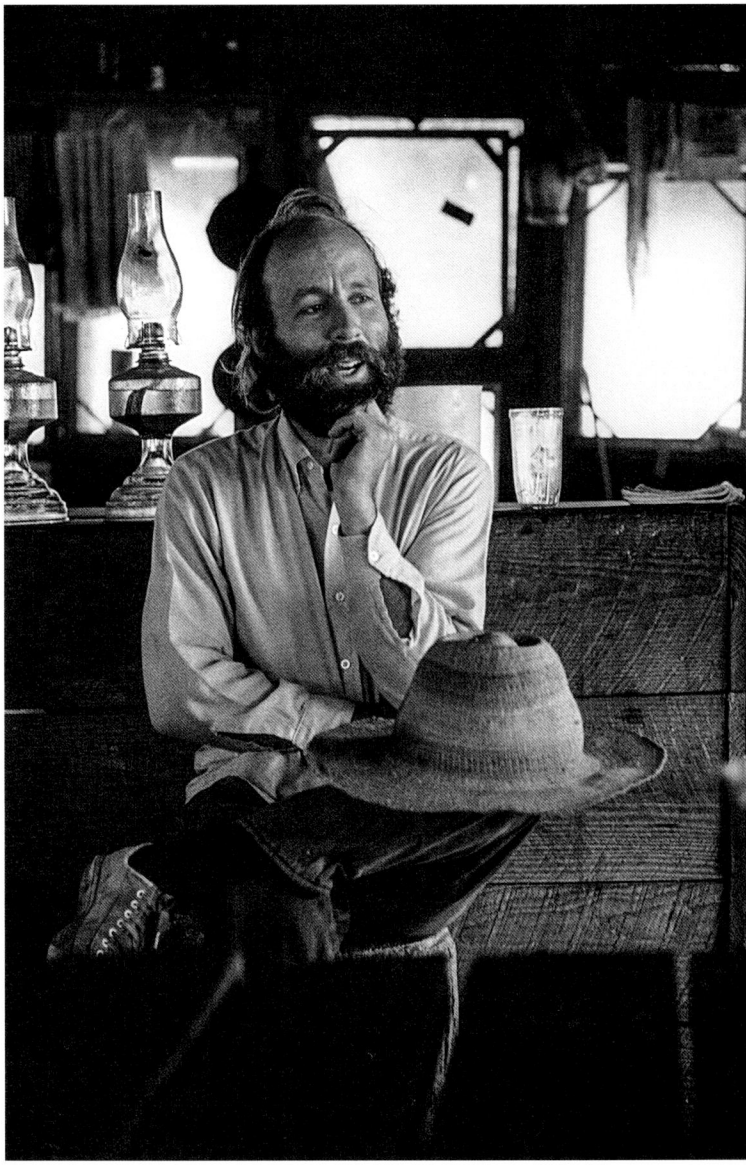

Justin West on Ossabaw Island, c. 1973.
Photograph by Clifford B. West

Al Bradford in the Cookshack at Genesis, 1977.
Photograph by Robert Lockhart

OSSABAW ISLAND— IDEA AND SOLUTION: A CONVERSATION

AL BRADFORD AND JUSTIN WEST

The Ossabaw Island Project and Genesis are not only notable for the creativity that they facilitated, but also for the many lasting relationships that came out of them. Al Bradford and Justin West first met through the OIP and have remained friends over the last fifty years. Justin grew up spending his school vacations on Ossabaw with his parents Eleanor "Sandy" Torrey West and Clifford B. West. He was seven years old when they founded the Ossabaw Island Project, and he watched the evolution of the OIP and later Genesis throughout his childhood and early adulthood. Al came to Ossabaw as a Project member in 1974 and lived on the island for the better part of the next eight years. He was a Genesis member and sometimes director from 1974 to 1977, and director of the OIP from 1978–1982. Justin and Al reunited on March 30, 2025 to reflect on their memories of both programs and the enduring resonance of Ossabaw Island.

Al Bradford:
Why do you think your parents started the Ossabaw Island Project?

Justin West:
What happened was very organic. I think it all started because my mother felt that having inherited the island, she had also inherited a responsibility to share it. So, initially, she thought about opening it up to the public and making it into a state park, but my father said, "If you do that, it's going to become like every other state park—it has a lot of unique qualities that could really benefit the artistic community."

My father was a painter, so that was, of course, his viewpoint.

Then they looked into two existing artists colonies, Yaddo and MacDowell, and saw that Yaddo seemed focused on writers, and MacDowell on painters. They said to themselves, "I wonder what would happen if we had both writers and painters, and if we're going to do that, let's have philosophers, and could we have people in business? I guess so. How about religion? Sure. Government? Yes, but will this work?" So that's when they invited a group of prominent people that they knew from a variety of disciplines down to the island

and asked them what they thought, and they said, "Yes, it sounds like a great idea." That's how the OIP began.

Then one day several years later, a group of people were sitting around in the living room at the Main House and somebody said, "You know, all the people at the Project are older and pretty established. We should do something for young people." Someone suggested Middle Place, and that was how Genesis was started. It was this organic thing that happened. The ideas sparked solutions.

A1: That instinctive way of thinking continued over the years. When I directed Genesis and the OIP long after those early days, opportunities often arose that inspired ideas, and we had to use our intuition to find solutions.

Justin: So, how did you become OIP director?

A1: Well, I was still living at Genesis while being Chuck and Anne's assistant at the OIP, and then they decided to retire.[1] I'll never forget it. I was living in the A-frame.[2] I was taking a nap one day when suddenly, I heard this Jeep pull up outside my door. Your mom was driving and she's calling out,

"Albert, Albert." Groggily, I poked my head out, "Oh, hi there, Mrs. West." She said, "I have something to ask you. Albert, I want you to be the new director of the Project." Just like that. I said, "Really?" At the time, Sandy had already started a national search for a new director, but then Roman Jakobson[3] came to her and said, "You are wasting your time. Your director is right there at Genesis. It's Albert Bradford." I became the director in 1978, and it was so difficult. I was all alone, and it was an unrelenting job. But I loved it [(fig. 1)].

Justin: Many people have said Ossabaw had a quality that none of the other colonies had. It inspired artists and writers and musicians, people in business, philosophers, and linguists. You and I would say, well, that's because it's Ossabaw, right? So, if you had to explain it to somebody, what do you think it was that made the island so special, made it different, made it inspiring?

A1: OK, I do have some thoughts on that. I remember a woman who was a writer—I can't remember her name now—but we were sitting around on the patio and she said that she'd been to all the other colonies and really enjoyed them and had

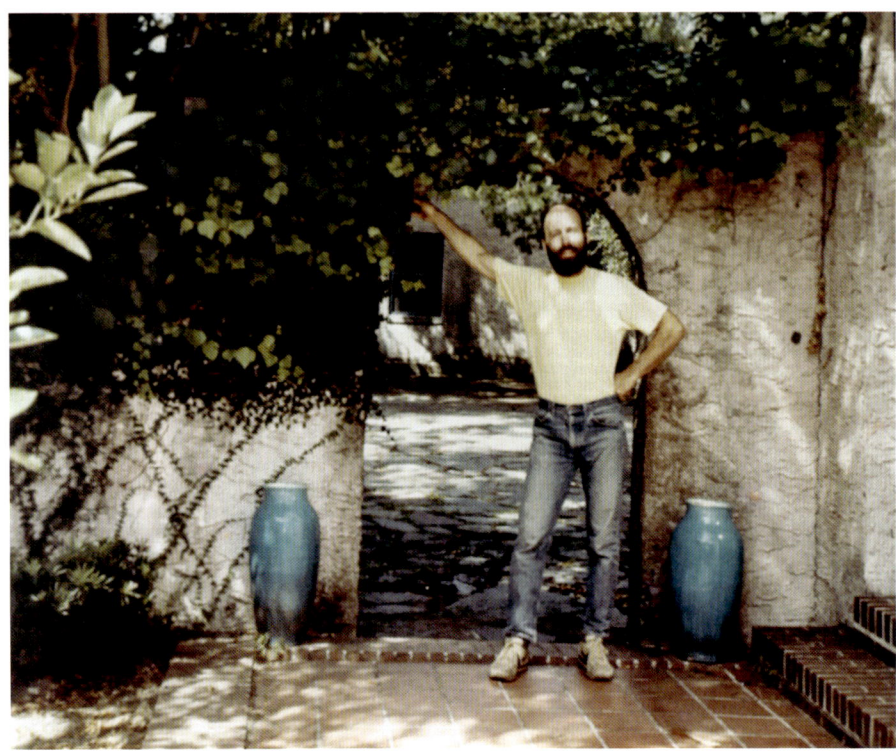

fig. 1.   Al Bradford on the patio at the Main House, c. 1978

gotten a lot of good work done. But when she came here to Ossabaw, she was really struck by the fact that we were living in a wilderness. The elemental activities of nature—the destruction, the creation, the births, the deaths, the storms, the dangers, the beauties—were all around us. And she said that began to touch her work. She told me that she realized there were things in her writing that were not elemental and should be discarded.

I think another aspect of this is that Ossabaw made people feel more protected than most colonies because it was an island, so naturally you're cut off from the regular world. Being so far away from their everyday lives, they could really release their minds and do their creative work.

I think another part of it was that Ossabaw was interdisciplinary. Project members found themselves surrounded by a world of disciplines that they'd never even imagined interacting with. They were meeting other creative people they might never have otherwise met.

Justin: It's almost like being on an ocean liner. When people went across the Atlantic, they did all kinds of things that they wouldn't normally do.

Al: I think that's true. The microcosm that a ship provides gives you permission to move outside the norms of your regular life. You are in another little world on Ossabaw, where you see things differently. You can reach out more creatively.

Justin: Do you think there was something about the island itself? Some inherent power?

Al: Yes, I do. I think the island has a personality. It certainly affected Stanley Hollingsworth.[4] He was a composer who came to the island, and almost immediately, he told me, "I'm probably going to have to leave. I'm so isolated and the phone is too far away," and so on. And I said, "Well, Stanley, if you end up having to leave, we accept that." He was fairly unhappy for several days, and then one day I realized that he wasn't at breakfast, and he wasn't at lunch. I went looking for him, and he was in his studio just working away. And

he said, "Oh, I asked the cook to make sandwiches for me so that I didn't have to waste time on meals because I'm really at a good place in my work right now." The island, in that way, is kind of like a person who charms you. When you meet them, you fall under their spell.

Then there was another guy named Jon Friedman,[5] an abstract painter from New York, who later told me that he was overwhelmed by the visual impact of Ossabaw. He said that the environment was so different from what he was used to, with the sunlight coming through the Spanish moss, the palmetto leaves, the arching oak trees.

He spent his whole time on the island not doing abstract paintings, but very photorealistic paintings instead. And he said, "I'm doing this because I want to try to understand what I'm seeing here, what I'm experiencing here with all of these amazing shapes and colors that I've never experienced before."

Justin: And even if you're not a painter, I mean, the shock of Ossabaw, the magic of Ossabaw, and the differentness of Ossabaw—I think that refreshed people.

Al: What was it like growing up on the island?

Justin: I have known Ossabaw since before I even knew I knew it. I came there as a baby when my grandparents were alive; I have memories of sitting on my grandmother's lap and eating the cherry from her old-fashioned, riding in her Packard touring car. My grandparents had purchased Ossabaw as a place to live at a time when it seemed reasonable that two people would own an island, but a generation later, my parents inherited a situation that seemed unfair to them, and they wanted to share Ossabaw with others. I remember them wondering what to do with this island they had just inherited.

From that time on, I led a dual life. I was a kid who had the run of an island, with my own pony cart to explore the woods [(fig. 2)], a small outboard bateau to explore the creeks [(fig. 3)], and a whole community of people who looked out for me, kept me safe, and taught me carpentry,

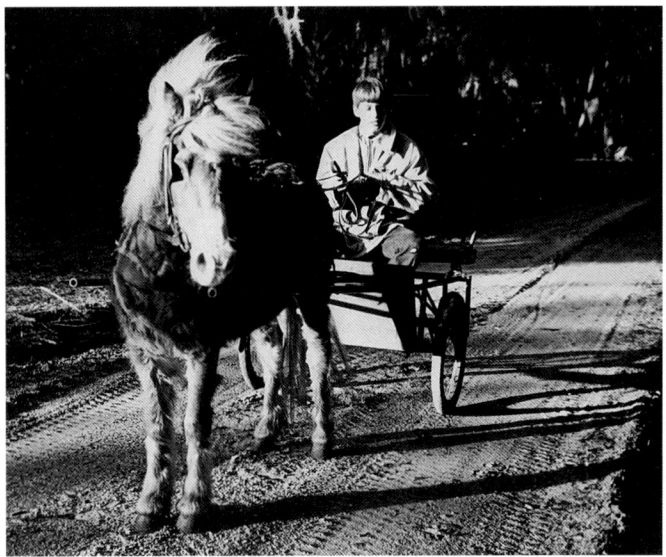

fig. 2.   Justin West with his pony, King, c. 1965.
           Photograph by Clifford B. West

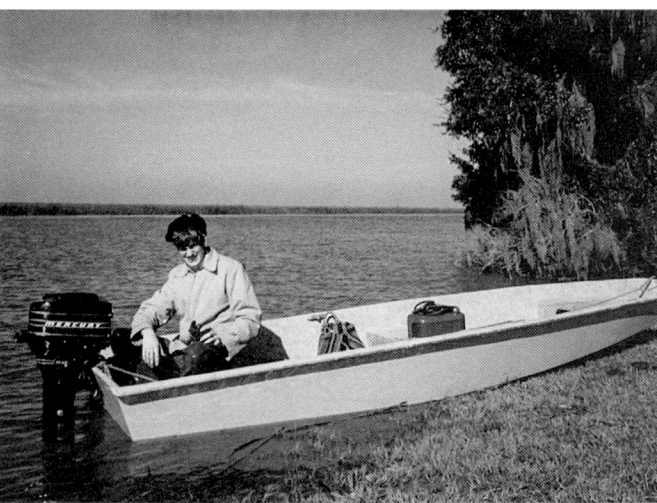

fig. 3.   Justin West in his boat on Middle
           Place Creek, 1971. Photograph by
           Eleanor Torrey West

electricity, animal care, woodcraft, and navigation. The people who lived and worked on Ossabaw were like a large family. Arthur Graves, Eugene Graves, and Roger Parker were superintendents from whom I learned about boats and how to repair just about anything. James Brownlee and Cyrus Martin helped me understand island lore, Queenie Williams told me about potions, and Agnes Graves taught me how to make her biscuits. Yet I had to share all this with the people who came to the Ossabaw Island Project—give up my room, not make a mess in the kitchen, and be quiet. Later, when I was in college and returned to the island for holidays, I was amazed that the authors of my textbooks would sometimes be sitting next to me at breakfast.[6]

Then, when we knew we couldn't keep Ossabaw and it was sold to the state, that was hard. Now I know that Jimmy Carter and others helped forge a unique private/public partnership that saved the island, but at the time, it felt like losing my home.[7]

Al: I can imagine.

Justin: You spent a lot of time at Genesis. (fig. 4)
        How was that different from the OIP?

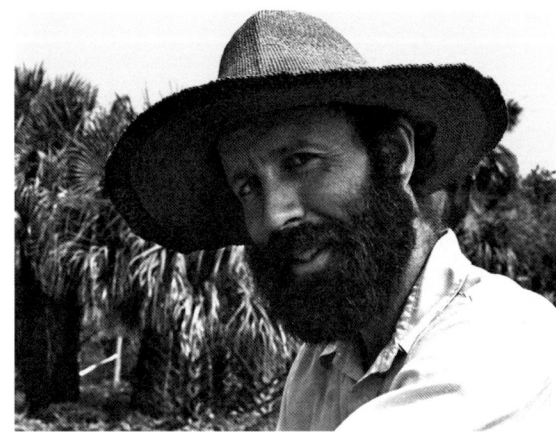

fig. 4.   Al Bradford on Ossabaw Island,
           c. 1976. Photograph by Ann Jones

Al: I think Genesis members often bonded more quickly and deeply because they worked together on gardening, cooking, and things like that. They were living a more elemental and demanding outdoor life. Genesis brought members closer to nature, closer to the island, and closer to each other because we depended on one another to keep things going. There was this sense at Genesis that we had it all, that we could be milking the cow in the morning, and we could be listening to Margaret Atwood[8], or a future Margaret Atwood, at night at the Main House.

Justin: Part of the impetus for Genesis was about sharing Ossabaw with people who didn't yet have an established field or way of working or didn't yet have a muse. I remember that the OIP didn't require you to work on a specific project, but Genesis required that you have a project in mind to do on the island. It could be a scientific project. It could be writing poetry. It could be anything, but you had to have a project. And I think the idea there was to allow the island to help people who were not yet at the point where the Project members were.

A1: Yes. I think that is an important distinction that I had forgotten about. I'm glad you brought that up because that really made a difference at Genesis.

While the programs were distinct, they both made it easy for their members to interact with the island. When I was a project member at the OIP, I remember feeling like I wasn't getting anywhere with my writing after about two weeks or so. Anne Wood saw me frowning one day, and she said,

"How are you, Albert?" I could just tell that she was really asking me a serious question. And it all poured out. "I'm just not getting anything done," I said. "I feel really guilty." And she replied, "Well, Albert, what would you like to do? Don't worry about anyone else's expectations of you." My immediate answer was, "I want to explore this island." She said, "Then that's what you should do." And that was it for the writing. Anne understood that the OIP was about allowing the island to be a catalyst.

Justin: Once again, that's Ossabaw. Because the island was there, it drew you out, and Anne gave you permission.

A1: Yes, she did.

Justin: And because of that, you went on to become the OIP director and the Genesis director, helping artists who influenced other artists, linguists who worked with filmmakers, and people exploring a new field. Ossabaw has that kind of cascading effect.

Notes

1. Charles and Anne Wood were co-directors of the Ossabaw Island Project from 1968-1978. They were also Justin West's aunt and uncle, as Anne was Clifford West's older sister.

2. The A-frame was a building designed and constructed by Genesis member and architecture student Efton J. Thomas and others on the bank of Middle Place Creek.

3. Roman Jakobson (1896-1982) was a world-renowned linguist and sixteen-time OIP member. He served on the OIP's Advisory Board from 1970 until his death.

4. Stanley Hollingsworth (1924-2003) was an American composer of stage, orchestral, chamber, and choral music. He was an OIP member in 1974 and designed a piano studio for the Project that was built in 1975.

5. Jon Friedman (b. 1947) was an OIP member in 1979.

6. For instance, the Russian American art historian H. W. Janson (1913-1982) authored the seminal textbook *History of Art* in 1962, which was extensively used in art history curricula in the ensuing decades. Janson was an OIP member in 1967, 1968, and 1972, and served on the Advisory Board.

7. For more information on Ossabaw's conveyance to the State of Georgia in 1978, see Megan Mayhew Bergman's essay on p. 112 of this volume.

8. The Canadian author Margaret Atwood (b. 1939) was an OIP member in 1982.

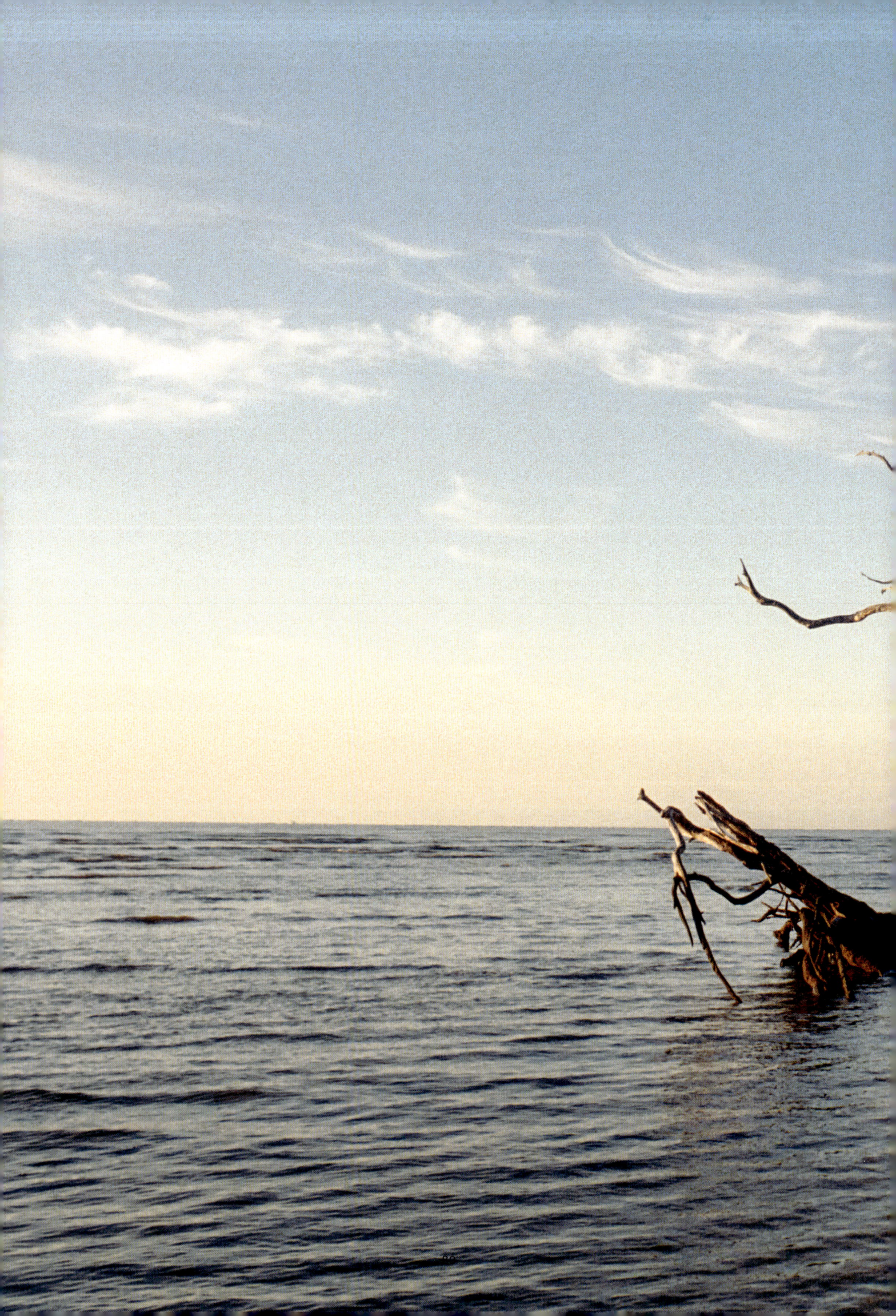

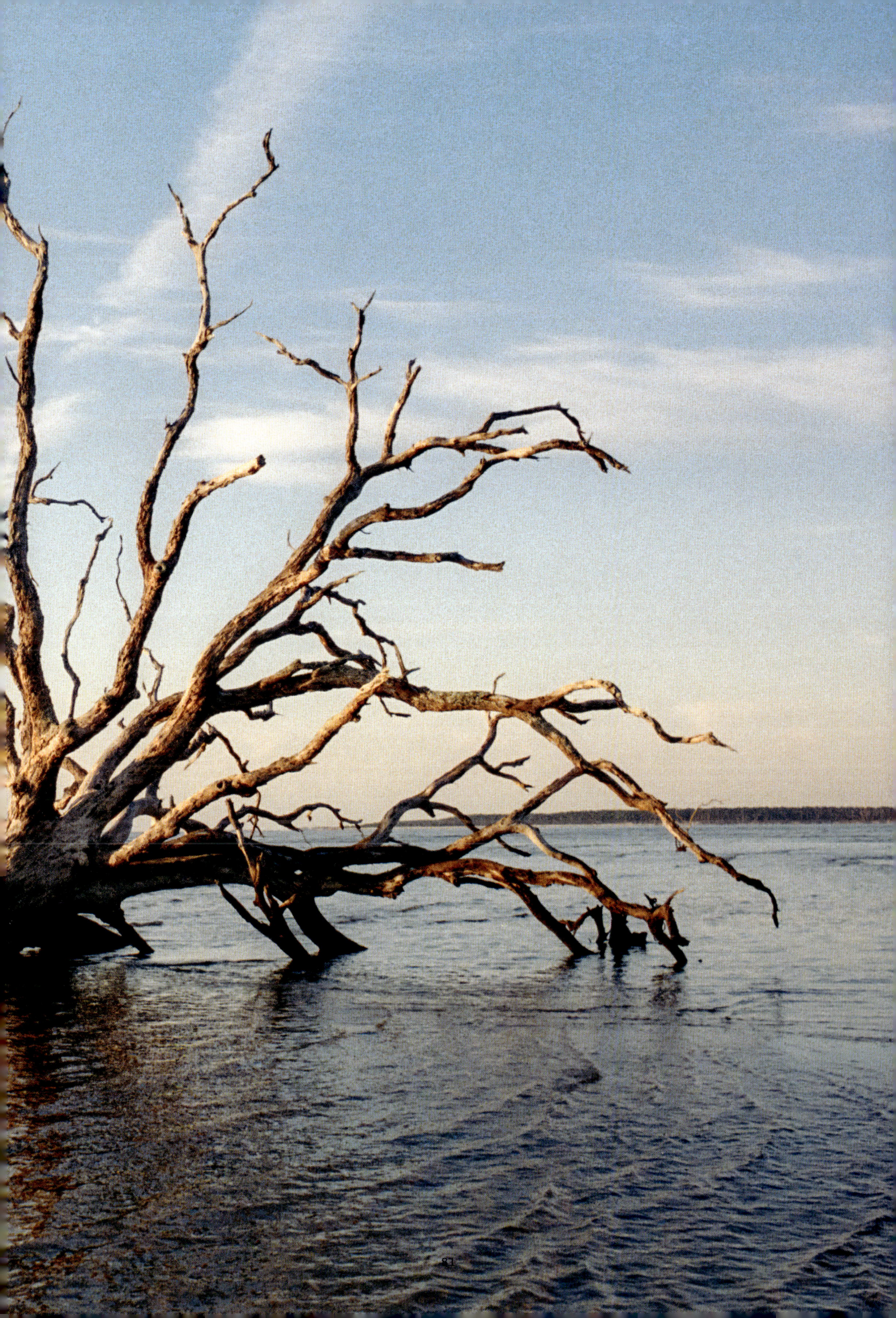

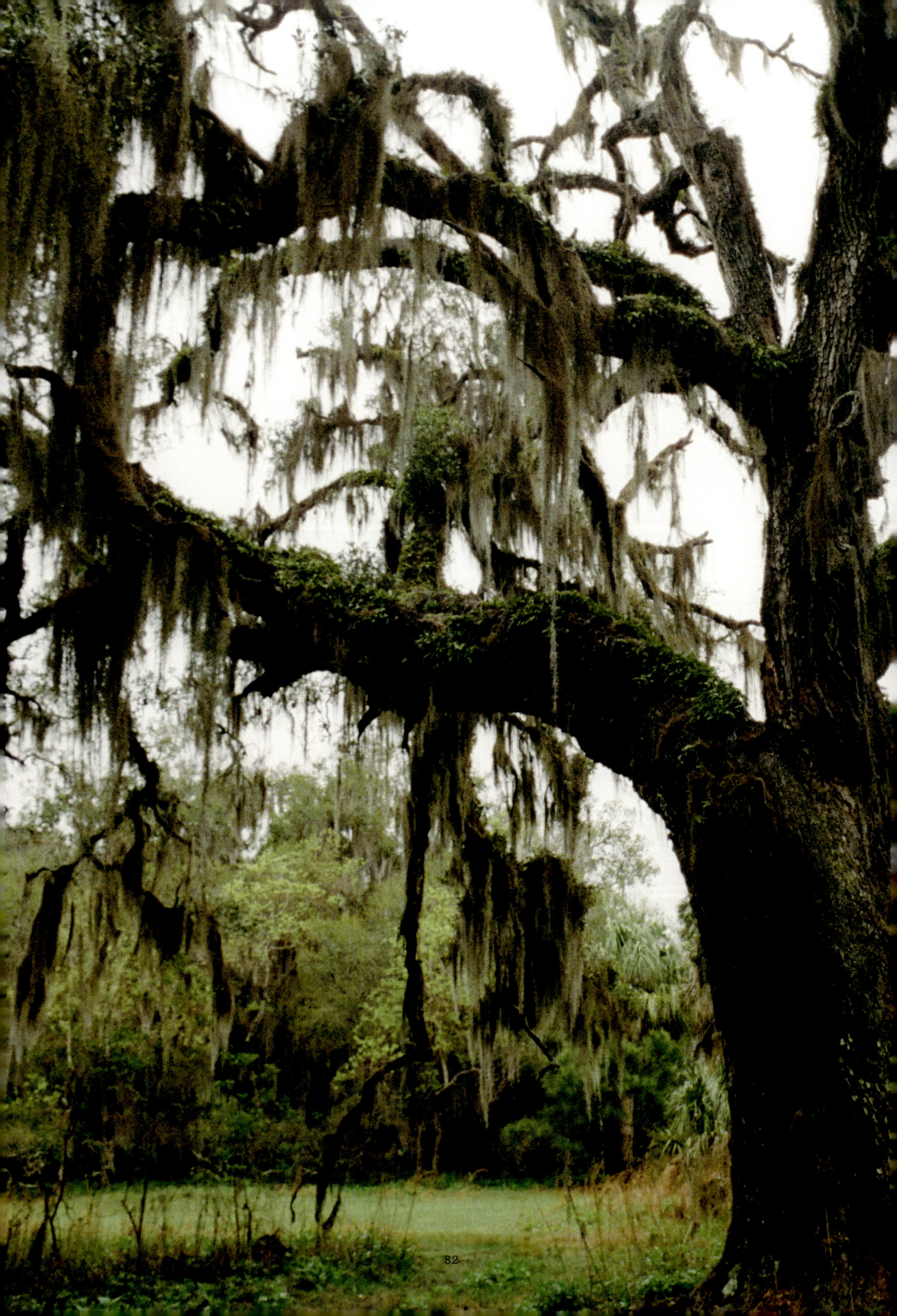

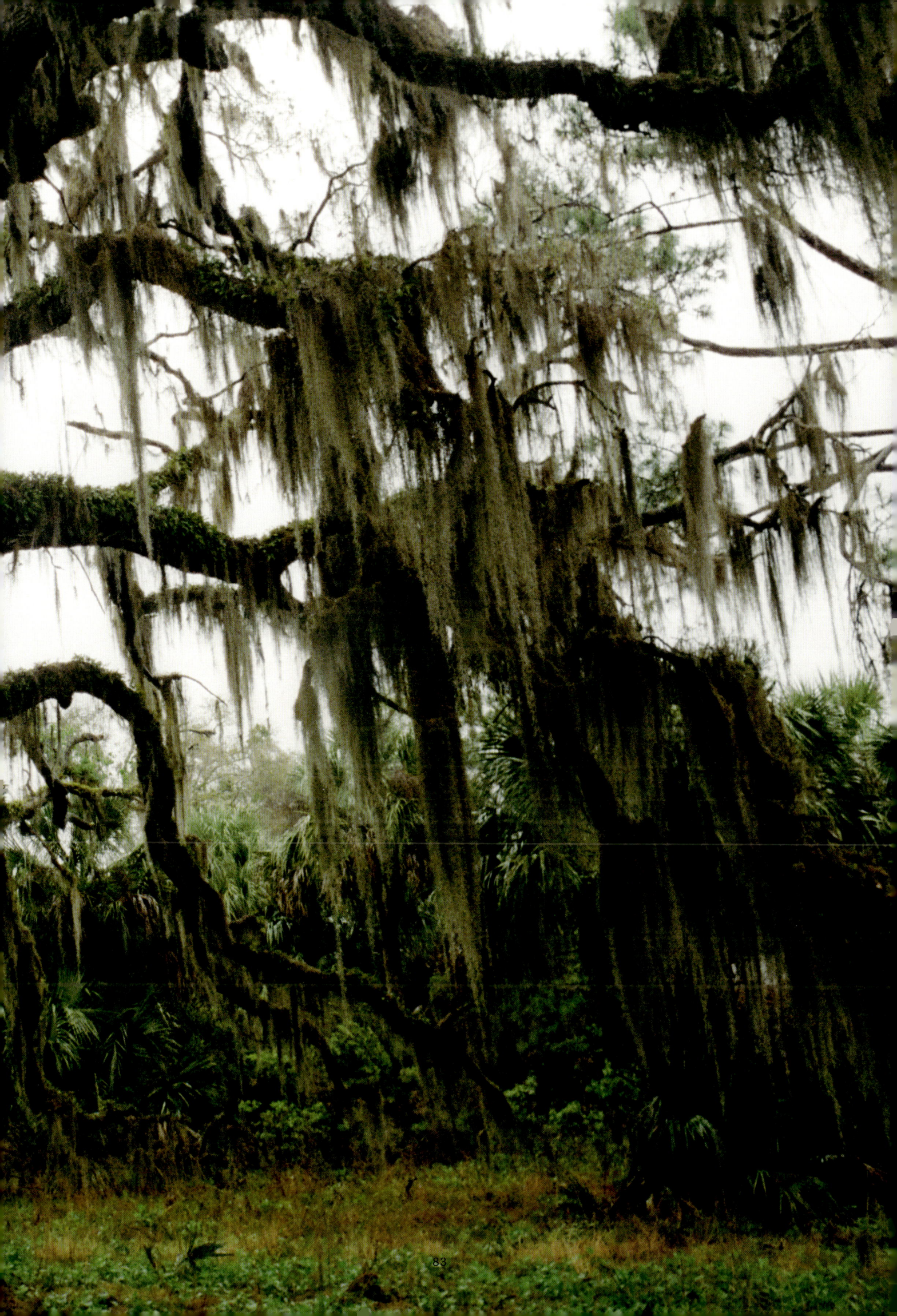

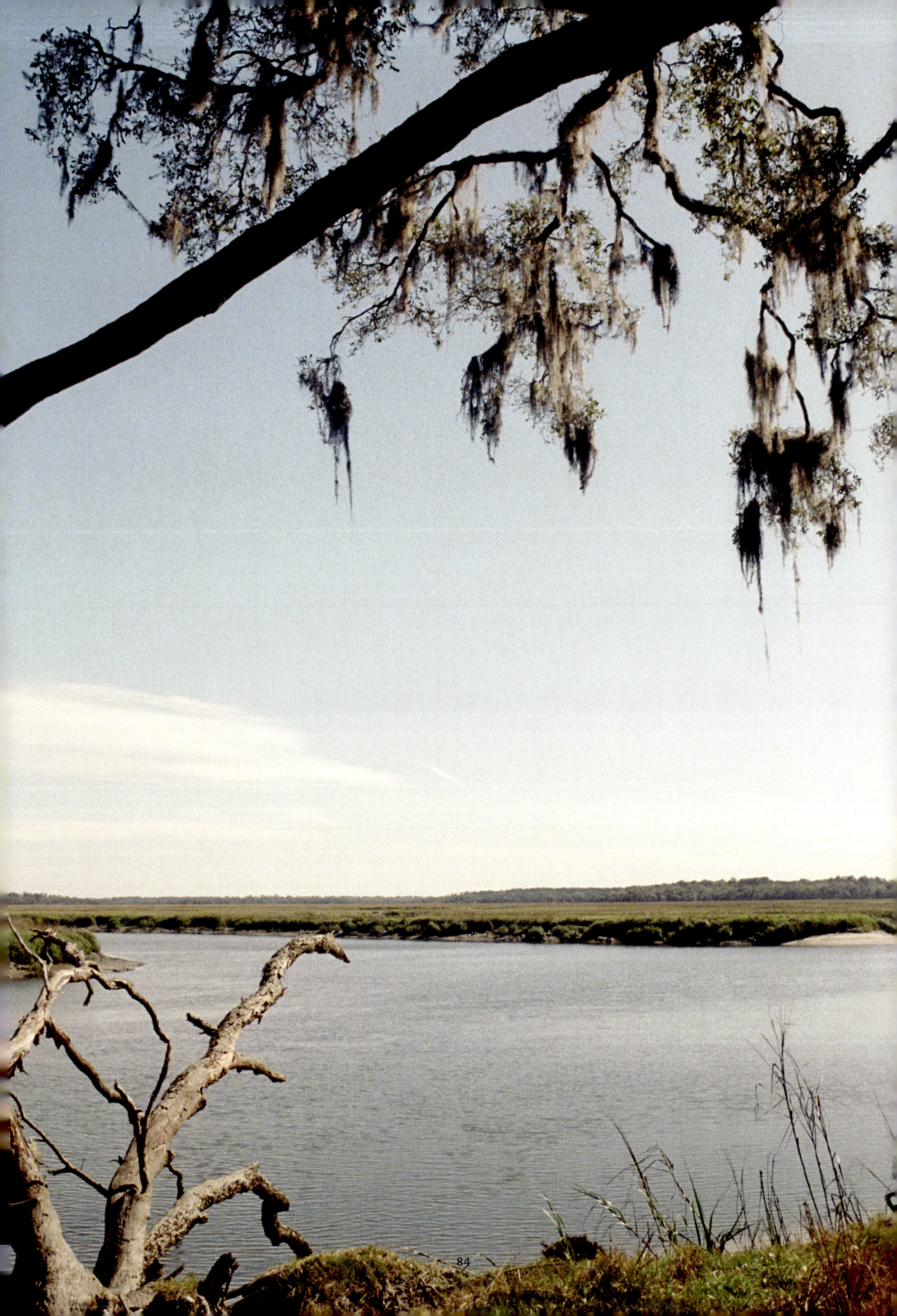

THE TERRAIN

Ossabaw's landscape contains multitudes, a mixture of dense maritime forest, flat sand beaches, and endless expanses of marsh. It is as beautiful as it is dangerous, with venomous snakes, alligators, and swarms of mosquitoes appearing when you least expect them. The contradictory nature of Ossabaw's terrain, eluding straightforward interpretation, is catnip for many of the visual artists who explore the island.

ARNOLD BLANCH (1896–1968)

Arnold Blanch was a painter and key figure in the Woodstock, New York, art community from the 1920s until his death. He studied at the Minneapolis School of Arts and the Art Students League in New York and taught at the California School of Fine Arts in San Francisco, the Colorado Fine Arts Center in Colorado Springs, and the Art Students League, among other institutions. In the 1930s during the Great Depression, Blanch worked as a muralist on government-sponsored art projects. From his home in Woodstock, Blanch helped define the look and feel of rural modernism in New York with his pastoral paintings. In the 1950s and 1960s, he drastically simplified his forms into barely recognizable shapes in increasingly abstract landscape and still life paintings. Around 1939, he began a lifelong relationship with the painter Doris Lee, though they never married. Close friends of Clifford and Sandy West, Blanch and Lee were both on the founding Advisory Board of the Ossabaw Island Project.

p. 88

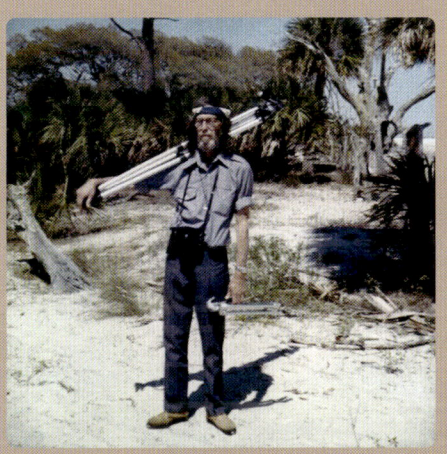

JOHN EARL (1921–2008)

John Earl was a nature photographer and jazz musician based in Savannah, Georgia. A native Georgian, Earl attended the University of Miami under the G.I. Bill, obtaining a degree in music and earning a reputation as a skilled jazz drummer. In his 40s, Earl pivoted to nature photography under the tutelage of photographer James Valentine. He first visited Ossabaw Island with Valentine and Robert Hanie, founder of the Georgia Conservancy, in 1969 when the three men were working together on the environmental publication *Guale, the Golden Coast of Georgia* (1974). Earl frequently returned to Ossabaw as both an OIP and a Genesis member and served for many years on the Advisory Board for the former program. He also met his second wife, Susan Earl, at the OIP. A lifelong advocate for conservation and the power of nature and wilderness, Earl's landscape photographs graced the pages of magazines such as *National Geographic*, and he published several books, including *John Muir's Longest Walk* (1975), an account of his trip tracing the footsteps of Muir's 1867 journey from Louisville, Kentucky, to Cedar Key, Florida. Earl taught photography and the history of jazz at the Savannah College of Art and Design for 25 years.

pp. 90–91

MARCY HERMANSADER (B. 1951)

Marcy Hermansader creates drawings that convey her sense of the world as a place of great mystery and complexity. Her purposeful and experimental use of common materials—such as thread, colored pencils, paper, and paint—grows out of the sylvan, otherworldly landscapes that make up much of her work. Built from a collection of intuitive and deeply personal images and symbols, her images alternate between inward focus and engagement with issues in the larger world. Her pieces seamlessly blend inner and outer worlds to conjure alternative realities. Hermansader holds a BFA in sculpture from the Philadelphia College of Art in Pennsylvania, and lives and works in southern Vermont. During her time on Ossabaw as a Genesis member in 1982, she encountered "a wild and unfamiliar world, forests of towering live oak trees draped with Spanish moss, salt marshes with winding streams, and abundant wildlife," all of which found its way into a series of Ossabaw-related works she made over many years.

pp. 92–93, 134

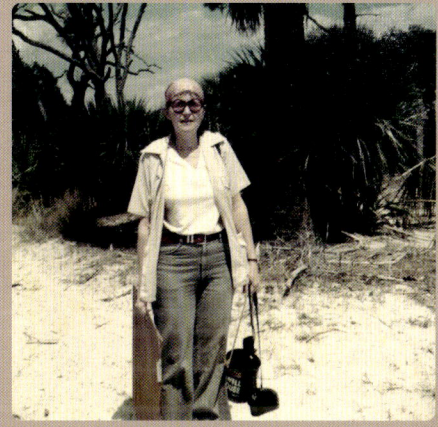

ELLEN LANYON (1926–2013)

Ellen Lanyon's meticulously realized paintings often combine animal, vegetal, and floral motifs into fantastical and semi-autobiographical compositions that reflect her private mythology. Her frequent depiction of everyday objects with simultaneously domestic and sinister connotations—including scissors, sewing needles, and cutlery, objects that evoke Victorian Americana as well as Surrealist dream objects—has elicited comparisons between her work and Metaphysical painting of the 1910s and 1920s. It has also situated her among a generation of feminist artists whose embrace of intimacy and sentiment offered a counterpoint to modernism's supposed neutrality. Born in Chicago, Ellen Lanyon received a BFA from the School of the Art Institute of Chicago in 1948, an MFA from University of Iowa in 1950, and was awarded a Fulbright Fellowship to pursue postgraduate work at the Courtauld Institute of Art in London. She received a Department of Interior commission to work in Everglades National Park in 1975 and attended the Ossabaw Island Project from March 26–April 9, 1976, experiences that brought the urgency of environmental concerns into her work. Lanyon worked between Chicago, where she was often identified with Chicago Imagism, and New York City, where she became a member of the *Heresies* magazine collective.

pp. 94–95

DORIS LEE (1904–1983)

Doris Lee's work spans easel paintings, murals, prints, illustrations, and costume, textile, and ceramic design. She first garnered attention in 1935 when her painting *Thanksgiving* (c. 1935) won the prestigious Logan Prize at the Art Institute of Chicago. Her work from this period concerned life in rural America, and in a stylistic and ideological sense, has much in common with Regionalism. She portrayed the simple joys of American life in touching, nostalgic, and sometimes fanciful ways. In the 1940s and 1950s, Lee's work became more stylized and concerned with pure form and color. Her simple, flat paintings portrayed gardens, seasonal landscapes, and women and children on the beach. Lee produced a significant body of abstract work during the 1960s that celebrated her private experience of the world and synthesized her personal and emotional response to her subject matter. Lee and her long-term partner Arnold Blanch were key figures in the Woodstock, New York, art community for many decades. Close friends of Clifford and Sandy West, Lee and Blanch were both on the founding Advisory Board of the Ossabaw Island Project.

p. 97

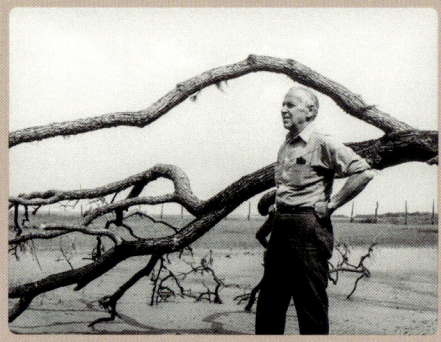

THOMAS MARKER (1901–1978)

Thomas Marker was a prominent Michigan artist, widely known in the Detroit area for his watercolors of the American West, marine studies of the Great Lakes, photography, and printmaking. Marker served in the Army during World War II and for several years worked in hard rock and placer mining in Colorado and Idaho. A graduate of the Cleveland School of Arts, he was associated with the Cranbrook Academy of Art in Bloomfield Hills, Michigan, and knew and worked with many prominent Midwestern artists, including Marshall Fredericks and William Sommer, whom he assisted with the creation of the Brett Hall murals at the Cleveland Public Library. A close friend of Clifford and Sandy West, Marker was executive director of the Ossabaw Island Project from 1961–1967. During his years at Ossabaw, he painted numerous works of its natural life and photographed all aspects of the island, particularly the driftwood, trees, and wildlife.

pp. 102-3

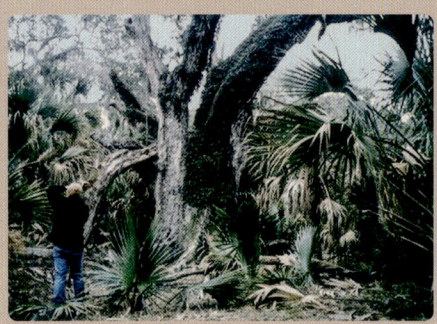

JACK LEIGH (1948–2004)

Savannah-born photographer Jack Leigh spent more than thirty years documenting the rapidly changing landscape and way of life in the rural South. He studied at the University of Georgia, where he discovered his primary medium in a documentary photography course. After traveling in Europe and living in Virginia, Leigh returned to Savannah in the 1970s. He patiently recorded Southerners and their surrounding landscape through black-and-white photographs that he published in a series of books. This distinct perspective influenced author John Berendt to recommend Leigh for the cover commission for *Midnight in the Garden of Good and Evil* (1994), a runaway bestseller. His photograph of Sylvia Shaw Judson's bronze sculpture *Bird Girl* (1936) has stood as an iconic depiction of Savannah ever since. In 2004, Leigh collaborated with painter Alan Campbell and writer James Kilgo on the book *Ossabaw: Evocations of an Island*, a tribute to the island through their respective lenses.

pp. 98–101

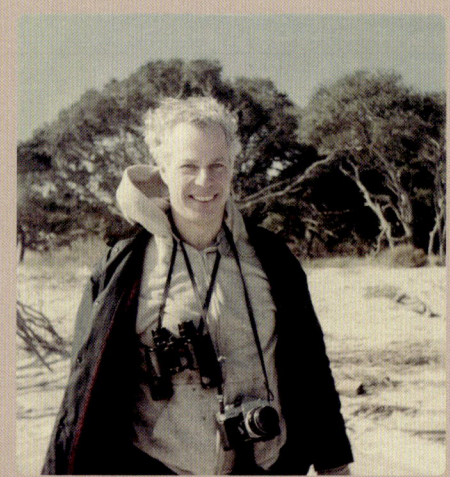

MICHAEL MAZUR (1935–2009)

Michael Mazur was a painter and printmaker whose lifelong interests pursued a balance between the narrative power of observation and the nonrepresentational expression of gesture. Throughout his five-decade career, he reveled in the physicality of his chosen medium, relishing the process of making. He approached his work through the constructive vocabulary of observation, deftly capturing fleeting moments in nature, human tragedy, and rapture. Broad themes in his work encompassed social documentation, psychological portraiture, and passionate landscapes that moved back and forth aesthetically between figuration and abstraction. Born in New York City, Michael Mazur received a BA from Amherst College in 1958, followed by a BFA and MFA from the Yale School of Art and Architecture in 1960 and 1961, respectively. In 1975, he received a Department of Interior commission to work on Wassaw Island, but completed the work primarily on Ossabaw during his residency at the OIP from January 3–17 of that year. He later returned to the OIP from March 9–April 2, 1979.

pp. 104–5

MARTHA ODUM (1917–1995)

Martha Odum was a watercolorist whose paintings evoke the diverse beauty of landscapes all over the world. With her paints in tow, she often accompanied her husband Eugene P. Odum, widely considered the founder of modern ecology, on his travels across the world, including to New Mexico, California, Oregon, Maine, Portugal, and Japan. "I've always enjoyed painting on the spot—feeling the wind and sun, becoming a part of the environment—trying to find its essence," she wrote. Despite her international travels, Odum's primary subject was the coastal marshes and beaches of the Southeast and she created several paintings of Ossabaw Island when she and her husband were members at the OIP from April 2–10, 1969; Eugene Odum later sat on the Advisory Board. Together, the Odums created a partnership that showcased how art and ecology could work together to communicate the power and fragility of the natural environments that surrounded them.

p. 106

DAGA RAMSEY (1907–1997)

Daga Ramsey was a graphic artist who specialized in serigraphs and Scandinavian wool rya (rugs). Born in Stockholm, Sweden, Ramsey studied in New York City at the National Academy of Design, the Art Students League, the Pratt Graphic Art Center, and the New School, and in Bloomfield Hills, Michigan, at the Cranbrook Academy of Art. She and her husband Jack Ramsey, a Texas-born painter, lived in Sag Harbor, New York, and opened the Ramsey Workshop, where Daga taught classes and earned her reputation as a printmaker. They were neighbors and friends with the writer John Steinbeck, who wrote about their practice, "It has been a privilege to watch my friends, Jack and Daga, reduce the world to its ingredients of light, color, form and their relationships, and then rebuilding them with the tools of mind, imagination and unrelenting discipline until what sometimes emerges is new and wonderful, for painting is creation in its truest sense." Ramsey attended the Ossabaw Island Project from October 31–November 14, 1969, where she made a rya rug with a long pile based on her sketches of the island that abstracted the landscape into a study of color, shape, and form. She later made a series of serigraphs inspired by Ossabaw and returned to the OIP from February 26–March 26, 1971.

p. 107

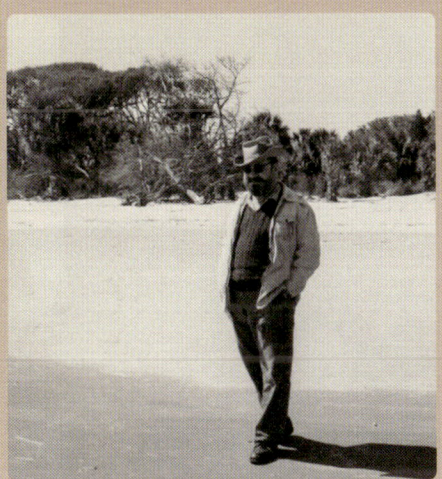

TEX SCHIWETZ (1909–1971)

Tex Schiwetz was a sculptor and educator who worked primarily in stone and bronze, creating mythologically-inflected sculptures of animals imbued with a cheeky whimsicality. "Tex had wisdom, warmth, and wit," wrote the architect Robert Venturi. "In his work these qualities helped him catch the reality of his subjects with a gentle, intense, sad humor." Born Berthold Schiwetz in Cuero, Texas,

he studied sculpture at the Museum of Fine Arts, Houston, under William McVey and at Cranbrook Academy of Art under Carl Milles during the 1930s. From 1945–1955, Schiwetz worked in Milles's studio first at Cranbrook and later at the American Academy in Rome. Schiwetz undertook a series of public commissions for large-scale sculpture, which he executed for such institutions as Oakland University in Rochester, Michigan; Good Samaritan Hospital in Portland, Oregon; the Flint Institute of Arts in Michigan; and the Ossabaw Foundation in Georgia. A close friend of Clifford and Sandy West, Schiwetz was an inaugural member of the Ossabaw Island Project Advisory Board and remained closely involved with the program until his death. He made many bronze sculptures inspired by Ossabaw wildlife, including pelicans and shore birds, as well as the Wests' dogs Bomper and Sean.

pp. 108–9

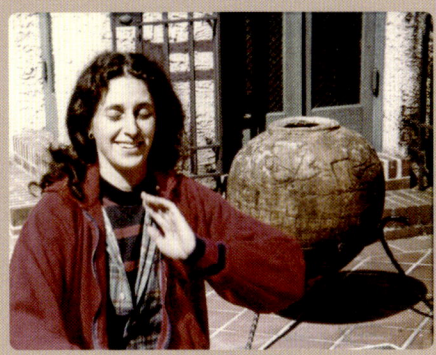

BETTY TOMPKINS (B. 1945)

Known for her unabashed portrayals of the female body, sexual desire, and objectification, feminist artist Betty Tompkins became notorious in the art world for questioning the rules of representation of women's bodies and what governs them with her *Fuck Paintings* series beginning in the late 1960s. In the late 1970s, Tompkins began a series of paintings of cows, birds, dogs, and other animals that were "obsessively reconstructed in a grid of words." Tompkins intricately rendered each animal using repetitions of its English moniker. Ossabaw, with its panoply of wild and domesticated animals, was an ideal environment to expand on this body of work, and she she did so during her residency at the OIP from October 8–19, 1979. During her time on the island, Tompkins also became friendly with the Allen Memorial Art Museum's legendary curator Ellen H. Johnson, who acquired *Ayrshire Class D* (1979) that same year for the museum's collection.

pp. 110–11

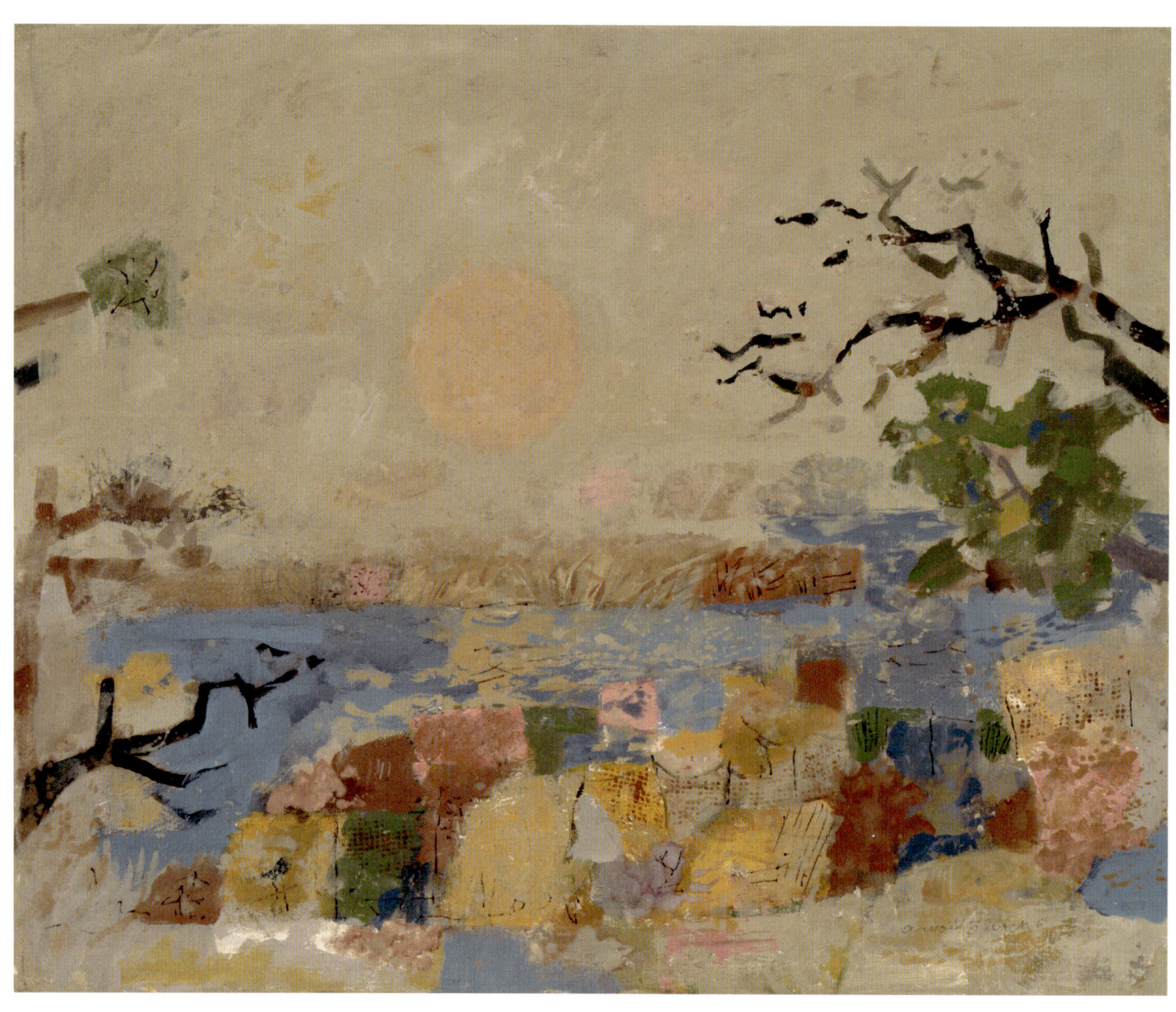

Arnold Blanch (1896–1968)
Ossabaw, 1964
Polymer on canvas
28 × 34 in.
Collection of Justin P. West and Eileen McGowan

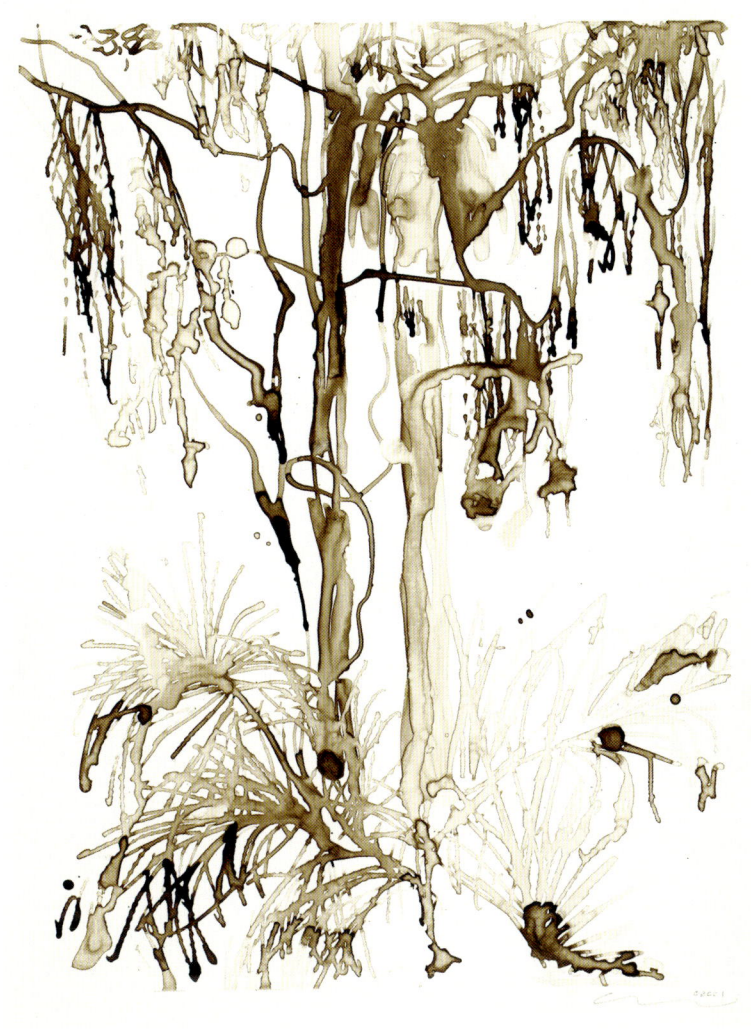

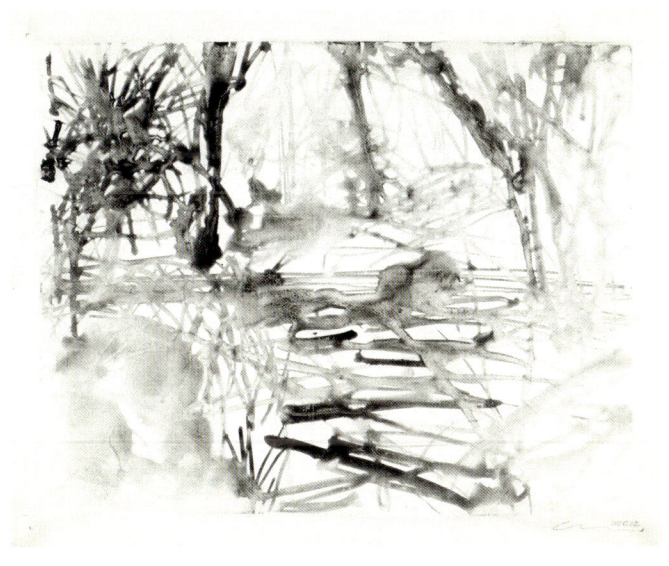

Betsy Cain (b. 1949)
Vines and Moss, 2021
Artist-made walnut ink on Yupo paper
14 × 11 in.
Private collection

Betsy Cain (b. 1949)
Cabbage Garden road (looking in the forest), 2022
Liquid graphite on Yupo paper
9 ½ × 12 ½ in.
Collection of Lisa and Mason White

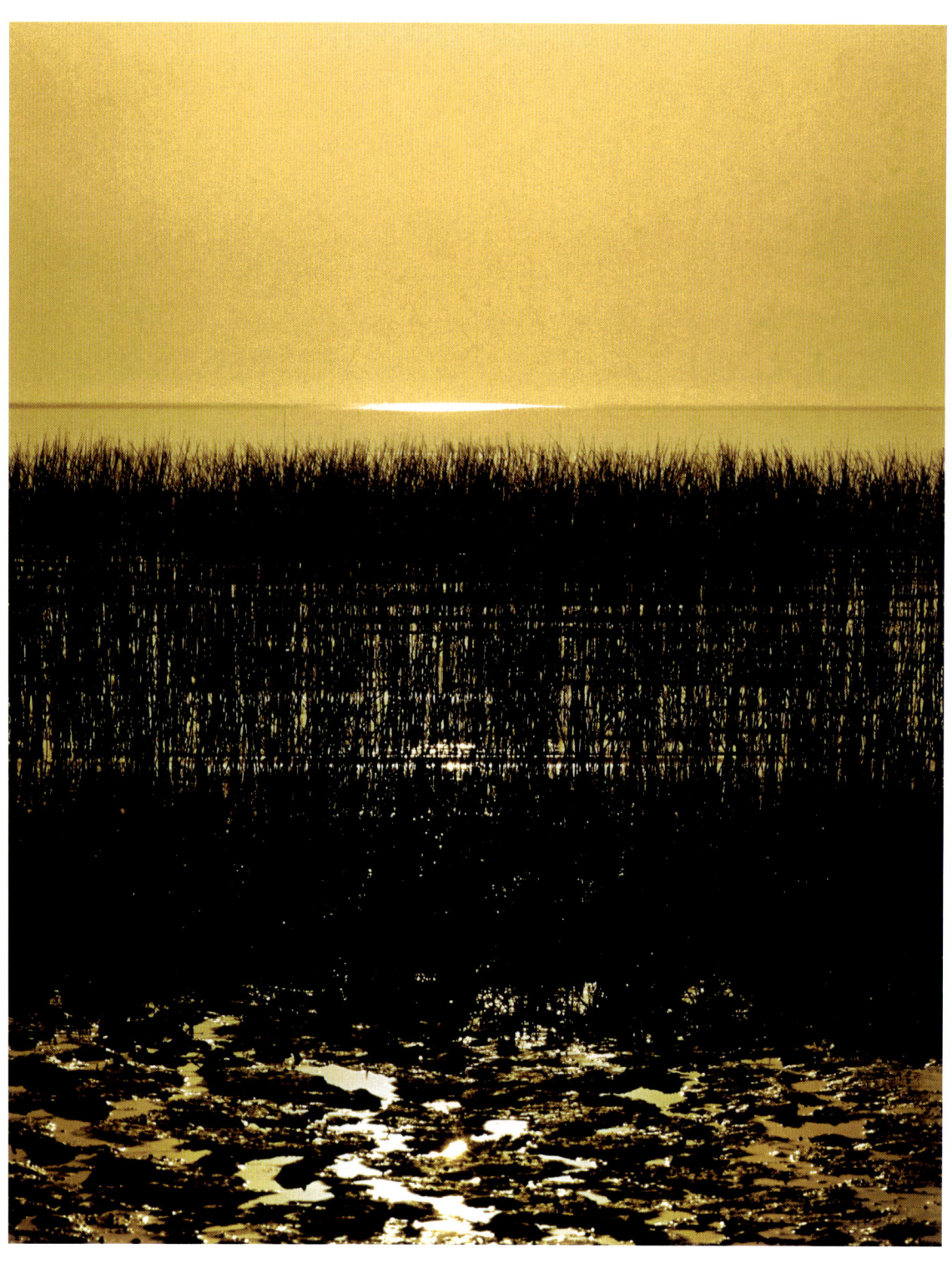

John Earl (1921–2008)
Ossabaw Sunset, c. 1974
Archival pigment print
24 × 16 in.
Collection of the Earl Family

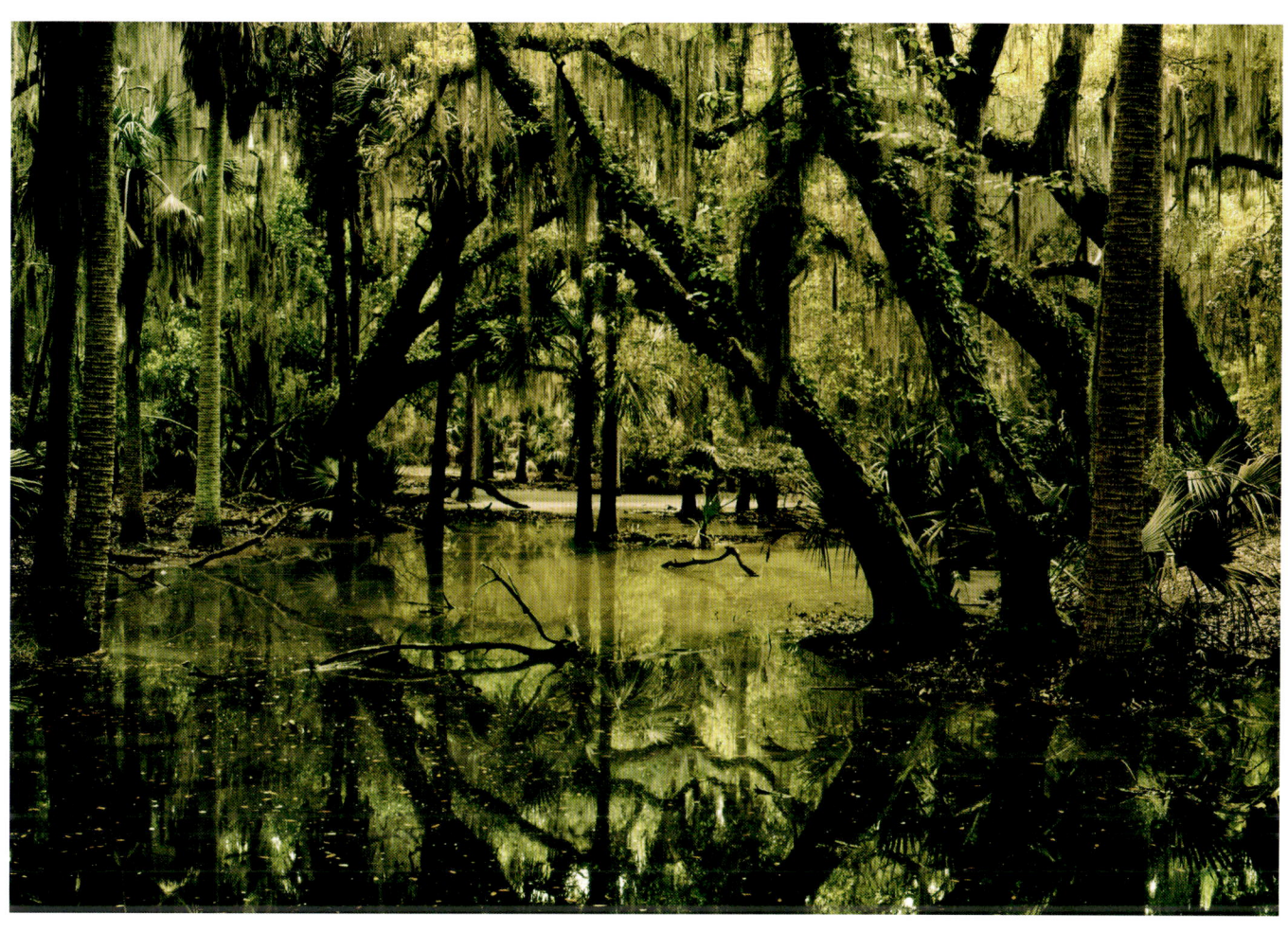

John Earl (1921–2008)
Mule Run, c. 1974
Archival pigment print
16 × 24 in.
Collection of the Earl Family

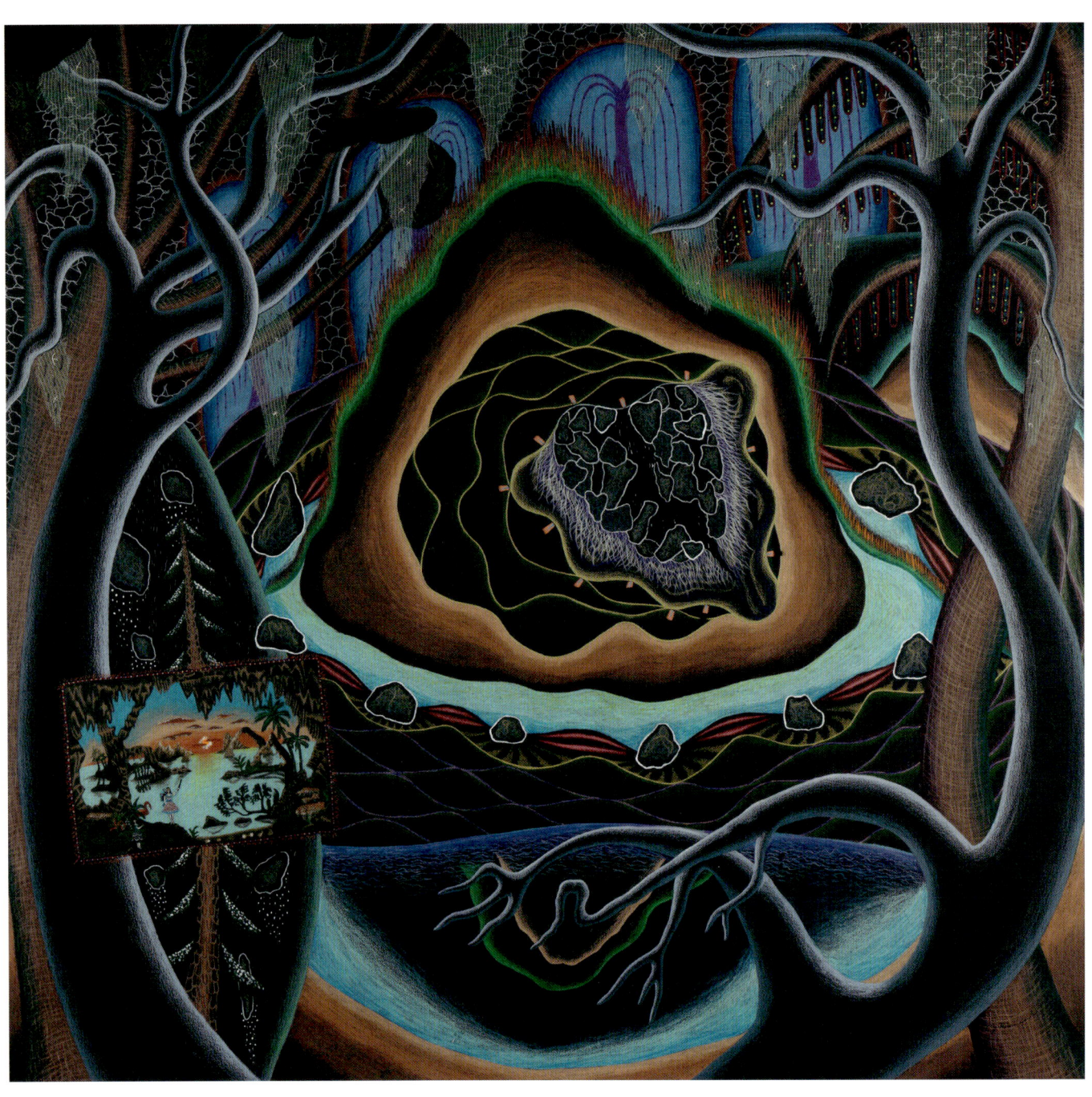

Marcy Hermansader (b. 1951)
Secrets of the Heart, 1983
Colored pencil, crayon, acrylic, mosquito
netting, and thread on black wove paper
29 × 30 in.
Pennsylvania Academy of the Fine Arts,
Lambert Fund Purchase, 1984.4

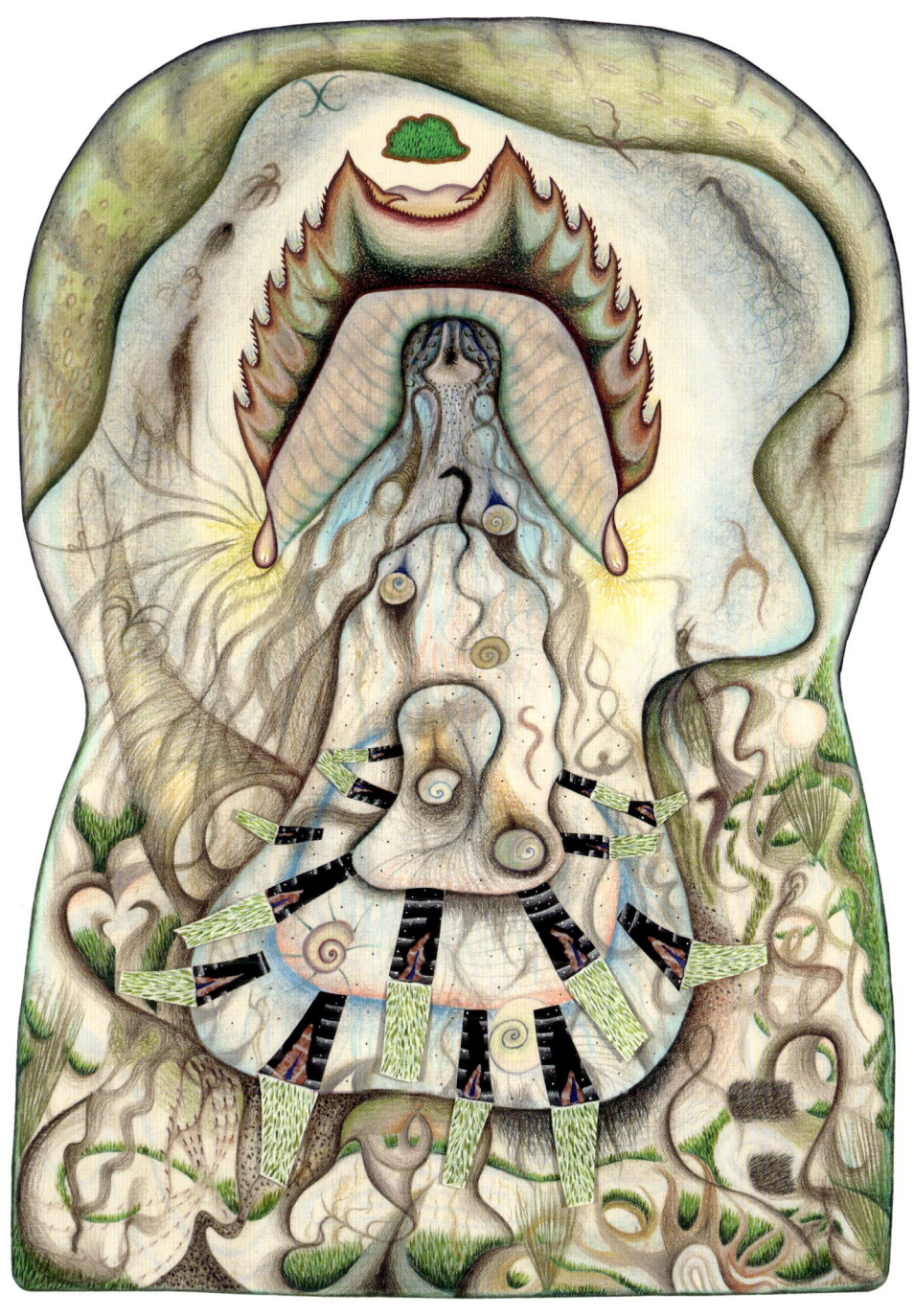

Marcy Hermansader (b. 1951)
The Marsh and the Sea, 1982
Colored pencil and acrylic on paper
with pinpricks and cut flaps
29 ½ × 21 ½ in.
Private collection

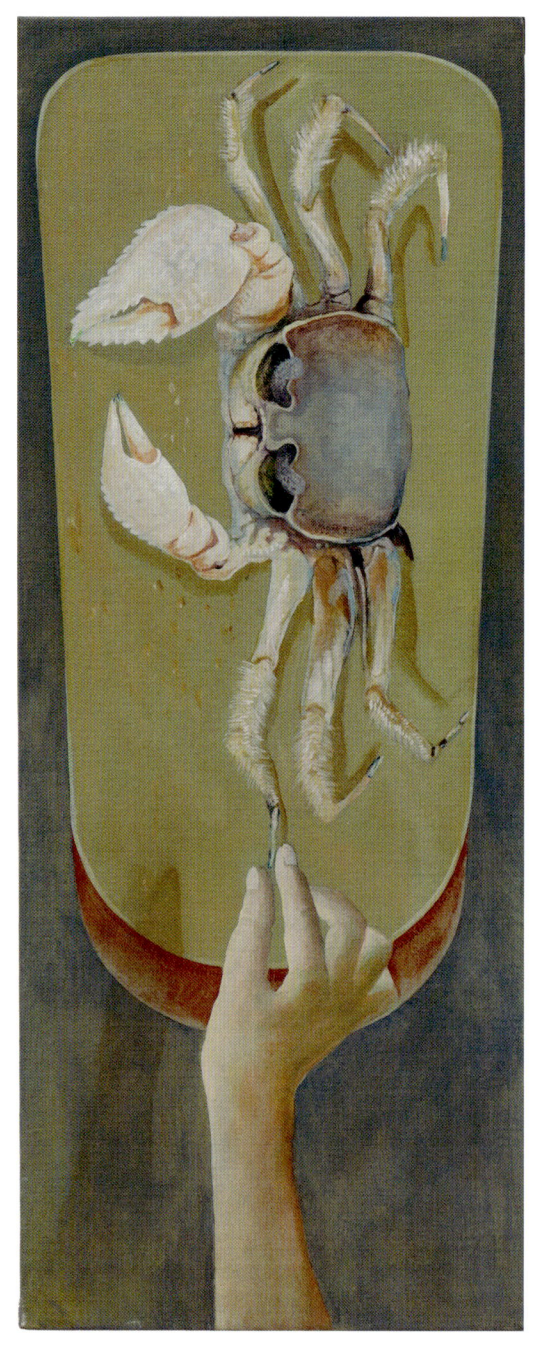

Ellen Lanyon (1926–2013)
Fan Ossabaw, c. 1978
Acrylic on canvas
30 × 12 in.
Estate of Ellen Lanyon, courtesy of
GRAY, Chicago/New York

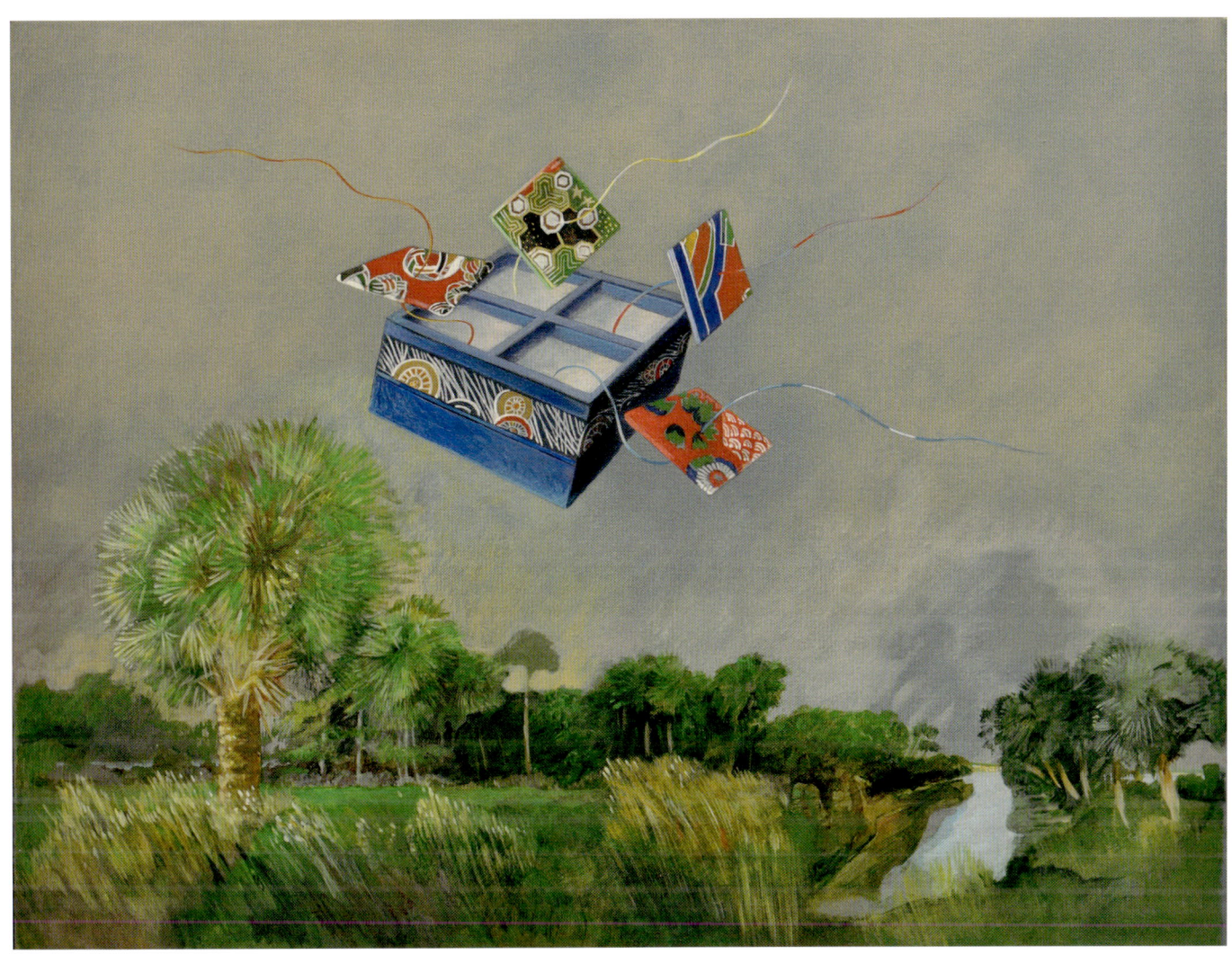

Ellen Lanyon (1926–2013)
Ossabaw Storm Warning, 1979
Acrylic on canvas
24 × 32 in.
Collection of Andrew Ginzel

Doris Lee (1905–1983)
Untitled, c. 1964
Oil on canvas
33 ½ × 41 ½ in.
Collection of Justin P. West and Eileen McGowan

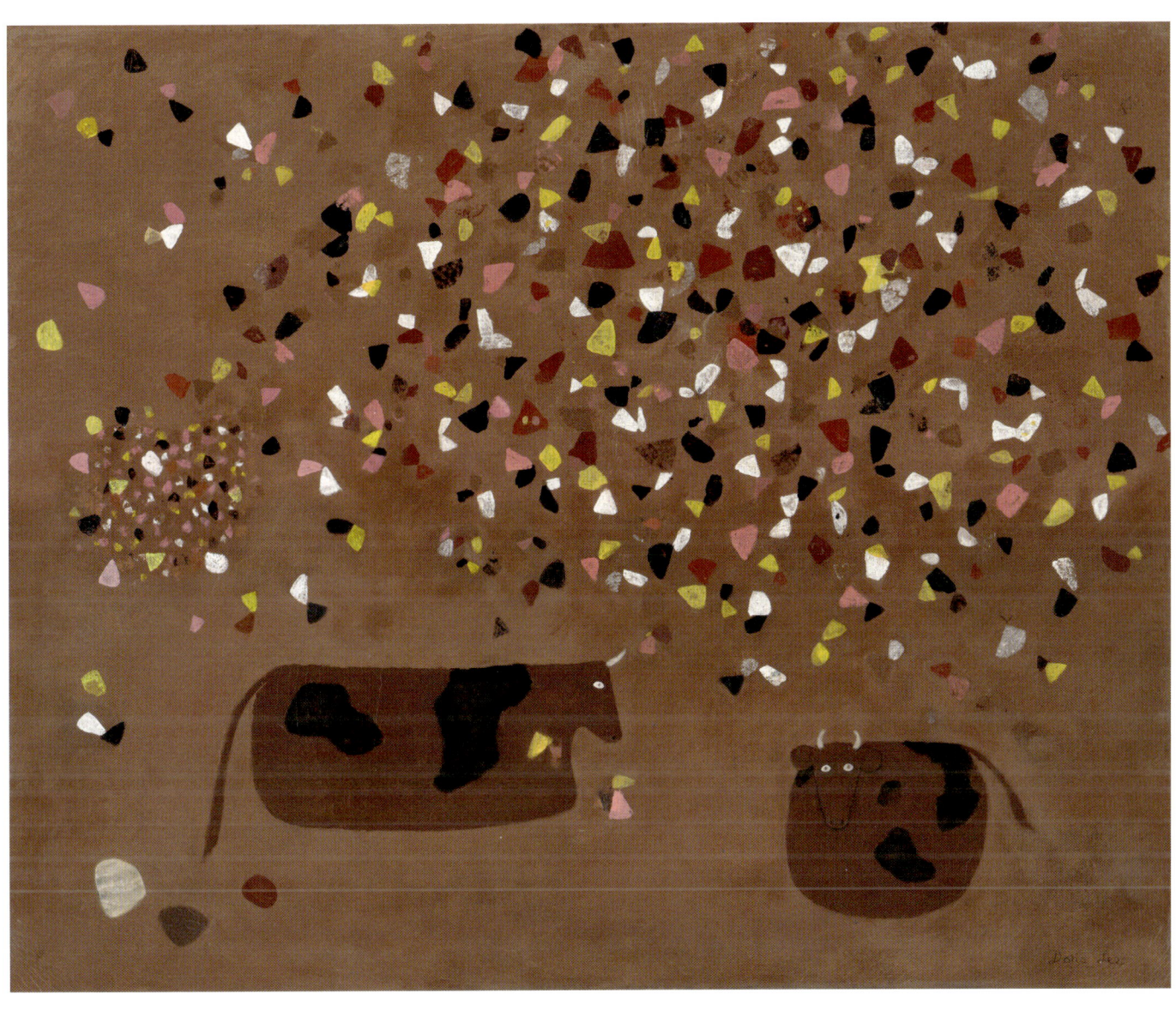

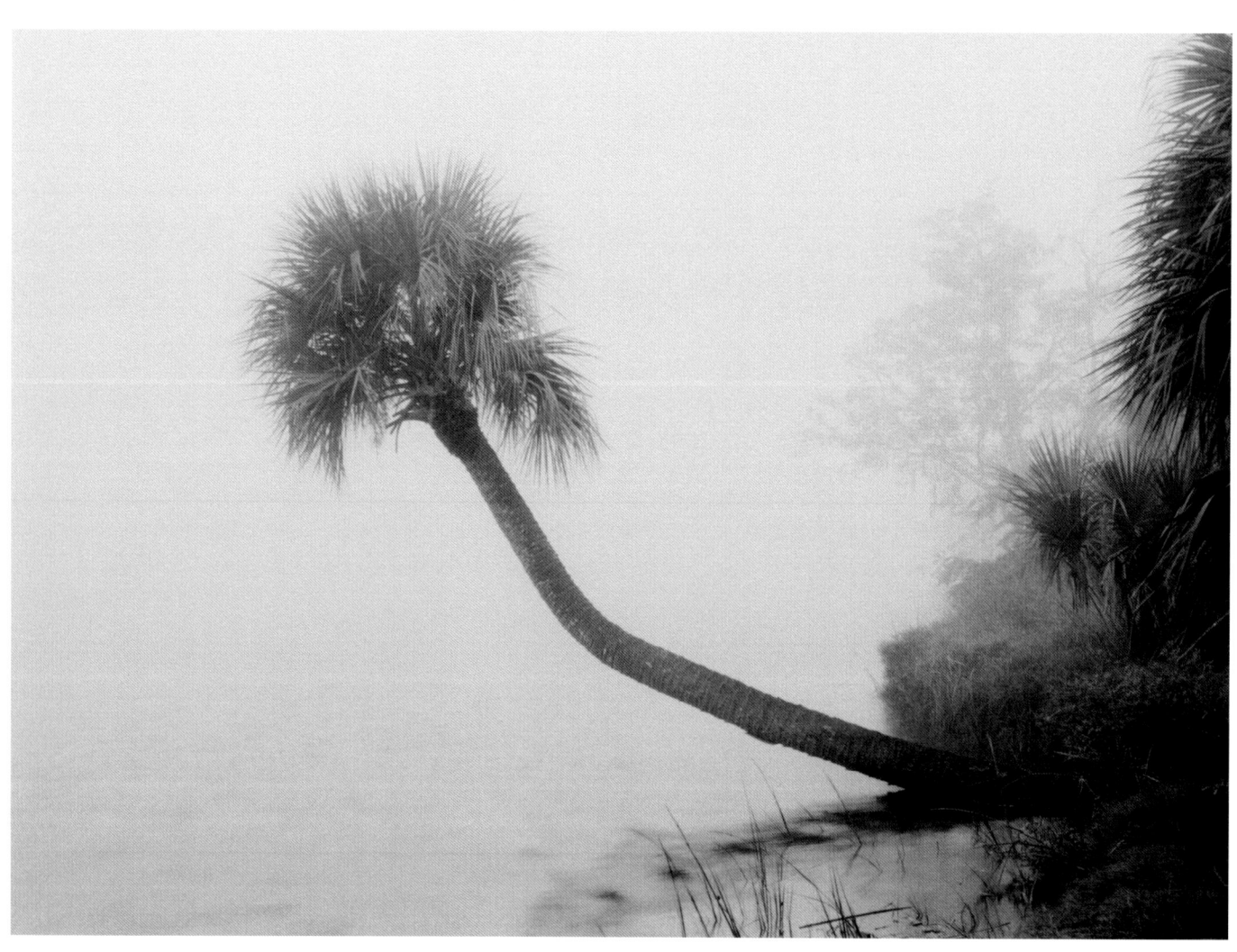

Jack Leigh (1948–2004)
Palm Tree in Fog, 2002
Carbon pigment print
15 ⅛ × 22 in.
Telfair Museums, museum purchase with funds
provided by Mr. and Mrs. Lawrence Dunn in memory of
Kirk Varnedoe and David DeLong, 2006.53

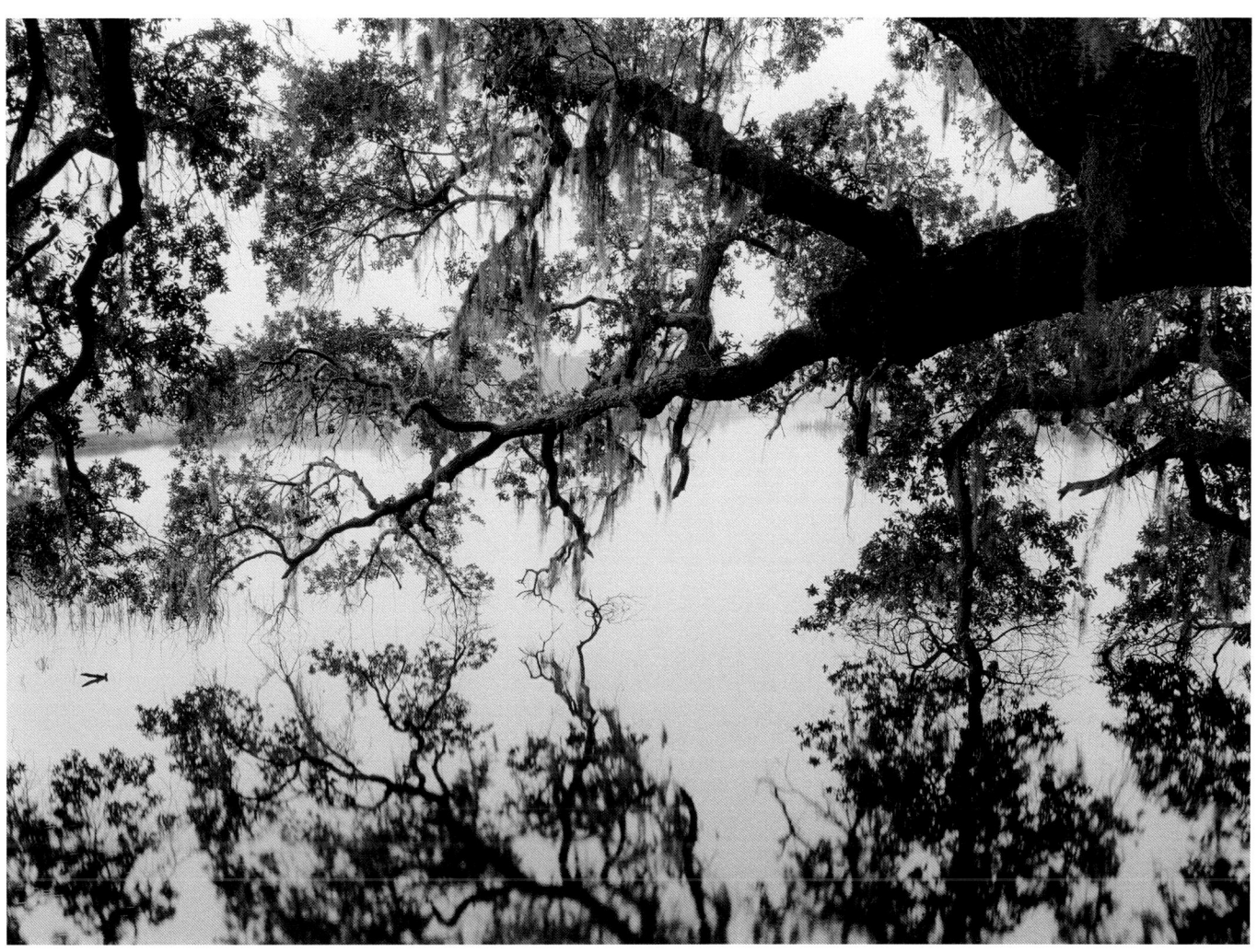

Jack Leigh (1948–2004)
Oak Limb Reflections, 2002
Pigmented inkjet print
15 ⅛ × 22 in.
High Museum of Art, Atlanta; Purchase with funds
from Paul Miller, Mrs. Robert O. Levitt, Phillip and
Patricia Laney, and V. Tomm Frungillo, 2021.364

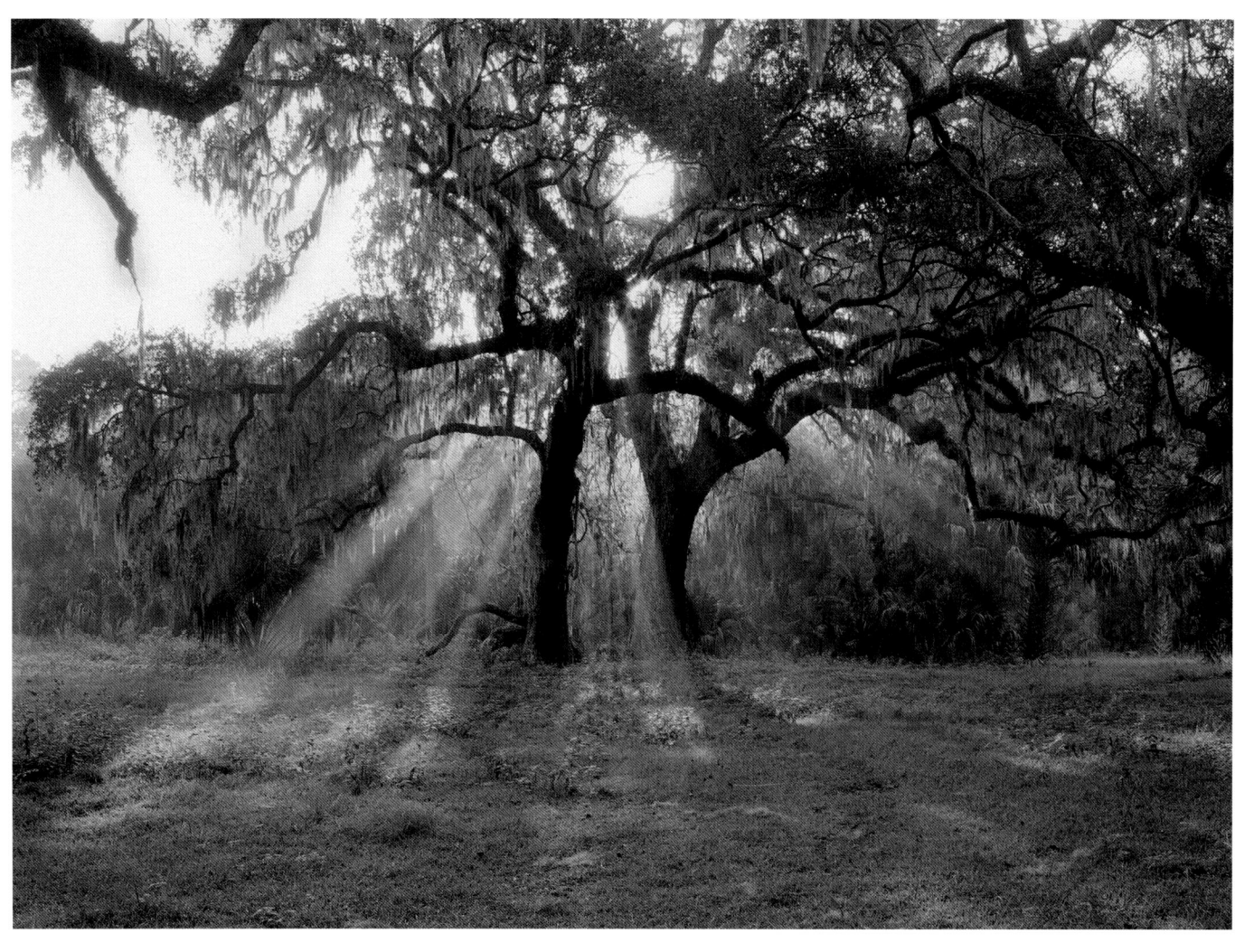

Jack Leigh (1948–2004)
Live Oak and Light Beams, 2002
Pigmented inkjet print
15 ⅛ × 22 in.
Collection of Elizabeth DuBose and Mark Frissell

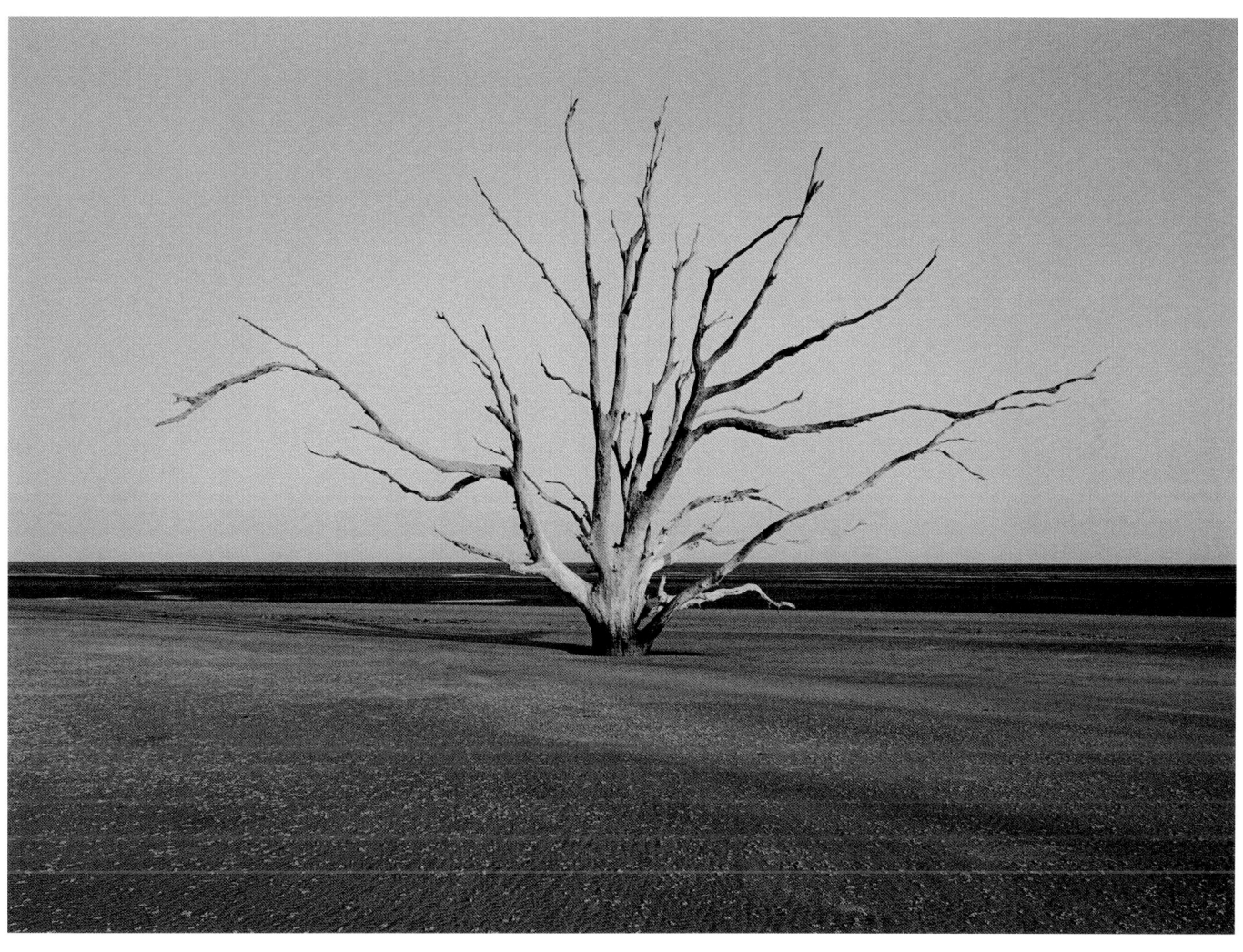

Jack Leigh (1948–2004)
Lone Tree at Sunset, Ossabaw, 2001
Silver gelatin print
16 ⅛ × 22 in.
Collection of Deborah Stroud

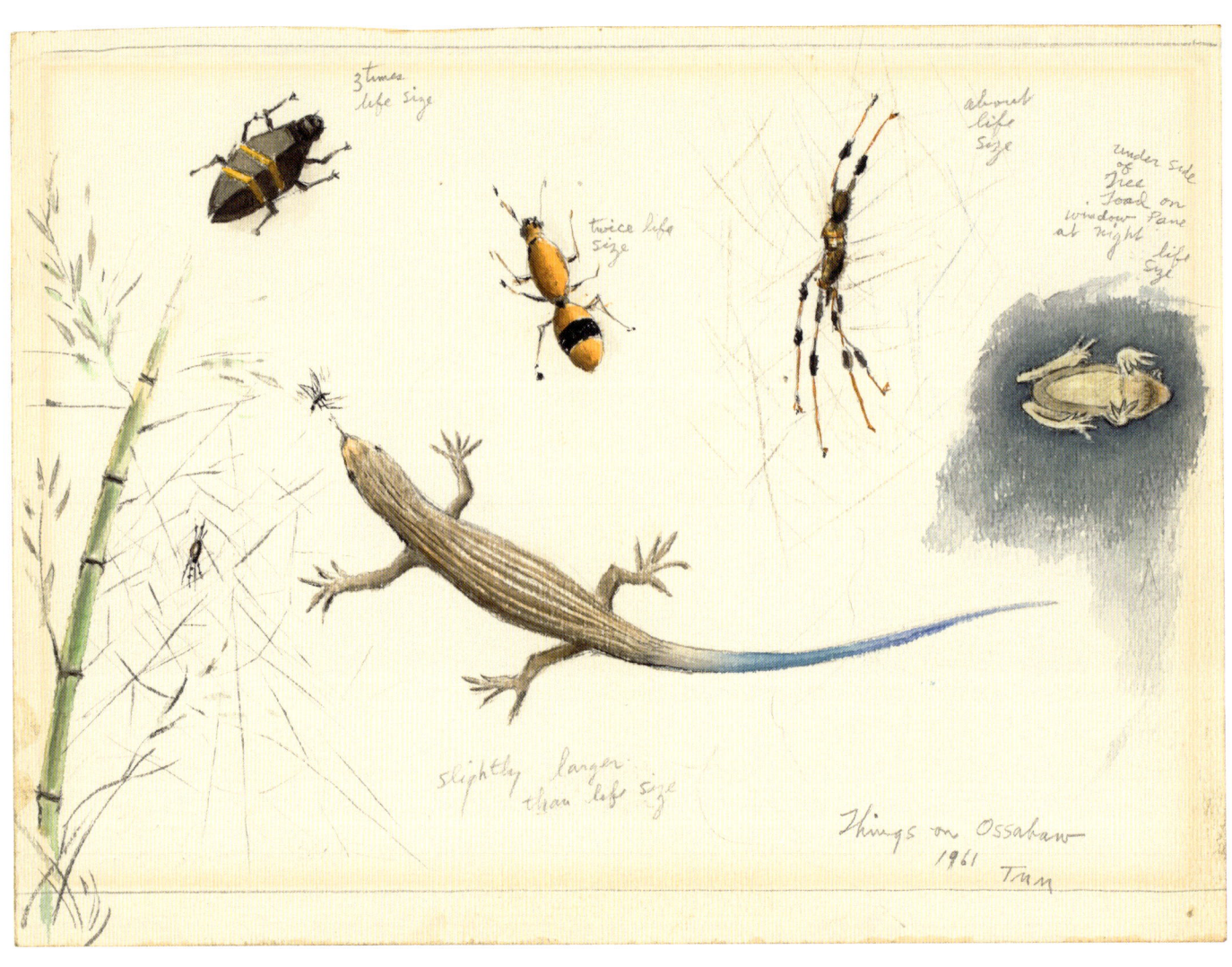

Thomas Marker (1901–1978)
Things on Ossabaw, 1961
Watercolor and pencil on paper
8 × 11 ½ in.
Private collection

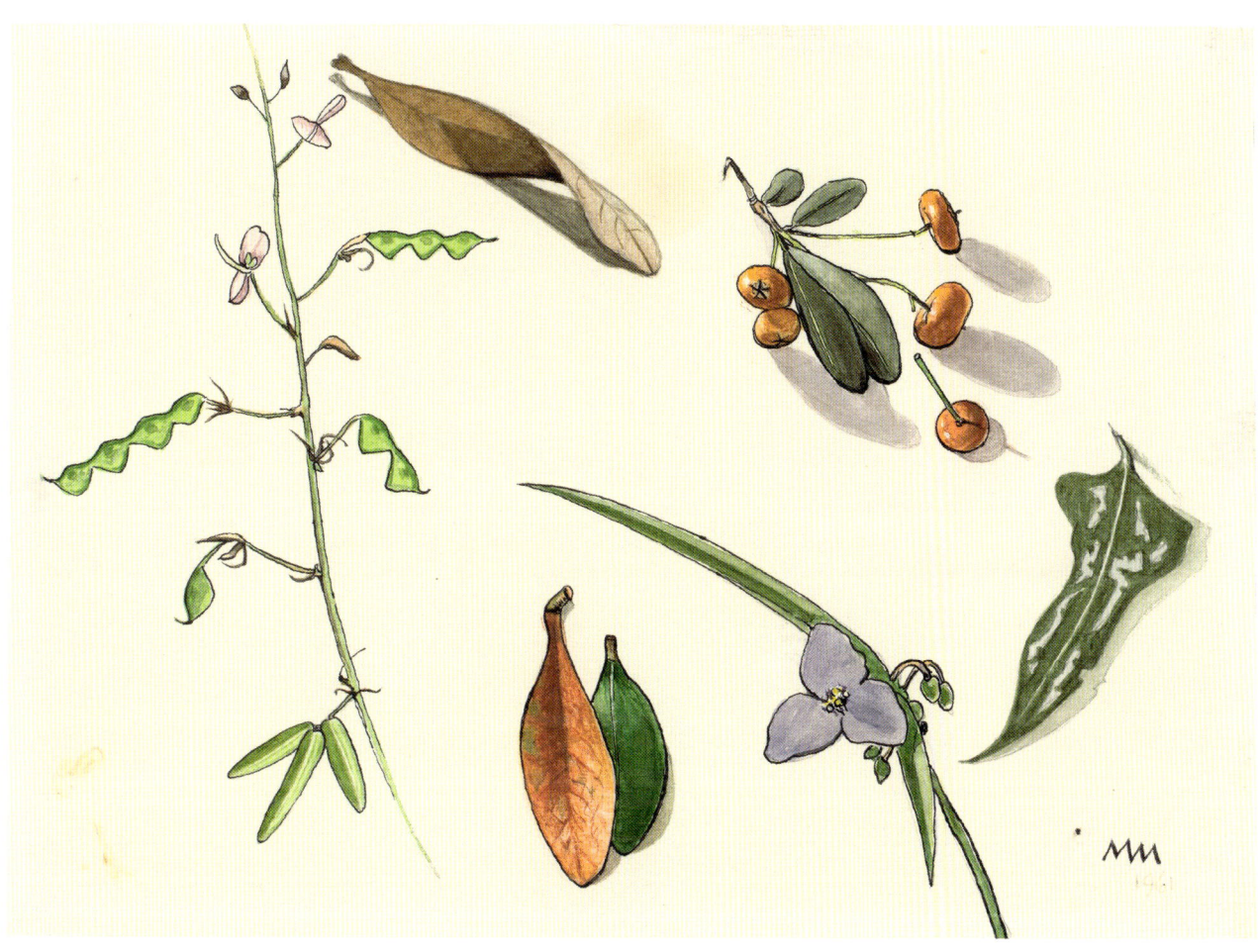

Thomas Marker (1901–1978)
Ossabaw Study, 1961
Watercolor and pencil on paper
6 ½ × 9 in.
Private collection

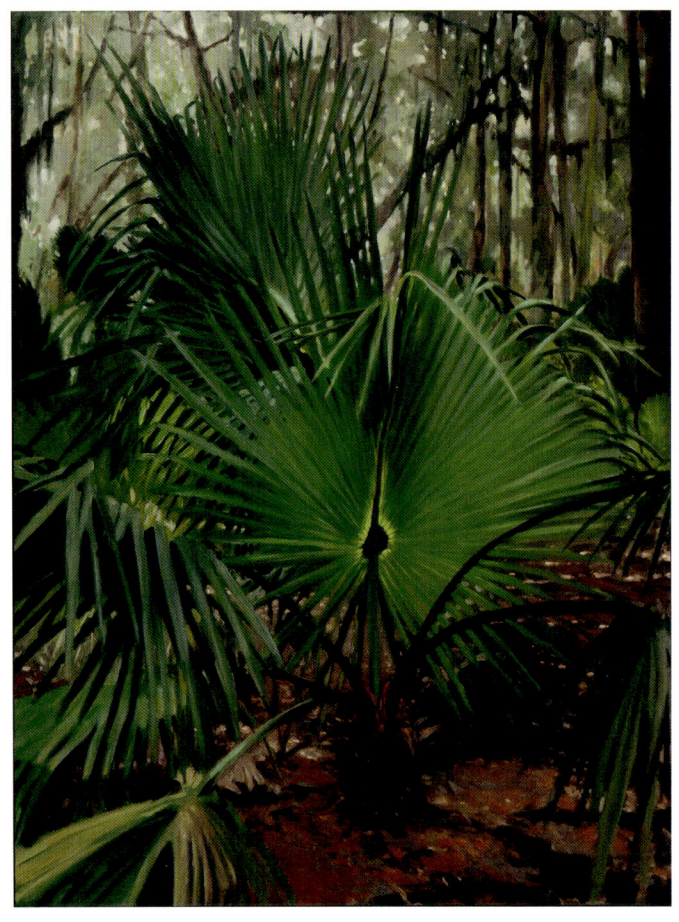

Michael Mazur (1935–2009)
Palmetto-Ossabaw, 1975
Oil on panel
39 × 29 ½ in.
Courtesy of the Estate of Michael Mazur

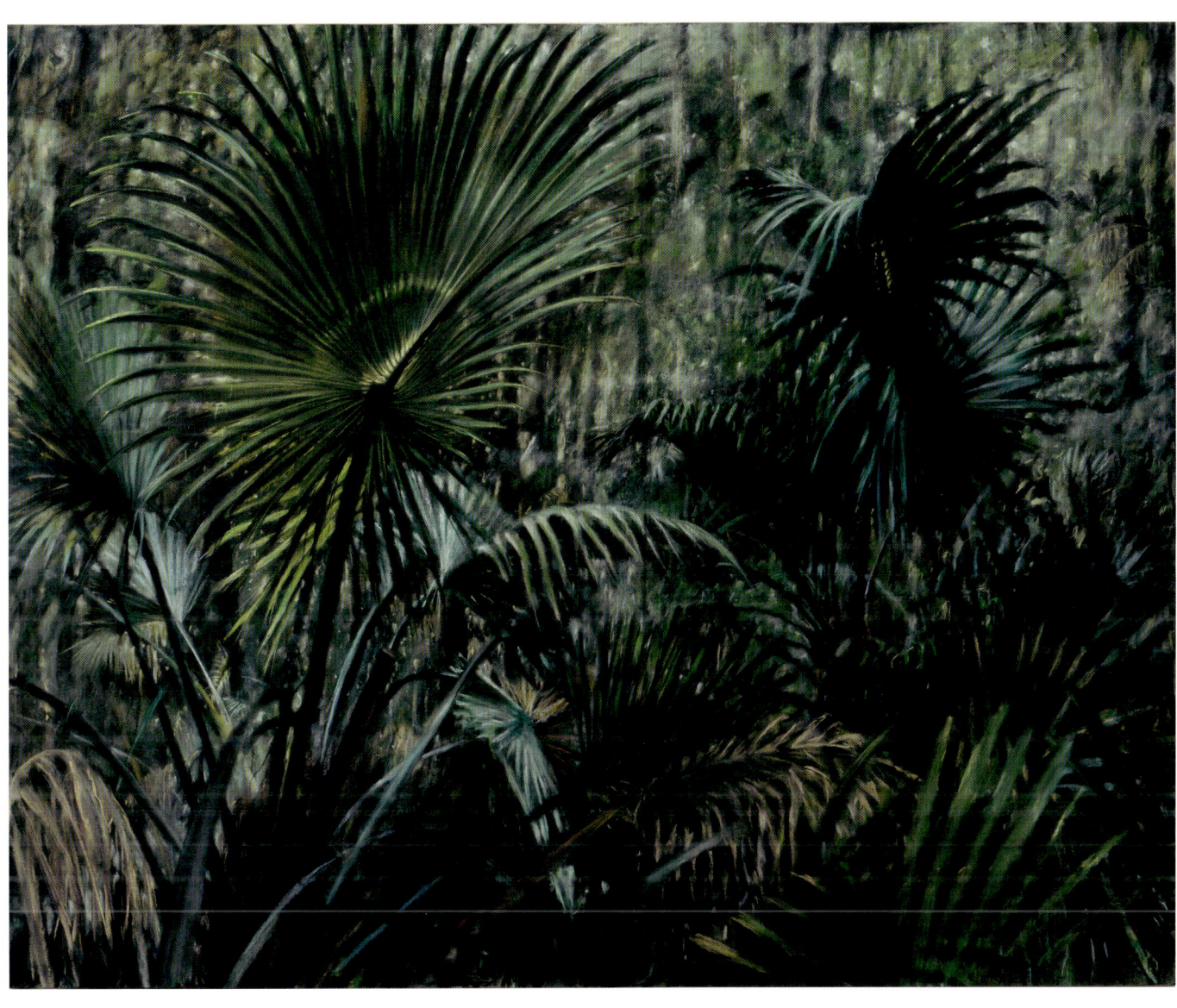

Michael Mazur (1935–2009)
Palmetto, 1975
Pastel on paper
71 × 89 ¾ in.
The Museum of Contemporary Art,
Los Angeles, Gift of Jim Dine, 82.36

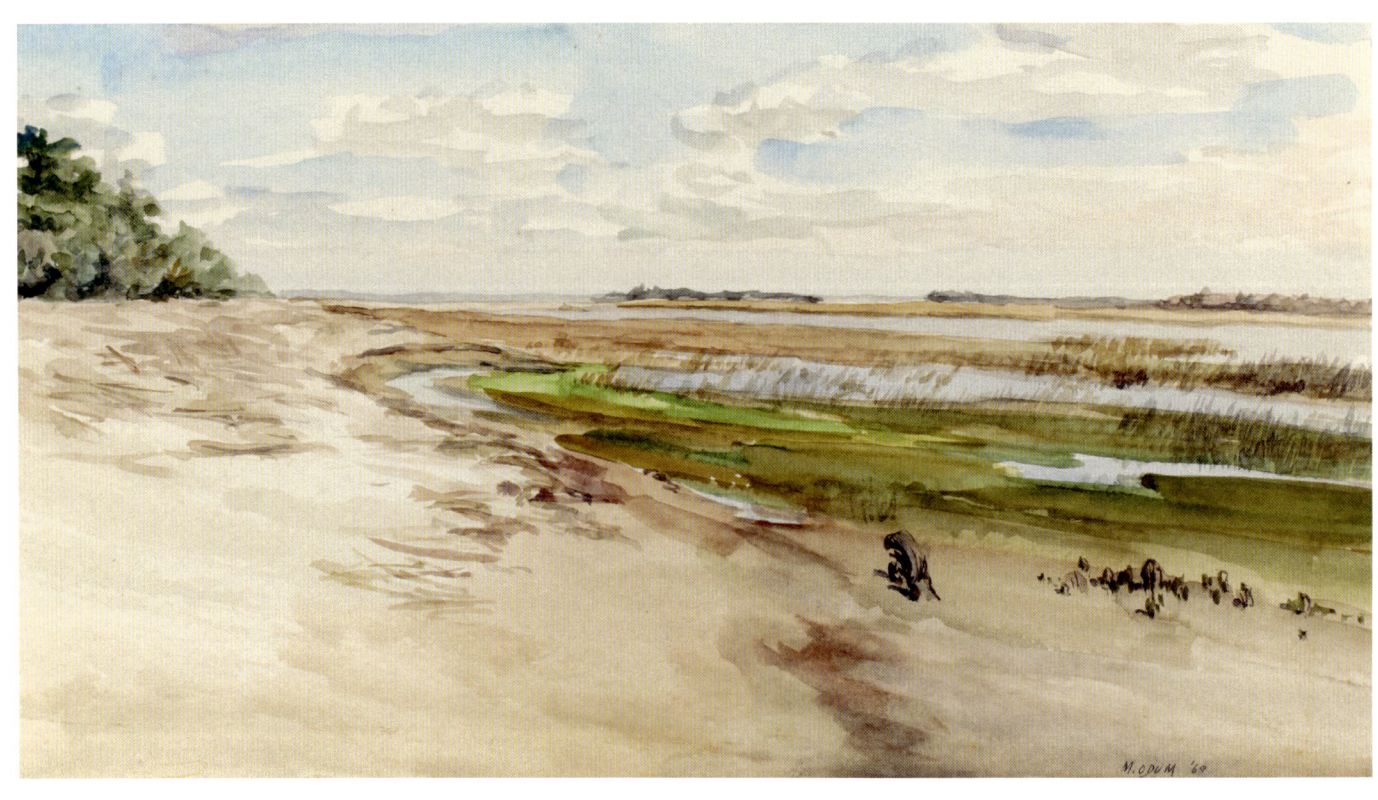

Martha Odum (1917–1995)
Untitled, 1969
Watercolor on paper
11 ¾ × 20 in.
The Ossabaw Island Foundation

Daga Ramsey (1907–1997)
Queen Bess Creek, c. 1969–71
Wool and canvas
71 × 36 in.
The Ossabaw Island Foundation

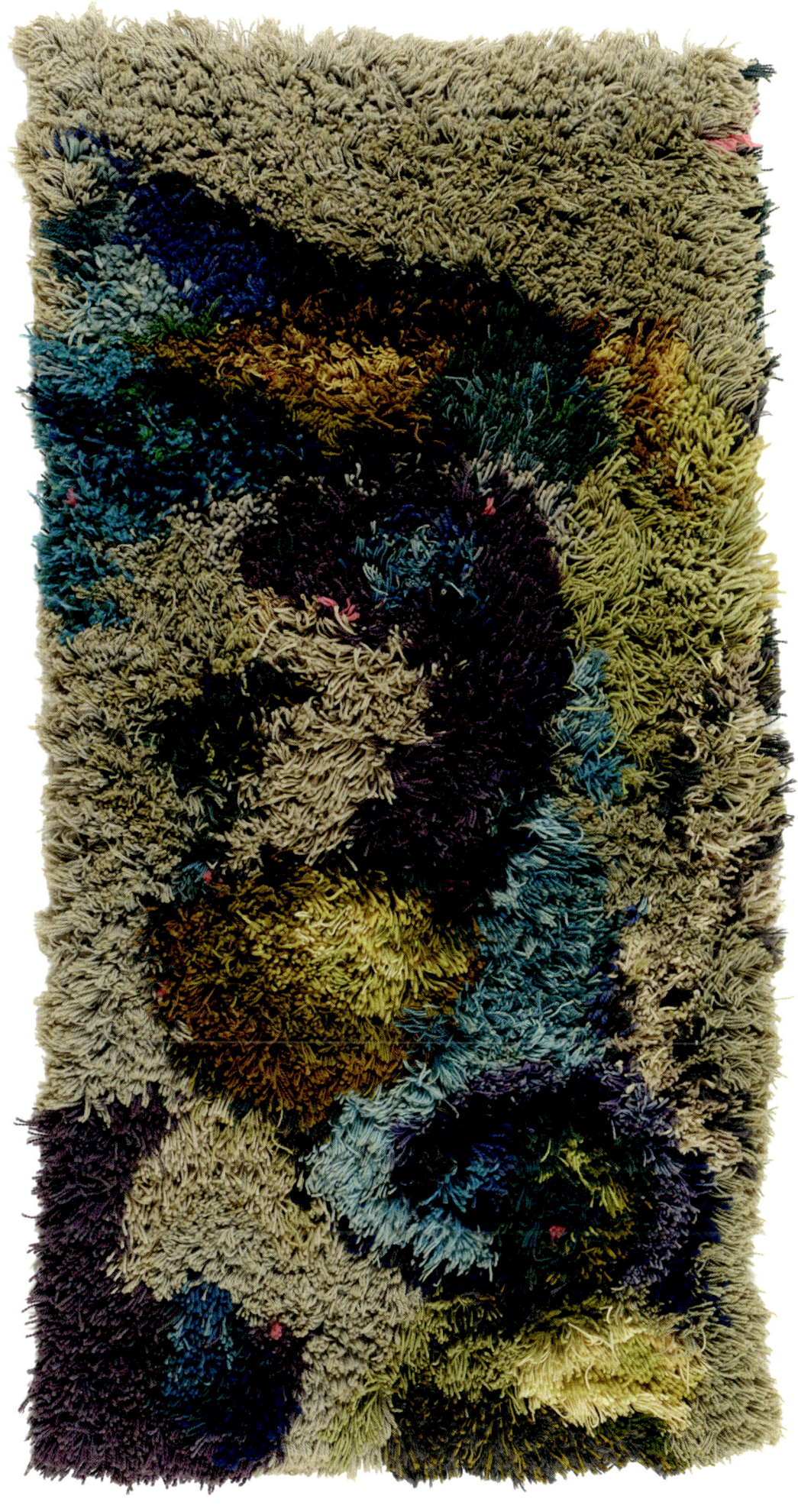

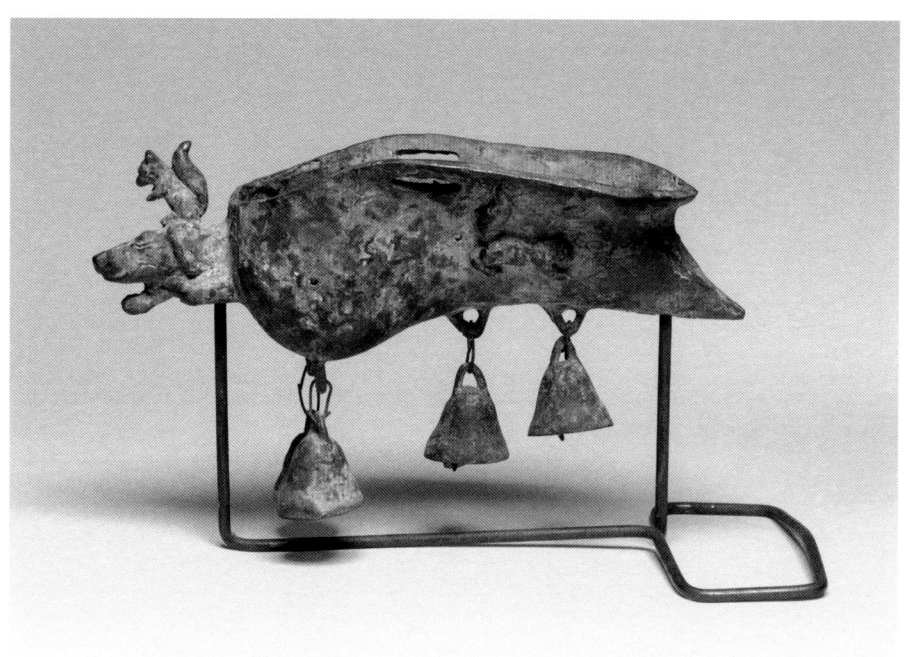

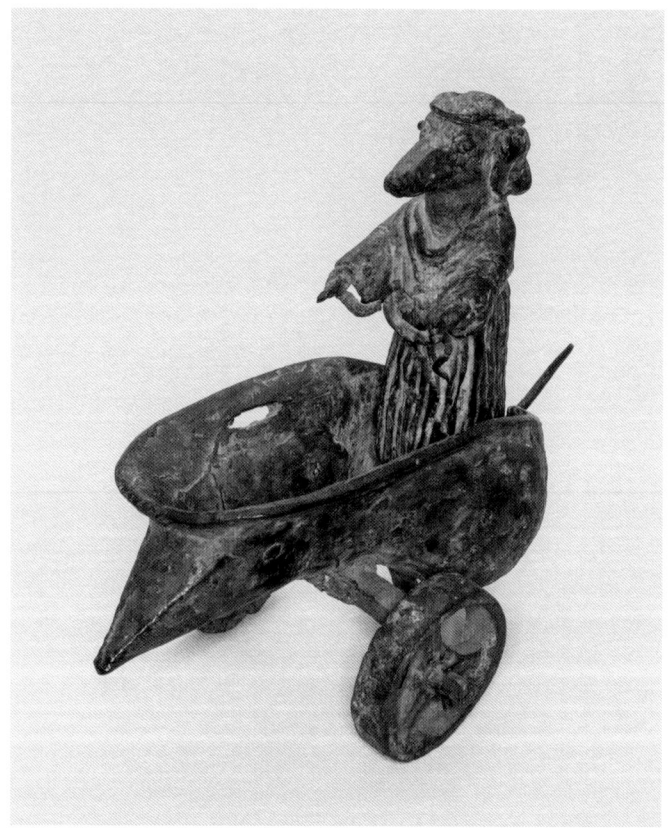

Tex Schiwetz (1909–1971)
Winter Underwear for Bomper, 1962
Bronze
4 × 6 ½ × 2 in.
Collection of Justin P. West
and Eileen McGowan

Tex Schiwetz (1909–1971)
Winter Underwear for Sean, 1962
Bronze
5 ½ × 3 ¾ × 6 ¼ in.
Private collection

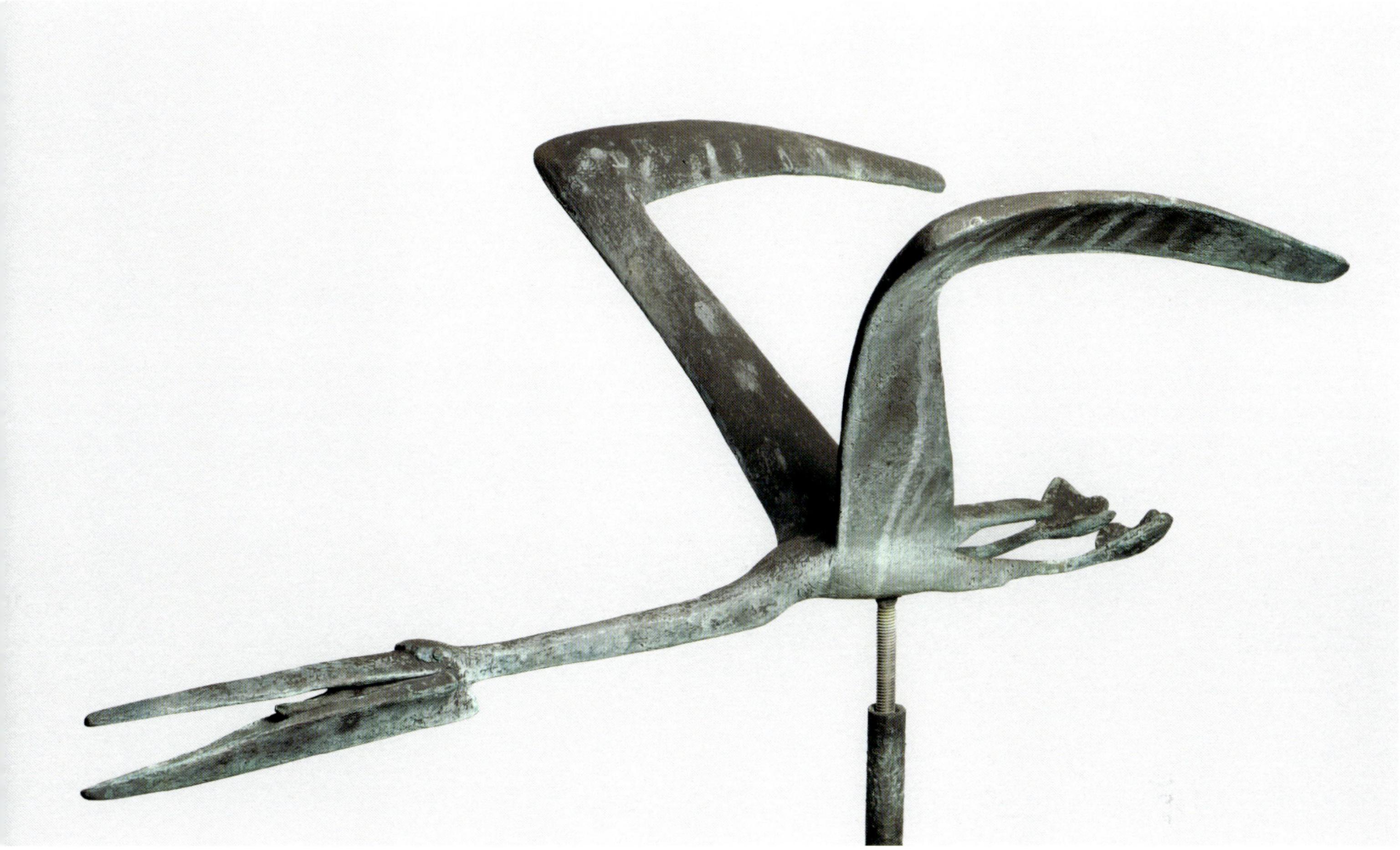

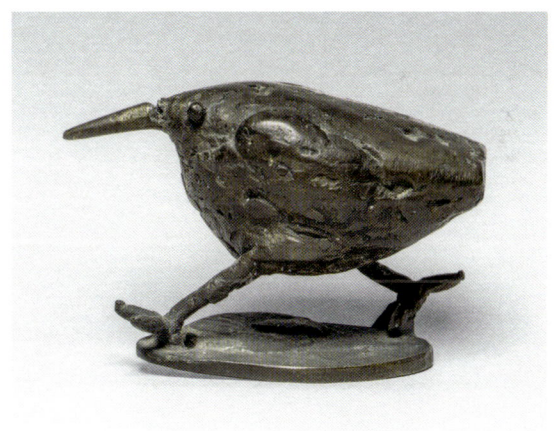

Tex Schiwetz (1909–1971)
Ossabaw Pelican Weathervane, 1965
Bronze
19 × 29 ½ × 19 in.
Collection of Burdine Giese and the late Lester Giese

Tex Schiwetz (1909–1971)
Running Bird, c. 1961
Bronze
1 ¹⁄₁₂ × 2 ¾ × 1 ¼ in.
Collection of Justin P. West
and Eileen McGowan

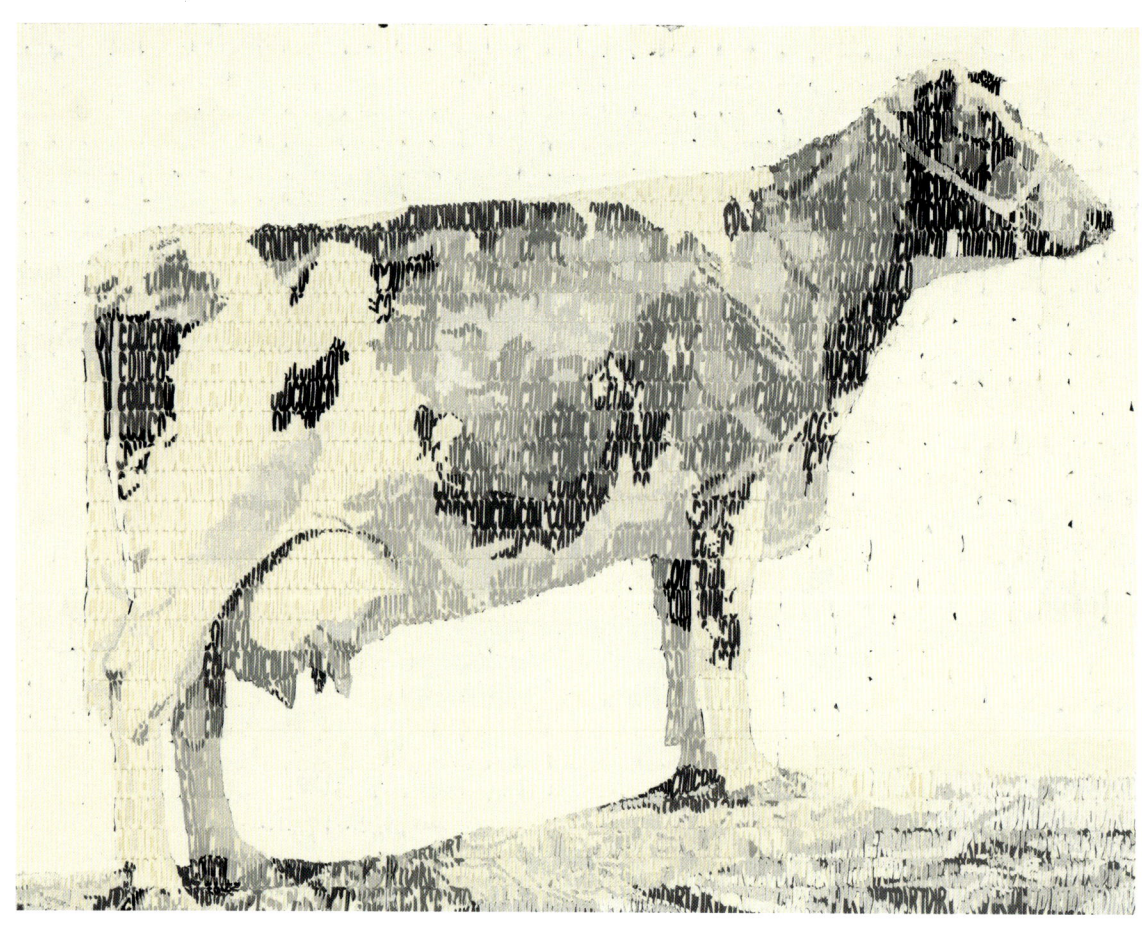

Betty Tompkins (b. 1945)
Ayrshire Class D, 1979
Gouache on cardboard
15 × 20 in.
Allen Memorial Art Museum, Oberlin College, Oberlin,
OH. Art Rental Collection Fund, RC1979.5

Betty Tompkins (b. 1945)
Impending Disaster I (Duetus Interuptus), 1982
Watercolor on paper
39 ½ × 26 in.
Courtesy of Betty Tompkins and P·P·O·W, New York

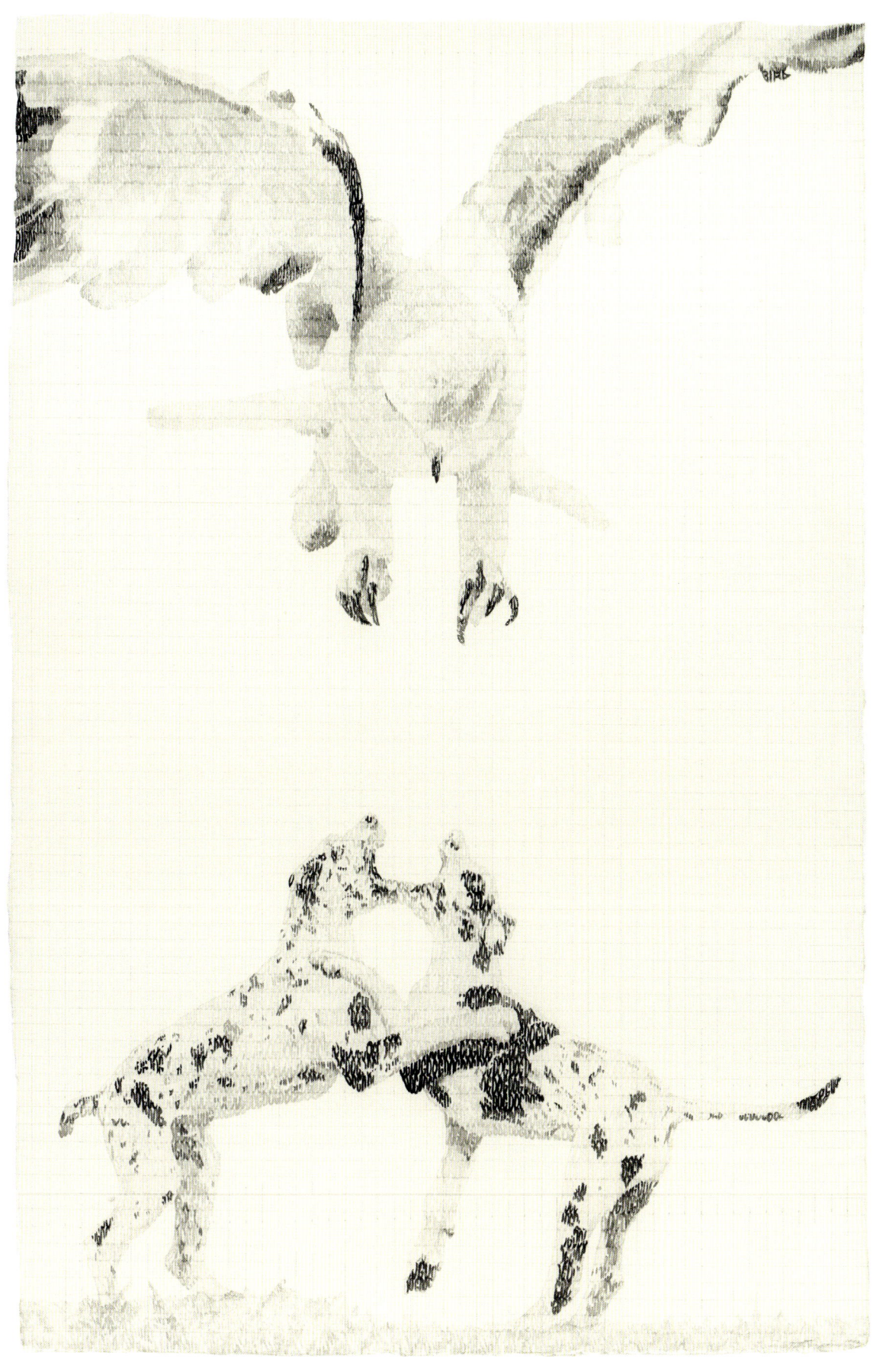

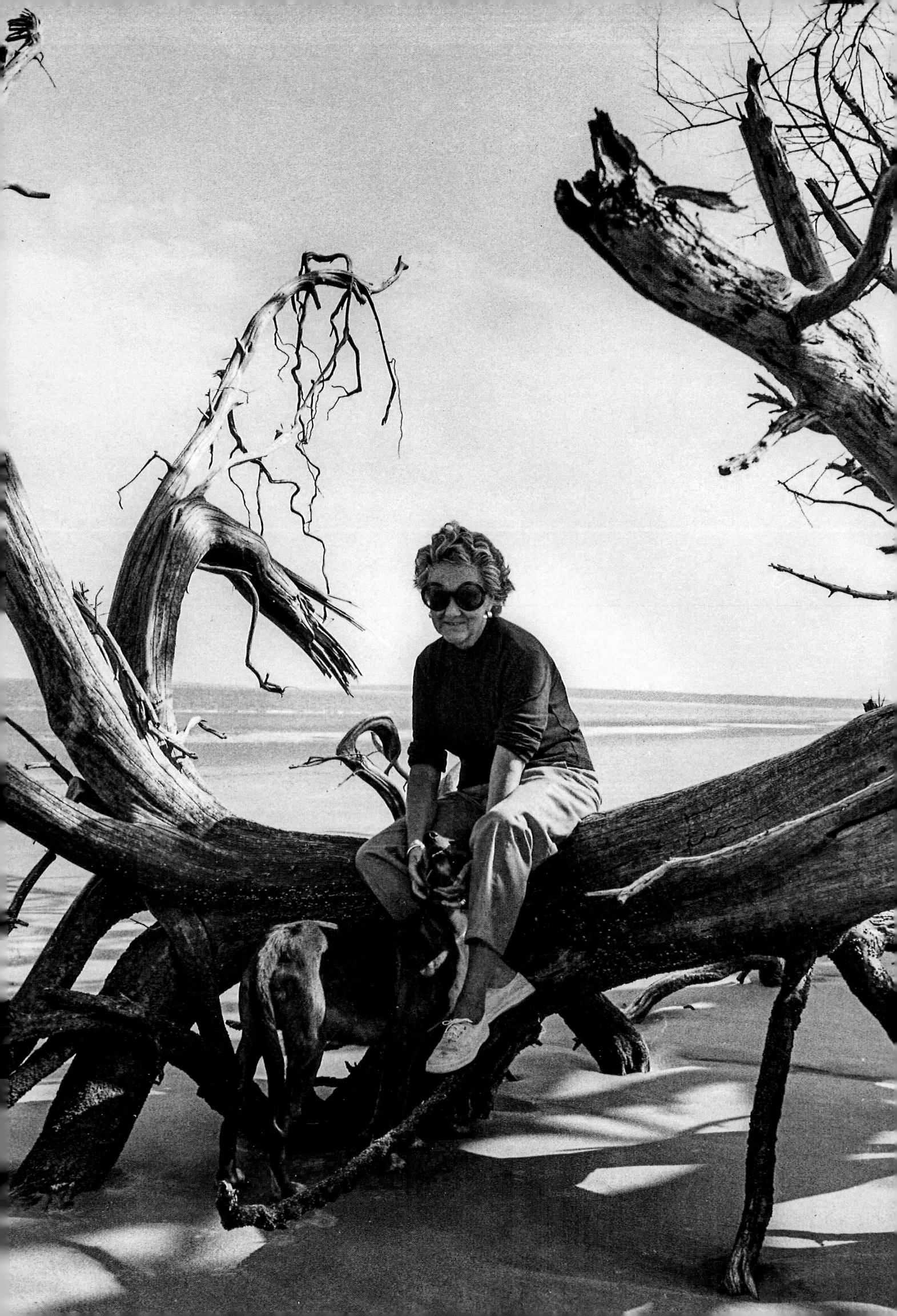

WILD GENEROSITY: SANDY WEST'S ECOFEMINIST VISION ON OSSABAW ISLAND

MEGAN MAYHEW BERGMAN

Before ecofeminism[1] became a recognized term, Eleanor Torrey West was living it. A patrician turned radical steward of Ossabaw Island, she wove conservation with curiosity, feminine leadership with land protection, and solitude with collaboration.

Sandy, as she was known to all, inherited a southern barrier island wrapped in beauty and historical trauma—and chose not possession, but shared purpose. With great blue herons fishing in the marsh, alligators raising their heads from the water, and wild boar traipsing through dense stands of live oaks, Sandy carefully watched over the wilds of Ossabaw, preserving the island not only as a living ecosystem but as an ecological workshop for human creativity. Ossabaw Island, with its ancient maritime forest, tidal creeks, 15-mile sand beach, and storied ruins, is a place of contradiction and revelation. As Sandy hurtled her truck down her personal avenue lined with ancient live oaks, nearly unreachable by the hustle of modern culture, she felt the island's truths. She understood the island was both lush and haunted—a landscape marked by natural splendor and the human pain of enslavement, plantation life, and extraction. Its landmarks and non-human inhabitants presented a tapestry of complexity: Indigenous shell middens and archaeological sites, tabby cabins built and inhabited by enslaved people, a 700-year-old oak tree, eastern diamondback and timber rattlesnakes, nesting sea turtles, and sea views for miles.

When Sandy and her brother's children inherited Ossabaw following her mother's death in 1958, she was faced with a crisis of purpose and identity: should she keep this gem of an island all to herself? Over time, Sandy recognized her belief in stewardship, not ownership. She and her second husband, Clifford B. West, built a program that underscored her conviction. They trusted that time, space, and refuge could give rise to art, ideas, ecological reverence, and social change. What the Wests envisioned was not a public park with the floodgates thrust open, but a sanctuary—for the island itself and

Sandy West on South End Beach with her dog William Rodgers, 1972 (detail). Photograph by John Pennington

for those invited to reckon with it creatively and intellectually. "There is a quality about Ossabaw," Sandy wrote, "that is as unmistakable as it is powerful; remote, beautiful, wild, peaceful, creative."

Born into wealth, Sandy's early life was defined by etiquette, marriage, and tradition, following the arc of many women in her social class. But during the 1950s, her world broadened. Clifford, who was a well-connected painter, burgeoning filmmaker, and teacher at Cranbrook's Kingswood School for Girls in Michigan, encouraged her to think more expansively. Increased exposure to artists, writers, academics, and a changing cultural climate opened her eyes to the possibility of Ossabaw as more than a private idyll. As the environmental movement gained momentum nationally, and her own spiritual and intellectual desires deepened, West began to imagine the island as a site of possibility—one that could catalyze work, reflection, and change for "people of creative thought and purpose... artists, scientists, sculptors, musicians, naturalists, writers."[2]

Sandy and Clifford moved intuitively and began a series of conversations to further inform their vision of Ossabaw's future as a haven for multidisciplinary thinkers. The couple invited the musician Samuel Barber, sculptor Harry Bertoia, and painter Arnold Blanch to the island in June 1961 to experience its splendor and discuss their idea for the Ossabaw Island Project, along with a biologist, a banker, and two lawyers, among others. "We just let them stay at Ossabaw," Sandy explained to Margaret Keister in a 1992 interview: "I think for three days, and didn't tell them what they were going to do or anything. And the thing that happened then is what made the Ossabaw Island Project successful: that Ossabaw is a total catalyst...We just let these people go...They just became absolutely carefree and childlike."[3] In her notes from that weekend, Sandy observed that the invited guests appreciated the value of overlapping with people from different countries and ages. They also liked the idea of allowing stays on the island to range from a week to several months.[4]

The Wests decided not to orchestrate a curriculum or direct outcomes. Instead, they invited people who were serious about their work—scientists, philosophers, ecologists, religious leaders, businesspeople, and artists—and trusted that the island itself would teach them. They respected the independence of creative inquiry. There was no detailed strategic plan, no elaborate branding. There was only the land, the time, and the invitation to engage. "It seems tremendously exciting to us," Sandy and Clifford wrote in 1961, "that people, such as these, so indispensable to the peace and value of man, could not only think and work in a place like Ossabaw, but would have, as well, the opportunity to interpret, to listen and gain understanding in ordinarily distant fields."[5] Sandy possessed an understanding of what it meant to be collaborative and creative, and what authentic support looked like. "A creative person," she scrawled in her notebook after one conversation during the summit in 1961, seeking to articulate her vision of whom the program might serve, was someone who "makes inquiries into the unknown, seeks proper relationship to his environment, seeks a sense of well being, and does things for the love of doing them."[6] Sandy didn't care if her inhabitants created a bestselling product on her island; she wanted Ossabaw to inspire true creative transformation.

As the first artists and scientists moved through the island, Sandy made notes about windy beaches, mice, fishing equipment, transport, Nor'easters, and how to make breakfast for eleven people, including 36 eggs and 54 cups of coffee.[7] The group had pig roasts underneath the stars on the isolated beach, and gathered for drinks, dinner, and stimulating conversation in the Wests' dining room. This early visit informed the design of the Ossabaw Island Project, where participants moved with maximum independence but came together at the end of the day to share food and ideas. Sandy often asked visitors not about what they had accomplished, but what they had *seen* on the island that day. In 1978, she wrote in the University of Georgia's *Research Reporter* that she believed that people of all disciplines, ages, and expertise "should endeavor to look at *everything* before *disturbing* anything."[8]

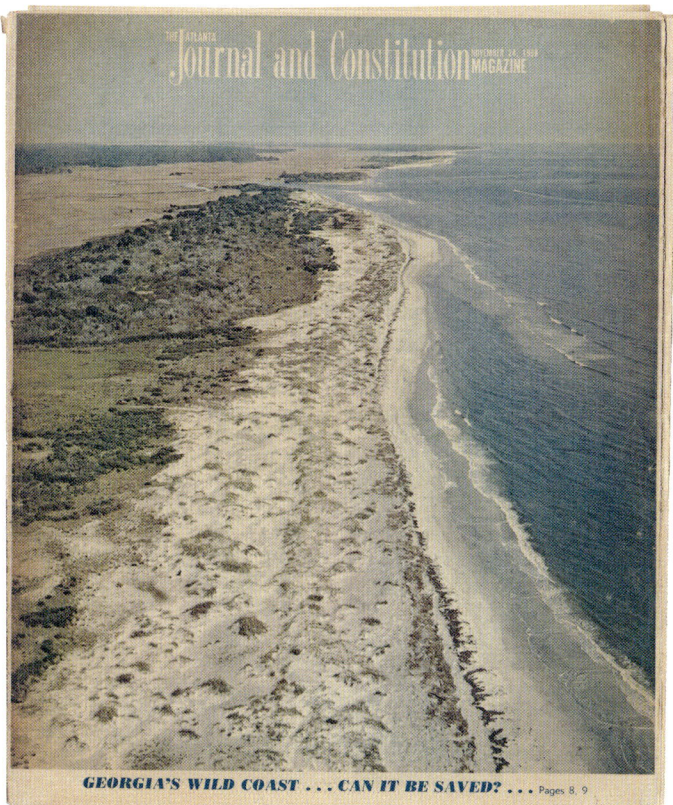

Cover of *The Atlanta Journal and Constitution Magazine*, November 24, 1968. The accompanying article chronicles "The Future of the Marshlands and Sea Islands of Georgia" conference at Sea Island, October 13-14, 1968

Concurrently, Sandy began making efforts towards protecting the island's future. In October of 1968, a conference took place on Sea Island that focused on the future of Georgia's marshlands and islands. Sandy—the only woman among a list of male speakers, including her husband—spoke publicly for the first time about the island's ecological importance. She began her speech by talking about the "grave responsibility" she and Clifford felt as owners of the island. "We have tried to share Ossabaw in a way which will not destroy that which is most precious to preserve," she explained. "We have shared the power and inspiration of something inescapably natural with top thinkers and doers... their influence is unquestionable."[9]

Sandy joined a small but potent group of environmentally-minded public voices. Rachel Carson and E. B. White were just beginning to make a case for environmental stewardship in *The New Yorker* in the early 1960s, with Carson's landmark *Silent Spring* book published in 1962. A post-war population and technology boom, along with increased land development, led to greater awareness that wilderness needed to be defined—as it was by the 1964 Wilderness Act—and protected. Locally, Georgia's farms had been carved up by highways, and old fields and swamps were converted and drained to support pine plantations for the paper industry. Phosphate companies hoped to mine Georgia's wetlands, leading to increased concern for the protection of the state's swamps and marshes and the passing of the Coastal Marshlands Protection Act in 1970.

Sandy, a significant land owner and private citizen, stood in front of a group of Georgia's decision makers and offered a speech that would read as progressive even in 2026. While many environmentalists called for conservation—such as the establishment of parks and wilderness or the prevention of dams—Sandy evoked the concept of interconnectedness and a landscape's or species' right to exist in a healthy state for its own sake. She noted that Ossabaw was essential to the interdisciplinary Project, but it was also "essential to shrimp and fish, to trees and plants, to migrations of birds and the life of wild animals, to Georgia history, and to you and me."[10] Citizens, especially lawmakers, are still uncomfortable with views that oppose human exceptionalism, and six decades later, environmentalists are only rarely successful in their pursuit of legal rights for rivers and non-human species.

In the late 1960s, Sandy began to find her public voice—not just as a wife, hostess or patron, but as a leader and protector. She was brave and prescient in her concerns. "Why save the birds, the turtles, the fish and the thinkers?" she asked. "How can anyone or anything keep its head above the mindless stream of pollution, misguided urban planning, and the gobbling up of natural resources and overpopulation?"[11] She collaborated on a pair of films with her husband that tackled these issues head on, *Untitled Film: A Search for Ecological Balance* (c. 1970), which focused on the research of pioneering ecologist Eugene P. Odum along the Georgia coastline, and *"Give and Take": A Story of One Way to Preserve and Use this Diminishing Earth* (1974), which outlined the ethos of her programs on Ossabaw.

With expenses and taxes skyrocketing and her own savings dwindling in the 1970s, Sandy knew she was running out of time to save Ossabaw. By this moment, Clifford was making films abroad, and the couple was living apart (they divorced in 1976). While she still consulted him and shared ownership of Ossabaw with her brother's children, Sandy became the matriarch and protector of the island, the stalwart steward of its future. Developers, including Hilton Head Island mastermind Charles E. Fraser, and wealthy aristocrats, such as Jacqueline and Aristotle Onassis, began making generous offers that would make her and her family very wealthy. But Sandy—largely on her own, under pressure, and with her finances in peril—spent ten years looking for a workable solution that would not just preserve Ossabaw, but do so in a holistic way. For the future. For all species on the island. For the island's own health. Sandy sought sustainable solutions while refusing to compromise the island's integrity. At a time when few women were recognized as environmental leaders, she stood among them with clarity and resolve. She explored various custodians for Ossabaw, such as environmentalist David Brower's Friends of the Earth, the Audubon Society, and the Nature Conservancy, but it felt as if an ideal solution did not currently exist. With her resources diminishing, she knew a decision had to be made before she lost the island entirely. Jimmy Carter, then governor of Georgia, and himself a progressive agent of southern ecology, asked Sandy what she thought should be done about the island when negotiations began with the State of Georgia in 1972. Her answer was not prescriptive—it was philosophical. She believed in purposeful access. Opening Ossabaw carte blanche, she knew, would destroy what made it sacred. Her early work laid the foundation for one of the most innovative conservation agreements in American history.

In 1977, after long negotiations, Sandy and her brother's children agreed to donate half of Ossabaw's land and sell the rest to the State of Georgia under the pioneering Heritage Preserve model. This arrangement—rare and visionary—ensured that the island would be protected in perpetuity from development and maintained for "natural, scientific, and educational purposes."[12] Despite finding a manager for Ossabaw that fulfilled most of her desires for the island's future, Sandy was miserable on the day in May 1978 when she signed away her rights to the island at a bank in Savannah. Joe Tanner, who was a key architect of the sale for Georgia's Department of Natural Resources, remembered her angrily throwing her check on the floor.[13] In addition to an act of creativity and governance, the sale was one of selflessness.

A key component of the agreement was an innovative public-private partnership model, which allowed a private foundation to oversee access to the island under the stipulated terms despite it being state-owned land. Sandy immediately reinvested the money she made from Ossabaw's sale into her foundation, leasing the island back from the state and continuing her programs in full force. Unfortunately, it didn't take long for her funds to run out. She was forced to close the Ossabaw Island Project and its satellite programs in 1982 after twenty-one years as their guiding light. Sandy could easily have remained a socialite and snowbird, moving between society and a mansion on a private island, then sell-ing it off for development, reaping millions. Instead, she actively fought to find a solution for a type of conservation agreement that had never existed before, risking her financial future—and that of her family—in the process. But such was the depth of her passion. She never stopped questioning the predominant stewardship mentality of the day, writing in 1978, "I believe man would do well to watch where he treads, as he is the only creature that leaves indelible footsteps that keep on running uncontrollably without him."[14]

Once the Department of Natural Resources took charge of managing Ossabaw, Sandy was relentless in her oversight of their activities on the island. She used her voice—the most powerful tool at her disposal—whenever she felt that the stipulations of the sale agreement weren't being upheld. Much to the DNR's chagrin, she did so by giving in-terviews to the *Washington Post*, *The Atlanta Journal / The Atlanta Constitution*, and the *Savannah Morning News*, among other publications. "I expect the state to keep its word," she told *National Geographic* in 2001.[15]

When we reflect on the legacies of unusual women, we tend to center our curios-ity on their bohemian tendencies. What circles did they move in? Who were their lovers? While these questions might yield fascinating answers, our ear for the sensational tends to miss what is most valuable. Sandy oversaw a landmark interdisciplinary movement that combined arts and environmental practice decades before anyone else was doing so, and she spearheaded a pioneering conservation agreement that safeguarded 26,000 acres of land from certain development and degradation.

Sandy's environmentalism was distinctly feminine—not because it was soft or maternal, but because it was relational, intuitive, and collaborative. She was part of a lin-

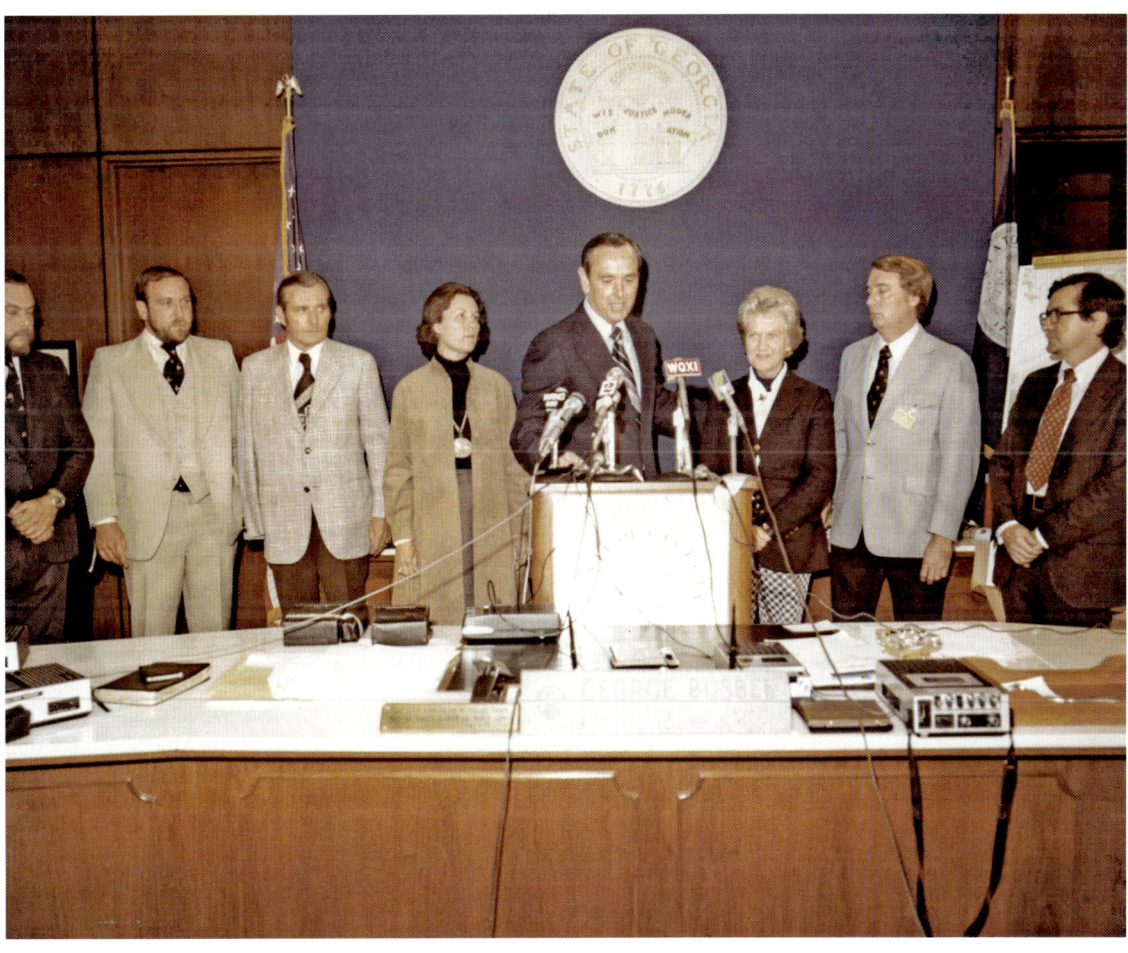

Georgia Governor George Busbee announces the State of Georgia's acquisition of Ossabaw Island, Atlanta, Georgia, April 7, 1977. From left: Emory Torrey, Randall Torrey, William Ford Torrey Jr., environmentalist Jane Yarn, Busbee, Sandy West, Director of Georgia's Department of Natural Resources Joe Tanner, and attorney Allison Wade

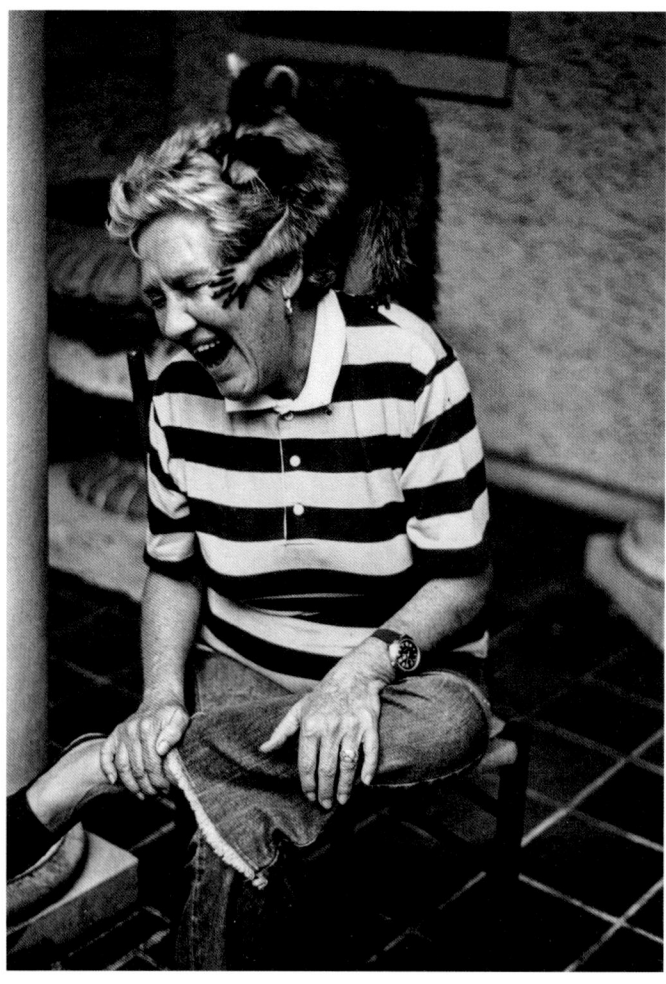

Sandy West and Clyde the raccoon at the Main House, c. 1975

eage of powerful southern women who linked ecology and liberation: Mary Musgrove, a half-Indigenous woman who fought for her right to land on Georgia's coast in the 18th century; Carol Ruckdeschel, who advocated for Cumberland Island with fierce independence and scientific precision; Cornelia Walker Bailey, the Geechee matriarch of Sapelo Island, who protected cultural memory with the same vigor others used to guard forests. West was in conversation—spiritually if not always directly—with these women, thinking not only about ecology, but about what it meant to protect space, voice, and legacy.

Sandy's ideas were elegantly revolutionary—about how art and thinking might come together and how conservation played a significant role in everyone's well-being. Her interviews from the 1970s on are frank, inspired, and pointed. "We believe that the only way to survive is through harmony with the universe, and it takes a 'whole' man to understand."[16] Sandy believed that freedom and ecology were interlinked, and that artists, scientists, historians, and leaders needed time, seclusion, and space to do their best work. She knew such sanctuary was increasingly rare in a modern, extractive world. Ossabaw offered a counterpoint to speed and productivity. Those who visited often found themselves irrevocably changed. Their work took new directions; their thinking deepened. The island, as this exhibition attests, was not a backdrop—it was a collaborator. Ossabaw was a wild muse to many of the contemporary creatives whose work remains on our shelves, in our ears, and on our walls.

Sandy's Ossabaw stewardship was not just environmental or artistic. It was *ethical*. It asked the essential question: how do we live responsibly with our inheritance of land, history, and power? Her answer was one of radical generosity. Not the kind that floods the gates, but the kind that creates sacred thresholds that preserve rather than restrict. Today, as we face climate collapse, mass extinction, and a crisis of meaning, West's model of interconnectedness, stewardship, and cross collaboration—looking before disturbing—feels prescient. Her work prefigured current movements around rewilding, slow scholarship, land acknowledgment, and creative ecology. She knew that protection and exploration could coexist. That wildness, when overseen intelligently and with love, could be a source of both individual transformation and collective insight.

Here are ideas that are both iconic and transferable: Ossabaw Island remains protected because Sandy West chose not to hoard her inheritance, but to share it wisely for posterity. She forged her own path to become a leader. She trusted her instincts about the value of place and the natural world. She allowed herself to evolve. She turned a privately-owned island into a public legacy—not by throwing open the doors, but by opening them just enough.

Notes

1. Ecofeminism is a philosophical and political movement that links ecological degradation and gender inequality, viewing both as consequences of patriarchal systems. The term was first coined by Françoise d'Eaubonne in her 1974 book *Le Féminisme ou la Mort* (Paris: P. Horay, 1974).

2. Sandy West's notes from the first meetings about the Ossabaw Island Project in a notebook labeled "Mrs. Clifford B. West; Ossabaw Island; June 22, 1961," introductory page, West family archives.

3. Margaret Ann Keister, "The Ossabaw Island Project, a Program Fostering Creative Production and Experience," (PhD diss., University of Georgia, 1992), 199-200.

4. "Mrs. Clifford B. West," entry from Saturday, June 24, 1961.

5. "Mrs. Clifford B. West," preliminary dossier on the Ossabaw Island Project.

6. "Mrs. Clifford B. West," entry from Friday, June 24, 1961.

7. "Mrs. Clifford B. West," entry from Saturday, June 23, 1961.

8. Eleanor Torrey West, "Viewpoint: Ossabaw Island," *Research Reporter* 11, no. 3 (1978): 9.

9. Mrs. Clifford West, "The April Conference, Ossabaw Island," in *The Future of the Marshlands and Sea Islands of Georgia*, eds. David S. Maney, Frederick C. Marland and Clifford B. West. (Sea Island: Georgia Natural Areas Council and the Coastal Area Planning and Development Commission, 1968), 67.

10. Mrs. Clifford West, "The April Conference, Ossabaw Island," 67.

11. Mrs. Clifford West, "The April Conference, Ossabaw Island," 70.

12. "Ossabaw Island: Heritage Preserve," The Ossabaw Island Foundation, accessed July 17, 2025, https://ossabawisland.org/island/heritage-preserve/.

13. Ann Hardie, "The Old Lady of Ossabaw," *Atlanta Magazine*, March 1, 2011.

14. West, "Viewpoint: Ossabaw Island," 9.

15. "Ossabaw Adrift," *National Geographic* 200, no. 5 (November 2001).

16. West, "Viewpoint: Ossabaw Island," 9.

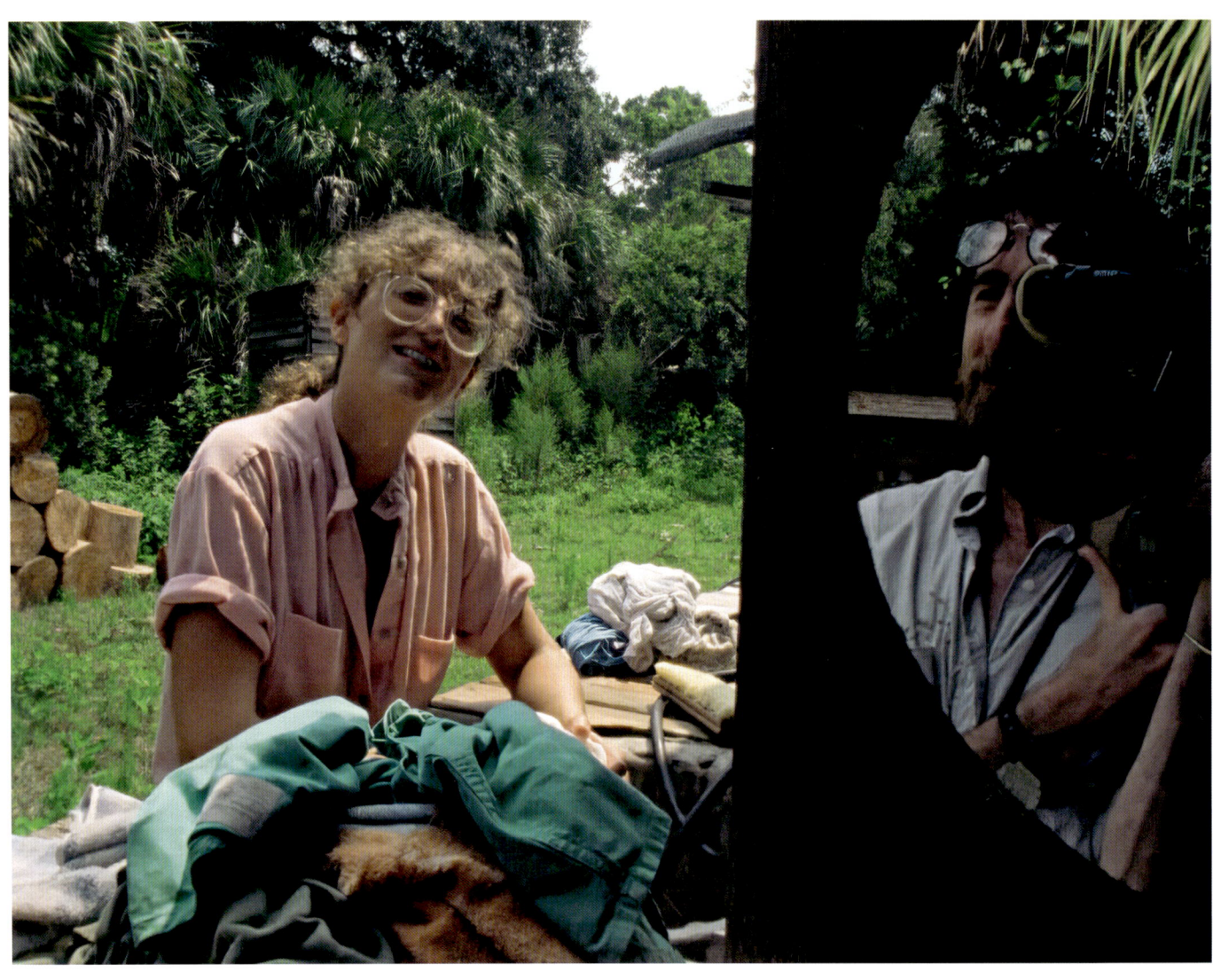

Ross McElwee filming Genesis member Wini Wood while she does
laundry, 1981. Film still from *Sherman's March*, 1986

ROSS MCELWEE, ME, AND *SHERMAN'S MARCH*

WINI WOOD

I don't remember exactly how I met Ross McElwee. Perhaps it was when we Genesis members went up to Ossabaw's Main House for a screening of one of his films. Or maybe he came to Middle Place on one of those outings Ossabaw Island Project members liked taking, and I led the tour. Whatever the occasion, we struck up a conversation that led to a fateful question: *Would you mind if I filmed you?* And that led to *Sherman's March*.

The filming unfolded over the next year (1981–82), with Ross making two return visits to the island. When he wasn't on the island, he was busy filming six other women. (Or, as Ross insists, he was back in Boston trying to earn money. Filmmaking is expensive.) I'm pretty sure I believed that film would never see the light of day. Little did I imagine that, when it was eventually finished, *Sherman's March* would win the Best Documentary award at Sundance (1987), much less that it would be preserved in the Library of Congress's National Film Registry (2000), that it would influence so many other filmmakers, or that whole articles and even books would be written about Ross's work.[1] It was not until 2011, when I was reviewing materials for a course on documentary film I planned to teach, that I realized how canonical this film—the film I was in—had become.

Ross initially described his filmmaking style as cinema vérité, a term that meant nothing to me then, but that I took to mean something like "cinema truth." The French expression is in fact a direct translation of the early Soviet film term *kino pravda,* a style that 1960s French documentary filmmakers much admired. Ross in fact had some experience in France. After finishing a degree in creative writing at Brown University, he spent a year working as a travelling wedding photographer in Brittany, a journey he later revisits in his film *Photographic Memory* (2012).He then studied filmmaking at the Massachusetts Institute of Technology (MIT) under the mentorship of vérité filmmakers he much admired, including Richard Leacock, whose voice you hear reading the opening lines of *Sherman's March*. Cinema vérité films favored the ordinary lives of ordinary people, and eschewed the overbearing style of early documentaries—voice-of-God narration, for example, or any other interfering presence of the filmmaker. The idea was, more or less, to turn the camera on and let people go about their business.

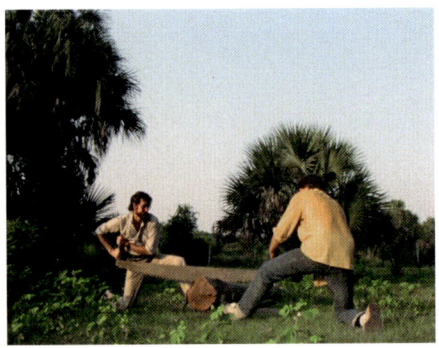 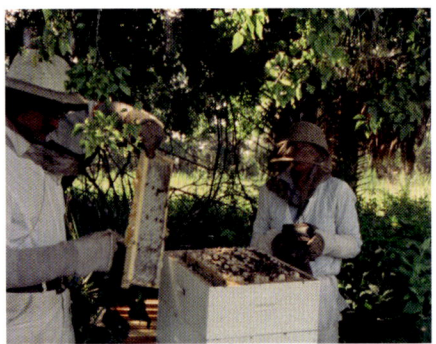 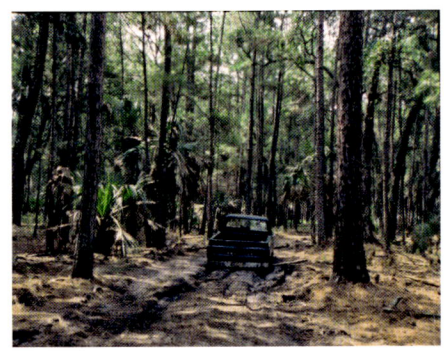

I could see how that worked in the film Ross showed at the Main House: his *Space Coast* (1980) was shot at Cape Canaveral, but avoided the spectacular subjects of space travel to focus on the ordinary people who lived and worked nearby.[2] The approach was intended to show a more truthful version of life. But as Ross is quick to remind me now, he (to great humorous effect) intentionally subverts all the strictures of cinema vérité in *Sherman's March*, most notably through his ever-present narration and, well, his ever-present self in the film.[3] Indeed, the question people most frequently ask me is: Is Ross *really* like that?

So, you wonder. How truthful is *Sherman's March*?

There are plenty of things you don't see in that film (at least, in the scenes where I appear) that might be construed as untruths by omission. For one thing, I wasn't on the island as an itinerant graduate student, and I certainly wasn't the only person there. I had a job (the job of a lifetime, a life-changing job), co-directing Genesis with Michael Billa, who appears in the film and is now my husband of 40 years. I still "can't imagine my life without Michael."[4]

For another, I was not unfamiliar with film; as a linguistics student at the University of Iowa, I'd spent much time with film studies majors, even appearing in student films. I'm certain I thought of Ross's enterprise as just another student film. When Ross outlined his ideas to me, I hardly took him seriously—I mean, would *anyone*? He proposed to follow Sherman's route to the sea, meanwhile expounding on his own fears of nuclear war...oh, and also searching for just the right relationship with a woman.[5] It sounded preposterous! I think I let him know that, as did most of the other women who ultimately appeared in the film.

Maybe most importantly, what the film does not reveal is the constant stimulating conversation that flowed between Ross and me over many months (and over a lifetime now). I know I peppered him with questions, perhaps asking *him* far more questions off-screen than he asks me on camera.[6]

And yet there is a deep truthfulness that emerges—for me, at least—in the film. It's important, I think, to understand Ross's role as provocateur. In the French notion of cinema vérité, the filmmaker has both presence and function to provoke a response that will, in the end, be more truthful than the self-conscious performance of subjects before a camera.[7] Indeed, Ross is the master of provocation, with a kind of teasing nudge that I felt often while he was filming me, but most especially in a scene when I was milking a cow, or later, when he kept pressing me about my new relationship with Michael. These are scenes that I have rewatched over the years with emotions ranging from embarrassment to wistful nostalgia, but never without a sense that: This was real. This happened.

When I sought time on Ossabaw—first, over a series of short visits as a Genesis member, then, finally, when I moved there to take a year-round job—it was for the ineluctable allure of the place. I was drawn to the island as if to home. I left everything for that job—my graduate studies, my identity as a Midwesterner, my home and family. Yet unlike almost everyone else who visits, I came without a camera. I sought not to *record* experience, but to *have* experience. I wanted nothing more than to breathe that place into my

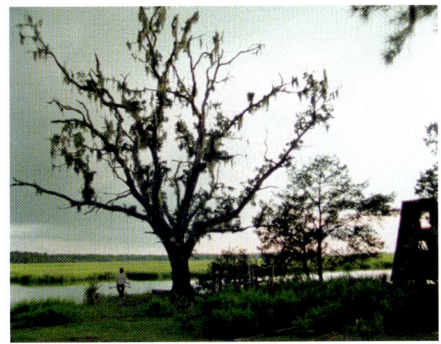
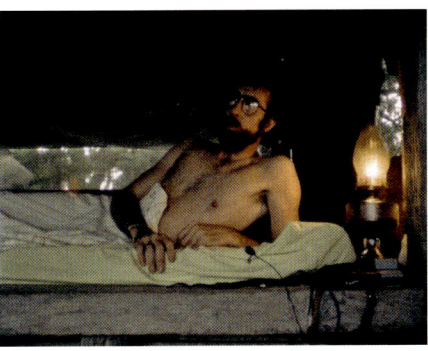
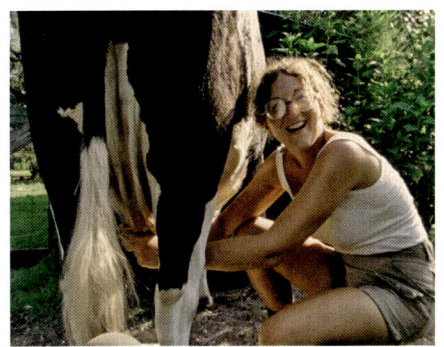

soul, to watch the light change from early morning to late afternoon, when Middle Place clearing felt like a bowl of light as I surveyed it, improbably, from the top of a sawdust pile. I wanted to inhabit the darkest nights of the new moon and the brightest nights of the full moon, to feel winter move into spring into summer, to watch the marsh grasses change from brown to yellow to green to gold, and to hear the corresponding movements of the rails and the dolphins and the alligators and the herons. I wanted to feel the air on my skin, to inhale what Michael once called "the fullness of life and the stench of death." I consider myself the luckiest person in the universe to have experienced that fullness, that continuity of time and space. No photograph can capture what I felt there.

And so I am grateful for the tiny slice of life that Ross captured with his motion picture camera, with his provocations, his questions, his own eye. I can look at myself milking that cow, and I can feel the warmth of her body, the softness of her teats, the strength of my hands and fingers; I can feel my nose buried in her fur, smell her smell. I can hear the soft gabble of the turkeys as they mill around, stealing bits of grain from Genie's[8] bin, and her soft, patient chewing as she eats her meal while she endures my milking. All of this exceeds the image.

But I know so much more about Ossabaw now, after years of return visits following the closing of the two projects, after walks and conversations with the hired help (of which I was one), with wildlife managers, Georgia state archaeologists, historians and scientists, and—to no small effect—with Mrs. West. The island is a perfectly preserved palimpsest of histories—natural histories, cultural histories, personal histories. I now know much more about who preceded me on the island—I've been shown evidence in the middens of native peoples who lived there some 5,000 years ago, in the drainage ditches dug along the roadsides and tabby buildings constructed around the island by enslaved Africans and their descendants, in the changing configuration of the beaches and vegetation and bird migrations, in the longings of every human, Black, white, and Indigenous, who thought, as I did, "this is home."

I know now that the allure of this island for me has always been deeper than the personal allure—it is the call of history. And that complex relationship between personal desire and the larger movements of history is what Ross's crazy, improbable film expresses. In the beginning and the end that was the allure for Ross himself. When Ross first arrived on Ossabaw, he did not plan to be filming; he had proposed to write an essay about his personal interest in General Sherman's march to the sea. But few people end up doing what they think they'll be doing on Ossabaw. The island intervenes—as it did for me, as it did for Ross, as it has done for so many other artists represented in this exhibition.

When we look at a place, what do we see? When we look at a film, what do we see?

When I look at *Sherman's March* now, I still see "my" island, "my" home—indeed, "my" self. But what I now also see is an astonishingly prescient portrait of today's South, of many of the forces and peoples that have mingled there, all products of its histories, all seeking either to preserve or move forward from those histories.[9] Intriguingly, in *Sherman's March*, it is a portrait painted entirely through women. Even me.

Acknowledgment

I'm grateful to Ross McElwee for reading a first draft of this essay, for filling in a few blanks, and for allowing me to play fast and loose in characterizing him as a cinema vérité filmmaker. All taken in stride with characteristic Ross-humor. Thanks, too, to Mike Billa for doing the same.

Notes

1. Ross's work has now also been officially canonized by the French Ministry of Culture, which in 2025 awarded him the rank of *Chevalier de l'ordre des Arts et des Lettres*. Sir Ross!

2. *Space Coast*, directed by Ross McElwee and Michel Negroponte (1980), 16mm, 90 min.

3. *Sherman's March* is now most frequently regarded as an exemplar of the "essay film," or sometimes as a "poetic documentary."

4. I'm quoting myself from *Sherman's March* here (01:16:47-55).

5. All this is embodied in the full title of the film: *Sherman's March: A Meditation on the Possibility of Romantic Love in the South During an Era of Nuclear Weapons Proliferation*.

6. Not to get too wonky, but what I'm really describing here gets at the essence and power of cinema vérité film. These were not drive-by filmmakers; they took much time getting to know their subjects as people and getting to know the spaces they inhabited. The best of these filmmakers—and Ross counts among the best—were superb cinematographers, skillful at adapting the camera to unpredictable environments and changing situations.

7. This version was first defined and enacted by anthropologist-filmmaker Jean Rouch and his sociologist co-director Edgar Morin in the groundbreaking *Chronique d'un été/Chronicle of a Summer* (Paris, 1960). The more restrictive correlate in the U.S. is often referred to as "direct cinema." An exemplar of a direct cinema filmmaker is Frederick Wiseman, whom Ross much admires.

8. The Genesis cow's name is spelled both as Genie and Jeanie in materials from the early 1980s. This spelling comes from Michael Billa and Wini Wood, "Genesis," *The Ossabaw Foundation 1979–1981* (Ossabaw Foundation, 1981), 9.

9. It is never lost on me, nor was it on Ross, that the cast of characters in *Sherman's March* is overwhelmingly white. One sees his sensitivity to race in other scenes from the film, and indeed, throughout his work, but themes of race are more fully articulated in some of his later autobiographical films.

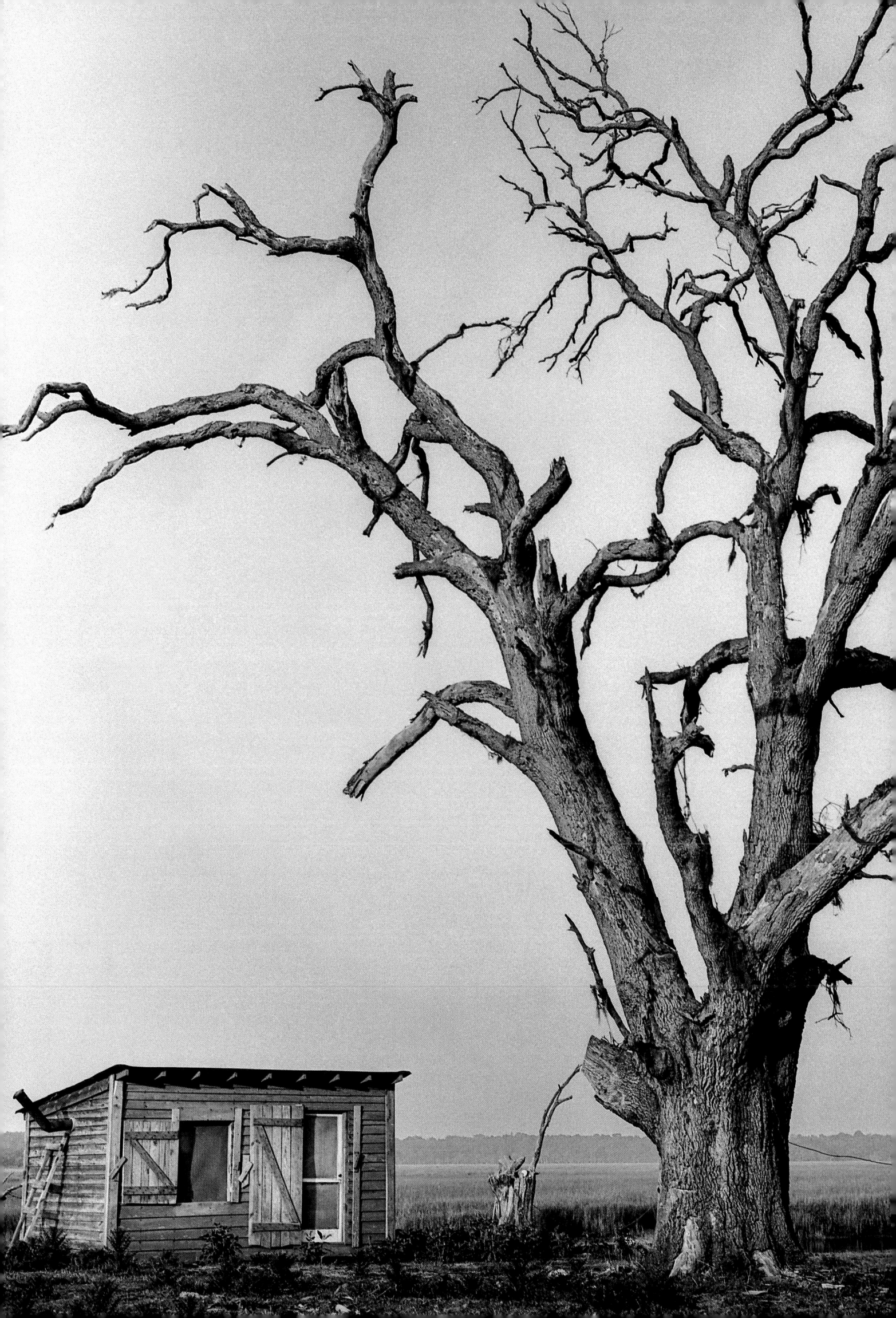

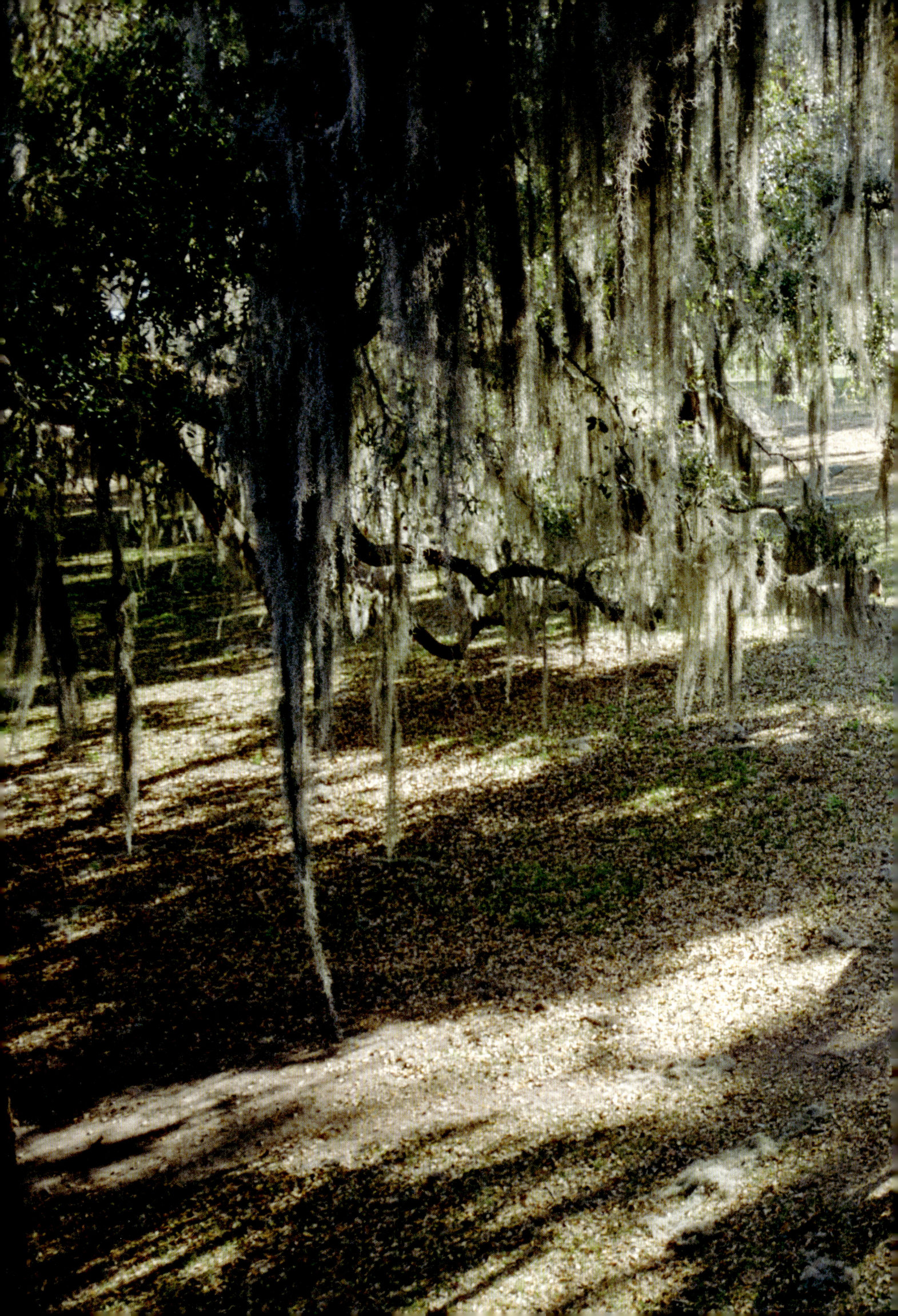

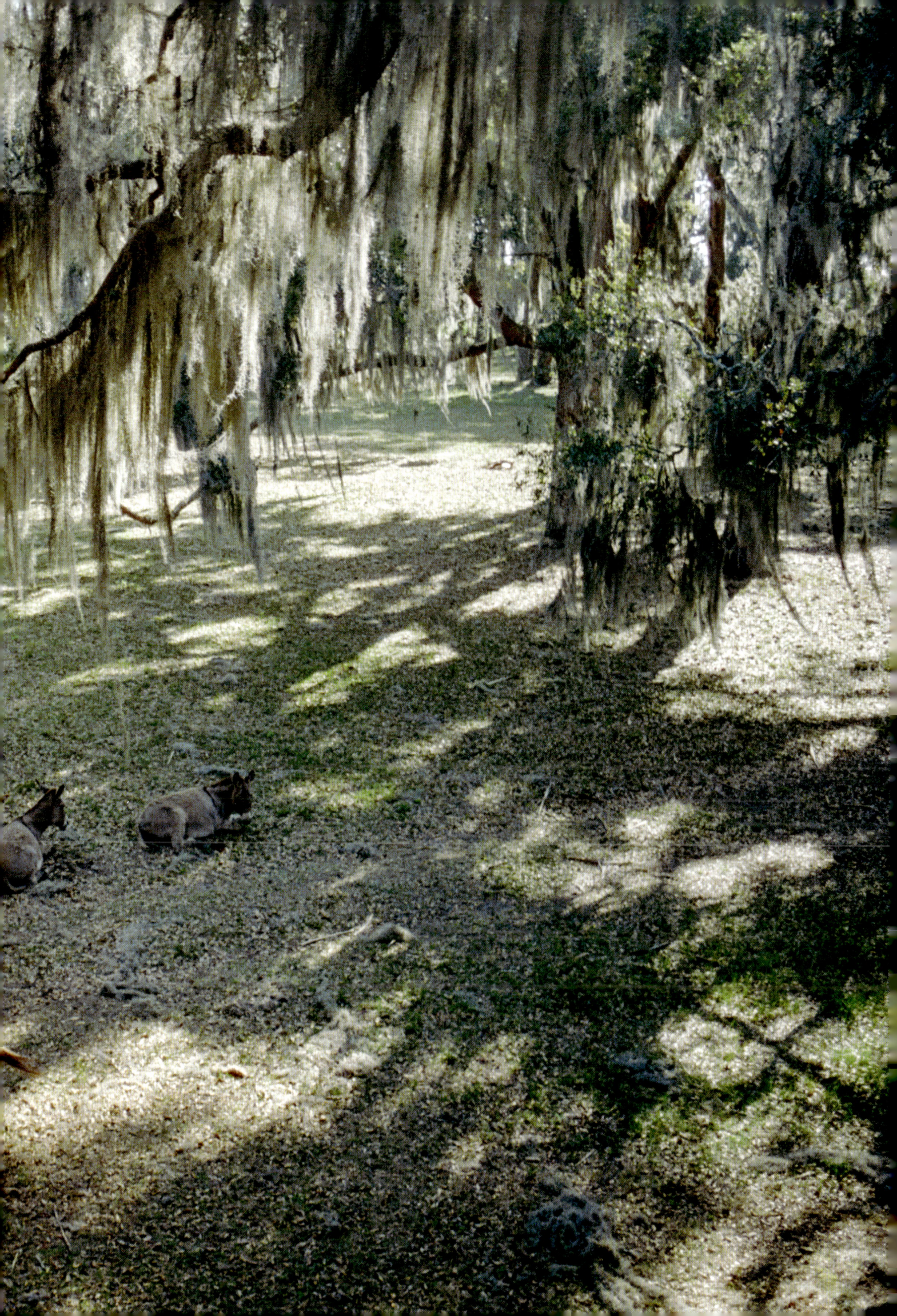

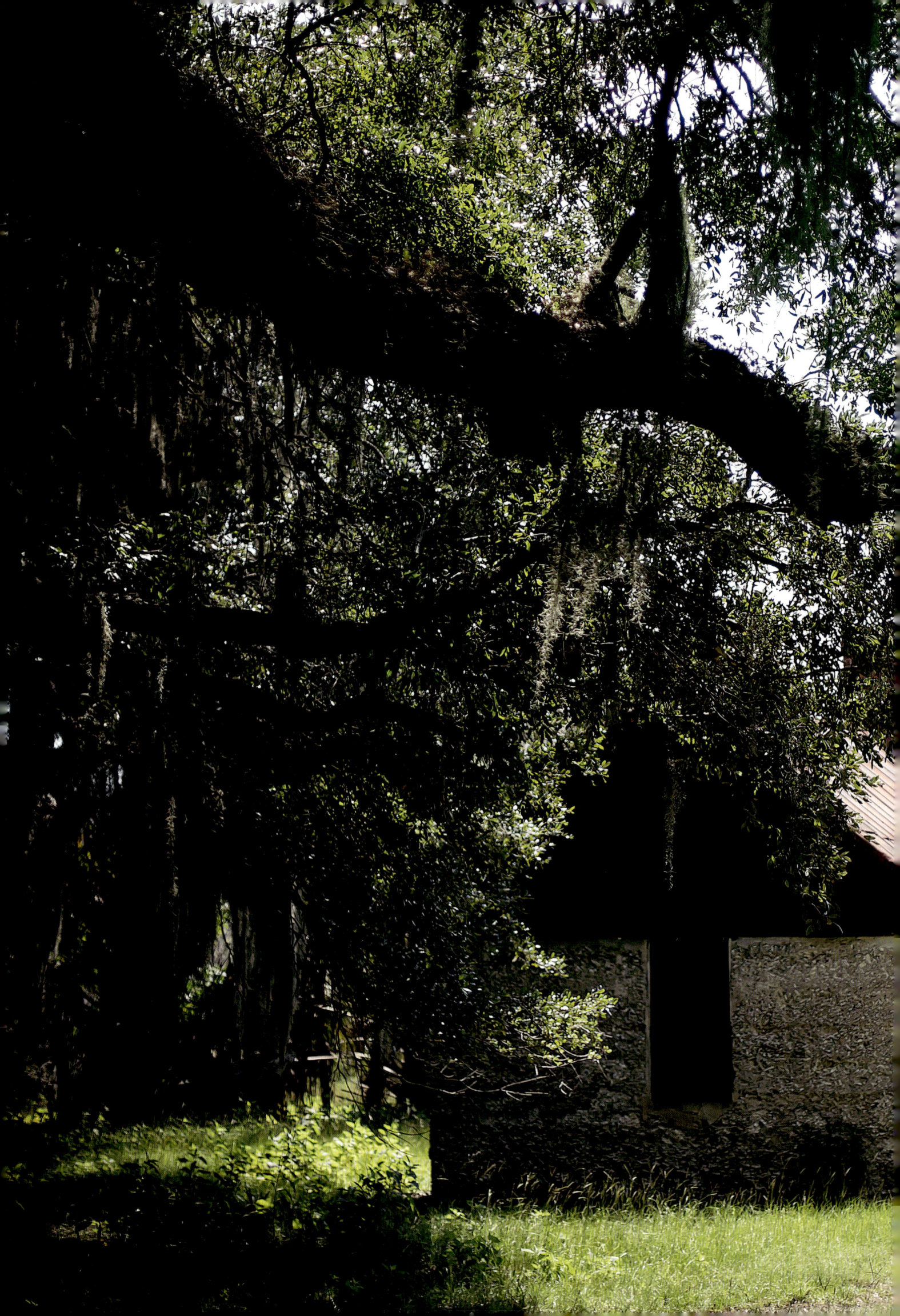

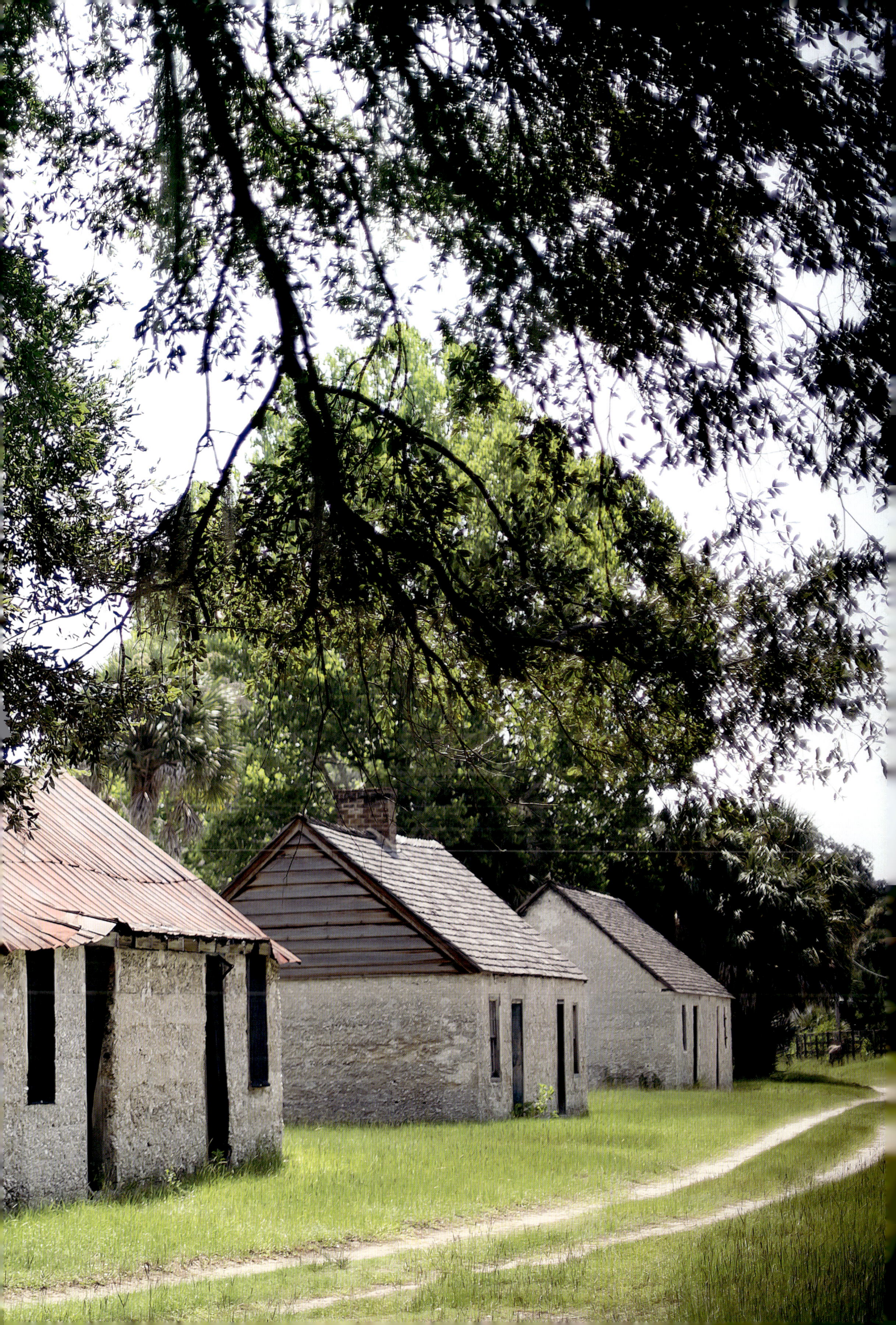

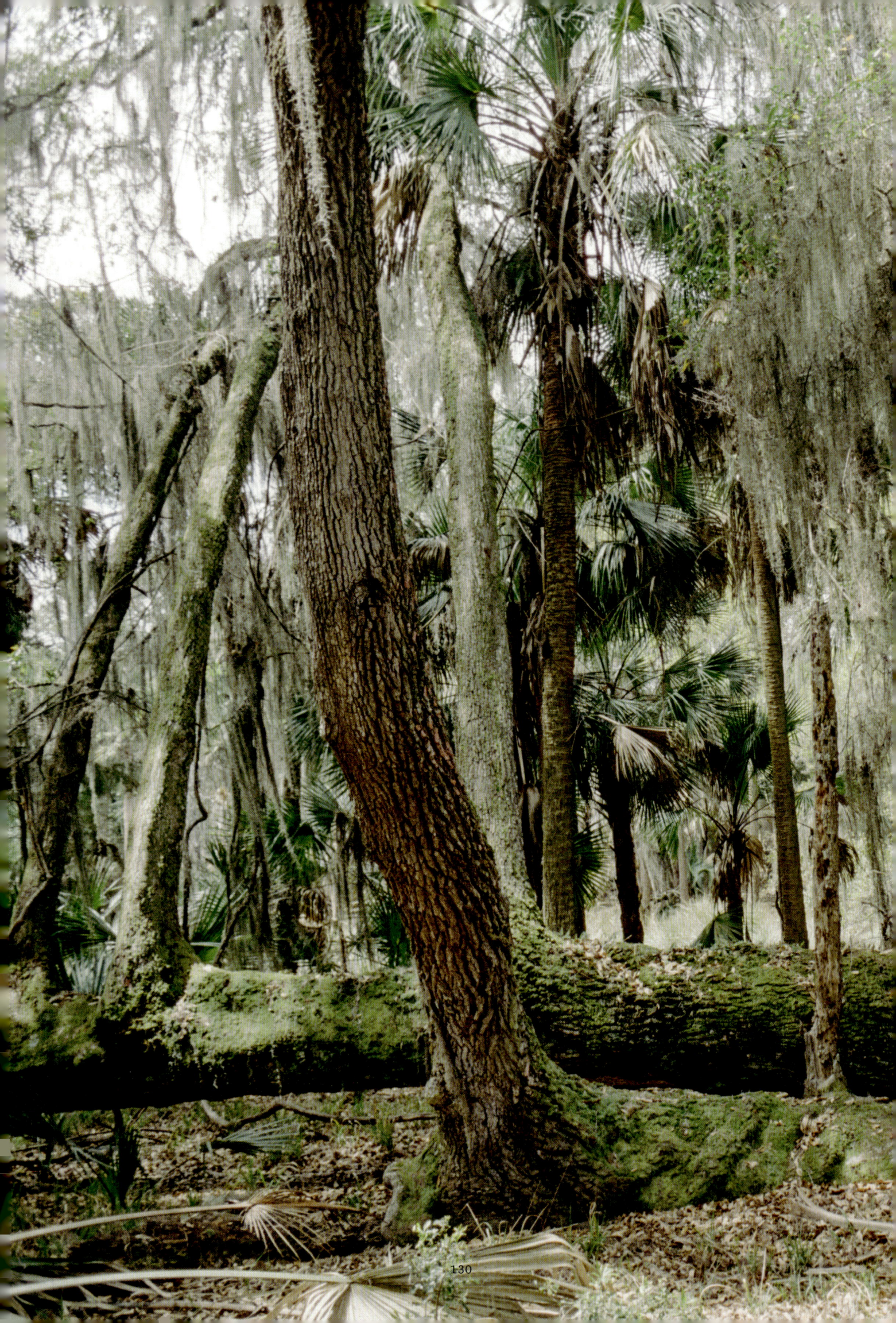

THE PARADOX

Ossabaw's rare beauty and unvarnished wildness cannot be fully experienced without understanding its complex human history. The island has both a rich cultural heritage and a legacy of violence, displacement, and enslavement. Many visual artists engage with this paradox in their work, often considering Ossabaw as a microcosm of the American experience.

ALLISON JANAE HAMILTON (B. 1984)

Allison Janae Hamilton is a New York-based visual artist working in sculpture, installation, photography, and film. She was born in Kentucky, raised in Florida, and her maternal family's farm and homestead lies in the rural flatlands of western Tennessee. Hamilton's relationship with these locations forms the cornerstone of her artwork, particularly her interest in landscape. Using plant matter, layered imagery, complex sounds, and animal remains, Hamilton creates immersive spaces that consider the ways that the American landscape contributes to our ideas of "Americana" and social relationships to space in the face of a changing climate, particularly within the rural American south. Through blending land-centered folklore and personal family narratives, she engages haunting yet epic mythologies that address the social and political concerns of today's changing southern terrain, including land loss, environmental justice, climate change, and sustainability. Each work contains narratives that are pieced together from folktales, hunting and farming rituals, African American nature writing, and Baptist hymns. Hamilton engages with the history of marronage along the Georgia coast in her narrative and atmospheric film *Venus of Ossabaw*, which was commissioned by Telfair Museums for *Off the Coast of Paradise* and primarily filmed on the island in November 2025. Hamilton received her PhD in American studies from New York University and her MFA in visual arts from Columbia University.

pp. 164–65

SALLY MANN (B. 1951)

Sally Mann is one of America's most renowned photographers, known for her photographs of intimate and familiar subjects rendered both sublime and disquieting. Her projects explore the complexities of familial relationships, social realities, and the passage of time, capturing tensions between nature, history, and memory. At a moment when many other photographers were creating large-scale color prints, Mann looked to photography's past, investigating the visual and metaphorical potential of employing 19th-century technologies. She has long used an 8 × 10 in. bellows camera and has explored platinum, bromoil, and wet-plate collodion processes for making prints. Born in Lexington, Virginia, Mann began to study photography in the late 1960s, attending the Ansel Adams Gallery's Yosemite Workshops in Yosemite National Park, California, and the Putney School and Bennington College, both in Vermont. She received a BA in literature in 1974 and an MA in creative writing in 1975, both from Hollins College in Roanoke, Virginia. Mann visited Ossabaw Island in late March 1996 during a four-day trip to Savannah to complete her *Picturing the South* commission for the High Museum of Art, Atlanta.

pp. 138–39

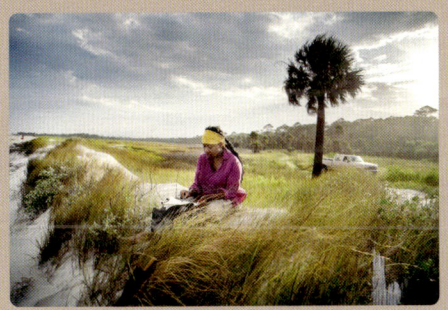

SUZANNE JACKSON (B. 1944)

Suzanne Jackson works experimentally across many media, including drawing, painting, printmaking, bookmaking, poetry, dance, theater, and costume design. In her lyrical work from the 1960s and 1970s, figures and recurring symbols are built up through multiple layers of acrylic wash on canvas. Jackson's recent "environmental abstractions," made with layers of pure acrylic, are partially structured with netting, rods, and paper fragments, and strewn with cast-off color and other elements. Jackson grew up in San Francisco and in the remote natural environment of pre-statehood Alaska, later returning to the Bay Area to study painting and theater at San Francisco State University and dance at the Pacific Ballet. From 1968 to 1970, she worked as an artist and teacher and engaged a community of artist peers through Gallery 32, which she ran from her studio. She received an MFA in theater design in 1990 from Yale University in New Haven, Connecticut, and lives and works between Savannah, Georgia and St. Remy, New York. Jackson spent ten days on Ossabaw Island in 2010 as part of The Ossabaw Island Foundation's Visiting Artists Program.

pp. 135–37

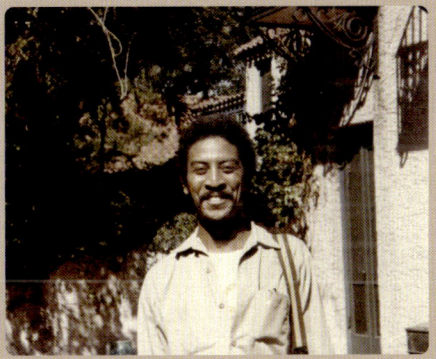

TYRONE MITCHELL (B. 1944)

Tyrone Mitchell is an abstract sculptor who works primarily with wood and metal, marrying the spirituality imbued in ritual objects such as those made by the Dogon people of Mali and the Yoruba people of Nigeria with contemporary notions of artmaking. Mitchell evokes his ideas and personal experiences in his sculpture through his thoughtful use of materials—incorporating found objects, applied stains, industrial paint, metal sheets, and fabrics into his works. In the words of curator Beryl J. Wright, "the challenge for Mitchell has been to find forms that encapsulate his belief that contemporary art can be psychically revelatory and healing." Born in Savannah, Georgia, Mitchell received the equivalent of a BFA in 1965 from the Art Students League of New York and the equivalent of an MFA from the New York Studio School in 1967. He attended the Ossabaw Island Project from October 10–27, 1980, during which time he collected objects from the landscape that later became part of his *Sea Island Recollections* series.

p. 141

T. J. REDDY (1945–2019)

T. J. Reddy was an artist, poet, musician, and civil rights activ-
ist whose interests were rooted in nature, education, and human
ecology. While he began investigating these ideas in the late 1960s,
they took on a deeper meaning in the 1970s. "As I began exploring,
it became obvious to me that human beings are part and parcel of
a much larger dimension of life," he explained. During this time, he
began creating socially-minded, mixed-media paintings that incorporated found objects—such as *From the Window of the Tower House,
Middle Place, Ossabaw Island, GA* (1981)—and he published two collections of poetry, *Less than a score, but a point* (1974) and *Poems in
One-part Harmony* (1979). Everything that he produced connected
back to those who came before him. "I am a being whose connection
is associated with my ancestry—an African origin," he explained.
"My Blackness, my African-ness, my color is infused in every pore
of my being. The source of the art comes from me." Reddy was born
in Savannah, Georgia, and received a BA in history and sociology
in 1974 and an MA in education in 1977, both from the University
of North Carolina, Charlotte. Reddy went to Ossabaw Island as a
Genesis member in 1981.

pp. 142–43

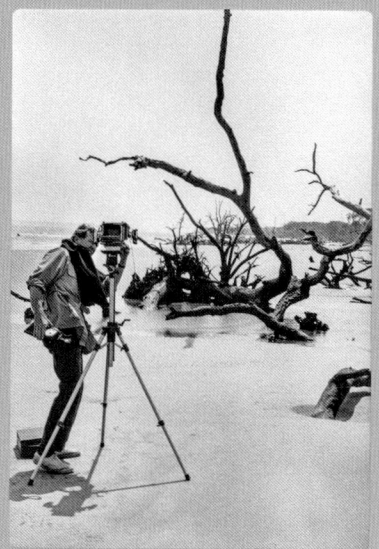

CLIFFORD B. WEST (1916–2006)

Clifford B. West was a filmmaker, painter, muralist, designer, photographer, and teacher whose seventy-year career encompassed a wide
range of styles, mediums, and points of entry. Born in Cleveland,
Ohio, he received a BA from Adams State College in Colorado and
a MFA from the Cranbrook Academy of Art in Bloomfield Hills,
Michigan, where he remained closely connected for many years as a
teacher. West co-founded the Ossabaw Island Project with his second
wife, Eleanor Torrey West, in 1961, and began exploring the use of
a 16mm camera around the same time, primarily on the island. This
was the beginning of a quarter-century career as an independent documentary filmmaker. The topics of his more than thirty films range
from contemporary artists such as Harry Bertoia, Arnold Blanch,
Carl Milles, Rolf Nesch, and Tex Schiwetz, to Italian Renaissance
sculptors and architects, to the legendary Norwegian artist Edvard
Munch. He made several films about Ossabaw, including *The Ossabaw
Island Project* (1962), *Synthesis: Travis, Tiger, and Wild Boars* (1962),
Time Form Color (1962), *Untitled Film: A Search for Ecological
Balance...* (c. 1970), and *"Give and Take": A Story Of One Way To
Preserve And Use This Diminishing Earth* (1974). Beginning in the mid-
1980s and through the end of his life, West was closely associated
with the AVA Gallery and Art Center in Lebanon, New Hampshire,
where he was a senior member of the faculty.

p. 146

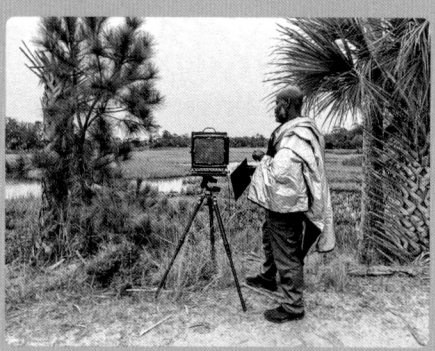

RASHOD TAYLOR (B. 1985)

Rashod Taylor is a photographer who explores themes of family,
intimacy, legacy, and the Black experience. Born and raised in
Bloomington, Illinois, Taylor resides in the Midwest, and his son
LJ is one of his most frequent subjects, especially in his long-form
series *Little Black Boy*, which won the 2021 Arnold Newman Prize for
New Directions in Photographic Portraiture. His current series, *My
America*, considers the weight of history on the contemporary Black
experience in the United States. Using a historic photographic process known as wet collodion, which requires a large-format camera
and portable darkroom, Taylor creates tintypes of landscapes with
racially charged histories, such as Ossabaw Island, which he visited
in February 2024.

pp. 144–45

ELEANOR TORREY WEST (1913–2021)

Eleanor Torrey West, known as Sandy, was an environmental preservationist, philanthropist, writer, and artist best known as the matriarch of Ossabaw Island. The great-granddaughter of the indus-
trialist Captain John Baptiste Ford, West grew up between Grosse
Pointe Shores, Michigan, and Savannah, Georgia. In 1924, her parents purchased Ossabaw Island as their winter estate, and the island
became the great love of her life. With her second husband, Clifford
West, Sandy co-founded the Ossabaw Island Project in 1961, followed by the Genesis, Public Use and Education, and Professional
Research programs. West was instrumental in facilitating the State
of Georgia's acquisition of the island in 1978 as its first Heritage
Preserve. She wrote and narrated many of her husband's documentary films, including *Untitled Film: A Search for Ecological Balance...*
(c. 1970) and *"Give and Take": A Story Of One Way To Preserve And
Use This Diminishing Earth* (1974), which focused on the preservation
of Georgia's coastline. West published the children's book *Maria
Bosomworth and William Rodgers* in 1976 and the memoir *The God of
the Hinge: Adventures in Cloud Cuckoo Land* with Elizabeth Pool in
2006. West also painted casually, capturing Ossabaw's historic buildings in her expressive watercolors.

p. 147

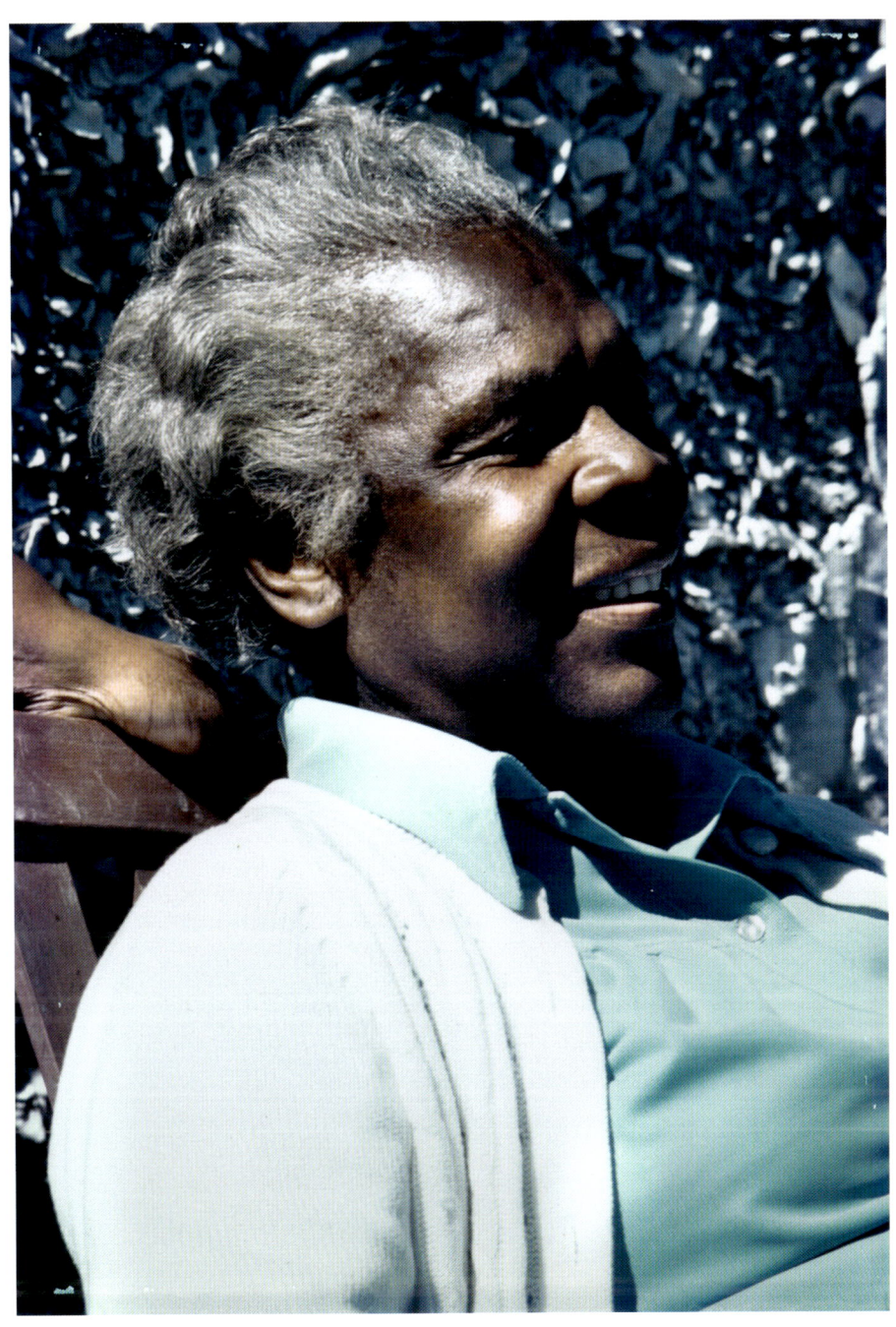

John Earl (1921–2008)
Untitled (Portrait of Queenie Williams), c. 1982
C-print
13 ½ × 9 ⅛ in.
Collection of Justin P. West and Eileen McGowan

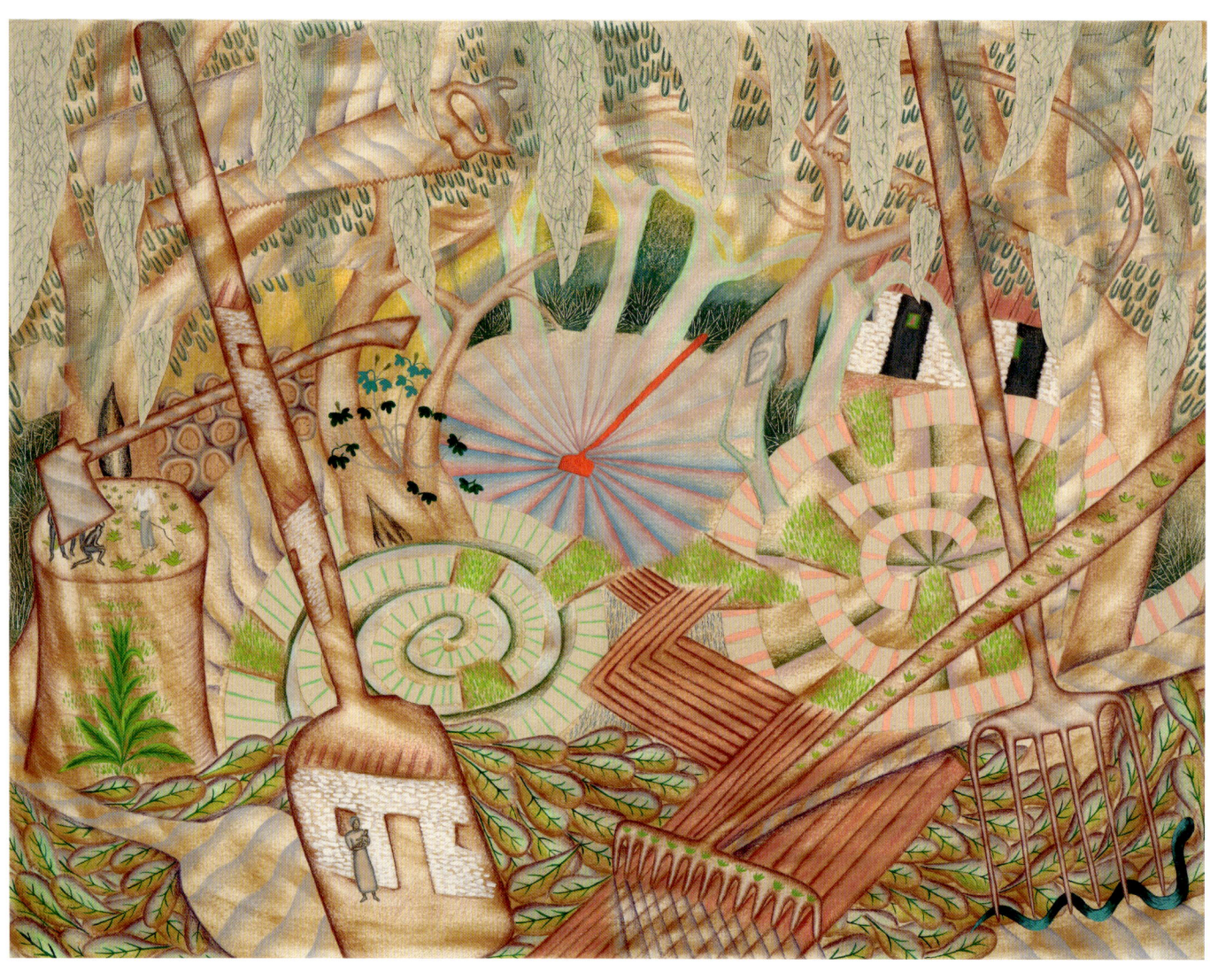

Marcy Hermansader (b. 1951)
The Magic Hoe, 1982
Colored pencil, acrylic, paper collage, mosquito netting,
and thread on paper rubbed with red clay soil
21 ¾ × 28 ½ in.
Collection of the artist

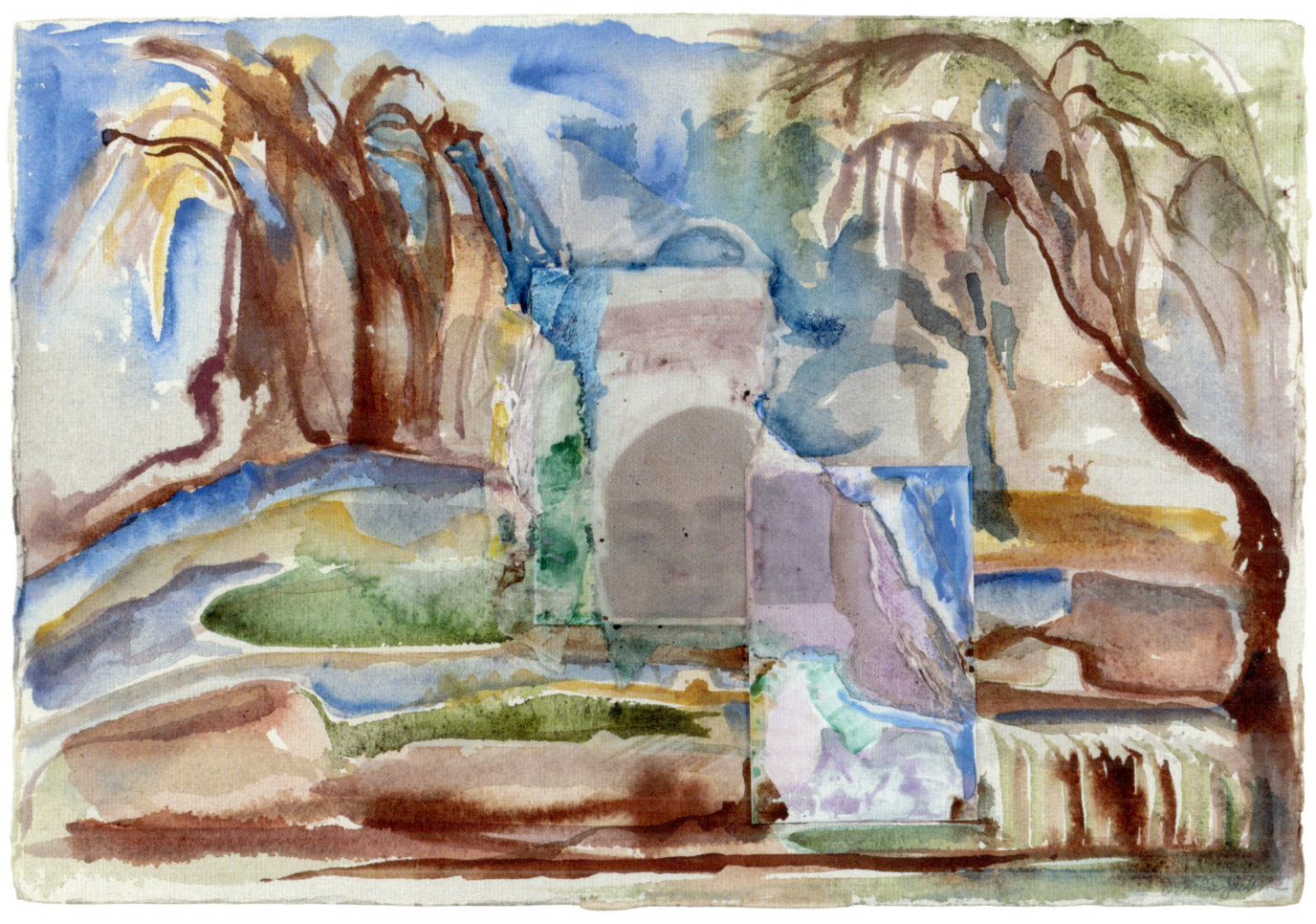

Suzanne Jackson (b. 1944)
Origins, 2010
Watercolor, acrylic on inkjet photo-paper, nylon,
D'Arches 300 lb. paper
15 × 22 in.
Martin and Rebecca Eisenberg

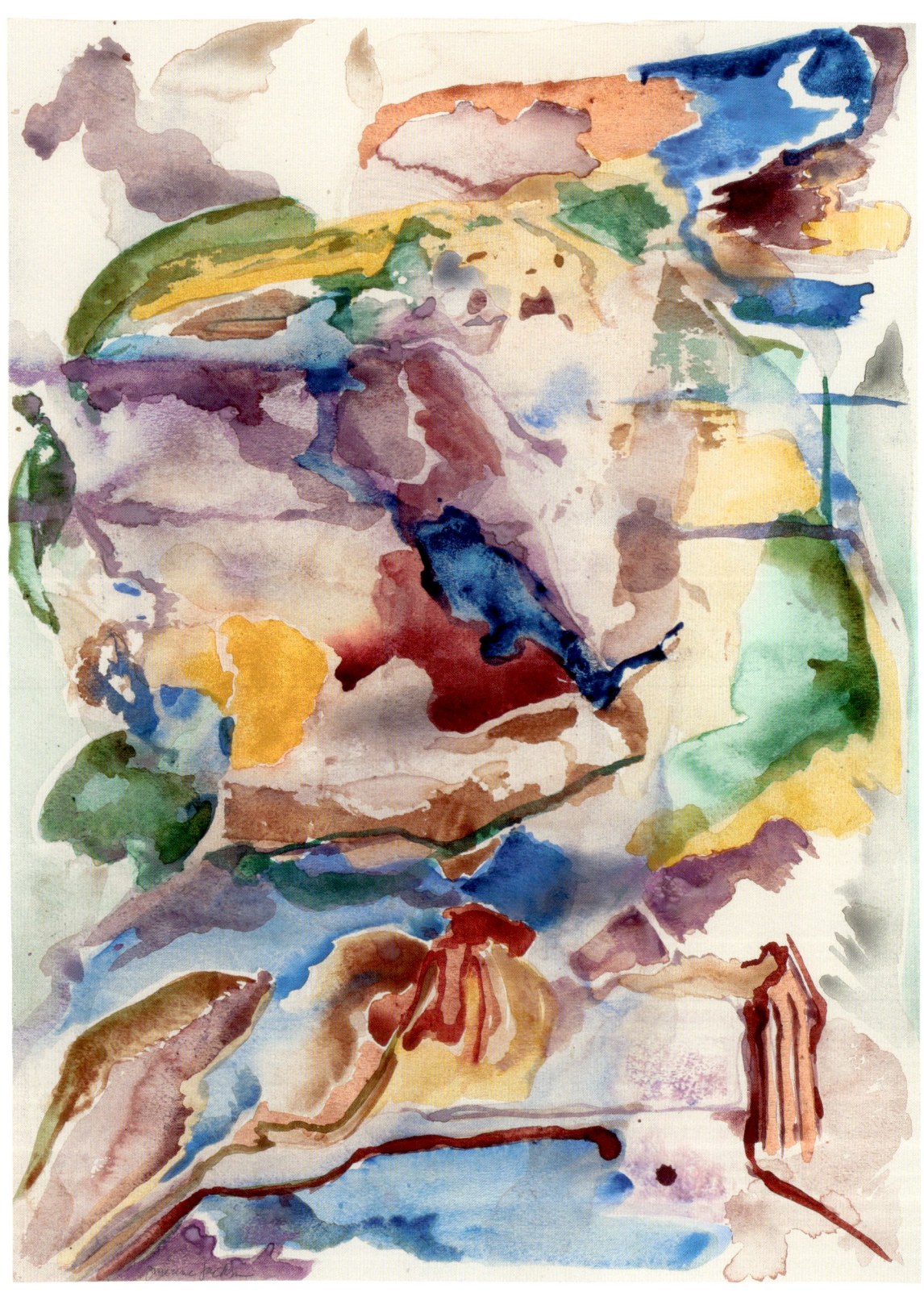

Suzanne Jackson (b. 1944)
a little path to paradise, 2010
Watercolor on Strathmore paper
24 × 18 in.
Martin and Rebecca Eisenberg

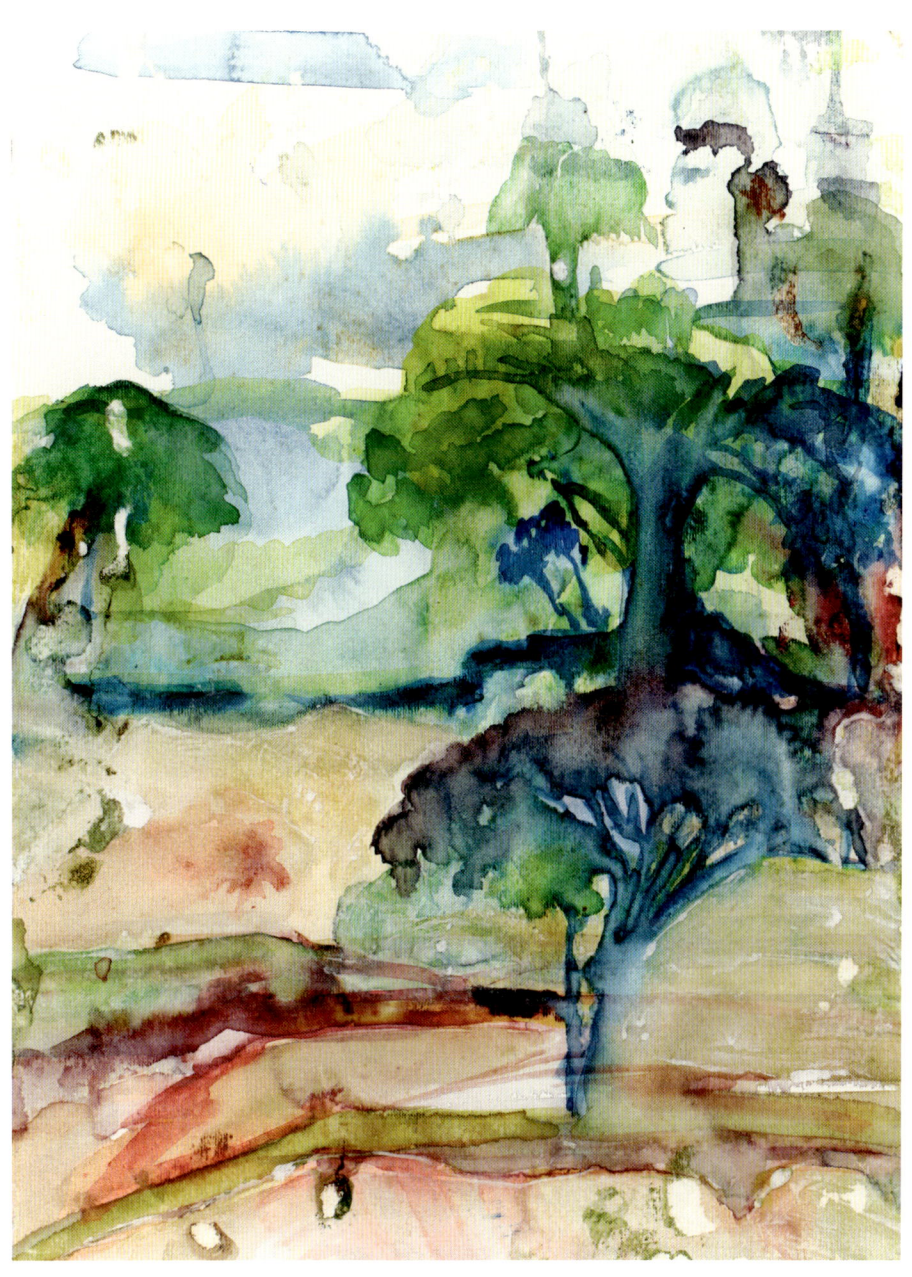

Suzanne Jackson (b. 1944)
Ossabaw Meadow, 2010
Acrylic wash on paper
15 × 11 in.
Courtesy of the artist and Ortuzar, New York

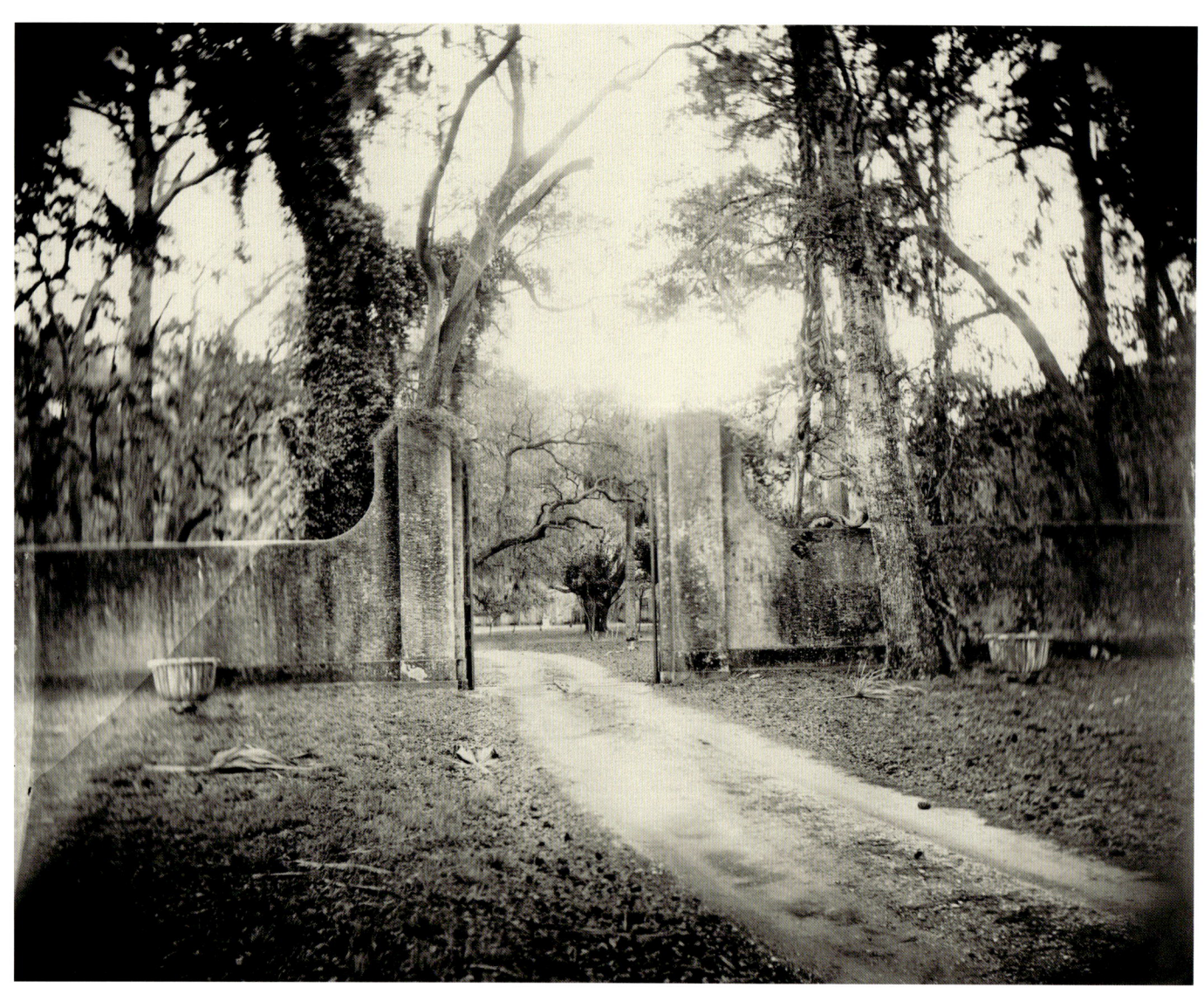

Sally Mann (b. 1951)
Georgia, Untitled (Ossabaw Gates), 1996
Gelatin silver print
40 × 50 in.
Telfair Museums, museum purchase

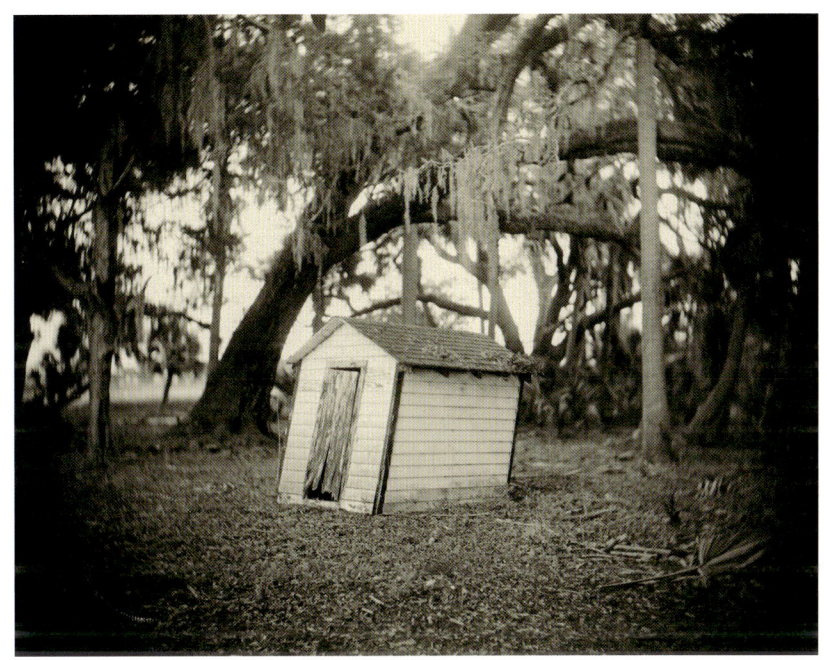

Sally Mann (b. 1951)
Untitled, 1996
Gelatin silver print
7 ¾ × 10 in.
Private collection

Tyrone Mitchell (b. 1944)
Buzzard's Vine, 1983
Wood, aluminum, and pigment
9 × 9 × 26 in.
Courtesy of Alitash Kebede Arts, Los Angeles, CA

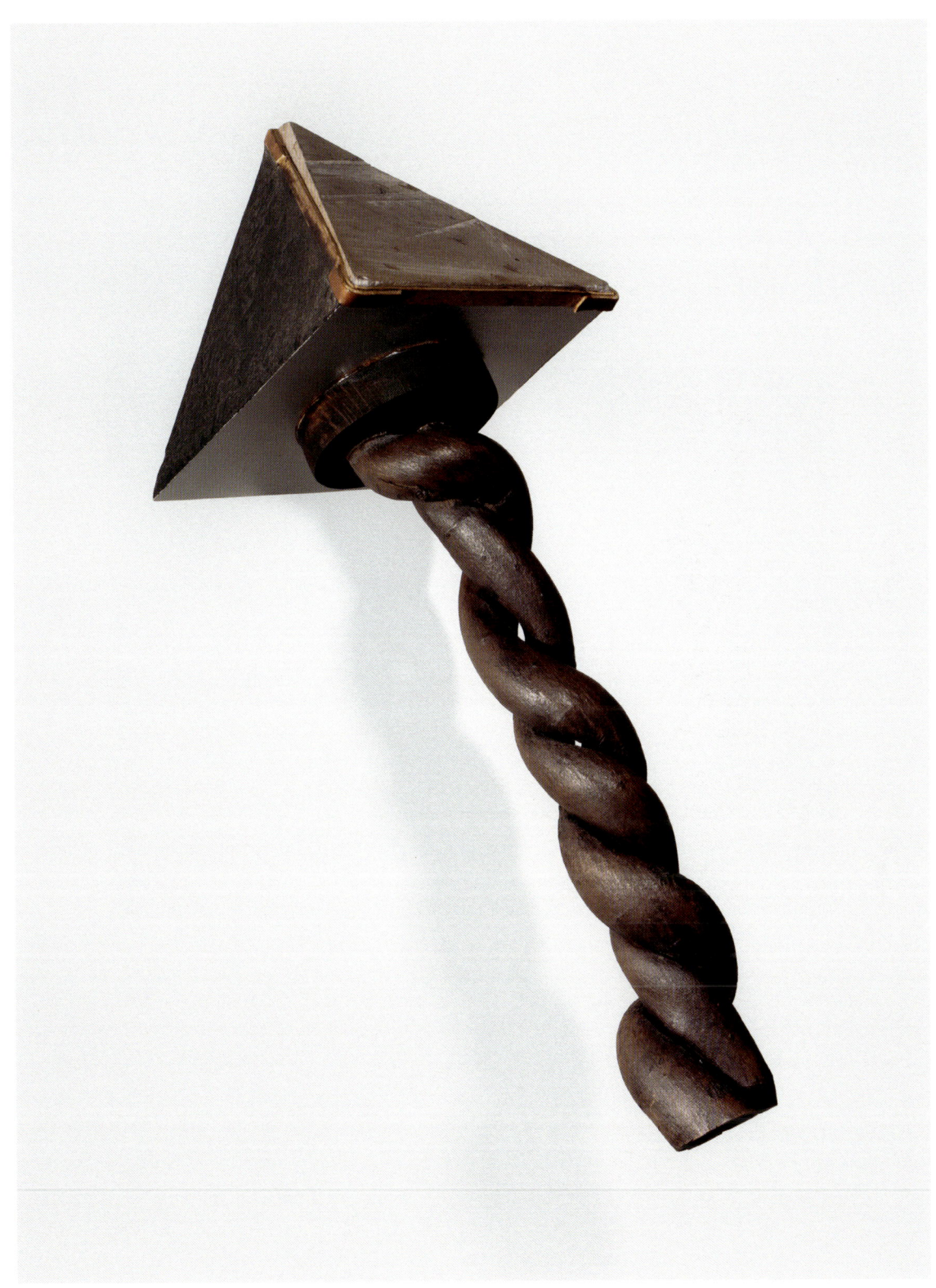

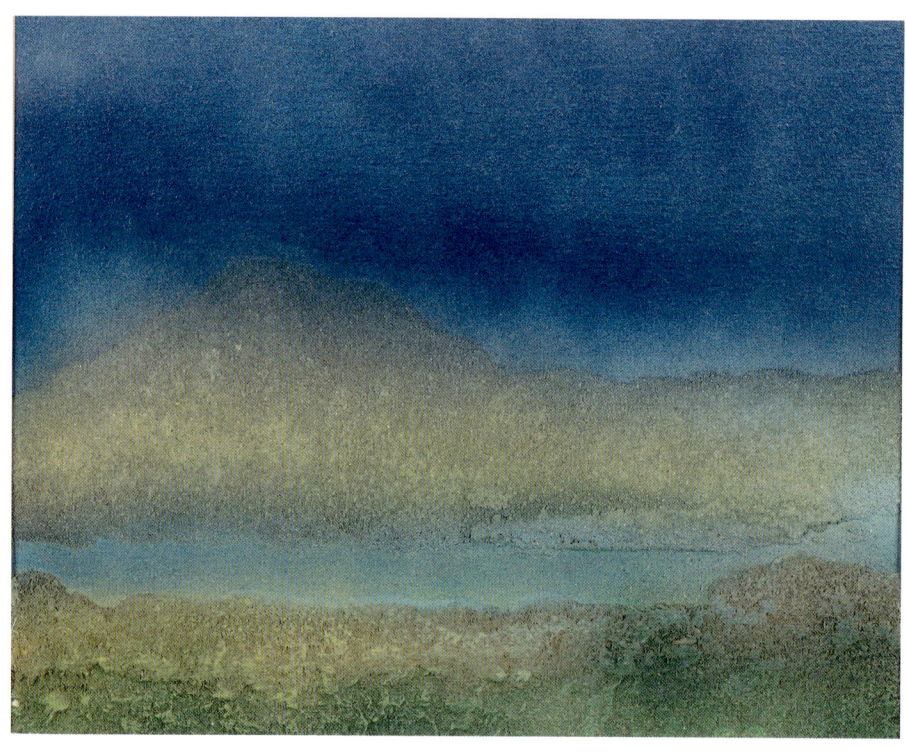

T. J. Reddy (1945–2019)
From the Window of the Tower House, Middle Place,
Ossabaw Island, GA, 1981
Sawdust, sand, modeling paste, and oil on panel
7 ⅜ × 9 ½ in.
Collection of the University of North
Carolina at Charlotte

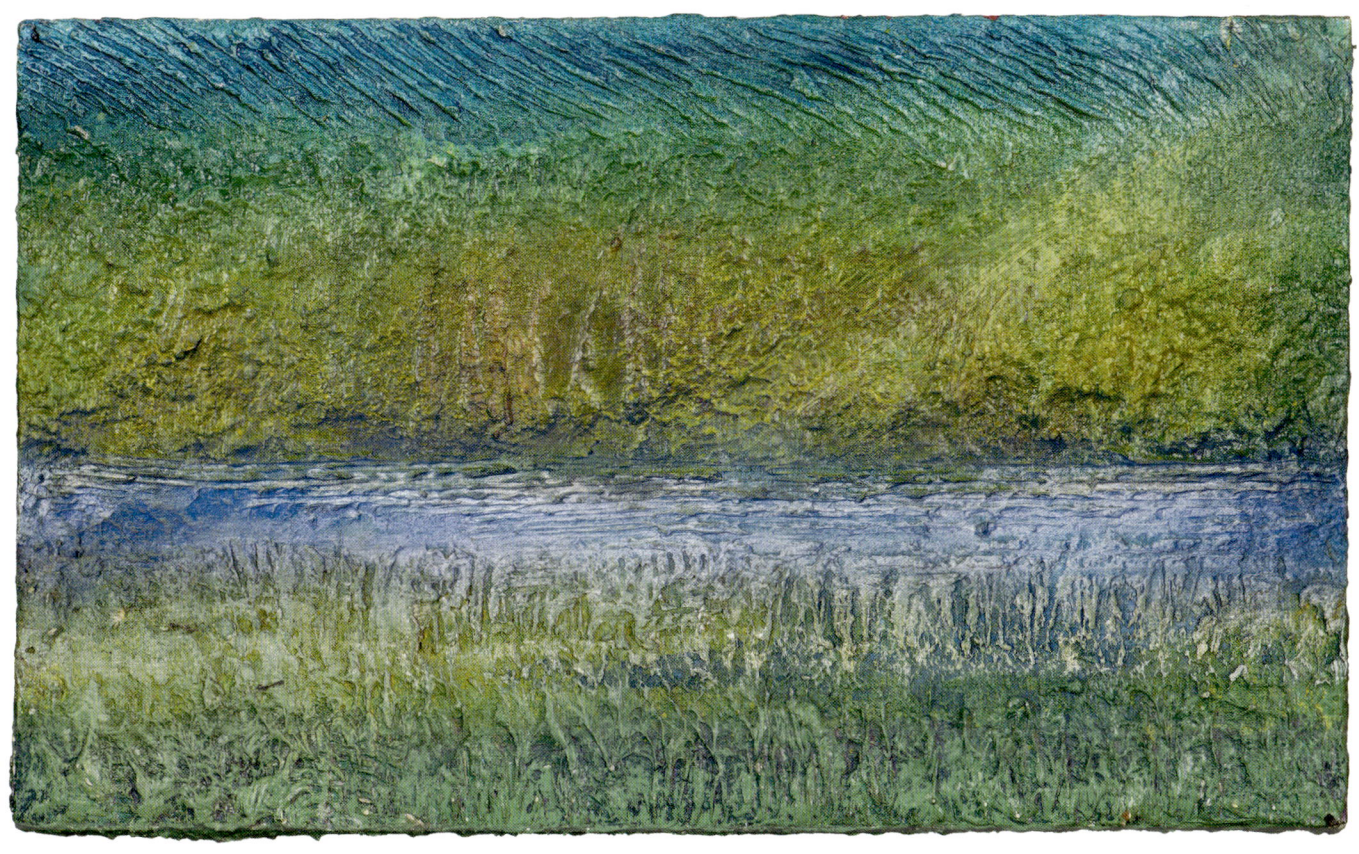

T. J. Reddy (1945–2019)
Scenes for the Maroon, 2011
Acrylic and mixed media on paper
12 × 20 in.
Private collection

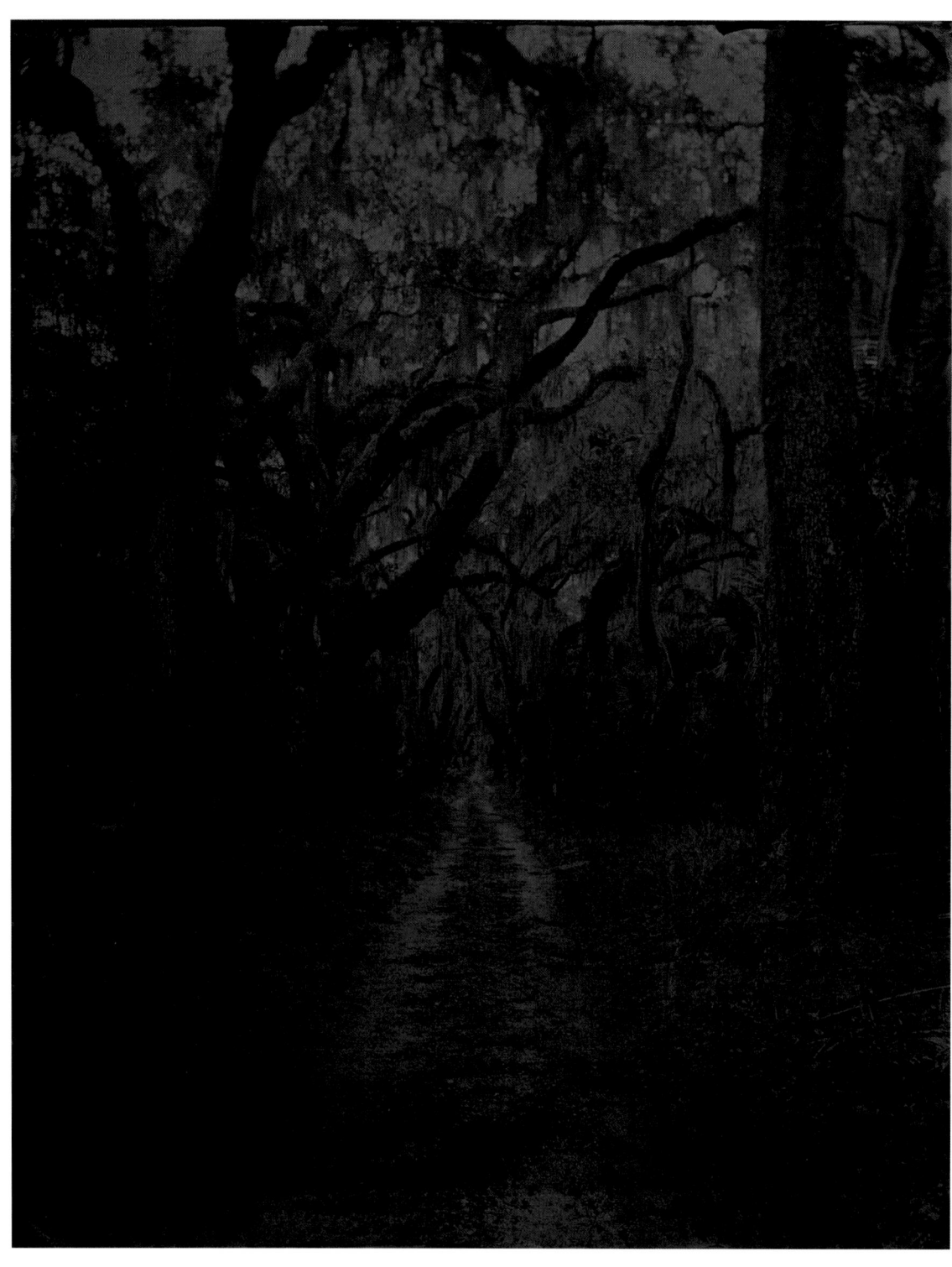

Rashod Taylor (b. 1985)
Road to the South, Ossabaw Island, GA, 2024
Tintype
10 × 8 in.
Library of Congress, Prints & Photographs
Division, LC-DIG-ppmsca-98419

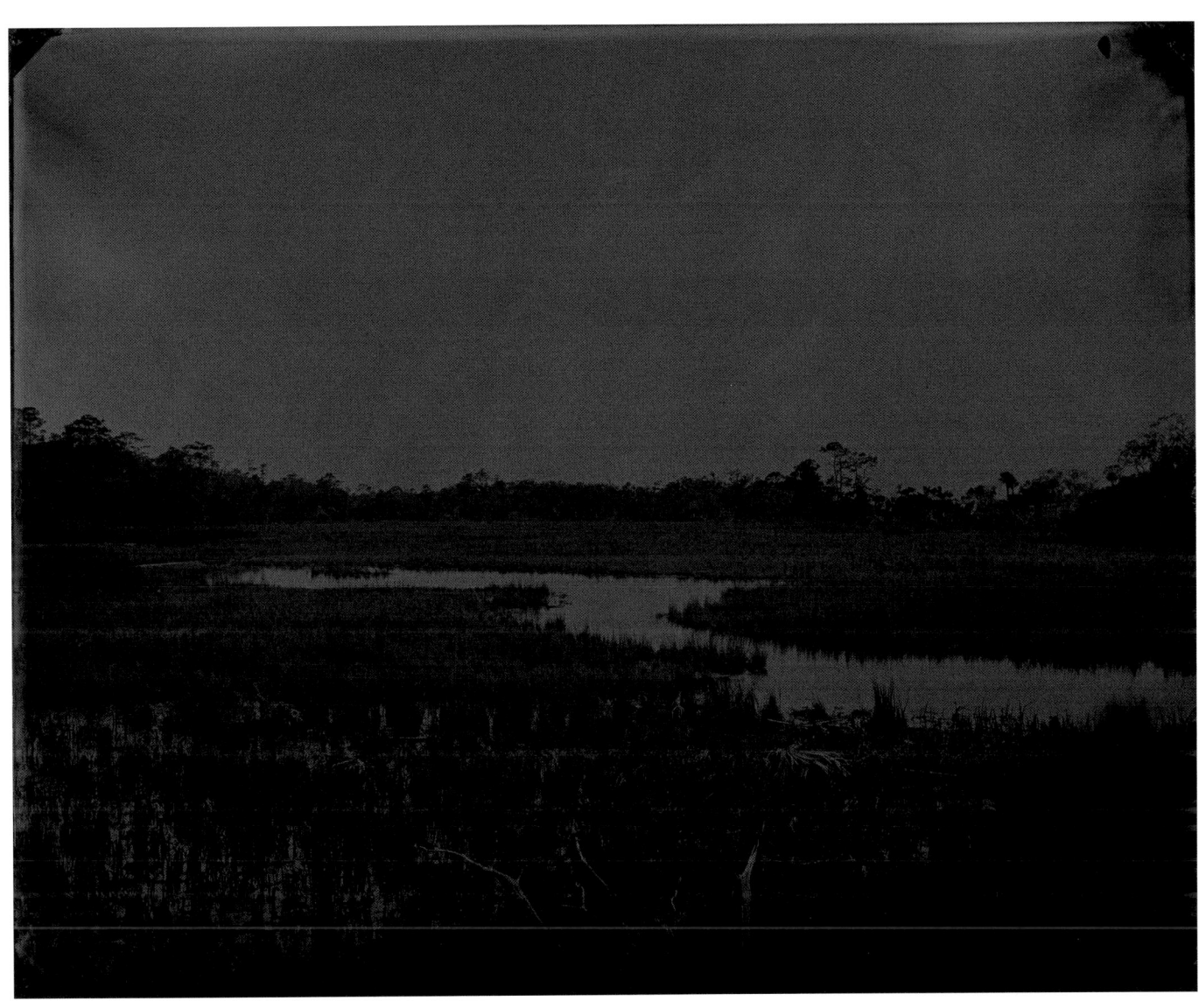

Rashod Taylor (b. 1985)
Marsh Land, Ossabaw Island, GA, 2024
Tintype
8 × 10 in.
Library of Congress, Prints & Photographs
Division, LC-DIG-ppmsca-98421

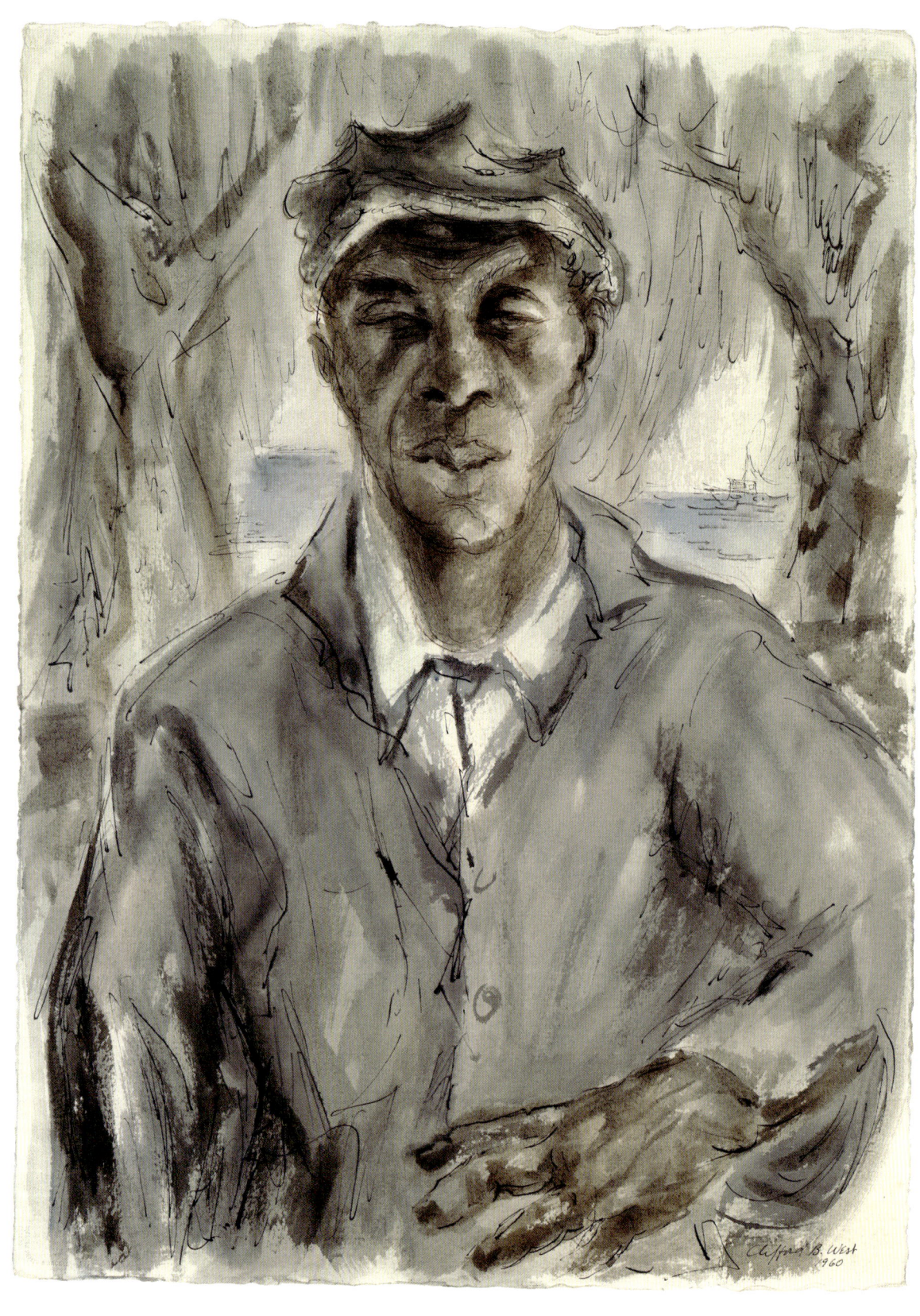

Clifford B. West (1916–2006)
Untitled (Portrait of Cyrus Martin Sr.), 1961
Watercolor and ink on paper
29 ½ × 22 in.
Collection of Justin P. West and Eileen McGowan

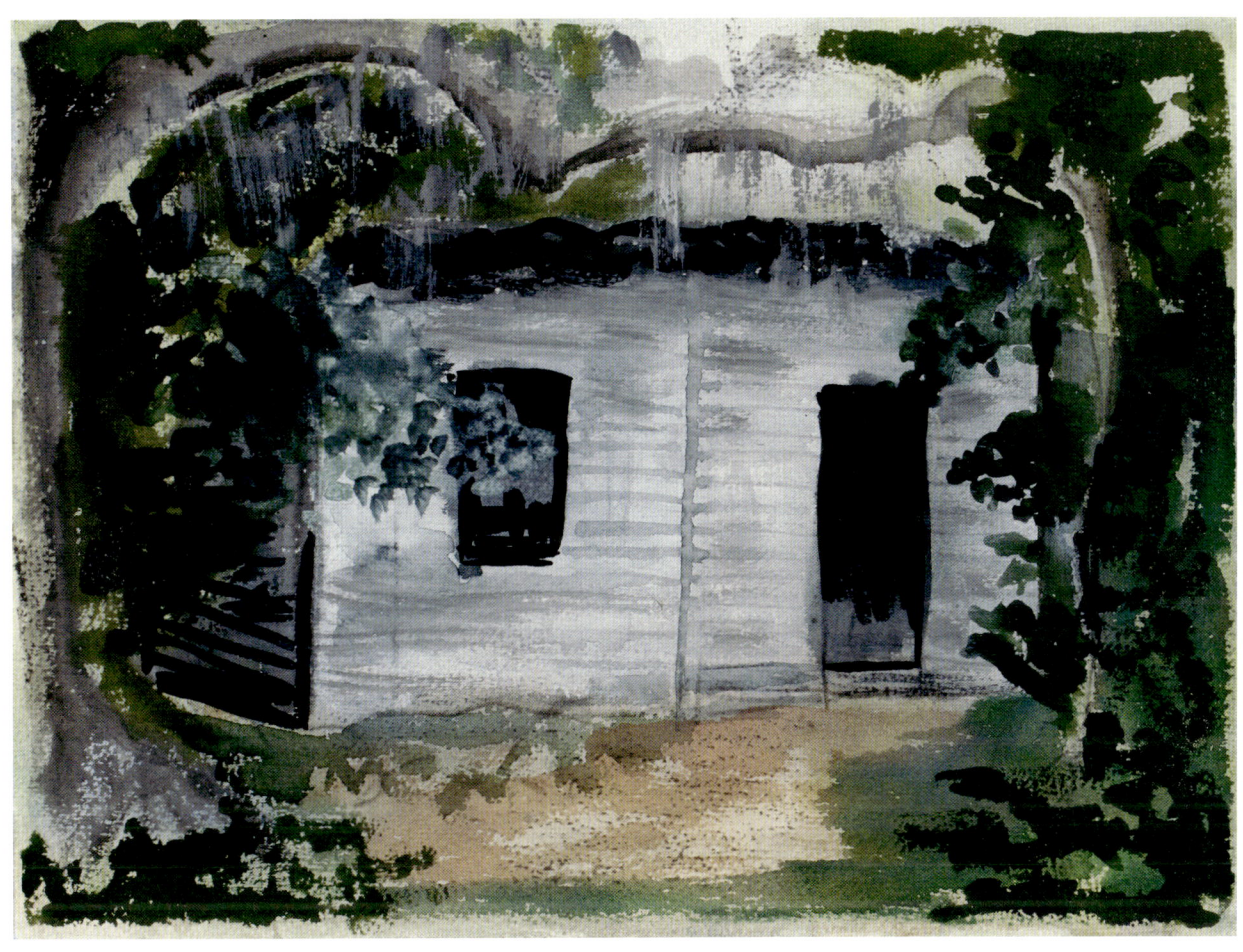

Eleanor Torrey West (1913–2021)
Untitled (Par Tank House), c. 1979
Watercolor on paper
10 ¼ × 14 ³⁄₁₆ in.
The Ossabaw Island Foundation

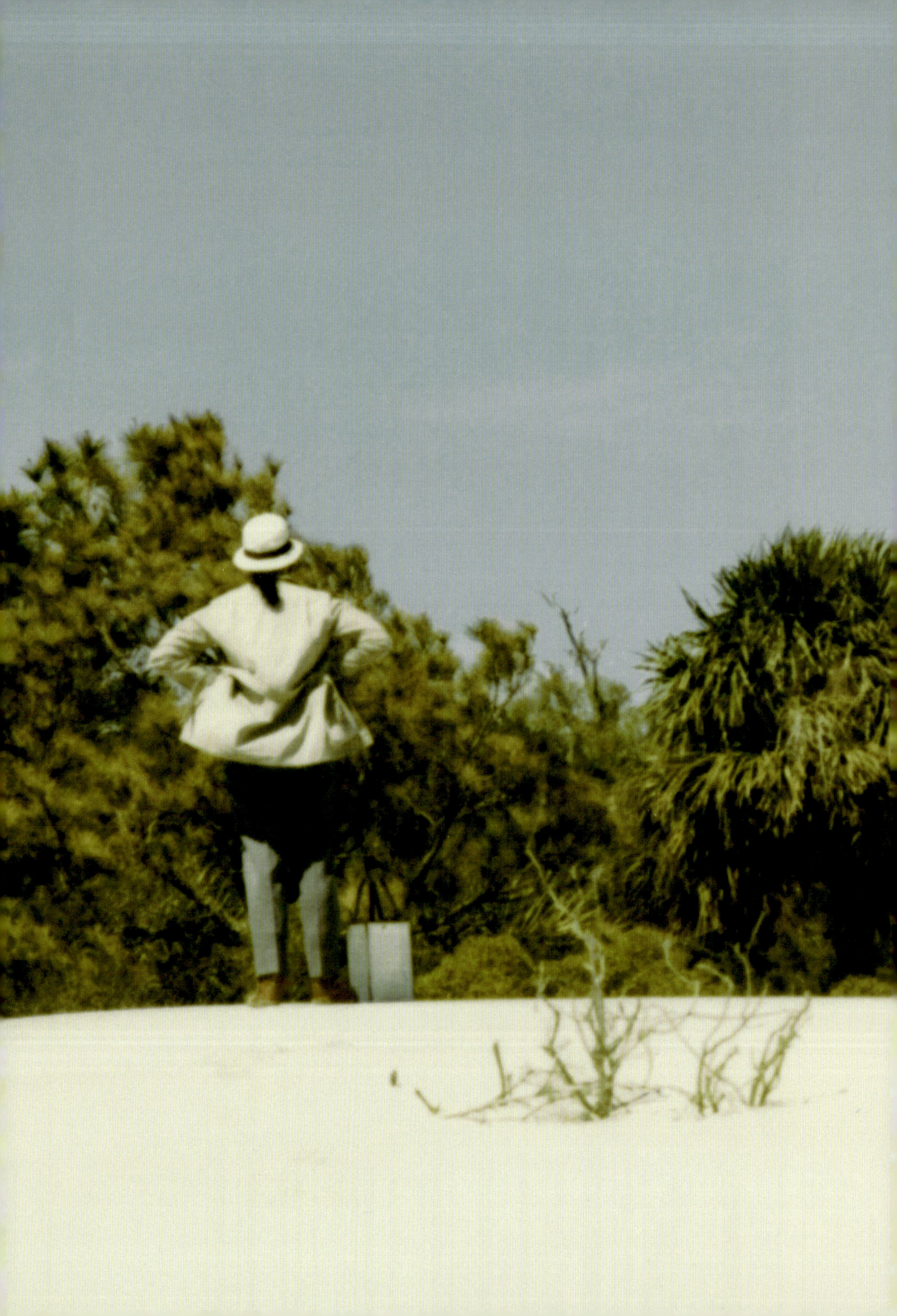

EACH FAMILY SHALL HAVE A PLOT

THOMAS LAX

THE PRESENCE OF BLACK

In just over three minutes, Linda Goode Bryant's 2022 essay film *The Presence of Black* [(fig. 1)] interweaves three centuries of Black space, deftly linking the Sea Islands to the Midwest and New York City.[1] The concise video juxtaposes black-and-white archival footage of Just Above Midtown—the art gallery and self-described laboratory for Black art that Goode Bryant started in midtown Manhattan in 1974—with still photographs of young farmers at Project EATS, the small-plot, high-yield urban farms in Black and Brown neighborhoods across New York City she founded in 2009. By intersplicing across time, the video implicitly knits one claim to Black space with another, the capacity to make art with the capacity to feed oneself.

The silent video is captioned by a letter Linda received from Zula Foster Goode [(fig. 2)], her paternal grandmother; Grandma Goode penned it at age 79 in the months leading up to her death. She wrote—and the film then relays—the following missive:

> I am among the first generation after slavery...My father bought land at 10
> and 15 dollars an acre. He bought a slaveowner's home. It was plenished
> with orchards and vegetation...They made deep trenches, and we came
> from a long, long ways. We are still finding new way and means. Means to
> *will* our ancestors the light, the right, the way to make a life worthwhile.

The text underscores our unfinished relationship to those who precede us; the essential connection between practicing freedom and nourishing ourselves; and the unexpected way that a slaveowner's house can be transformed into a source of plenishment by the descendants of enslaved people. By pairing this letter with a documentation of David Hammons lighting candles directly in front of the projected image of an ocean's waves and young Black and Brown farmers digging, harvesting, and eating fresh produce, Goode Bryant links the untold creative drive of her community over the past fifty years with her family's history of land use and the building of a subsistence economy.

The Presence of Black ends with a dedication to Grandma Goode, who was born in South Carolina to a Gullah Geechee-identified family. In an interview, Goode Bryant

Fanny Ellison on the beach at Ossabaw, 1971 (detail). Photograph by Ralph Ellison

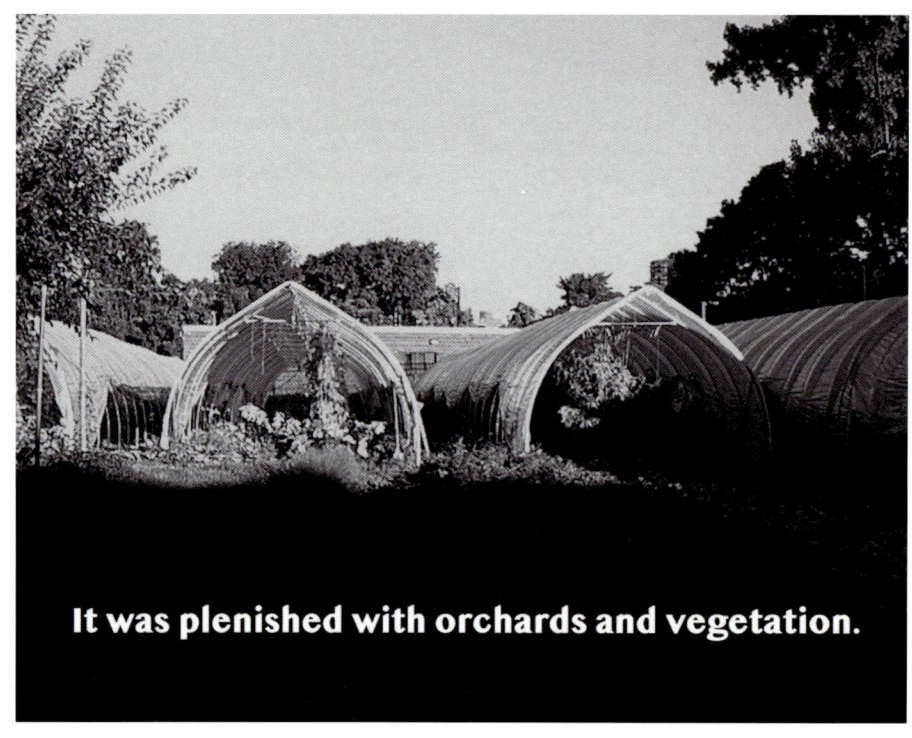

fig. 1.   Film still from Linda Goode Bryant, *The Presence of Black*, 2022

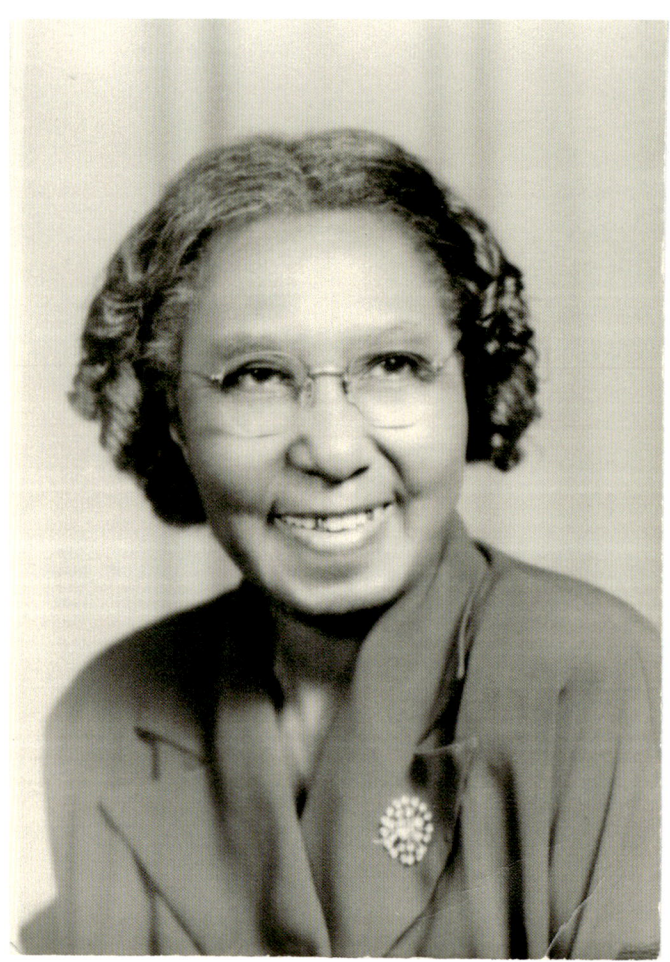

fig. 2.   Zula Foster Goode, Linda Goode Bryant's paternal grandmother

described one of her earliest memories of her grandmother, an experience that made her want to become an artist:

> I noticed she had a tendency to go downstairs into the kitchen early in the morning. One morning I heard her get out of bed and go downstairs, and I decided to go downstairs too. I followed her and attempted to open the door. It was locked, and I hadn't remembered it ever being closed. Then I heard this noise that sounded like sand being thrown against the wall. I lay down on my stomach and looked under the door. I could see what looked like a white pit of salt, and I could smell vinegar. I called 'Grandma Goode, let me in, let me in.' But she wouldn't. She was singing. I understood that there was some magic going on behind that door and I wanted to be part of it.[2]

Behind the closed door, peering under its crack, Goode Bryant imagines how Grandma Goode transformed basic cooking ingredients into a concoction—a skill she brought with her to Ohio from the South Carolina coast. In so doing, Grandma Goode not only alchemized the materials she had readily available to her, but in the process, transposed a model for an autonomous Black space into a new location. In this space, Black was not simply "the absence of white" but "the presence of Black," Goode Bryant tells us in the opening lines of her film. Could this motto for her ancestral home and, later her gallery, which displayed the work of artists of African descent alongside their counterparts of all racial backgrounds, be used as a motto for integrated spaces of other kinds?

RESERVED AND SET APART

Goode Bryant is one of many contemporary artists who has turned to the hundred-plus islands that stretch 300 miles across the coast of what is now South Carolina, Georgia, and Florida in the Southeastern U.S. What is it about the Lowcountry that has made it at once a testing ground and zone of contestation for the idea of Black autonomy? How have Black folks negotiated their relation to white landowners both in the wake of the promises of emancipation and since the beginning of the civil rights era? How have artists in particular reimagined their relationship to this dispossessed place?

In her essay, "Visible Roots and Visual Routes," art historian Lisa Gail Collins analyzes how artists across media have looked to the tidal and barrier island reef "for evidence of a cultural past" and, in so doing, have "illuminate[d] oppositional meanings and values."[3] Her essay describes the contributions of African American and white European artists in the 20th century, including Leigh Richmond Miner, Winold Reiss, Doris Ulmann, Eldzier Cortor, Jeanne Moutoussamy-Ashe, Carrie Mae Weems, Beverly Buchanan, and Martha Jackson Jarvis. By training her eye on the study of African "retentions" in the United States, Collins analyzes how the dialectic of loss and invention are expressed visually. This includes contemporary conflicts over land ownership on Hilton Head Island, or more recently, at Hog Hammock on Sapelo Island, as residents have been forcibly removed from places they have lived for generations to make room for condos, resorts, golf courses, and private gated communities. Ultimately, Collins concludes that artists who have made work on the Sea Islands have looked to the past to "offer resources for the future."[4]

Ossabaw Island's 26,000 acres, located midway through the archipelago, have been a destination for artists since the early 1960s, including Tyrone Mitchell, Suzanne Jackson, and Ralph Ellison, who are discussed in this essay and included in the exhibition accompanying this catalogue. Ossabaw is located approximately twenty miles south of Savannah. In Muscogee, the word translates into "land of holly" or "holly bush growing place" and refers specifically to yaupon holly, the green shrubs that grow red berries across the island and have been used to make the tea-like caffeinated beverage Black Drink.

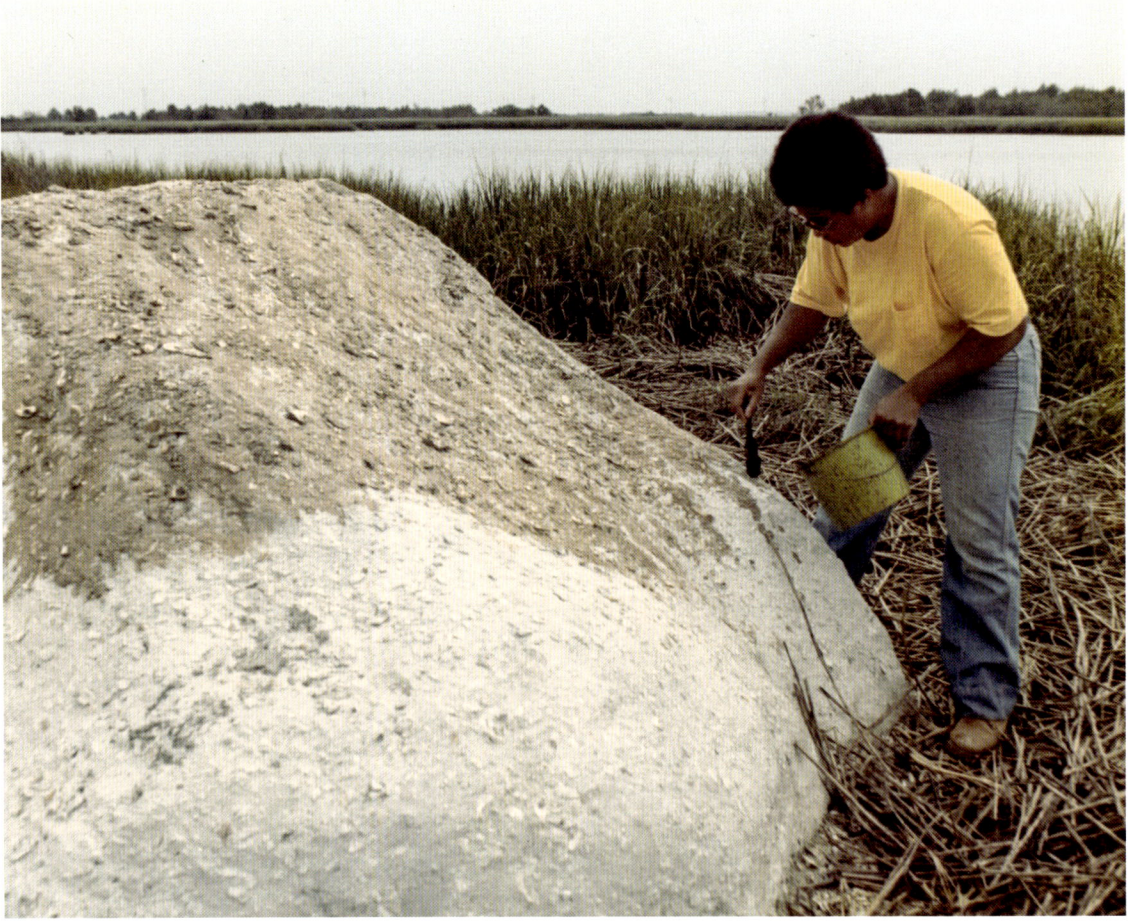

fig. 3.   Beverly Buchanan, *Marsh Ruins*, 1980, Brunswick, Georgia

Indigenous people took up residence on Ossabaw Island in small villages at least 5,000 years ago and established agricultural settlements 1,500 years ago. In the mid-16th century, the Spanish Crown set up missions across coastal Georgia; while no archaeological evidence of those structures has been found, Spanish pottery fragments from the time remain on the island, suggesting European presence dating back before British colonization. The arrival of Spaniards heralded the forcible displacement of Indigenous people inland, beginning with the burning of the Guale village of Azapo, which may have been located on the island's South End. After the English took control of the Georgia coast from the Spanish in the late 17th century, European settlers and enslaved Africans took up residence on Ossabaw, which they farmed and timbered beginning in 1763—the earliest record of Black folks living and working there involuntarily, which continued until and after the end of enslavement.[5]

Artists across generations have responded to these long and varied histories of Black and Indigenous land use in the Sea Islands and along the Atlantic coast. Consider the work of Beverly Buchanan, who grew up accompanying her father on his surveys of rural farming communities in the Southeast. For her 1980 work *Marsh Ruins*, for example, Buchanan used tabby concrete, which she applied to littoral rock mounds by hand [fig. 3].[6] At the time of European colonization, the Timucua had left oyster shells in large quantities in neat heaps; enslaved people secured the lime from them and then used the tabby to build houses and walls in 19th-century plantations across South Carolina, Georgia, and Florida—including the ones on Ossabaw.[7] Buchanan's use of tabby to mark existing rock formations in a work like *Marsh Ruins* offers a second life for the historically laden substance, reusing the very material out of which dwellings for enslaved people were constructed as a sign for this taint of dispossession.

Artists have continued to heighten the tensions of land use in the Sea Islands. In 2018, Cameron Rowland made their conceptual artwork *Depreciation* by buying—and then

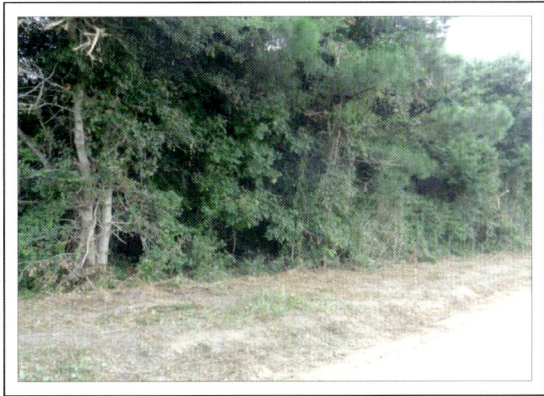

APPRAISAL REPORT

OF THE REAL PROPERTY LOCATED AT

8060 Maxie Road
Edisto Island, SC 29438

fig. 4.　Cameron Rowland, *Depreciation*, 2018. Restrictive covenant; 1 acre on Edisto Island, South Carolina. Extended loan, Dia Art Foundation

40 acres and a mule as reparations for slavery originates in General William Tecumseh Sherman's Special Field Orders No. 15, issued on January 16, 1865. Sherman's Field Order 15 was issued out of concern for a potential uprising of the thousands of ex-slaves who were following his army by the time it arrived in Savannah.[1]

　　The field order stipulated that "The islands from Charleston south, the abandoned rice fields along the rivers for thirty miles back from the sea, and the country bordering the St. Johns River, Florida, are reserved and set apart for the settlement of the negroes now made free by the acts of war and the Proclamation of the President of the United States. . . . Each family shall have a plot of not more than forty acres of tillable ground."[2]

　　This was followed by the formation of the Bureau of Refugees, Freedmen, and Abandoned Lands in March 1865. In the months immediately following the issue of the field orders, approximately 40,000 former slaves settled in the area designated by Sherman on the basis of possessory title.[3] 10,000 of these former slaves were settled on Edisto Island, South Carolina.[4]

　　In 1866, following Lincoln's assassination, President Andrew Johnson effectively rescinded Field Order 15 by ordering these lands be returned to their previous Confederate owners. Former slaves were given the option to work for their former masters as sharecroppers or be evicted. If evicted, former slaves could be arrested for homelessness under vagrancy clauses of the Black Codes. Those who refused to leave and refused to sign sharecrop contracts were threatened with arrest.

Although restoration of the land to the previous Confederate owners was slowed in some cases by court challenges filed by ex-slaves, nearly all the land settled was returned by the 1870s. As Eric Foner writes, "Johnson had in effect abrogated the Confiscation Act and unilaterally amended the law creating the [Freedmen's] Bureau. The idea of a Freedmen's Bureau actively promoting black landownership had come to an abrupt end."[5] The Freedmen's Bureau agents became primary proponents of labor contracts inducting former slaves into the sharecropping system.[6]

　　Among the lands that were repossessed in 1866 by former Confederate owners was the Maxcy Place plantation. "A group of freed people were at Maxcy Place in January 1866. . . . The people contracted to work for the proprietor, but no contract or list of names has been found."[7]

　　The one-acre piece of land at 8060 Maxie Road, Edisto Island, South Carolina, was part of the Maxcy Place plantation. This land was purchased at market value on August 6, 2018, by 8060 Maxie Road, Inc., a nonprofit company formed for the sole purpose of buying this land and recording a restrictive covenant on its use. This covenant has as its explicit purpose the restriction of all development and use of the property by the owner.

　　The property is now appraised at $0. By rendering it legally unusable, this restrictive covenant eliminates the market value of the land. These restrictions run with the land, regardless of the owner. As such, they will last indefinitely.

　　As reparation, this covenant asks how land might exist outside of the legal-economic regime of property that was instituted by slavery and colonization. Rather than redistributing the property, the restriction imposed on 8060 Maxie Road's status as valuable and transactable real estate asserts antagonism to the regime of property as a means of reparation.

　　8060 Maxie Road is not for visitation.

Notes

1.　Eric Foner, *Reconstruction: America's Unfinished Revolution, 1863–1877*, updated ed. (New York: Harper & Row, 1988; New York: HarperCollins, 2014), p. 71.
2.　Headquarters, Military Division of the Mississippi, *Special Field Orders* No. 15 (1865).
3.　Foner, *Reconstruction*, p. 71.
4.　Charles Spencer, *Edisto Island 1861 to 2006*: Ruin, Recovery and Rebirth (Charleston, SC: The History Press, 2008), p. 87.
5.　Foner, *Reconstruction*, p. 161.
6.　Foner, p. 161.
7.　Spencer, *Edisto Island 1861 to 2006*, p. 95.

revaluing—a tract of land on Edisto Island [fig. 4].[8] Rowland proceeded to use a restrictive covenant—a provision that reassessed the value of the one-acre plot located on Maxie Road at $0, effectively eliminating its market value, decreasing the market value of the surrounding plots, and threatening the capacity for developers to build on this island.

Rowland's revaluation is documented in the appraisal report that makes up the component of the work that is visible when it is shown in a gallery and is accompanied by an object label that the artist writes themself. *Depreciation*'s text reads, "Rather than redistributing the property, the restriction imposed on 8060 Maxie Road's status as valuable and transactable real estate asserts antagonism to the regime of property as a means of reparation." Instead of conceiving of reparations as redistribution, Rowland empties out the value terms of the property altogether, connecting racial capitalism's ongoing valuations to the institutions of slavery and colonization. Put glibly, Black or Indigenous ownership of a golf course on Edisto would not redress its history. In the same text, Rowland contextualizes the work within the undelivered promise of General Sherman's Field Order No. 15, which in the wake of abolition in 1865 stipulated that "Each family shall have a plot of not more than forty acres of tillable ground."[9] Although tens of thousands of former slaves tilled the soil and ran an experiment in self-governance for a year following the order, President Andrew Johnson rescinded it in 1866, returning the lands to their previous Confederate owners. Redistribution—or other forms of government-sanctioned reparations—remain deferred in Edisto, as they do in the rest of the Sea Islands.

FUGITIVE JUSTICE

Even if local, state, and federal governments have failed to redress the histories of expropriation in the Sea Islands, artists have used the materials available to them to seek other forms of remedy. They have looked to art to ask how we might collectively "compensate for centuries of violence that have as their consequence the impossibility of restoring a prior existence, of giving back what was taken, of repairing what was broken," as Stephen Best and Saidiya Hartman have described the task of fugitive justice.[10]

In her classic 1991 film *Daughters of the Dust*, for example, Julie Dash calls attention to recourses that have existed in excess of what the law or state have offered [fig. 5]. "African captives of the Ibo tribe, when they were brought to the New World, they refused to live in slavery," Dash relayed to writer bell hooks. "And then there is the story—the

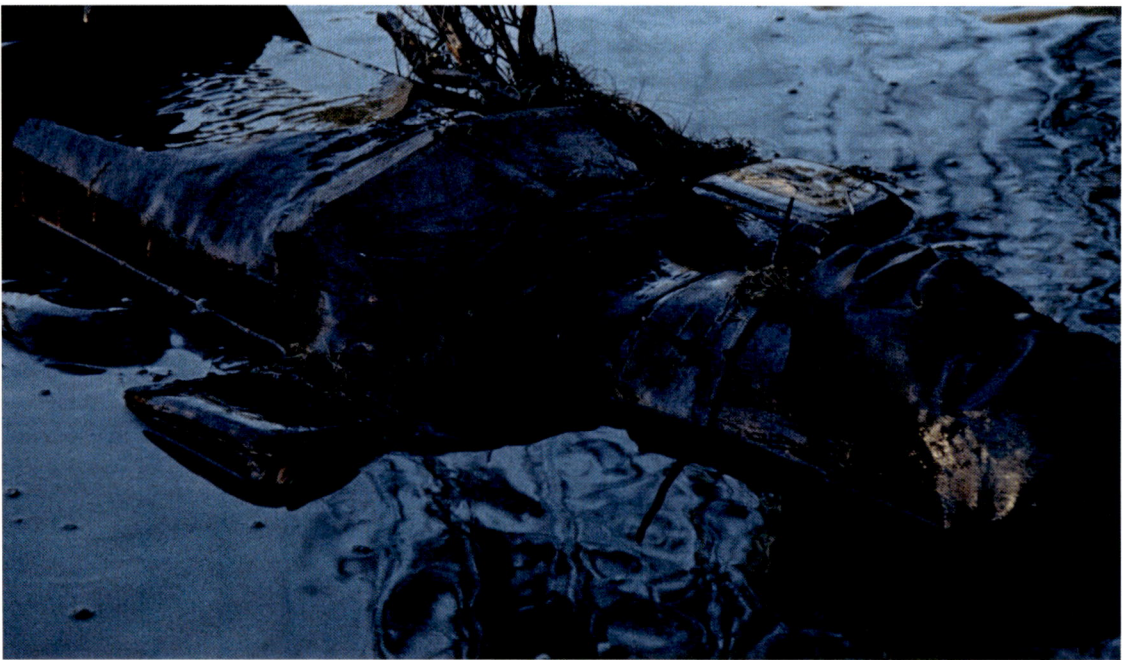

fig. 5.   Film still from Julie Dash, *Daughters of the Dust*, 1991

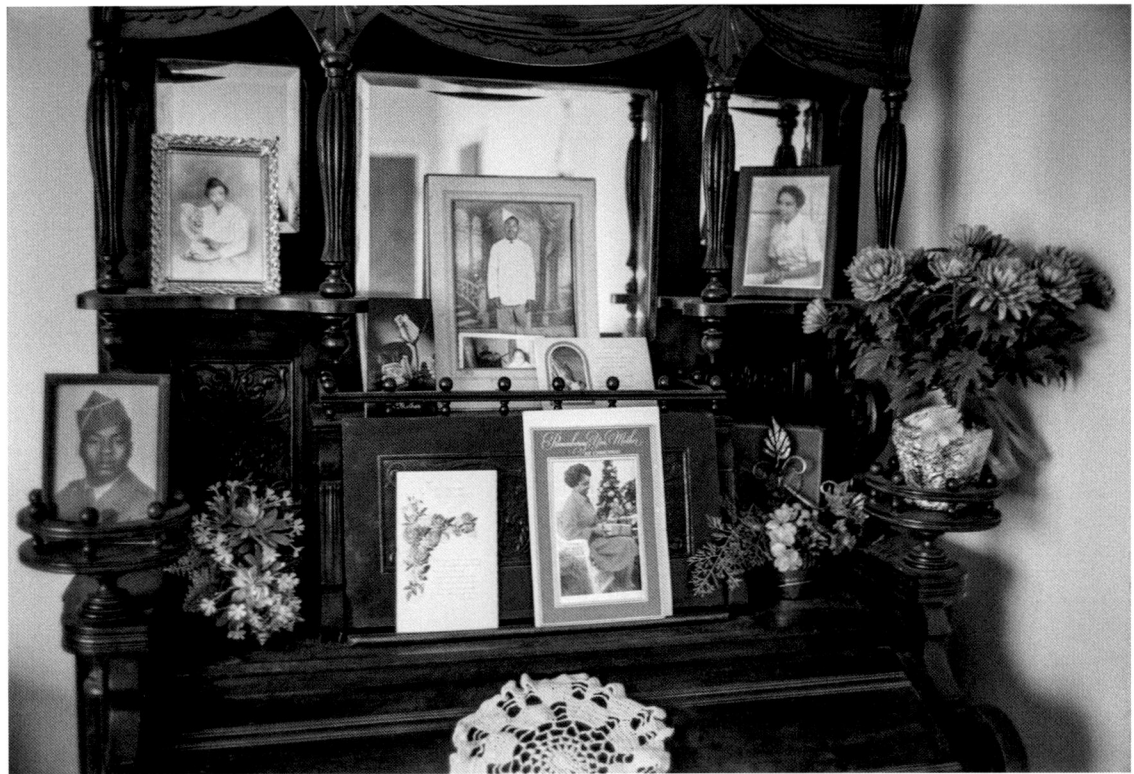

fig. 6. A 1979 photograph in Jeanne Moutoussamy-Ashe's series *Daufuskie Island*, named after
the Muscogee word for "sharp feather." It portrays some of the island's 84 residents
by picturing framed portraits on a wooden armoire amidst potted flowers and decorative
doilies. Like her photographs of the fishermen's nets and wedding scenes that she made
over the several years she visited the island, the photograph imagines an existing
network of relations as a claim to space.

truth or the myth—of them walking into the water and drowning themselves in front of
the captors."[11] While scouting for the film, Dash realized that across the Sea Islands, inhabitants in each had designated a place, "a little inlet, or a little area" they called Ibo
after the infamous site of disembarkation. "It's because that message is so strong, so
powerful, so sustaining to the tradition of resistance, by any means possible, that every
Gullah community embraces this myth."[12]

The movie evokes this specific past in one particular scene of loss. Eula Peazant,
played by Alva Rogers, bears witness to a figurehead (a wooden sculpture once affixed
to the bow of a European slaving shape) of an African man shackled by an iron collar
around his neck and iron chain around his waist as he is returned to the water. A sign
that reads "Ibo Landing" locates this enactment in space. Peazant, who was raped by a
white man and is pregnant with the child who narrates the film, recounts the story of Ibo
Landing: "They seen things that day that you and I don't have the power for see," she
relays of what the Ibo men, women, and children knew of the future that awaited them.
Eula's husband Eli Peazant (Adisa Anderson) walks into the water, and after performing a
purifying ritual, sends the sculpture back beneath the depths immediately before the community gathers to celebrate the Peazants' nuptials.

Artist Tyrone Mitchell made the figurehead depicted in the film at the invitation of cinematographer Arthur Jafa along with Kerry James Marshall, the production designer for *Daughters*, who added finishing touches to the sculpture on set
and worked with a team of visual artists that included David Hammons. Mitchell was
born in Savannah and was a member at the Ossabaw Island Project in 1980, an experience the late curator Beryl Wright described in an exhibition catalog on his work as
"a new source for [the artist's] continuing interest in myth and folklore."[13] In particular, Mitchell explained that visiting somewhere that "was a holding place for slaves"
made "the island seem to be habituated by the spirits or ghosts of these former slaves."[14]

fig. 7.   Suzanne Jackson. *Ossabaw Elder*, 2010.
          Acrylic wash on paper, 12 × 16 in.
          Courtesy of the artist and Ortuzar,
          New York

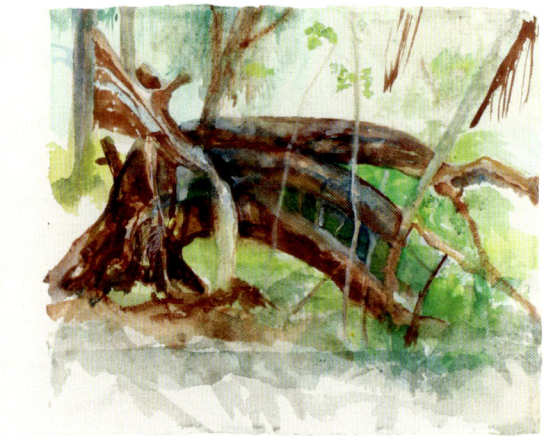

(Lisa Gail Collins cites a commonly held belief that enslaved Africans were smuggled to the United States through the Sea Islands as late as 1858, fifty years after the "Act Prohibiting the Importation of Slaves," which, in addition to the Islands' spatial isolation contributed to their real and perceived proximity to the African continent.)[15] Wright argued that it was the correspondence between time spent in West Africa (in particular, at the slave prison at Gorée Island) and Ossabaw that allowed Mitchell to "reestablish connections to an obscured cultural past." It was in the interval between these locations that Mitchell was able to meld "the spiritual power of traditional ritual objects with contemporary art theories and practices."[16]

PELTRIES, INDIGO, COTTON, RICE, AND LUMBER

For geographer Katherine McKittrick, "Black matters are spatial matters."[17] She extrapolates on this maxim suggesting that "space and place give Black lives meaning in a world that has, for the most part, incorrectly deemed Black populations and their attendant geographies as 'ungeographic'."[18] Black folks have responded to this paradox of place with insistence, claiming our thrown-out-of-the-world status as a source of meaning making. This contradiction is borne out in the Sea Islands, which for makers across time, have been at once an emblem of the South and of Africa, both real and imagined. They are at once a terminus and point of departure: a proxy in a narrative of deferred freedom and perpetual slavery, a midpoint between the past and its aftermath, and a place to reconcile an unknowable origin with an uncertain futurity.

This swirl of meanings unfurls in Suzanne Jackson's watercolor and photograph on paper, *Origins*, which she made on Ossabaw Island during a ten-day visit in August 2010 [(p. 135)]. Bands of cobalt, mustard, rust, and moss stack in a succession of horizon lines that resemble archaeological layers cascading at their edges. This lush, Edenic space is decidedly not one before man: In the center of the collage sits the handsome bald-headed, brown-skinned Lawrence Campbell, a nephew of Gullah historian Emory Campbell, who worked with Jeanne Moutoussamy-Ashe on her *Daufuskie Island* series [(fig. 6)19]. Campbell's face is flanked on either side by the foliage of two drooping evergreens, ever-present in their construction of place. "And that's when I could hear in the trees," Jackson remembered of her time spent in Ossabaw's landscape. "You can hear people talking, people who were there before and, you know, ancient times in the trees."[20]

In a sketchbook she kept over those ten days on the island, Jackson returned over and again to the live oaks: a species endemic to the wilderness of the Southeastern United States, iconic of the plantation architecture of the Old South, and the official state tree of Georgia [(fig. 7)]. In Jackson's hands, the trees' limbs seem to gnarl, buckle, and bend; their sinewy parts fall away from the majesty with which they are often depicted, emphasizing instead a network of knots tangled with the ground itself.

Jackson was not the only one who couldn't keep her eyes off the live oaks when she was at Ossabaw. In a handwritten note following his week-long residency at the Ossabaw Island Project in 1971, writer Ralph Ellison [(fig. 8)] jotted down the following remarks:

> At the South end...live oak, one of the largest growing along the coast.
> Estimated by experts to have stood for [600 yrs]...more than 30 feet in
> circumference and its great branches have a spread of over a hundred
> and fifty feet. If there is any truth in the old saying, about the age of
> the coastal live oaks—three hundred years in growing, three hundred
> years in living, three hundred years in dying......[21]

In seeking a term of measurement (years, feet) and then anxiously repeating them (years for growing, years for living, years for dying). Ellison attempts to count uncountable time. He holds open a place for the yawning sense of history that Jackson describes as "ancient," perhaps only assessable in what she names as the task of listening to the voices of "people who were there before."[22]

Ellison's notes on the land read as a material history of its flora and fauna, including its architecture and inhabitants. The next entry details the Main House, the two-story structure where Ellison stayed that is decorated with Bermuda-pink walls and a roof made of Castilian tile. It sits on the island's North End with a view of the sound. His note traces the connection between the island's commercial history and its structures for living:

> Massive mantel + chimney are made of a stone brought to the island in
> sailing vessels of the early days of the colony. There is no native stone on

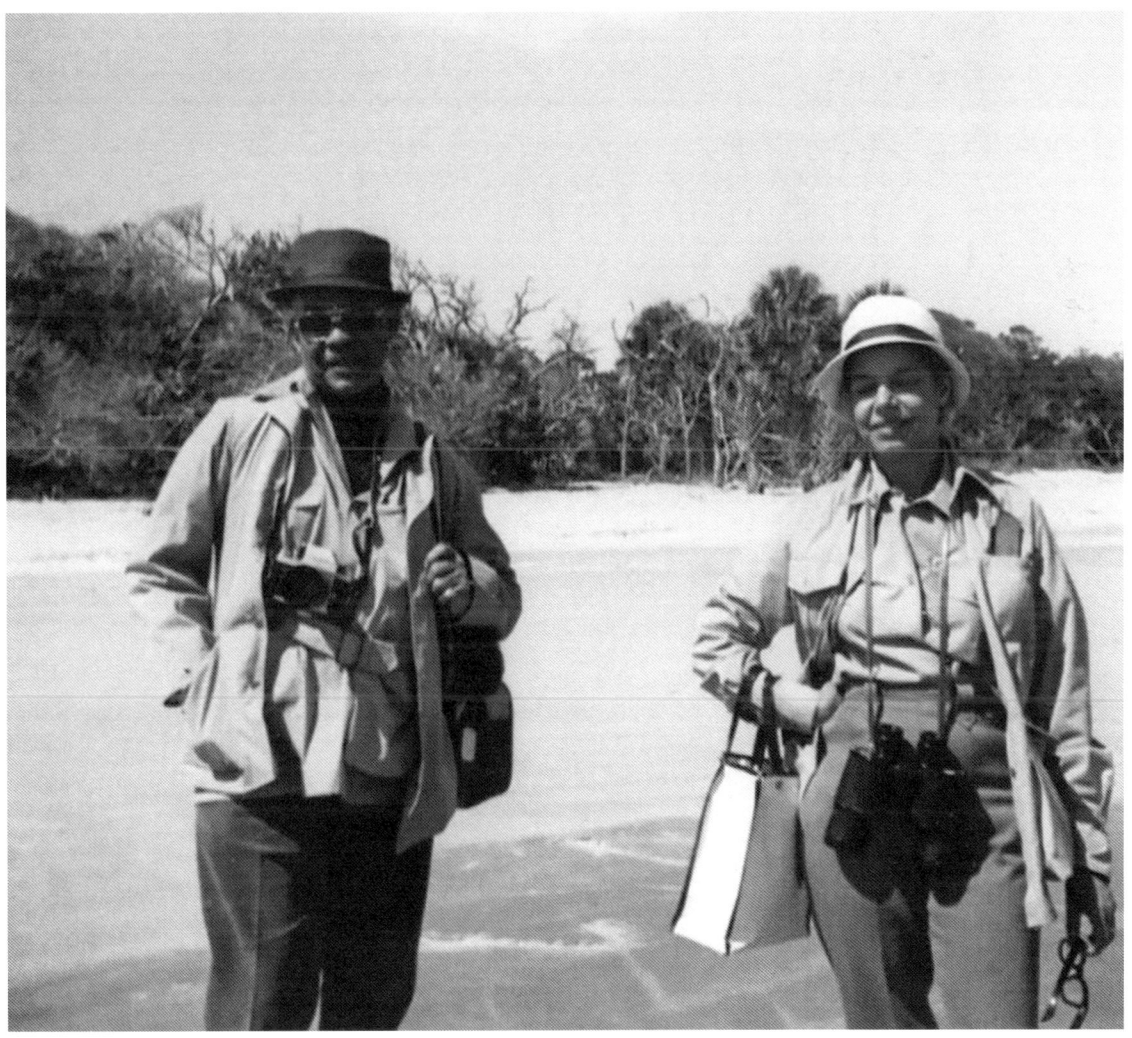

fig. 8.   Ralph and Fanny Ellison on the beach at Ossabaw, 1971

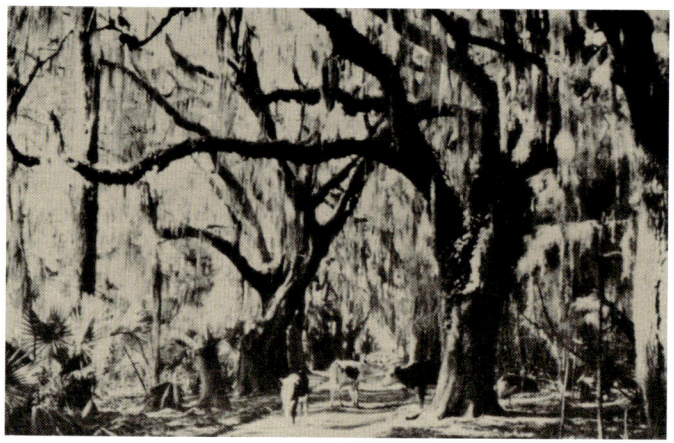

the Island; all rocks and stones were brought as ship ballast and dumped
to make room for cargoes of peltries, indigo, cotton, rice, and lumber[23]

The writer's summary connects the island's material residue to its position as a post in
the trade of goods produced by enslaved people. No native stones remain on the island.
Instead, we are left with a ship's ballast, made to hold the vessel down in the water,
turned into a fungible commodity that could be swapped in the boat for the products of
involuntary labor. Later, they were transformed into a home. It is not only amidst the
trees but through the building's stones that people can be heard.

Over the course of a decade, Ellison continued his exchange with the Ossabaw
Island Project's co-founder Eleanor "Sandy" Torrey West [fig. 9], which took the form of
dozens of letters and are part of the thousands he committedly wrote over his eighty years,
now held in the Library of Congress. The two shared a sense of welcome not just for the
biologists and philosophers who came as members to visit the island but also to the many
creatures and critters who found a more permanent home there. In the last entry in this
informal breakdown of the island, he lists the following "Inhabitants":

> Wild turkey, quail, blue + white heron. Migratory duck "by the thou-
> sand visit the fresh water lakes." And in "April more white egret [come]
> to the summer rookery at Egret Pond...." razor back pigs, deer, alliga-
> tors, poisonous snakes, donkeys [Durkee-tame] horses; Spanish moss,
> dogwood + magnolia trees, Palmetta [sic], + Palms, Camelias, azaleas...[24]

Despite their differences in affect, Ellison's litany of non-human animals mirrors the attention West would pay to them in an anecdote she reported to *The New York Times* in
1979 about the unlikely path some of these inhabitants had taken to arrive at Ossabaw:

> "There was a man named Crosley—he made cars or radios or something,
> and he owned Bull Island. He imported the donkeys and a buffalo and
> all sorts of other things, sort of a Noah's Ark, and then after he died,
> the buffalo appeared in somebody's duck pond, the donkeys were loose—
> that sort of thing—so we loaded four of the donkeys, a female, a jack, a
> gelding, and a baby into a Volkswagen bus and brought them here."[25]

In the absence of a plan for reproducing life, creativity offers a path for continuing on.
The strangeness of our world, revealed in the interval of death, offers up materials for us
to construct an impossible place for us to dwell—including in our bodies, which hold lives
lived in loss.[26]

Notes

1. *The Presence of Black*, directed by Linda Goode Bryant (United States: 2022), video. The film was included in the exhibition *Just Above Midtown: Changing Spaces*, which I co-organized with Goode Bryant at The Museum of Modern Art, October 9 2022-February 18, 2023.

2. Linda Goode Bryant and Thelma Golden, "Can JAM Be JAM at MoMA? A Conversation between Linda Goode Bryant and Thelma Golden," in *Just Above Midtown: Changing Spaces* (New York: The Museum of Modern Art, 2022), 13.

3. Lisa Gail Collins, "Visible Roots and Visual Routes: Art, Africanisms, and the Sea Islands," in *The Art of History: African American Women Artists Engage the Past* (New Brunswick and London: Rutgers University Press, 2002), 65.

4. Collins, 98.

5. "Ossabaw Island: Timeline," Ossabaw Island Foundation, accessed July 25, 2024, https://ossabawisland.org/island/history-timeline2/.

6. Tabby is an amalgam of sand, water, and shells—an accessible source of lime, the binding component of concrete. Harvesting it is a labor-intensive process of cleaning salt shells to prevent corrosion and then crushing as well as burning them to release the lime particles.

7. Jennifer Burris Staton and Park McArthur, "Beverly Buchanan's Artist," in *Beverly Buchanan: 1978-1981*, ed. Jennifer Burris Staton and Park McArthur (Mexico City: Athénée Press, 2015), 9-19.

8. Edisto Island is located 42 miles south of Charleston and named after the Edistow people.

9. The text further reads, "The islands from Charleston south, the abandoned rice fields along the rivers for thirty miles back from the sea, and the country bordering the St. Johns River, Florida, are reserved and set apart for the settlement of the negroes now made free by the acts of war and the Proclamation of the President of the United States." Headquarters, Military Division of the Mississippi, *Special Field Orders No. 15* (1865).

10. Stephen Best and Saidiya Hartman, "Fugitive Justice: The Appeal of the Slave," *Representations* 92 (Fall 2006): 2.

11. Julie Dash and bell hooks, "Dialogue between bell hooks and Julie Dash" in *Daughters of the Dust: The Making of an African American Woman's Film*, ed. Julie Dash (New York City: The New Press, 1992), 30.

12. Dash and hooks, 30.

13. Beryl J. Wright, *Tyrone Mitchell* (New Jersey: The Newark Museum, 1990), 10.

14. Wright, 10.

15. Collins, 66.

16. Wright, 3-4.

17. Katherine McKittrick, *Demonic Grounds: Black Women and the Cartography of Struggle* (Minneapolis: University of Minnesota Press, 2006), xii.

18. McKittrick, xii.

19. Beryl Gilothwest, email to author, July 23, 2024.

20. Gilothwest, email to author.

21. Ralph Ellison, *Ossabaw Foundation*, manuscript, Ralph Ellison papers, box 92, folder 5, Library of Congress. Shortly after his death, Fanny McConnell Ellison deeded her husband's books, manuscripts, drafts, letters, and papers of all kinds to the Library of Congress. John F. Callahan, "General Introduction," in The *Selected Letters of Ralph Ellison*, ed. John F. Callahan and Marc C. Conner (New York: Random House, 2019), 13.

22. Beryl Gilothwest, email to author, July 23, 2024.

23. Ellison, *Ossabaw Foundation*.

24. Ellison, *Ossabaw Foundation*.

25. Wayne King, "Donkeys Get Vasectomies And Escape a Worse Fate," *The New York Times*, June 6, 1979, A14.

26. This is a variation on words written by Veena Das in "Language and Body: Transactions in the Construction of Pain," in *Social Suffering*, ed. Arthur Kleinman, Veena Das, and Margaret Lock (Berkeley: University of California Press, 1997), 69. As cited in Best and Hartman, 2.

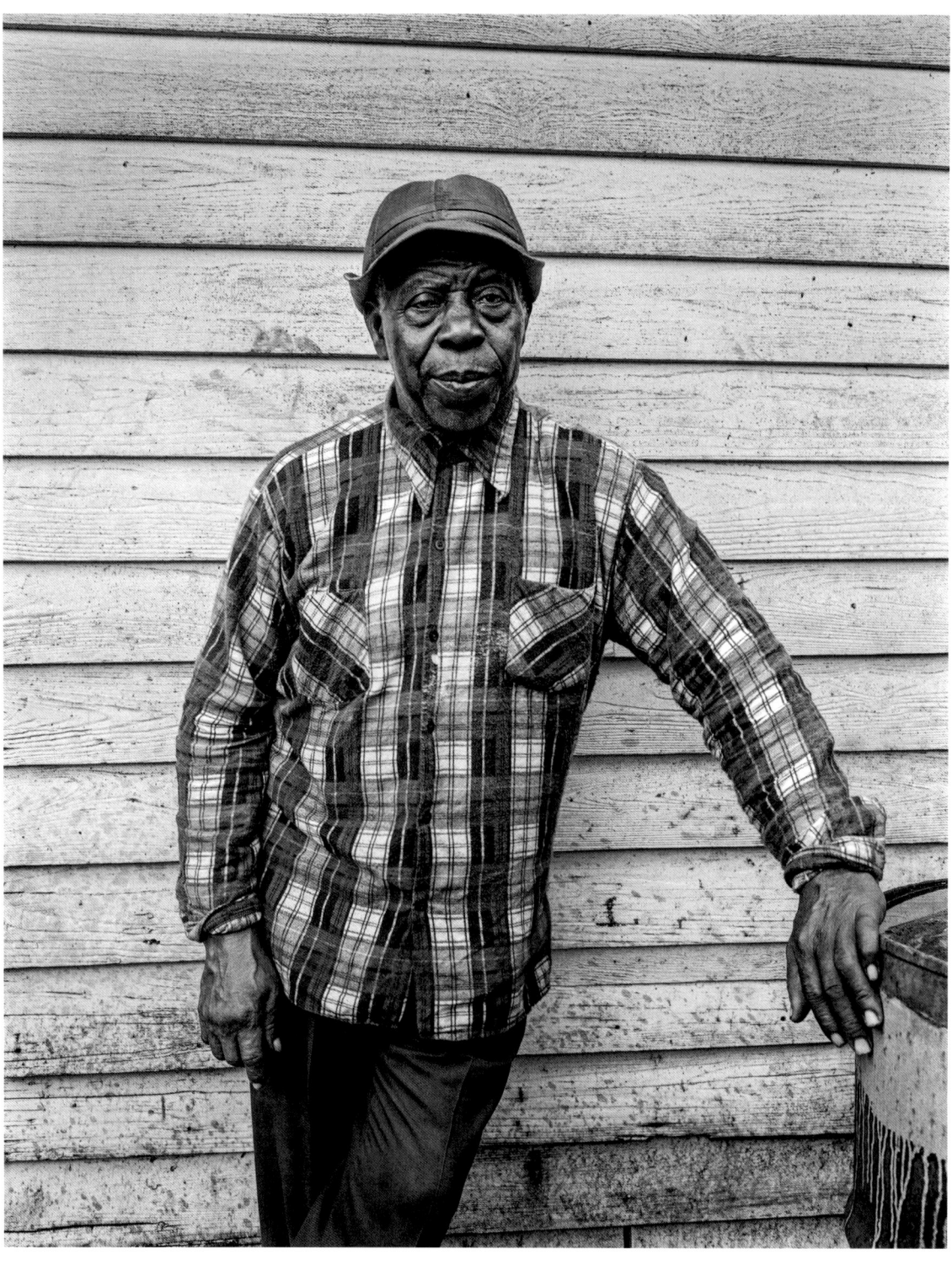

Cyrus Martin Sr. on Ossabaw Island, 1977. Photograph by Susan Earl

THE STORY OF CYRUS MARTIN AND PAR TANK

VAUGHNETTE GOODE-WALKER

Cyrus Martin was a Gullah Geechee man; his heritage claimed him by the "basket name" Jimbo.[1] His language was Gullah, a creolized form of English spoken by Black Americans on the Sea Islands and coastal areas of South Carolina and Georgia.[2] Martin was born May 23, 1900, on Skidaway Island, a barrier island south of Savannah. He lived and worked on nearby Ossabaw Island for most of his 94 years, which spanned the beginning of segregation through the civil rights era.

Martin was a "griot," or master storyteller, who told his many stories of Ossabaw in a direct and straightforward manner, including those about his encounters with spirits. Ossabaw's former co-owner Eleanor "Sandy" Torrey West first met Martin when she was eleven years old. In the late 1970s, several decades after she first heard his Ossabaw stories, West and her son Justin began recording them. Martin told them about when he first came to the island in 1913 to work for John Harrison, a caretaker at Middle Place:

> This man, Mr. Harrison get me to come over here you know. Mr. Harrison was, he's the butcher off Skidaway, see, we had a lot of cows, you know, and we don't sell no cows to nobody but him. So, he come and buy about ten from this one, four from this other one, four, five from the other one like that. Every time I see him, he tell me, he say he gon carry me, take me off, on the boat. I used to take off. He had me scared he was gon bring me over here and not bring me back.[3]

Martin stayed on Ossabaw when the island was sold to Sandy West's parents, Dr. and Mrs. Henry Norton Torrey, in 1924. He moved to the North End, where he took care of the horses and lived in one of the tabby cabins that housed island employees until the 1980s and were originally inhabited by enslaved people. The typical work schedule was ten days on the island and four days off, which gave employees time to visit with family and friends.[4] Martin spent his time off in Savannah, where his wife, Beatrice, lived with their six children, Cyrus Jr. (known as Bubba), Charles (known as Billy), Annette, Harold (known as Al), Jacqueline, and Eunice on East Hall Lane in the Beach Institute neighborhood. At the time, it was a community primarily populated by Black households headed by men who worked for the Atlantic Coast Line Railroad. They later moved further east to the city's Benjamin Van Clark neighborhood.

"Jimbo" embodied his griot persona most of all when he told his signature story of Par Tank, a malevolent ghost or "hant" that he first heard about from his uncle and encountered twice on the island when he was a young man. In recordings of his story, Martin reveals the "spirit" was named for a round water tank lying on its side in the Ossabaw woods, which may have been the spot where his uncle first encountered it.[5] While Par Tank bothered his brother and uncle every time they were alone on the island, Martin was the only one to actually see the hant. Gullah Geechee people believe that hants "ride you" at night while you are sleeping, an apt description of Martin's first interaction with Par Tank one night in the cabin[p. 147] where he often slept at Middle Place.[6] In this transcription of a recording from the late-1970s, he tells the story to Sandy West:

Cyrus Martin Sr.:

I tell you I come in that night about ten of eight. I had been working on the road. I had this mule and wagon, like I tell you all the time...So, I come in, nobody had been here but me and Miss Gatehouse and they husband.[7] So, I come in this night, and I had my little .22 rifle in the wagon. I didn't carry it in the house. I just leave it in the wagon there. So, I gone in there, I had a little wood stove and I put some wood in the stove and I lay down on my back, flat. So, I decided to get up and put some more wood in the stove and just as I started to get up, he clapped me cross the arm just like that. I just stand up and he hang on to me and I just keep shaking him, you know, just shaking him like that, and he just pick that cot up, the foot of the cot that I been laying on and throw it like that and come down and it folded up. So, I could see him then, he had the whole room light up. I could see him there, I could show you the hole right now, it's about that big. It had a little cover over it.[8] He went back down in that hole, and I could see the dust flying and I went right back, right on back to take my mattress off the cot, put the mattress on the floor. I say well, if he pick up me he pick up me and the mattress all together. So, I stayed there, and I went over to Miss Gatehouse, and I tell them about it the next morning. Miss Gatehouse, she say, "Jim you take a little salt and sprinkle it around your house," and she say, "He not gon worry you no more." "Yes ma'am."[9]

Sandy West:

What did it look like?

Cyrus: I couldn't see nothing, but it had a big black arm. I couldn't see no head or nothing.

Sandy: And was it a hairy arm?

Cyrus: Just a big old bare arm.

Sandy: A man's arm?

Cyrus: A man's arm. I could see him. He had his hand cross mine. I could see his arm so I grab his arm.

Sandy: You did?

Cyrus: Yes, I grab his arm and hang on to it. I hang on to it til he shake me off and I went outside and get the rifle and came back in to look all underneath the bed, I could see nobody. I say well, so I take the mattress off the bed (laughs).

Sandy: And then when did he go down the hole? After you came back?

Cyrus: It gone down the hole after it shake me. I went outside after he done went in the hole.

Sandy: Then after you put the salt around the thing, around the house, then he never came back?

Cyrus: No ma'am, he never come back no more.[10]

Martin worked for Sandy West into his late eighties. He was on the island throughout the Ossabaw Island Project and Genesis years, and the members of those programs knew him well. He appears often in their art, writings, and memories, including those of sculptor Tyrone Mitchell, photographers John and Susan Earl, and painter and filmmaker Clifford B. West[p. 146]. Martin knew every corner of Ossabaw, having worked most of his life there. When a journalist asked how he felt about the island in 1977, he replied:

> It means a lot to me...And I enjoy being over here. You can get anything you want here. Any kind of meat: deer, possum, coon, pork— good pork—anything you want over here...If I was on the other side, I'd have to buy whatever I wanted. But not over here.[11]

On his eightieth birthday in 1980, Martin was commissioned as Aide de Camp by Georgia Governor George Busbee and was presented with a scroll featuring the gold seal of the State of Georgia. After he passed away on Christmas Eve in 1994, The Ossabaw Island Foundation adopted a resolution in his memory, written by Sandy West and presented to his widow, Beatrice. "For seventy years Cyrus Martin has been a dedicated worker, a leader and an example of decency, honesty and courage," she wrote. "[He] sort of retired in his late eighties but he never really left Ossabaw and never will."[12]

Notes

1. A "basket name" is given to Gullah Geechee babies when they are still in a bassinet, which was historically a basket. It is the name by which they are known in the community, rather than in government records. See Emory Campbell, *Gullah Cultural Legacies*, 3rd ed. (Hilton Head Island, SC: Gullah Heritage Consulting Services, 2008), 20.

2. In 1949, linguist Lorenzo Dow Turner published the results of his research into the origin of the Gullah language. See Lorenzo D. Turner, *Africanisms in the Gullah Dialect* (Chicago: The University of Chicago Press, 1949).

3. Cyrus Martin Sr., interview with Sandy West, c. late-1970s, West family archives.

4. Ann Foskey, *Images of America: Ossabaw Island* (Mt. Pleasant, SC: Arcadia Publishing, 2001), 20.

5. Cyrus Martin Sr., and Queenie Williams interview with Sandy and Justin West, c. late-1970s, West family archives.

6. "Hants" are spirits in the African tradition who bother you in the dead of night while you are sleeping. "The old folks call this being 'ridden by a hant.' Hants are the spirits of people who died suddenly, unpleasantly, and/or without proper burial. They are ghosts, really, to be pitied and feared." Luisa Teish, *Jambalaya: The Natural Woman's Book of Personal Charms and Practical Rituals* (San Francisco: HarperCollins, 1985), 216.

7. The Gatehouses were a white family that lived at Middle Place from 1921-1937. *Ossabaw Oracle* X, no. 3 (Fall 2005): 2.

8. In another recording of Martin telling this story, he describes the hole as about the size of the top of a can of condensed milk. See Cyrus Martin Sr. and Queenie Williams interview with Sandy and Justin West, c. late-1970s.

9. In the African diaspora, salt is commonly used for repelling hants. See Teish, 218.

10. Cyrus Martin Sr. interview with Sandy West, c. late-1970s. In another recording of Martin telling this story, he describes a second, later experience that he had with Par Tank. He was sleeping in a shack built for drying millet at Middle Place (he often slept there on hot nights because of the breeze from the Middle Place Creek that came through the slats) when the house began shaking violently despite a complete lack of wind, causing it to fall off the cinder blocks it was propped up on. Martin ran outside and saw Par Tank escaping into the woods. See Cyrus Martin Sr. and Queenie Williams interview with Sandy and Justin West, c. late-1970s.

11. Cyrus Martin Sr. quoted in Fred Powledge, "Island Fever," *Esquire*, March 1977, 114.

12. Leopold Adler II to Mrs. Cyrus Martin, March 1, 1995, West family archives.

LISTENING TO THE LAND: CRAFTING UNTOLD HISTORIES WITH *VENUS OF OSSABAW*

ALLISON JANAE HAMILTON

As an artist deeply engaged with the landscapes and layered histories of the American South, Ossabaw Island holds a profound and personal resonance for me. My practice has long been rooted in exploring the entangled archive embedded in landscape and the natural environment—especially within the complex terrain of this part of the country. Across my work, I return to the land as a site of ancestral intimacy, political struggle, and spiritual resistance. The coastal environments of Georgia—its barrier islands, swamps, and estuaries—are not only places I'm drawn to visually but also emotionally and historically, as spaces where Black life has endured, adapted, and flourished under relentless pressure.

Within Ossabaw's rich landscape lies its nuanced and dense history: from the Guale people who first stewarded the land, to the Spanish colonial presence of the 16th century, to its role as an indigo plantation during the transatlantic slave trade, the island has borne witness to centuries of transformation. Ossabaw has operated in many forms, even more recently as a sanctuary for multidisciplinary thinkers. This tension—between violence and refuge, ecological degradation and regeneration—is central to how I approach my work. I'm interested in the South as a living archive, and in artmaking as a way of listening to the stories the land still holds.

My film *Venus of Ossabaw*, commissioned by Telfair Museums for *Off the Coast of Paradise: Artists and Ossabaw Island, 1961–Now*, unfolds directly from my larger trajectory as an artist. A wilderness narrative set in the late 18th century, the film follows a teenage girl named Venus, who escapes captivity on Ossabaw and journeys through the treacherous terrain of South Georgia toward St. Augustine in Spanish East Florida. Her story draws inspiration from historical accounts of Maroons and freedom seekers who fled the Sea Islands in pursuit of liberation—particularly figures like Titus, a man formerly enslaved on Ossabaw who, in 1795, led a small group from the Georgia coast toward Spanish Florida, where the Catholic Church offered conditional sanctuary to fugitives.[1] While little is known about Titus beyond his brief appearance in the colonial archives, his decision to risk everything for freedom suggests a powerful mission toward autonomy and self-determination that I wanted to carry forward through Venus's story.

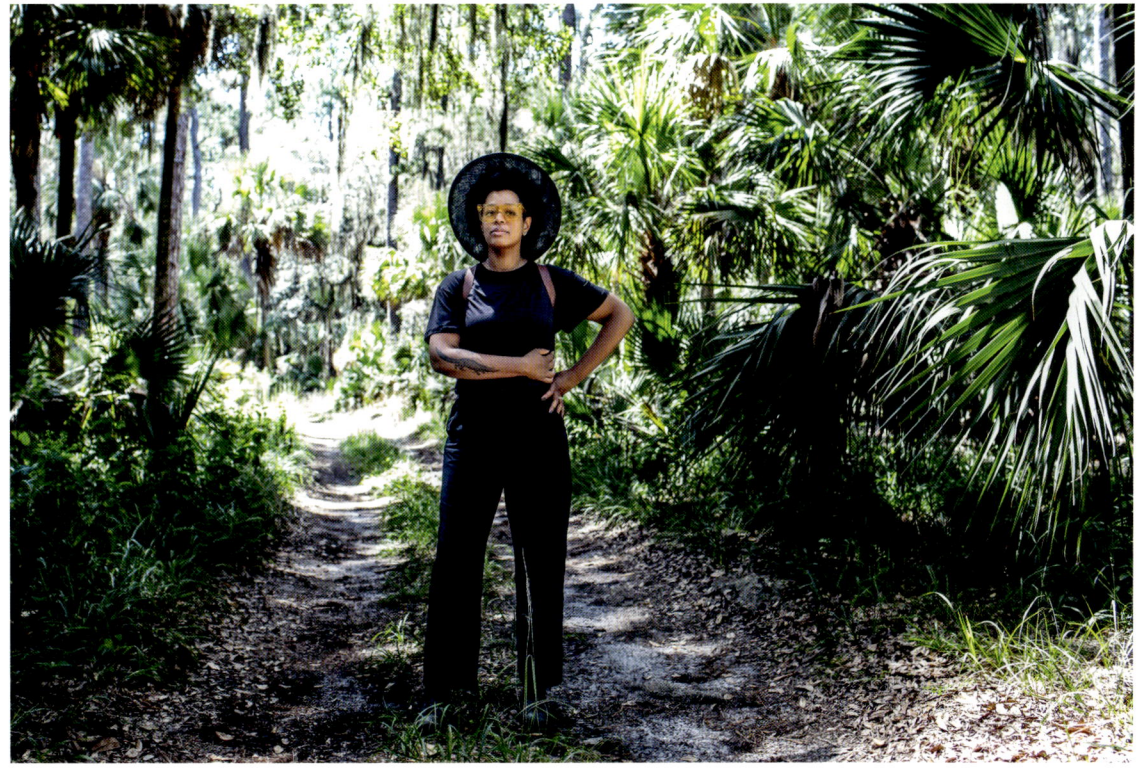

Allison Janae Hamilton on Pine Barren Road, September 2025

Shooting most of the film on Ossabaw Island itself was essential. The island, with its remote access and limited on-site resources, required me and the team to enact a creative openness to the production process. Ossabaw Island is not just the setting, it's a character and inevitably, a creative collaborator in the filming process. Being physically present on the land allowed me, the team, and the cast to engage deeply with the texture of place: listening and responding to the weight of the humidity, the movement of the tides, the density of the woods. All of these elements shape the tone and rhythm of the film. In this vein, the environment added layers of meaning that couldn't be written or planned. For Venus, the landscape is at once dangerous and familiar; it is a multifaceted space of haunting and healing. By filming on Ossabaw, we tapped into that duality. The island's presence infused every frame with a kind of ancestral charge that could not have been replicated elsewhere.

The environment in the film is alive: responsive, intimate, even conspiratorial. Its tidal creeks and moss-draped trees hold a memory far older than our own. The indigo plant, once cultivated there under severe and inhumane conditions, offers a visual and symbolic throughline as a color of both trauma and transformation. For this project, I chose to work with animation as a way to carry complex aspects of the story and create a visual language that I felt served the film's narrative in innovative ways. The soundscape furthers this motivation, as it weaves together environmental textures with layered vocals that not only reflect Venus's psychological state, but also fold time in on itself—evoking past, present, and ancestral futures all at once.

Venus of Ossabaw weaves together historical research, speculative fiction, and aesthetic experimentation to explore what liberation might look like as both an ecological and spiritual journey. For me, it's a way to honor those who fled, those who stayed, and those who continue forging life and resistance while the land continues to bear witness and remember. And through this film, I hope to share in that remembering not as a fixed narrative, but as an open-ended conversation between past and present, body and earth, loss and possibility.

1. Paul M. Pressly, *A Southern Underground Railroad: Black Georgians and the Promise of Spanish Florida and Indian Country* (Athens: The University of Georgia Press, 2024), 93-112.

THE OSSABAW ISLAND PROJECT, GENESIS, AND BEYOND

A SELECTED CHRONOLOGY

Art inspired by Ossabaw Island is powerful because the artists who have spent time there understand collectively that the island holds memory. Ossabaw's countless histories, many of which are imbued in the artwork on display in this exhibition and publication, reflect that memory. This focused chronology on the 20th and 21st centuries looks at the development, administration, and legacy of the Ossabaw Island Project and Genesis programs, which facilitated the creation of this diverse body of art.

This chronology represents a small part of the 5,000 years that humans have lived on Ossabaw. For a broader understanding of the island's complex and multifaceted history, please visit The Ossabaw Island Foundation's website: ossabawisland.org/island/history-timeline2

1924

Detroit-based couple, Dr. Henry Norton Torrey and Nell Ford Torrey—an heiress to the fortune of her grandfather, John Baptiste Ford, who founded the Pittsburgh Plate Glass and Wyandotte Chemical companies—purchase Ossabaw Island from partners of the Strachan Shipping Company for $300,000 after a fire destroys Greenwich, their winter estate on the Wilmington River in Thunderbolt, Georgia. Savannah-based architect Henrik Wallin designs a Spanish Colonial Revival-style home, known as the Main House, for the Torreys and it is constructed on the northwest side of the island over the course of two years [fig. 1]. The family utilizes several existing buildings on the site of a former plantation at the North End as living spaces for their staff and island caretakers. The Torreys continue to split their time between Detroit and Ossabaw.

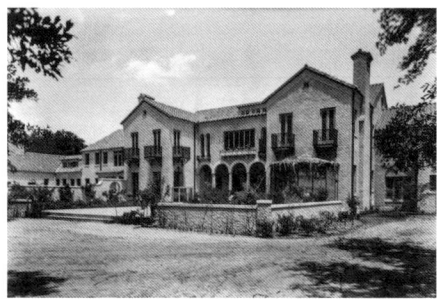

fig. 1.   The Main House, c. 1930

1952

March 21

The Torreys' daughter, Eleanor Torrey Shallcross, known as Sandy, marries her second husband, Clifford B. West [fig. 2]. He is a painter and art teacher at the Cranbrook Educational Community's Kingswood School for Girls in Bloomfield Hills, Michigan, where the couple lives.

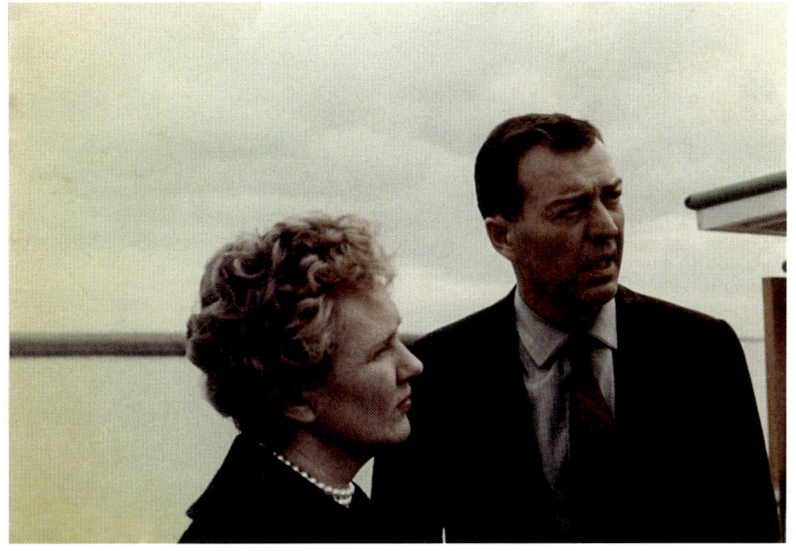

fig. 2.   Sandy and Clifford West on the dock on Ossabaw's North End, c. 1961

1958

November 10

Nell Ford Torrey dies in Detroit, thirteen years after her husband. Ossabaw is bequeathed to Sandy West and her late brother's children, Annette Torrey Peck, William Torrey Jr., Emory Torrey, and Randall Torrey.

1961

Conscious-stricken about keeping Ossabaw just for herself and her family, Sandy West considers how best to share the island with the public. Her husband urges her not to open the floodgates for recreational use, but rather think about how to share the island in a responsible way. They come up with the idea of a multidisciplinary residency program, utilizing the preserved wilderness of the island as a respite from the busy outside world. The Wests plan to open up the Main House for, as Sandy writes, "dedicated men and women of creative thought and purpose in the arts, the sciences, industry, education, and religion," to focus on projects without the expectation of a finished product at the end of their stay.

June 22–26

The Wests hold a summit on Ossabaw to finalize what they call the Ossabaw Island Project. They invite luminaries from their extended circle in a wide variety of fields to attend, including businessman Beekman Pool, banker Joseph Harrison, lawyers Julian Sipple and Reuben Waterman, composers Samuel Barber and Billy Jim Layton, sculptors Tex Schiwetz and Harry Bertoia, painters Arnold Blanch and Thomas Marker, journalist Edmund McKenzie, and biologist Colin Pittendrigh. The

Wests' young son Justin, Sandy's daughter Gilian Shallcross, and her niece Annette Peck are also present. The layout of the program is discussed at length, including the age range of the participants, the length of time for the stay on the island, and the size of each cohort on the island at one time [fig. 3].

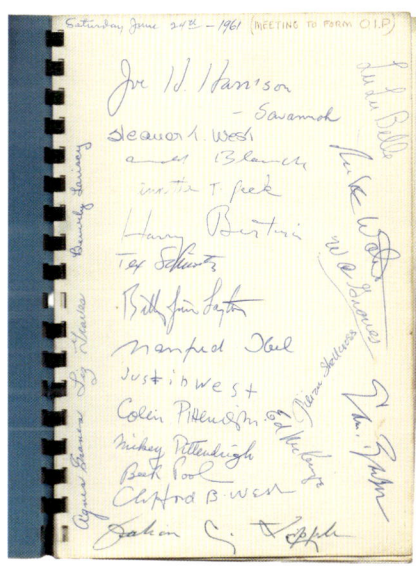

fig. 3.   Thomas Marker's journal from the meeting to set up the Ossabaw Island Project with signatures from the attendees, June 1961

July 2

Clifford's old friend, painter Thomas Marker, is named as the first executive director of the OIP, a role that he holds until the end of the 1966–67 season. He is the only fine artist to serve in this position. The Wests' staff on the island will also support the effort. They include Arthur and Agnes Graves, Eugene and Liz Graves, Queenie Williams and James Brownlee, and Cyrus Martin, among others [fig. 4].

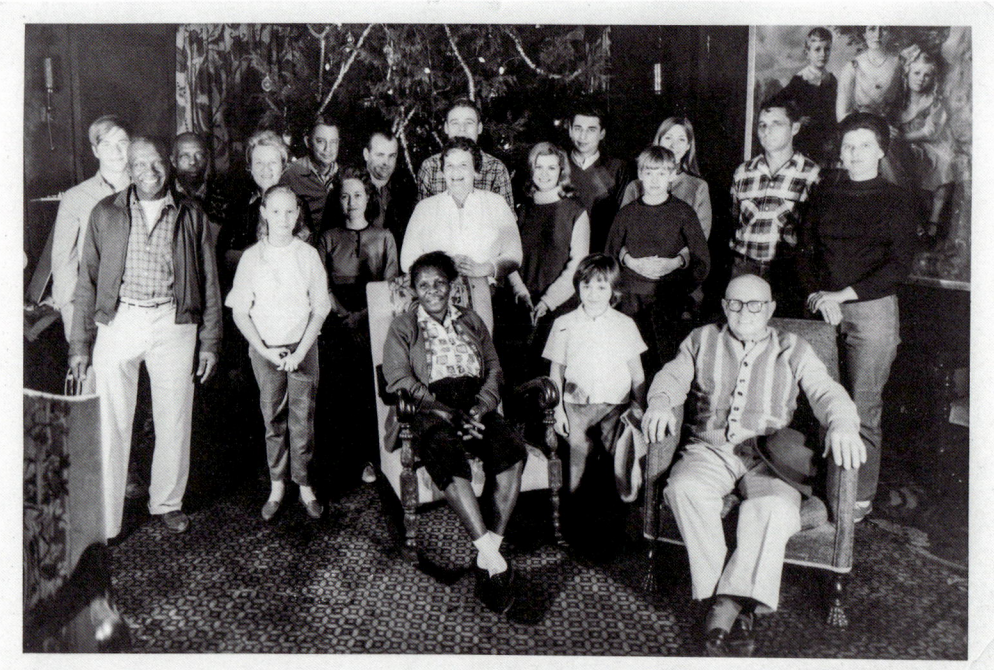

fig. 4.   The West and Shallcross family and Ossabaw Island staff at Christmas, c. 1966.
Back row: John Shallcross, Cyrus Martin Sr., Sandy West, Roy Cannon, Perry Hires,
Eugene Graves, Franco Roselli, Gilian Shallcross, Arthur Graves, Agnes Graves.
Middle row: James Brownlee, the daughter and wife of Perry Hires, Liz Graves, Pat
Garrish, Justin West. Front row: Queenie Williams, Sandy Graves, unknown

October

The first OIP members, painters Bruce Currie and
Ethel Magafan and multidisciplinary artist Bartow
Underhill, arrive on Ossabaw[(fig. 5)]. The Ossabaw
Island Project Foundation (later known as the
Ossabaw Foundation) is incorporated a few months
later[(fig. 6)]. During its first season, which runs until
April 1962, the OIP welcomes fourteen participants
(called members) from six different states who stay
on the island for an average of two weeks. All members are invited to apply at the recommendation
of the Advisory Board, which primarily comprises
those who visited the island in June. In order to run
the program on the island, the Wests negotiate a re-
newable lease with Sandy's niece and nephews.

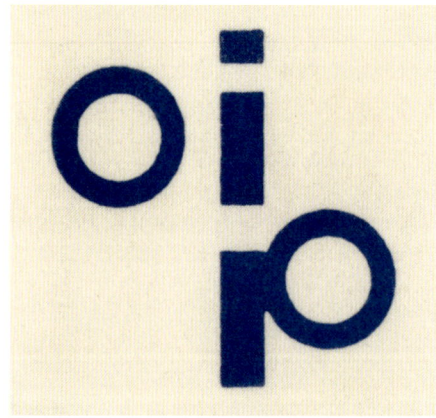

fig. 6.   Ossabaw Island Project logo

1962

Clifford West produces a film about the OIP through
the newly established production company, OIP
Films. Sandy West writes the narration, which is performed by OIP advisor Edmund McKenzie. Clifford
also makes a 15-minute film titled *Synthesis: Travis,
Tigers, and Wild Boars*, which follows OIP member
and painter Paul Travis as he makes a watercolor of a
tiger hunt[(fig. 7)]. The island staff and the West family
watch Travis work in one of the tabby cabins on the island's North End, which functions as his studio. In the
latter half of the film, island manager Arthur Graves
takes Travis on a boar hunt on the island. In ensuing
years, the Wests produce several films under the OIP
Films banner, with Clifford as director and cinema-

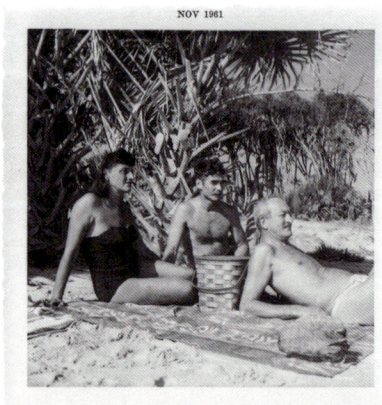

fig. 5.   Ethel Magafan, Bruce Currie, and Bartow
Underhill, South End Beach, November 1961

tographer and Sandy as a frequent scriptwriter. Many of them focus on artists, including OIP members such as Tex Schiwetz, Arnold Blanch, and Harry Bertoia, and historical figures such as Brunelleschi, Donatello, Verrocchio, Michelangelo, and Luca della Robbia, among others. These films are often screened in the Main House after dinner for OIP members.

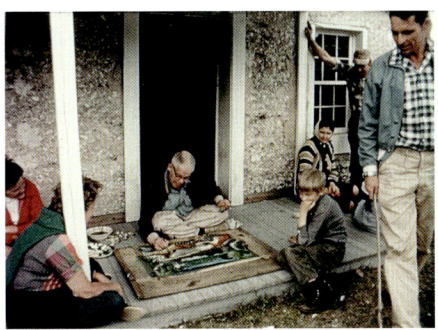

fig. 7.   Paul Travis (center) with the Ossabaw staff and West family, 1962. Film still from Clifford West, *Synthesis: Travis, Tigers, and Wild Boars*, 1962

March

OIP advisor Tex Schiwetz donates his sculpture *Sharks* (c. 1958) to the Ossabaw Island Project and installs it on the front lawn of the Main House (fig. 8). Schiwetz is the first of many artists to donate works of art to the OIP.

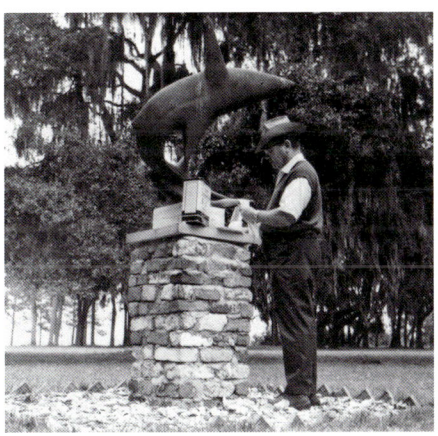

fig. 8.   Tex Schiwetz cleaning his *Sharks*, c. 1958, on the Main House lawn, 1966

1964

Fall

Sandy West contacts Allston Jenkins of the Natural Lands Trust for advice on how to approach preserving Ossabaw Island in the long term. The environmental writer Michael Frome later suggests to the Wests that they seek advice from Richard Pough, founder of the Nature Conservancy.

October 19–20

Joseph Harrison, Julian Sipple, and the Wests organize a conference on Ossabaw to educate the presidents of regional universities and other locally prominent people about the island and OIP (fig. 9). Discussion centers around bringing students to the island, and brainstorming how to expand the program's reach in a thoughtful and purposeful way. In a summary of the conference sent out to the Advisory Board, the Wests write, "Our trial years are behind us and we are able to operate at full capacity. We most vitally need [advisors'] recommendations to broaden our base and to ensure a continuing representation from many fields of creative thought and work."

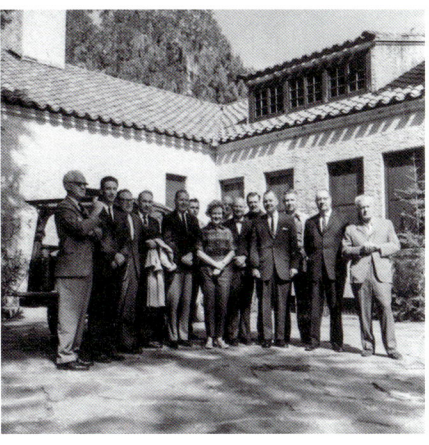

fig. 9.   Lamar Dodd, Charles D. Hounshell, William H. Patterson, Earl Mueller, Alan J. Robertson, Arthur R. Kelley, Sandy West, Joseph Harrison, G. H. Achenbach, Clifford West, Edwin D. Harrison, Julian Sipple, O. C. Aderhold, and Arnold Blanch at the Main House, November 1964

1967

To accommodate OIP's growth and allow for longer residencies, the Main House's garage is converted into additional artist studio spaces. Storage spaces on the back side of the house are also remodeled as two more smaller studios. Around this time, married Advisory Board members architect Olav Hammarstrom and textile designer and weaver Marianne Strengell donate plans for an Ossabaw museum. The blueprints call for three buildings to be constructed behind the Main House. The Wests write that "one building will be dedicated to the flora and fauna and formation of the Island, the second to the 4,000 years of history represented by the treasures we have found and the third to the accomplishments and donations of the O.I.P. Members." The first stake is driven in April 1969, but the museum is never completed (fig. 10).

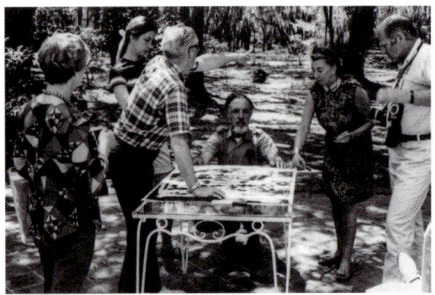

fig. 10.   Anne Wood, Gilian Wohlauer, Olav Hammarstrom, Charles Wood, Marianne Strengell, and William Saltzman discussing plans for the Ossabaw museum, 1969

12 January

The OIP Advisory Board decides to begin accepting recommendations from former Project members. Sandy writes, "Now that the Project and its pattern are well established it seems advisable that Project Members who have already experienced a stay on the Island should participate in recommending others."

1968

October

Clifford West's sister, Anne Wood, and her husband, actor Charles Wood, are named co-executive directors of OIP. Following Marker's retirement in June 1967, writer Jon Edwards directed the Project for one season.

October 13–14

Mounting pressure to commercially develop the nearby, privately owned Wassaw Island and a plan to begin mining for phosphate off its shores shines a light on the increasing endangerment of Georgia's coast. The Georgia Natural Areas Council and the Coastal Area Planning and Development Commission convene a Conference on the Future of the Marshlands and Islands of Georgia at the Cloisters on Sea Island, which the Wests help to organize. Sandy and Clifford both give impassioned speeches on the development of the OIP through the lens of creative work as a means of land preservation. "Ossabaw is essential to this Project, but Ossabaw is also essential to shrimp and fish, to trees and plants," says Sandy. "This too is part of our responsibility and so for ten years we have tried...to figure out a way of keeping Ossabaw intact and unspoiled." John W. Bright of the National Park Service highlights the Wests' programs on Ossabaw. "America depends on quality of thought to prompt and guide the actions and expression of individuals and organizations," he says. "I can imagine no higher use for a portion of the Golden Isles."

1969

March

Twenty-five biology students from Shorter College in Rome, Georgia, arrive on Ossabaw under the supervision of botany professors Dr. Philip Greear and Dr. Emma Lewis Lipps [fig. 11]. The students have specific projects planned for their trip, including studies of plant galls, fiddler crab populations, and pond grasses. They stay at a camp on Newell Creek that is later dubbed Fort Shorter. After the success of the inaugural visit, Dr. Greear brings students to the island each spring for 17 consecutive years under the Wests' Public Use and Education program.

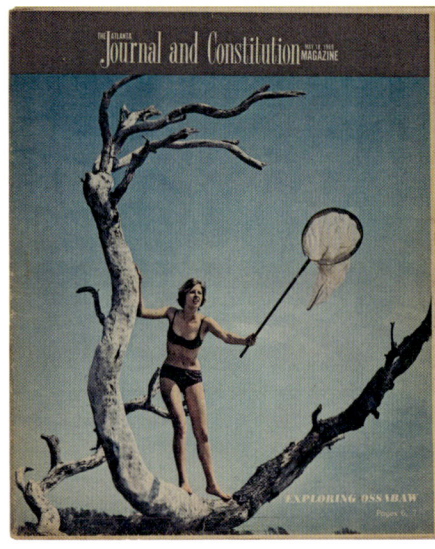

fig. 11.   A Shorter College student on the cover of *The Atlanta Journal and Constitution Magazine*, May 18, 1969

December 6

The Atlanta Journal and Constitution reports that the Wests are in talks with eight colleges and universities in Georgia to co-manage use of the island. The institutions would establish an ambitious Center for Ecological Studies at Middle Place, a site of one of the island's former plantations, to host educational and research activities. The initiative never materializes.

1970

The State of Georgia passes the Coastal Marshlands Protection Act.

April

After plans for the Center for Ecological Studies fall apart, the Wests dream up a program of their own for Middle Place that they call Genesis. In contrast to the OIP, which caters to established professionals, Genesis will invite multidisciplinary students to live together in a semi-sustainable community on the island: "The initial purpose of the Genesis Experiment is to provide a group of carefully selected individuals with an experience of basic living, in harmonious co-existence with and dependence on Nature, requiring multi-disciplinary problem solving." [(fig. 12)]

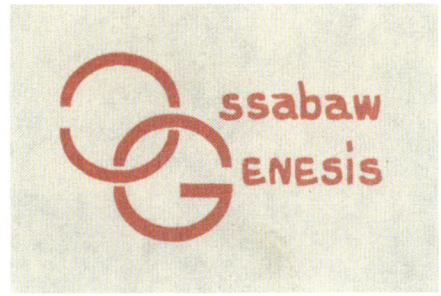

fig. 12.　Genesis logo

June 15–August 30

The first Genesis members spend the summer on Ossabaw. Thirty college students from universities across the country restore buildings left behind by a timbering operation at Middle Place and con-struct new buildings, including an A-frame, three treehouses, an outhouse, and a chicken coop. Four-member teams are formed to equally dispense chores, which rotate weekly. They help butcher cattle and pigs, tend a five-acre garden, harvest local seafood, and study the ecology of the island, among other projects. "I want to tell you all the things I've forgotten to say, but if I started I could go on for years and years," Maura Frank, who kept a log of the summer, wrote in her final entry. "I'll just say that it's been fine and beautiful and wonderful and, just as I thought, the life energies are flowing in me strong again."

September

The Wests are informed that Chatham County has reassessed Ossabaw Island and taxes will be raised from $6,790 to $48,000 per year. They are able to negotiate the taxes down to $27,000 per year by highlighting the nonprofit programs that they are running on the island, but the major increase puts their ability to financially support the Ossabaw programs in jeopardy.

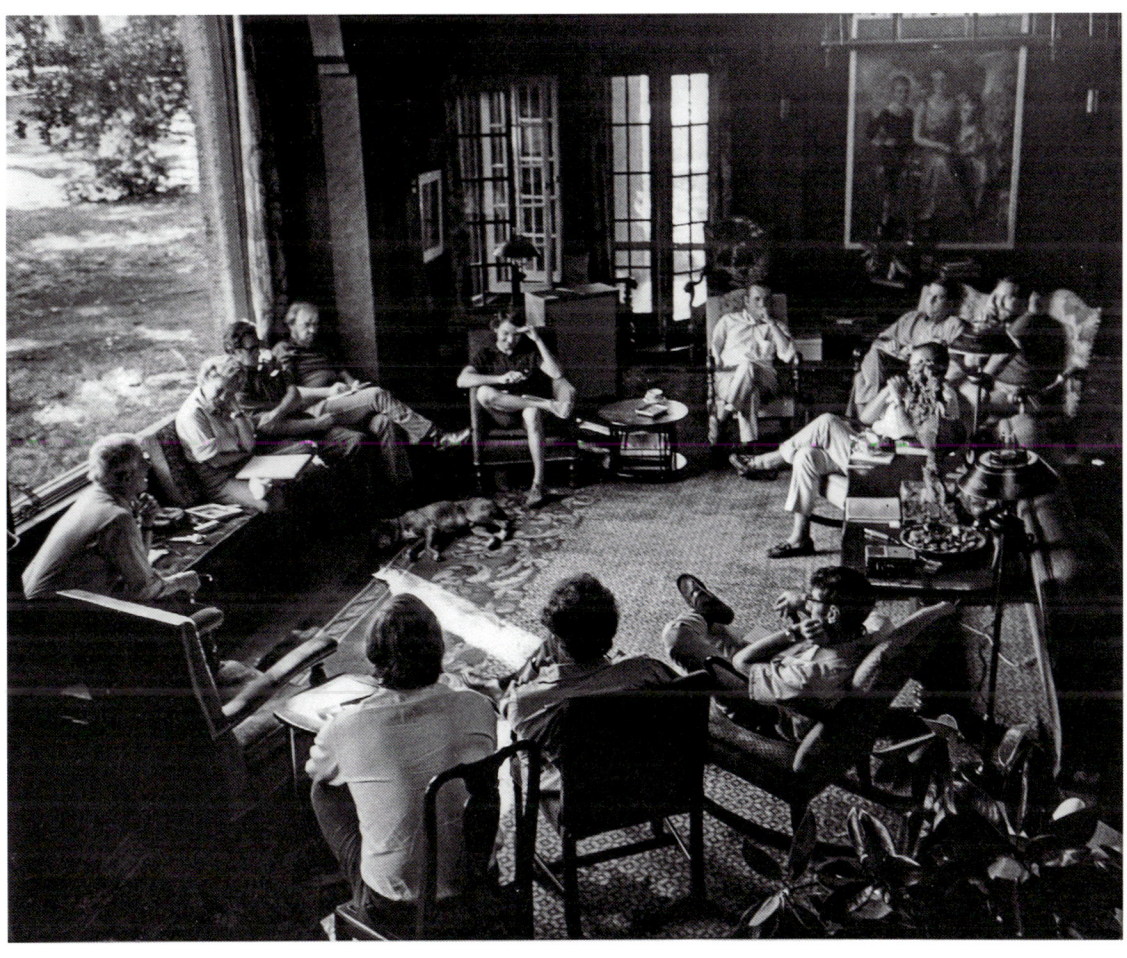

fig. 13.　Conference to discuss the future of Ossabaw Island in the Main House living room, 1972. Clockwise from left: David Brower, Sandy West, Dale Jenkins, Robert Jenkins, Robert Funicello, William Ford Torrey Jr., Philip Berolzeimer, Randall Torrey, Emory Torrey, Steve Keitey, Robert Hanie, and Charlie Hanie. Photograph by John Pennington

Based on learnings from the first year of Genesis, the second season is limited to July and August and features a smaller cohort. Applicants are required to submit a proposal for interdisciplinary study during their time on the island and the program is free of charge for those who are accepted. In contrast to the OIP, Genesis directors are hired on a short-term basis. Over the ensuing years, they include Jim Brown, Sandy West's son John Shallcross, Kathy and Omar Hendrix, Kevin Donovan, Virginia "Shorty" Boucher, Al Bradford, Stephen Schoenholtz, Helen Hamada, Bob Lockhart, David Bayne, Michael Billa, Jane Timmerman, Wini Wood, and Ann Jones.

June 22

Tex Schiwetz, OIP advisor and a close friend of the Wests, passes away in Michigan. In his will, Schiwetz leaves a fifth of his estate to the Ossabaw Island Project. This significant financial contribution helps to stave off the increased costs of running the programs on Ossabaw for the next few years.

June 1

At the urging of renowned conservationist and founder of Friends of the Earth David Brower, Sandy West hosts a conference on Ossabaw to discuss the protection of Georgia's last wild barrier islands from private development [fig. 13]. Her three nephews attend, as well as Joe Tanner of Georgia's Department of Natural Resources, and Robert Jenkins of the Nature Conservancy, among others. Brower proposes bringing 75 miles of Coastal Georgia, including Ossabaw, into a proposed World Heritage Trust. West expresses her approval of the proposal but cautions the group that something must be done fast as her niece and nephews have voiced their intention to sell their share of the island by July 1974. "We've as a family felt the need of preserving this island," West says. "But if in July of '74 or whenever the [money] runs out, and nobody else dies and leaves us [money, and] we have no more cattle to sell, we will have to sell this island to the highest bidder." As word spreads that West and the

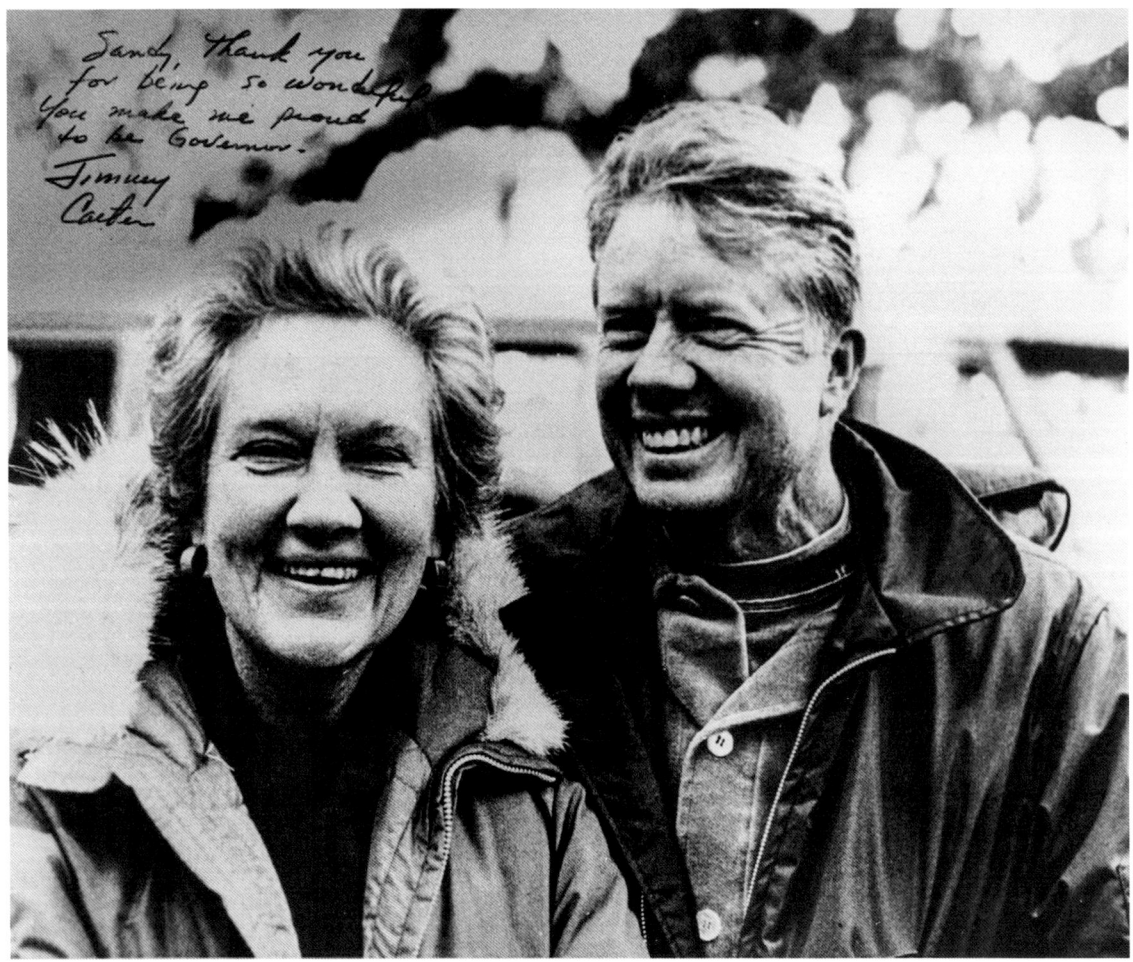

fig. 14. Sandy West and Jimmy Carter, c. 1973. Inscribed by Carter

Torreys are looking for a steward for Ossabaw, private buyers express interest in acquiring the island, from Charles E. Fraser, the developer of Hilton Head Island, to Jacqueline and Aristotle Onassis. In an article documenting the conference, the journalist John Pennington notes that Queenie Williams, while singing spirituals after dinner, inserts the island's name into her prayer: "Ossabaw needs you, Lord, come by here..."

Summer

Governor Jimmy Carter establishes the Georgia Heritage Advisory Commission. He asks its members to advise on "a program for the immediate acquisition of the most significant and endangered historical, environmental and recreational areas" in Georgia. At the end of August, the group approves a list of 38 places that includes Ossabaw.

Fall

Genesis becomes a year-round program and logs representation of over 20 colleges and 23 different fields of study. Research projects conducted by participants range from the study of the island's flora and fauna, painting, weaving, and turtle conservation. In later years, Genesis goes through a natural expansion to include members of all ages and those who are already active in their professional careers. People from around the United States and the world participate, including from Germany and Indonesia.

September 25

OIP advisor and renowned ecologist Eugene P. Odum urges Sandy West to consider the State of Georgia as a steward for Ossabaw rather than an international organization such as Friends of the Earth. He writes, "I estimate the lag time for political, and particularly international reforms in terms of land-use to be at least ten years." Given the urgency of her financial situation, he stresses that she will have more leverage in dictating the terms of the island's use if she is able to give it away rather than sell it.

December 16–17

Following initial meetings between Sandy West, the Torreys, and Joe Tanner of Georgia's Department of Natural Resources, Jimmy Carter spends two days on Ossabaw to discuss the island's potential acquisition by the state [fig. 14]. Sandy West takes him all over the island and shares her vision for its ongoing preservation. Immediately upon his return to Atlanta, Carter sends West and the Torreys a proposal for the state to acquire Ossabaw. Carter later wrote, "I grew to appreciate Sandy's deep spiritual connection to the island and all its living creatures, past, present, and future."

1973

The Wests publish an extended booklet that delineates the aims of the Ossabaw Foundation [fig. 15]. They highlight their expanded program, which includes Public Use and Education and Professional Research in addition to the OIP and Genesis. A wide range of scientists from universities around the country visit Ossabaw under the umbrella of Professional Research to conduct extended projects on the island. Local, regional, and national organizations come to the island through the Public Use and Education program, including Savannah's public schools, the Nature Conservancy, and the Audubon Society, among many others.

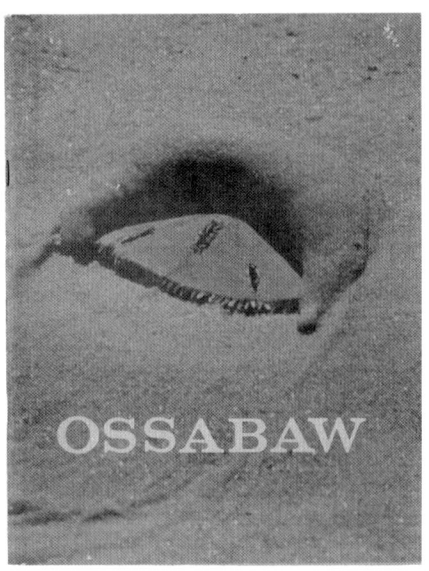

fig. 15.   Cover of a booklet outlining the Ossabaw Foundation's activities, compiled by Sandy and Clifford West, 1973

1974

As part of its effort to make the region a World Heritage Site, Friends of the Earth publishes *Guale, the Golden Coast of Georgia*, the seventh book in its "The Earth's Wild Places Series" [fig. 16]. The text is written by Georgia Conservancy founder, ecologist, and recurring OIP member Robert Hanie, with a foreword by David Brower, an introduction by Eugene P. Odum and John P. Milton, and photographs by OIP members John Earl and James Valentine—many of which were taken on Ossabaw.

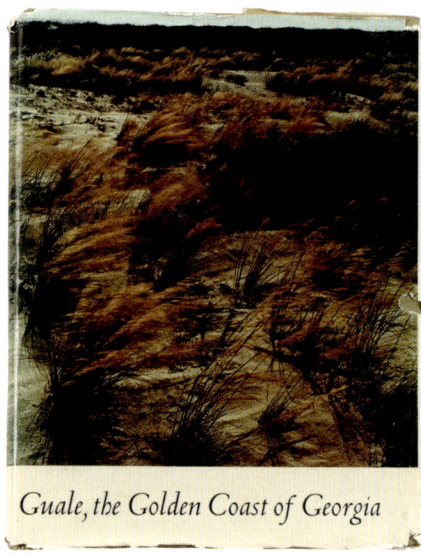

fig. 16.   Cover of *Guale, the Golden Coast of
Georgia* (Friends of the Earth, 1974)

1975

The OIP continues to grow and evolve. Sandy and Clifford West's son Justin constructs a new pottery studio with a gas-fired kiln in the old Delco plant behind the Main House[fig. 17]. The artist studios undergo repairs, a darkroom is set up in one of the Main House's closets, and a piano studio designed by OIP member and composer Stanley Hollingsworth is built. Meanwhile, Jimmy Carter signs the Georgia Heritage Trust Act to "preserve certain real property...that exhibits unique natural characteristics, special historical significance, or particular recreational value."

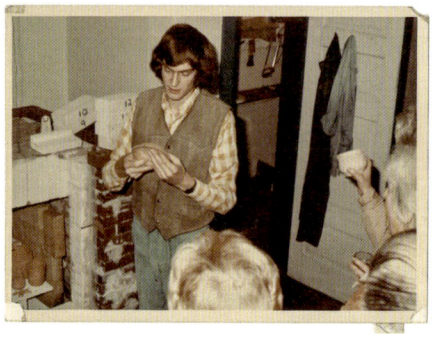

fig. 17.   Justin West holding a ceramic bowl
fired in the kiln at the Ossabaw Island
Project, 1975

1976

Sandy West publishes a children's book through The Beehive Press in Savannah titled *Maria Bosomworth and William Rodgers*[fig. 18]. It tells the tale of an unlikely friendship between a piglet and a puppy on Ossabaw. The piglet, Maria, was named after the first woman to lay claim to the island (known historically as Mary Musgrove). Half-English and half-Muscogee, she lived during the 18th century and became an important interpreter between the two communities. William, the puppy, was named after a writer who had been an OIP member in 1968 and 1969. A brochure for the publication claims, "All profits from the sale of the book will go to the Ossabaw Island Project, which is dedicated to education, research, and the preservation of this wild, natural land and its animals."

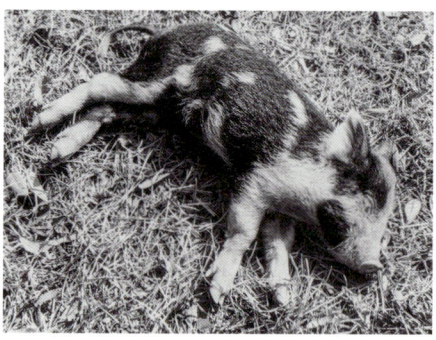

fig. 18.   Maria Bosomworth, 1976. Photograph by
Eleanor Torrey West

March 10

Sandy and Clifford West's divorce is finalized after years of the couple living apart.

1977

April 7

Sandy West, Annette Torrey Fraser (formerly Peck), William Torrey Jr., Emory Torrey, and Randall Torrey sign an agreement with Georgia's governor George Busbee to sell Ossabaw to the State of Georgia in the spring of 1978 for $8 million, half of its appraised value. A $4 million payment by the state is matched by a donation from Atlanta philanthropist and former Coca-Cola board chairman, Robert W. Woodruff. When the sale goes into effect, the island will become the state's first Heritage Preserve under the Heritage Trust Act. The sales agreement stipulates that the island shall "only (be) used for natural, scientific, and cultural study, research, and education, and environmentally sound preservation, conservation, and management of the Island's ecosystem." Sandy West also negotiates a use agreement that will allow the Ossabaw Foundation's programs to continue on the island[fig. 19]. In a note to the OIP Advisory Board, Sandy writes, "THE MIRACLE IN WHICH WE ALL BELIEVE HAS HAPPENED! AFTER 16 YEARS OF STRUGGLE AND FAITH OSSABAW ISLAND HAS BEEN SAVED!"

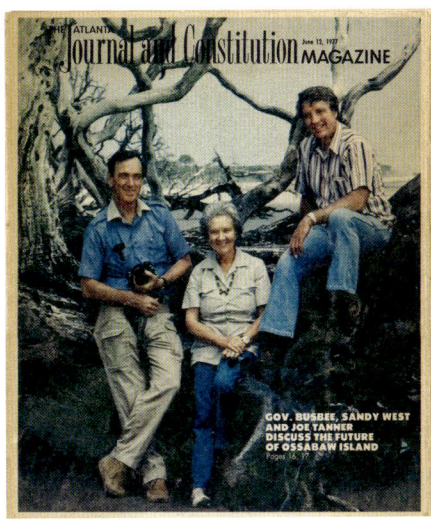

fig. 19. Cover of *The Atlanta Journal and Constitution Magazine*, June 12, 1977

organization's new relationship with the State of Georgia. Movius travels around the country to try to raise money for the organization without much success. Grants are later secured from the National Endowment for the Arts, the Georgia Council of the Arts and Humanities, the Ralph and Winifred Polk Foundation, and the Witter Bynner Foundation, among others, but the Foundation's programs remain funded primarily by Sandy.

October

Genesis members partner with the Savannah Science Museum to build a solar hot water heater to provide hot water for use in the Cookshack. Improvements are made on the treehouses, a tabby building from the pre-Civil War era, and the director's house. A raku-style kiln, woodworking shop, and toolshed-food-bin are built as well.

May 11

Ossabaw Island is officially purchased by the State of Georgia. Sandy West retains a life estate in the Main House and the approximately thirty acres surrounding it, with the stipulation that the house and grounds will transfer to the state upon her death. In a letter to the Ossabaw Foundation's Advisory Board announcing the sale, West writes, "Ossabaw is as safe as we can make it and the Coast has a reprieve."

June 1

Charles and Anne Wood retire after ten years. Sandy West asks former OIP member and Genesis co-director Al Bradford, who had been working as their assistant, to take over at the beginning of the 1978/79 season. Poet and two-time OIP member Carol Burdick joins Bradford as co-director the following year.

1978

March 22

In advance of Ossabaw's sale, Sandy West appoints former OIP member Geoffrey Movius as the first executive director of the Ossabaw Foundation. He is put in charge of fundraising and managing the

1980

Spring

Following the construction of a post-and-beam solar shower and sauna at Middle Place, Genesis members David Bayne and Mark Bromley spearhead a

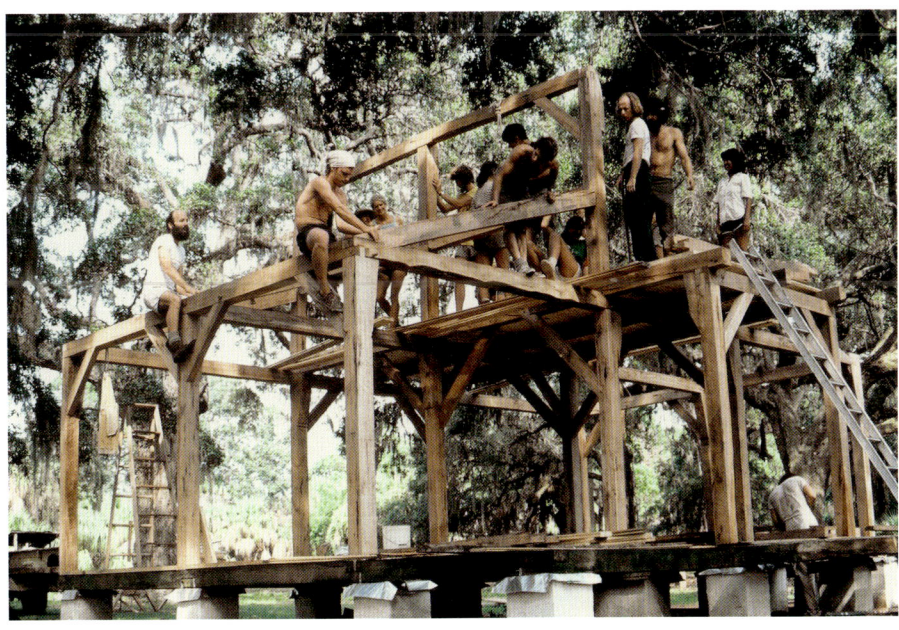

fig. 20. Genesis members building the Tower House at Middle Place, c. 1980. Photograph by Leslie Ferst

project to salvage felled trees from Hurricane David. They use a DIY-style sawmill powered by a chainsaw to mill the lumber necessary to build a new housing structure known as the Tower House on the foundation of an old barn. Genesis members begin living and working in the space in June 1981 [fig. 20].

April 6

The two-year-old Savannah College of Art and Design opens *Ossabaw Island Georgia: Painting, Drawing, Photography, Sculpture, Textiles* at Exhibit A gallery in Poetter Hall [fig. 21]. The first exhibition of art created on and about Ossabaw Island features 33 artists affiliated with the OIP, Genesis, and the Ossabaw Foundation's other programs working in a wide range of media. They include Harry Bertoia, Arnold Blanch, John Earl, Helen Hamada, Doris Lee, Nancy Marshall, Lorraine McCarty, Martha Odum, Daga Ramsey, and Tex Schiwetz, among others. The exhibition acts as a dual fundraiser for the Foundation and the College.

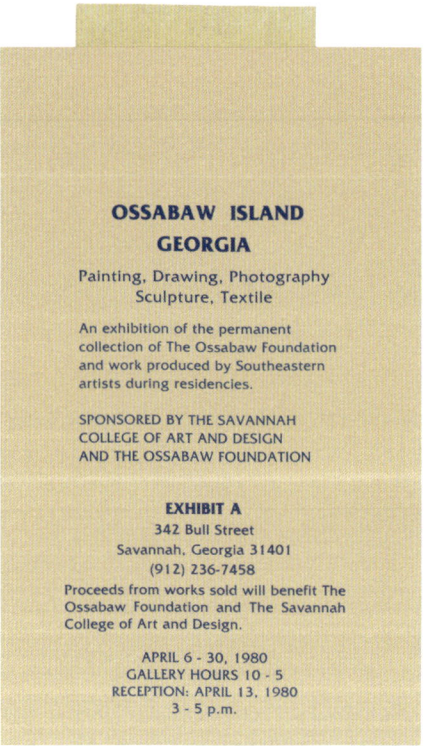

OSSABAW ISLAND
GEORGIA

Painting, Drawing, Photography
Sculpture, Textile

An exhibition of the permanent collection of The Ossabaw Foundation and work produced by Southeastern artists during residencies.

SPONSORED BY THE SAVANNAH COLLEGE OF ART AND DESIGN AND THE OSSABAW FOUNDATION

EXHIBIT A
342 Bull Street
Savannah, Georgia 31401
(912) 236-7458
Proceeds from works sold will benefit The Ossabaw Foundation and The Savannah College of Art and Design.

APRIL 6 - 30, 1980
GALLERY HOURS 10 - 5
RECEPTION: APRIL 13, 1980
3 - 5 p.m.

fig. 21. Invitation for *Ossabaw Island, Georgia: Painting, Drawing, Photography, Sculpture, Textile* at Exhibit A, Savannah College of Art and Design, April 6-30, 1980

September

Former OIP members Ellen H. Johnson, an art historian and Professor Emerita at Oberlin College, and David Hamilton, a poet, travel to Ossabaw for the inaugural admissions committee meeting for the

OIP. Sandy West, her children Gilian Wohlauer (née Shallcross) and Justin West, and OIP co-directors Al Bradford and Carol Burdick also participate. The committee is assembled to review the Project's rapidly increasing number of applications. Johnson suggests formalizing the process and using higher standards to assess applicants in the visual arts.

November

A wood-burning kiln is built at Middle Place as part of a workshop led by potters David Morgan and Leslie Ferst, a former Genesis member [fig. 22]. Costs related to the kiln are defrayed by a donation from former Genesis members Janice and Larry Payne.

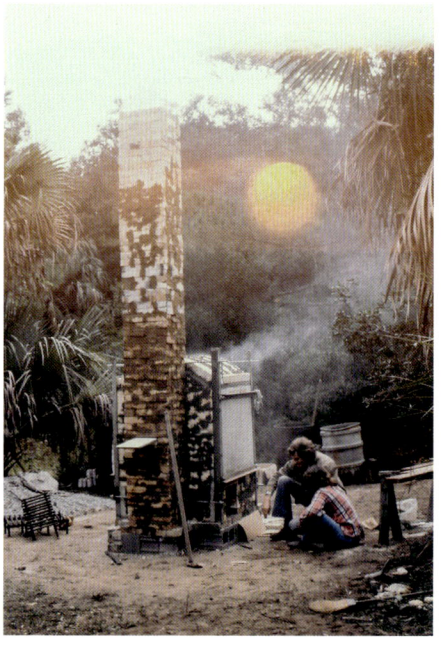

fig. 22. Justin West and Diana Nicholson with the wood-burning kiln at Middle Place, c. November 1980. Photograph by Leslie Ferst

1981

November 13

The one room River House [fig. 23], which faces Buckhead Creek at Middle Place, catches fire in the middle of the night. Genesis co-director Michael Billa, who was living there at the time, escapes with nothing but the clothes on his back. Billa and fellow Genesis member John Christenson rebuild the house on a nearby site the following spring.

1982

April 17

Having supported the Ossabaw Foundation primarily with money earned from the sale of the island, Sandy West sends out an urgent letter concerning

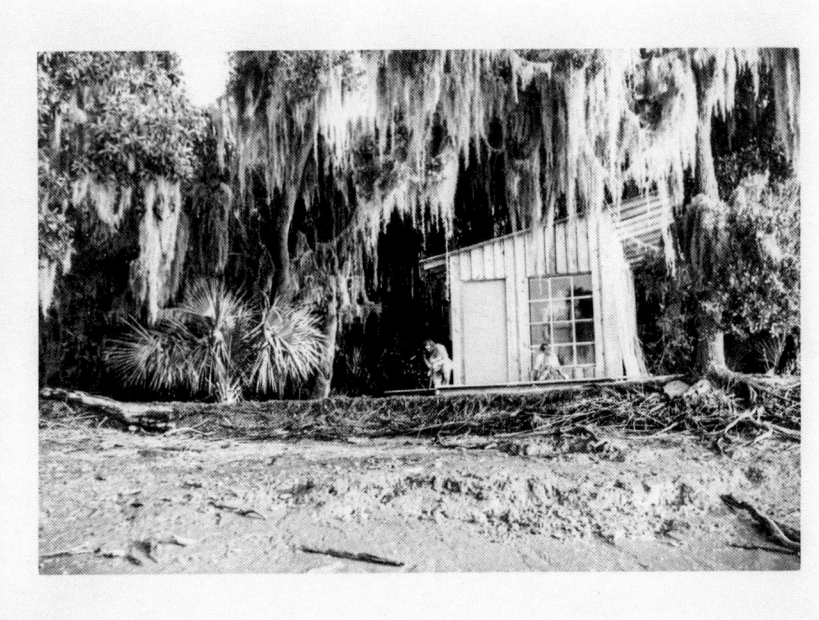

fig. 23.   Genesis members building the first River House at Middle Place, c. 1970

the Foundation's financial crisis. "We must have two donations or pledges of $25,000 or more before July 31, 1982...if we fail, the Foundation, after twenty years, will have to leave Ossabaw."

August 12

Sandy writes to the trustees of the Ossabaw Foundation to share that the deadline has passed to raise enough money to continue the organization's programs. OIP is closed for the year, and Genesis, Public Use and Education, and Professional Research await decisions on closure.

September 15

"In spite of the wonderful response to my letter in April, we have been forced to suspend some of our programs," West writes in a follow-up letter. She explains that OIP and Genesis will close for the year despite an increase in applications to both. The Foundation, though dramatically cut back, will continue to support both the Professional Research and the Public Use and Education programs. "The months ahead will be a time of rethinking," she writes. "I am convinced that we will find a long range plan that will be affordable and manageable."

1983

November 15

A year after their temporary closure, Sandy writes to the Ossabaw Foundation's Advisory Board to inform them that OIP and Genesis will close indefinitely. The Foundation continues to run its Public Use and Education and Professional Research programs in a very limited capacity.

1993

At the behest of Sandy West, Savannah-based historic preservationist Leopold Adler II spearheads an effort to revitalize the languishing Ossabaw Foundation. The organization changes its name to The Ossabaw Island Foundation (TOIF) and applies to become a public 501(c)3 for the first time. Inspired by the Wests' programs during the 1960s and 1970s but not aiming to emulate them, the new foundation focuses on facilitating programming on Ossabaw within the restrictions of its Heritage Preserve status and restoring the island's historic buildings. "We need to raise approximately six million dollars to put the properties in shape and support our public use and education programs," Adler says in a 1995 interview.

1995

The National Trust for Historic Preservation puts Ossabaw Island on its annual list of America's 11 Most Endangered Historic Places.

1996

September 13

Ossabaw Island is added to the National Register of Historic Places, which is dedicated to districts, sites, buildings, and structures significant in American history, architecture, archaeology, and culture.

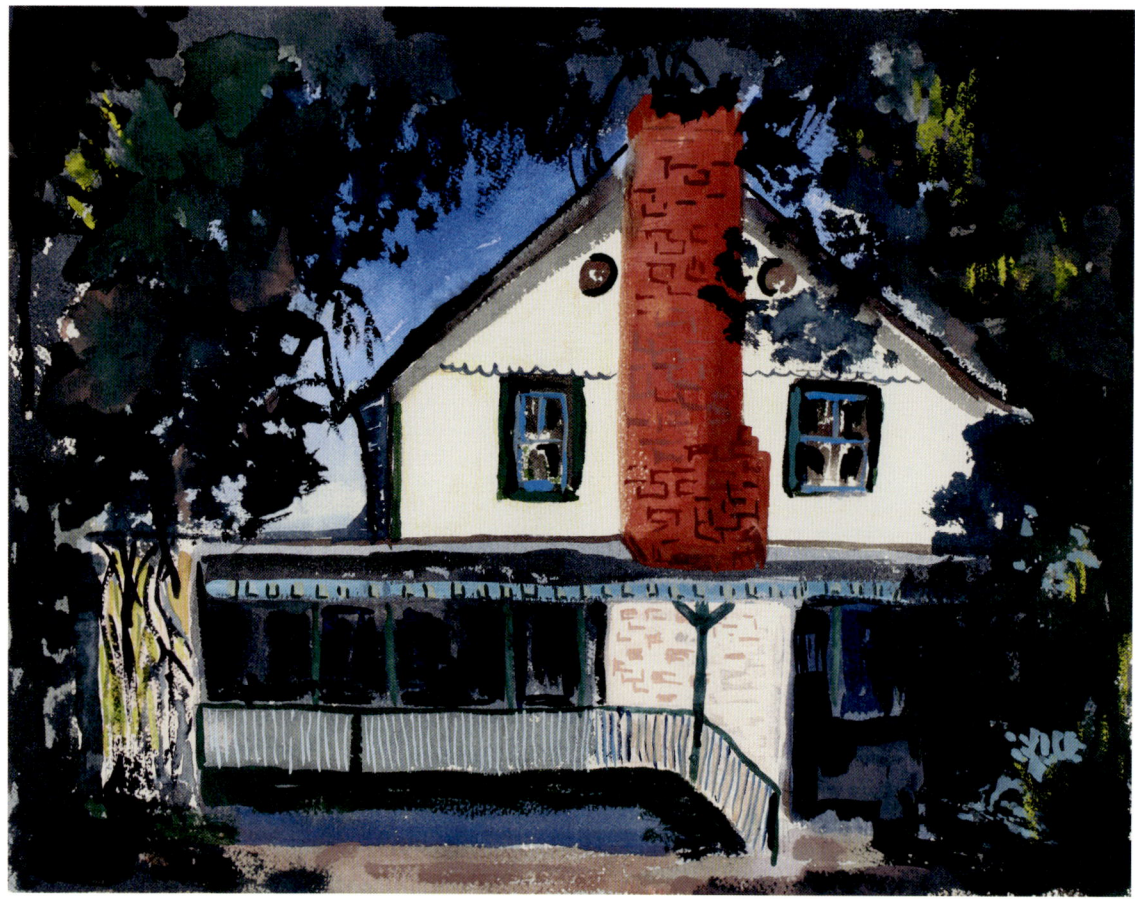

fig. 24.   Eleanor Torrey West. Untitled (Clubhouse), c. 1979. Watercolor on paper,
12 ³/₁₆ × 16 ¹/₈ in. The Ossabaw Island Foundation

1999

TOIF restores the Clubhouse—a large two story home built in 1887 on the site of a former plantation house at the North End—for use on day trips and to offer overnight accommodations for island visitors [fig. 24]. Eight years later, the Foundation rehabilitates the nearby Boarding House, built in 1918, to increase lodging capabilities on the island.

2002

March 2–17

The Jack Leigh Gallery in Savannah hosts *Ossabaw Island: Photographs and Paintings*, an exhibition of Leigh's photographs and OIP member Alan Campbell's paintings of the island. Two years later, the University of Georgia Press publishes *Ossabaw: Evocations of an Island*, featuring the work of both artists as well as essays by John Lane and James Kilgo [fig. 25]. A portion of the proceeds from the exhibition and the book are donated to Sandy West, whose precarious financial situation threatens her ability to continue living on Ossabaw.

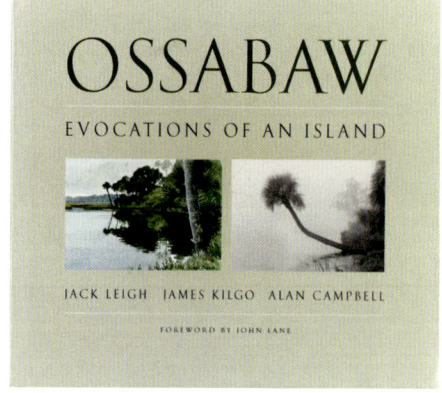

fig. 25.   Cover of *Ossabaw: Evocations of an Island*
(University of Georgia Press, 2004)

2004

TOIF establishes the Ossabaw Island Education Alliance with a "vision to make the island a nationally recognized education center focusing on many disciplines." The initiative fosters research into all aspects of the island under the tutelage of Dr. Paul Pressly, who organizes the symposia "The Atlantic World and African American Life and Culture in the Georgia Lowcountry: 18th to 20th Century" in 2008 and "Coastal Nature, Coastal Culture: Environmental Histories of the Georgia Coast" in 2016.

2005

TOIF facilitates the restoration of two of the three tabby cabins on Ossabaw's North End to reflect their original appearance and use. These houses were built in the first half of the 19th century by enslaved people who were skilled carpenters and tradesmen, using tabby, tabby bricks, clay bricks, shell mortar, and wood. The restoration is funded through a $400,000 Save America's Treasures grant from the U.S. Department of the Interior, matched with private donations.

2006

Summer

TOIF puts out a call for artists to gain "creative stimulation" from Ossabaw Island in their quarterly newsletter. They offer free overnight trips to the island for artists to spend time, make work, and learn about Ossabaw's natural and built environment under the supervision of on-island coordinator Jim Bitler during the low season in August and September. In return, the visiting artists are asked to donate artworks created on and about the island to the auction at the Foundation's annual fundraiser. Savannah-based artists Betsy Cain and Suzanne Jackson spend time on Ossabaw as part of the Visiting Artists Program, which continues until 2011. Cain, who is also actively involved in bringing artists to Ossabaw through the program, writes in TOIF's spring 2011 newsletter, "There is a pulse of the unknown on this island, ripe territory for the creative soul." [fig. 26]

2014

January

TOIF adapts a concrete structure on the North End originally built for meat processing into a new field lab. It includes a black-and-white photography darkroom and a work area for processing natural specimens collected on the island.

2016

May 3

At 103 years old, Sandy West leaves Ossabaw Island to move into an assisted living facility in Savannah.

2020

March 12

Georgia House Bill (HB) 906 is introduced in the Georgia House of Representatives and passes with just seven nay votes. The bill proposes to privatize historic structures in Georgia as a way to preserve them, putting such sites as the Ossabaw Island Heritage Preserve, Wormsloe Historic Site, and Skidaway Island State Park at risk.

June 15

Jimmy Carter releases a statement urging state leaders "to halt any further consideration of HB906," citing Georgia's acquisition of Ossabaw Island as its first Heritage Preserve. Carter states that passing the bill "would breach the commitments made to Mrs. West and many others who have conveyed land to the state as Heritage Preserves." West's son and

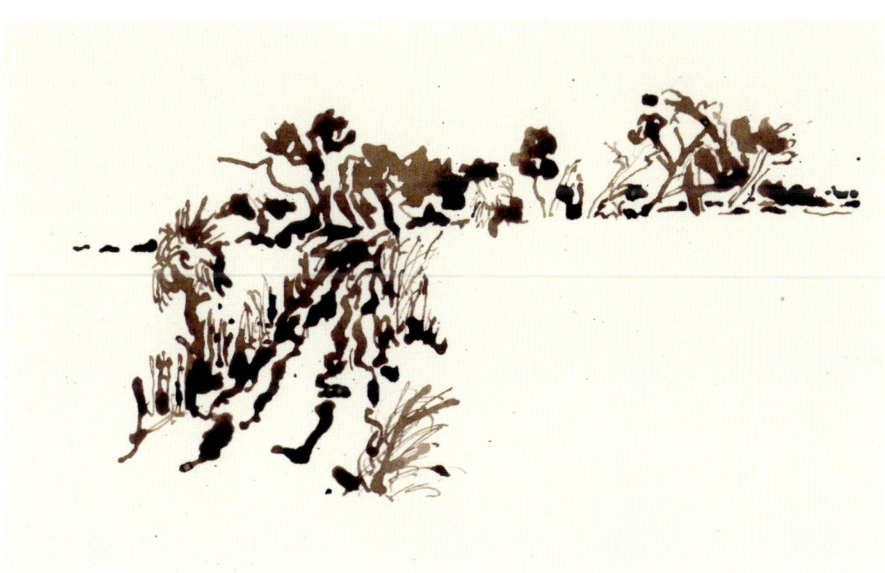

fig. 26.   Betsy Cain. *Cane Patch Road hammock*, 2012. Artist made walnut ink on D'arches paper, 4 ½ × 7 ¾ in. Suzanne Fitzallen Jackson Foundation

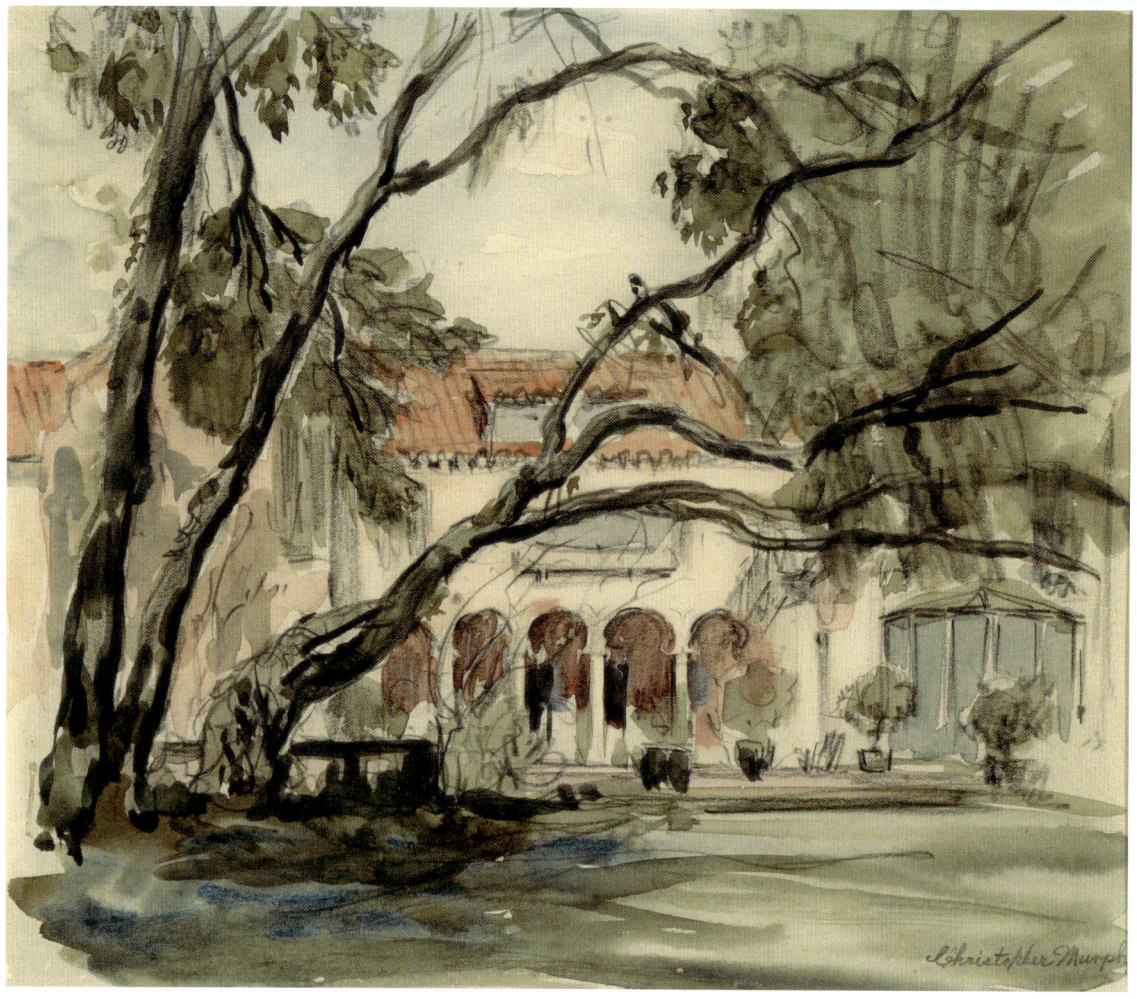

fig. 27. Christopher Murphy. *Main House, Ossabaw Island*, c. 1940. Watercolor on paper, 7 ¾ × 9 in. Collection of Justin P. West and Eileen McGowan

grandson, Justin West and Beryl Gilothwest, speak out on behalf of Sandy West, who is now 107, in the *Savannah Morning News*: "This dangerous bill threatens to undo the work that our family and countless others have done to preserve Ossabaw...by allowing portions of the island and Georgia's other 120 heritage preserves to be sold off to the highest bidder."

June 18
After extensive pushback and unsuccessful revisions, Georgia State Representative Jesse Petrea tells the *Savannah Morning News* that "(House Bill 906) is not coming back...the bottom line is, the language is no good. It needed to die. It's dead."

2021

January 17
Sandy West dies on her 108th birthday in Savannah. Upon her death, the Main House and its grounds become part of the Ossabaw Island Heritage Preserve.

2024

June 6
TOIF announces that $7 million has been allocated in the budget of Georgia's Department of Natural Resources to restore the Main House, where the Ossabaw Island Project was founded 63 years earlier[fig. 27]. The building's renovation will allow the Foundation to significantly expand its capabilities on the island.

2026

March 13–September 6
Telfair Museums presents *Off the Coast of Paradise: Artists and Ossabaw Island, 1961–Now*, the first major museum exhibition to explore the unique impact of Ossabaw Island on artists working over the last six decades.

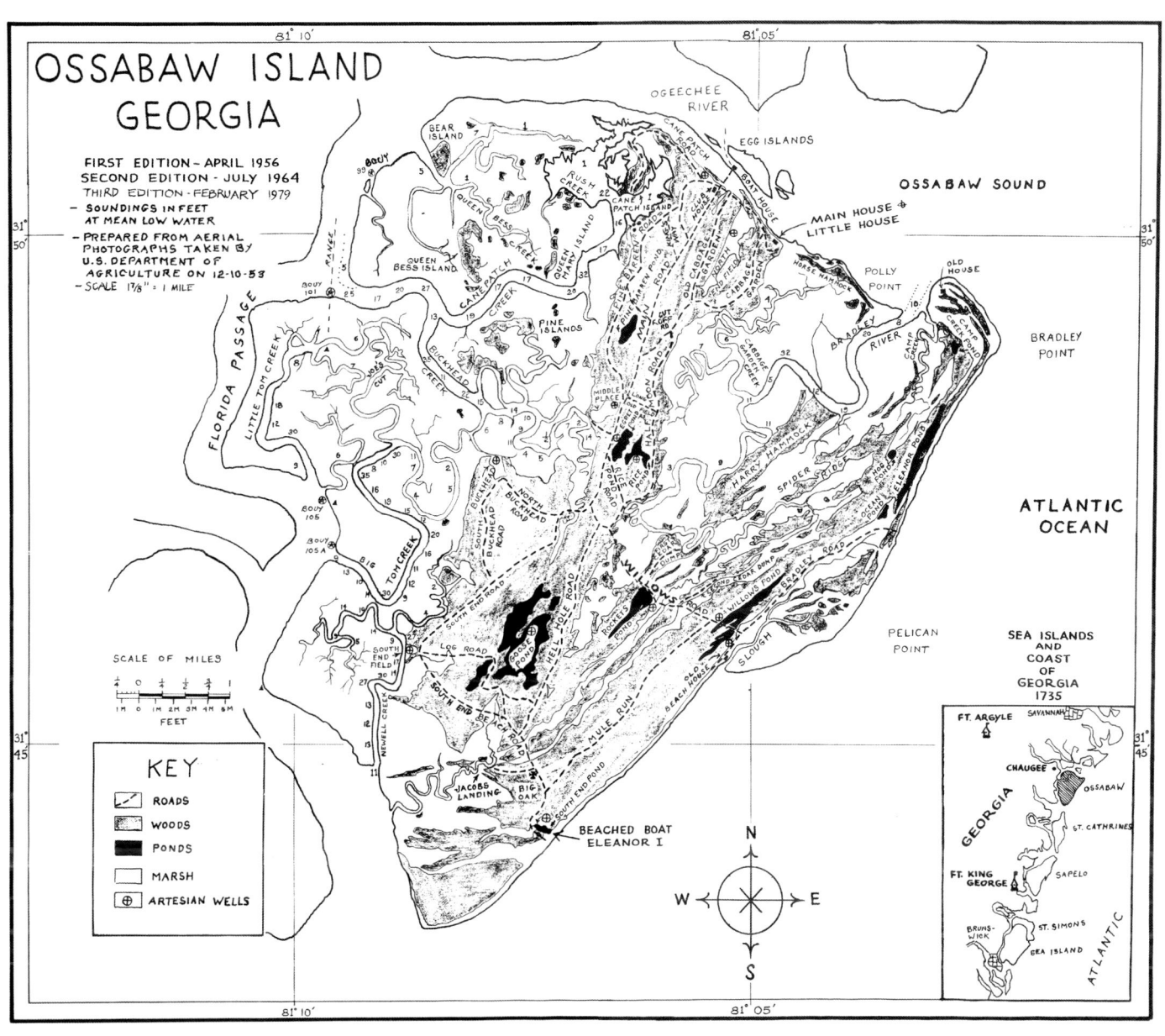

OSSABAW ISLAND GEORGIA

FIRST EDITION - APRIL 1956
SECOND EDITION - JULY 1964
THIRD EDITION - FEBRUARY 1979
– SOUNDINGS IN FEET
AT MEAN LOW WATER
– PREPARED FROM AERIAL
PHOTOGRAPHS TAKEN BY
U.S. DEPARTMENT OF
AGRICULTURE ON 12-10-53
– SCALE 1⅞" = 1 MILE

SCALE OF MILES

FEET

KEY

ROADS
WOODS
PONDS
MARSH
ARTESIAN WELLS

OSSABAW SOUND

ATLANTIC OCEAN

SEA ISLANDS
AND
COAST
OF
GEORGIA
1735

BEACHED BOAT
ELEANOR I

EXHIBITION CHECKLIST

Harry Bertoia (1915–1978)
Untitled, 1966
Bronze and stone
24 × 58 × 9 ½ in.
The Ossabaw Island Foundation
p. 34

Harry Bertoia (1915–1978)
Untitled, 1962
Monotype on laid rice paper
12 ¼ × 39 in.
Allentown Art Museum, SOTA
Print Fund, 1992.5.9
p. 35

Harry Bertoia (1915–1978)
Untitled (Spill Cast), c. 1962
Bronze
25 ½ × 51 × 6 ½ in.
Courtesy of Michael Rosenfeld
Gallery, LLC, New York, NY
p. 36

Arnold Blanch (1896–1968)
Ossabaw, 1964
Polymer on canvas
28 × 34 in.
Collection of Justin P. West and
Eileen McGowan
p. 88

Betsy Cain (b. 1949)
Fire Tree, 2010
Oil on Yupo paper
56 × 40 in.
Private collection
p. 37

Betsy Cain (b. 1949)
Cabbage Garden road (looking in the forest), 2022
Liquid graphite on Yupo paper
9 ½ × 12 ½ in.
Collection of Lisa and Mason
White
p. 89

Betsy Cain (b. 1949)
Vines and Moss, 2021
Artist made walnut ink on Yupo
paper
14 × 11 in.
Private collection
p. 89

Agnes Denes (b. 1931)
Life Beneath the Surface, 1981
Archival pigment print
12 × 18 in.
Collection of the artist
p. 38

Agnes Denes (b. 1931)
Silver Shores, 1981
Archival pigment print
12 × 18 in.
Collection of the artist
p. 39

Agnes Denes (b. 1931)
Patterns in Motion, 1981
Archival pigment print
12 × 18 in.
Collection of the artist
p. 40

Agnes Denes (b. 1931)
Sun's Reflection on Wet Sand,
1981
Archival pigment print
12 × 18 in.
Collection of the artist
p. 41

John Earl (1921–2008)
Ossabaw Sunset, c. 1974
Archival pigment print
24 × 16 in.
Collection of the Earl Family
p. 90

John Earl (1921–2008)
Mule Run, c. 1974
Archival pigment print
16 × 24 in.
Collection of the Earl Family
p. 91

John Earl (1921–2008)
Untitled (Portrait of Queenie
Williams), c. 1982
C-print
13 ½ × 9 ⅛ in.
Collection of Justin P. West and
Eileen McGowan
p. 133

Leslie Ferst (b. 1954)
The Circumnavigation, 1983
Clay and glaze
36 × 18 × 18 in.
Private collection
p. 42

Leslie Ferst (b. 1954)
Grotto, 2002
Clay and glaze
30 × 25 × 25 in.
Private collection
p. 43

Helen Hamada (b. 1951)
Ossabaw Island, 1974
Gelatin silver print
6 ½ × 6 ½ in.
The Ossabaw Island Foundation
p. 44

Helen Hamada (b. 1951)
Ossabaw Island, 1974
Gelatin silver print
6 ⁹⁄₁₆ × 6 ¼ in.
The Ossabaw Island Foundation
p. 45

Helen Hamada (b. 1951)
Bradley Beach, 1974
Gelatin silver print
6 ½ × 6 ½ in.
The Ossabaw Island Foundation
p. 46

Allison Janae Hamilton (b. 1984)
Venus of Ossabaw, 2026
Single channel video
Telfair Museums, museum com-
mission with funds provided by
VIA Art Fund
pp. 164–65

Marcy Hermansader (b. 1951)
Secrets of the Heart, 1983
Colored pencil, crayon, acrylic,
mosquito netting, and thread on
black wove paper
29 × 30 in.
Pennsylvania Academy of
the Fine Arts, Lambert Fund
Purchase, 1984.4
p. 92

Marcy Hermansader (b. 1951)
The Marsh and the Sea, 1982
Colored pencil and acrylic on
paper with pinpricks and cut
flaps
29 ½ × 21 ½ in.
Private collection
p. 93

Marcy Hermansader (b. 1951)
The Magic Hoe, 1982
Colored pencil, acrylic, paper
collage, mosquito netting, and
thread on paper rubbed with red
clay soil
21 ¾ × 28 ½ in.
Collection of the artist
p. 134

Suzanne Jackson (b. 1944)
Origins, 2010
Watercolor, acrylic on inkjet
photo-paper, nylon, D'Arches
300 lb. paper
15 × 22 in.
Martin and Rebecca Eisenberg
p. 135

Suzanne Jackson (b. 1944)
a little path to paradise, 2010
Watercolor on Strathmore paper
24 × 18 in.
Martin and Rebecca Eisenberg
p. 136

Suzanne Jackson (b. 1944)
Ossabaw Meadow, 2010
Acrylic wash on paper
15 × 11 in.
Courtesy of the artist and
Ortuzar, New York
p. 137

Ellen Lanyon (1926–2013)
Fan Ossabaw, c. 1978
Acrylic on canvas
30 × 12 in.
Estate of Ellen Lanyon, courtesy
of GRAY, Chicago/New York
p. 94

Ellen Lanyon (1926–2013)
Ossabaw Storm Warning, 1979
Acrylic on canvas
24 × 32 in.
Collection of Andrew Ginzel
p. 95

Doris Lee (1905–1983)
Untitled, c. 1964
Oil on canvas
33 ½ × 41 ½ in.
Collection of Justin P. West and
Eileen McGowan
p. 97

Jack Leigh (1948–2004)
Palm Tree in Fog, 2002
Carbon pigment print
15 ⅛ × 22 in.
Telfair Museums, museum
purchase with funds provided by
Mr. and Mrs. Lawrence Dunn in
memory of Kirk Varnedoe and
David DeLong, 2006. 53
p. 98

Jack Leigh (1948–2004)
Oak Limb Reflections, 2002
Pigmented inkjet print
15 ⅛ × 22 in.
High Museum of Art, Atlanta;
Purchase with funds from Paul
Miller, Mrs. Robert O. Levitt,
Phillip and Patricia Laney, and
V. Tomm Frungillo, 2021.364
p. 99

Jack Leigh (1948–2004)
Live Oak and Light Beams, 2002
Pigmented inkjet print
15 1⅛ × 22 in.
Collection of Elizabeth DuBose
and Mark Frissell
p. 100

Jack Leigh (1948–2004)
Lone Tree at Sunset, Ossabaw, 2001
Silver gelatin print
16 ⅛ × 22 in.
Collection of Deborah Stroud
p. 101

Sally Mann (b. 1951)
Georgia, Untitled (Ossabaw Gates), 1996
Gelatin silver print
40 × 50 in.
Telfair Museums, museum purchase
p. 138

Sally Mann (b. 1951)
Untitled, 1996
Gelatin silver print
7 ¾ × 10 in.
Private collection
p. 139

Thomas Marker (1901–1978)
Things on Ossabaw, 1961
Watercolor and pencil on paper
8 × 11 ½ in.
Private collection
p. 102

Thomas Marker (1901–1978)
Ossabaw Study, 1961
Watercolor and pencil on paper
6 ½ × 9 in.
Private collection
p. 103

Nancy Marshall (b. 1946)
Untitled, c. 1979
Palladium print
7 × 5 in.
High Museum of Art, Atlanta;
Gift of Ann and Ben Johnson,
2000.280
p. 47

Nancy Marshall (b. 1946)
Cookshack, 1979
Platinum palladium print
5 × 7 in.
Collection of the Artist
p. 48

Nancy Marshall (b. 1946)
*The Treehouse, Middle Place,
Ossabaw Island (Portrait of
Deborah Shepherd, Genesis
Project Member)*, 1979
Platinum palladium print
4 ⅞ × 6 ⅞ in.
Collection of the Artist
p. 49

Michael Mazur (1935–2009)
Palmetto-Ossabaw, 1975
Oil on panel
39 × 29 ½ in.
Courtesy of the Estate of
Michael Mazur
p. 104

Michael Mazur (1935–2009)
Palmetto, 1975
Pastel on paper
71 × 89 ¾ in.
The Museum of Contemporary
Art, Los Angeles, Gift of Jim
Dine, 82.36
p. 105

Lorraine McCarty (1920–2004)
Untitled, 1965
Oil on canvas
49 ¼ × 47 ⅛ in.
The Ossabaw Island
Foundation
p. 51

Ross McElwee (b. 1947)
Excerpt from *Sherman's March*,
1986
Video (color, sound)
16 min.
Courtesy of Little Field Films
pp. 120–24

Tyrone Mitchell (b. 1944)
Buzzard's Vine, 1983
Wood, aluminum, and pigment
9 × 9 × 26 in.
Courtesy of Alitash Kebede
Arts, Los Angeles, CA
p. 141

Irene O'Garden (b. 1951)
Easter Sunday, 1981
Higgins India ink on Bristol paper
11 × 8 ½ in. each
Collection of the artist
p. 52–53

Martha Odum (1917–1995)
Untitled, 1969
Watercolor on paper
11 ¾ × 20 in.
The Ossabaw Island Foundation
p. 106

Daga Ramsey (1907–1997)
Queen Bess Creek, c. 1969–71
Wool and canvas
71 × 36 in.
The Ossabaw Island Foundation
p. 107

T. J. Reddy (1945–2019)
*From the Window of the Tower
House, Middle Place, Ossabaw
Island, GA*, 1981
Sawdust, sand, modeling paste,
and oil on panel
7 ⅜ × 9 ½ in.
Collection of the University of
North Carolina at Charlotte
p. 142

T. J. Reddy (1945–2019)
Scenes for the Maroon, 2011
Acrylic and mixed media on paper
12 × 20 in.
Private collection
p. 143

Miriam Schapiro (1923–2015)
Ossabaw Heart, 1982
Acrylic and fabric on paper
31 × 32 in.
Estate of Miriam Schapiro,
courtesy of Eric Firestone
Gallery
p. 55

Tex Schiwetz (1909–1971)
Winter Underwear for Bomper, 1962
Bronze
4 × 6 ½ × 2 in.
Collection of Justin P. West and
Eileen McGowan
p. 108

Tex Schiwetz (1909–1971)
Winter Underwear for Sean, 1962
Bronze
5 ½ × 3 ¾ × 6 ¼ in.
Private collection
p. 108

Tex Schiwetz (1909–1971)
Ossabaw Pelican Weathervane, 1965
Bronze
19 × 29 ½ × 19 in.
Collection of Burdine Giese
and the late Lester Giese
p. 109

Tex Schiwetz (1909–1971)
Running Bird, c. 1961
Bronze
1 1/12 × 2 ¾ × 1 ¼ in.
Collection of Justin P. West and
Eileen McGowan
p. 109

Athena Tacha (b. 1936)
Windtracks (Ossabaw),
1980/2005
12 chromogenic digital prints
on metallic photo paper cold
mounted with UV protective film
37 ½ × 42 in.
Collection of Ingleside at Rock
Creek, Washington, DC
p. 56

Athena Tacha (b. 1936)
Tide Beach, 1980–81
Rag paper pulp relief
23 ⅞ × 29 ½
Collection of the artist
p. 57

Athena Tacha (b. 1936)
Tide Beach, 1980–81
Rag paper pulp relief
24 in. × 28 ½ in.
Collection of the artist
p. 57

Rashod Taylor (b. 1985)
*Road to the South, Ossabaw Island,
GA*, 2024
Tintype
10 × 8 in.
Library of Congress, Prints &
Photographs Division, LC-
DIG-ppmsca-98419
p. 144

Rashod Taylor (b. 1985)
Marsh Land, Ossabaw Island, GA,
2024
Tintype
8 × 10 in.
Library of Congress, Prints &
Photographs Division, LC-
DIG-ppmsca-98421
p. 145

Betty Tompkins (b. 1945)
Ayrshire Class D, 1979
Gouache on cardboard
15 × 20 in.
Allen Memorial Art Museum,
Oberlin College, Oberlin, OH.
Art Rental Collection Fund,
RC1979.5
p. 110

Betty Tompkins (b. 1945)
*Impending Disaster I (Duetus
Interuptus)*, 1982
Watercolor on paper
39 ½ × 26 in.
Courtesy of Betty Tompkins
and P·P·O·W, New York
p. 111

Anne Truitt (1921–2004)
Ossabaw Island, 25 March '75, 1975
Graphite and acrylic on paper
9 × 5 ¼ in.
Estate of Anne Truitt, Courtesy
Matthew Marks Gallery
p. 59

Clifford B. West (1916–2006)
Untitled (Portrait of Cyrus
Martin Sr.), 1961
Watercolor and ink on paper
29 ½ × 22 in.
Collection of Justin P. West and
Eileen McGowan
p. 146

Eleanor Torrey West (1913–2021)
Untitled (Par Tank House),
c. 1979
Watercolor on paper
10 ¼ × 14 3/16 in.
The Ossabaw Island Foundation
p. 147

SELECTED BIBLIOGRAPHY

ARTICLES/JOURNALS

"30 Students Work on Isle for 'Genesis.'" *The Atlanta Journal*, July 8, 1970.

Als, Hilton. "The Color of Humanity in Sally Mann's South." *The New Yorker*, February 28, 2018.

Ancrum, Nancy. "Ossabaw Is Not for Sale, Owner Informs Legislators." *Savannah Morning News*, November 10, 1969.

Best, Stephen, and Saidiya Hartman. "Fugitive Justice: The Appeal of the Slave." *Representations* 92 (Fall 2006).

Blumenthal, Michael. "Ossabaw Island—haven for both Man and animals." *Smithsonian* 12, no. 7 (October 1981): 124–33.

Bryans, Raleigh. "Enthusiasm of Carter gave Heritage Trust boost it needed." *The Atlanta Constitution*, November 15, 1981.

Burns, Olive Ann. "Ossabaw: An Atlanta writer working on her first novel discovers an unreal world of natural and intellectual wonders on this island by the sea." *Atlanta Weekly*, May 11, 1980: 14–17, 30–39, 41.

———. "Boy Howdy, Ma'am. You Have Sent Us a Fine Book." *The English Journal* 78, no. 8 (December 1989): 16–20.

Butler, Susan. "Sanctuary for Ideas." *The Irish Times*, February 22, 1974: 12.

Campbell, Alan. "The Ossabaw Experience." *Georgia Journal* 1, no. 6 (September/October 1981): 6–10.

Campbell, Lawrence. "Creative Casting." *craft horizons* 23, no. 6 (November/December 1963).

Cerruti, James. "Sea Islands: Adventuring Along the South's Surprising Coast." *National Geographic* 139, no. 3 (March 1971): 366–92.

Chapin, Louis. "Georgia Island Becomes Teacher." *Tallahassee Democrat*, August 1, 1973.

———. "Historic Ossabaw Island Remains Largely Unchanged By the Times." *The Greenville News*, November 23, 1973.

Chapman, Dan. "Keeper of the Island: Centenarian Sandy West Wants to Live Out Her Days on Ossabaw Island, but Time May Be Running Out." *The Atlanta Journal-Constitution,* March 16, 2016.

Cook, Charles R. "Islands of Georgia and Florida Hold Pensive Promise to All." *Jacksonville Journal*, July 1961.

Coulbourn, Keith. "Yerkes Primate Research Center experiments with Chimp Family On Bear Island." *The Atlanta Journal and Constitution Magazine*, July 30, 1972: 12–13, 16–17, 19.

Curry, Nan. "Ossabaw Island: A wealth of information is scattered over privately-owned island." *Rome News-Tribune*, April 11, 1971.

Daniels, Ann Marshall. "Ossabaw Exhibit Opens Monday At College of Art and Design." *Savannah Morning News*, April 6, 1980.

———. "State Buying Ossabaw." *Savannah Morning News*, April 8, 1977.

Davis, Jingle. "Near-pristine Ossabaw Island still at risk." *The Atlanta Journal-Constitution*, September 3, 1996.

Dillard, Annie. "Reflections on an Island." *Science '81* (April 1981): 63–67.

Domet, Sarah. "Ossabaw's Gift." *Savannah Magazine*, August 5, 2021.

Eason, Henry. "History-Filled Ossabaw Is Paradise for Wildlife." *The Atlanta Constitution*, April 8, 1977.

———. "Ossabaw Purchase Arranged by State." *The Atlanta Constitution*, April 8, 1977.

Edwards, Margaret. "Writer's Retreat: A Dangerous Paradise." *Bryn Mawr Alumnae Bulletin* (Spring 1980): 22–25.

Elliott, Daniel E. "North End Plantation, Ossabaw Island, Georgia. Preliminary Archaeological Investigations." *Lamar Institute Reports*, no. 76, 2005.

Ellison, Ralph. "The Little Man at Chehaw Station: The American Artist and His Audience." *The American Scholar* 47, no. 1 (1978): 25–48.

Erwin, John. "Georgia's Wild Island Fights to Preserve Itself." *Rodale's Environment Action Bulletin* 5, no. 16 (May 1974): 1–3.

Fishman, Jane. "'It's the joint': Roosevelt Brownlee feels at home on Ossabaw, filled with tales of food and jazz." *Savannah Morning News*, May 18, 2022.

———. "Keeping Sandy West's Ossabaw donkey line alive." *Savannah Morning News*, September 19, 2020.

———. "The magic of Sandy West, Ossabaw Island and the number 108." *Savannah Morning News*, January 20, 2021.

Gettleman, Jeffrey. "Fighting Against The Tide." *Los Angeles Times*, November 27, 2001.

Gillette, Jane Brown. "Enchanted Isle." *Historic Preservation* 47, no. 6 (November/December 1995).

Graves, Ralph A. "Marching Through Georgia Sixty Years After." *The National Geographic Magazine* 50, no. 3 (September 1926): 259–311.

Hagedorn, Hermann. "The Peterborough Colony: 'A Workshop, with a wonderland thrown in,' for creative workers in the seven arts." *The Outlook: An Illustrated Weekly Journey of Current Life* 129 (September–December 1921).

Hallahan, Huston. "An experiment on Ossabaw Island." *The Chronicle: Duke's Daily Newspaper*, April 17, 1974: 5.

Hallerman, Tamar. "Sandy West, doyenne of Ossabaw Island, dead at 108." *The Atlanta Journal-Constitution*, February 2, 2021.

Hardie, Ann. "Isle on the edge." *The Atlanta Journal-Constitution*, January 30, 2000.

———. "The Old Lady of Ossabaw." *Atlanta Magazine*, March 1, 2011.

Hendrix, Steve. "Sweet Georgia Coast: The millionaires are gone from these pristine barrier islands. But they left a rich legacy behind." *The Washington Post*, May 19, 2002: E1, E9–13.

Hunter, Anna. "In the beginning." *Savannah News-Press Magazine*, July 12, 1970.

Jones, Ann. "Georgia's Golden Isles." *National Geographic Traveler* (July/August 1996): 36–40.

Justus, Lucy. "Preserving an Island: Ossabaw." *Outdoors in Georgia* 9, no. 4 (April 1979): 16–22.

———. "Mrs. West Finds a Landlord." *The Atlanta Journal and Constitution Magazine* June 12, 1977: 16–17, 20–22.

King, Wayne. "Donkeys Get Vasectomies And Escape a Worse Fate." *The New York Times*, June 6, 1979.

Kinney, Jean. "Conserving the Barrier: A Dream to Save Ossabaw Island." *The Washington Post*, June 8, 1975: G1.

Koenig, John, Jr. "Georgia's Island Jewels." *Tampa Bay Times*, January 24, 1993.

———. "Ossabaw Island: Low Profile Georgia Getaway Is High on Wildlife, Natural Charm." *Athens Daily News*, November 1, 1992.

Kovalenko, Anne. "Lehigh Professor Takes Artistic 'Holiday.'" *Sunday Call-Chronicle*, February 16, 1969.

Krueger, Gail. "Ossabaw Island to be added to nation's historic sites list." *Savannah Morning News*, September 13, 1996.

———. "Island's donkeys braying for help." *Savannah Morning News*, March 28, 1999.

Landers, Mary. "Heritage preserves bill 'dead.'" *Savannah Morning News*, June 20, 2020: A1, A3.

———. "Ossabaw Island matriarch dies at 108." *Savannah Morning News*, January 18, 2021: A1, A9.

———. "Slideshow: Georgia to rehab Ossabaw mansion." *The Current*, June 11, 2024. https://thecurrentga. org/2024/06/11/georgia-to-rehab-ossabaw-mansion/.

Ledlie, Joe. "Fighting to Save the Golden Isles." *The Atlanta Constitution*, May 8, 1977: 1A, 12A.

———. "The big four for environment." *The Atlanta Journal and Constitution Magazine*, February 12, 1978: 16–17, 26.

"Life on Bear Island becomes to hazardous for Jiggs, other chimps from Yerkes Primate Center." *The Atlanta Constitution*, March 5, 1978: SM8.

MacDougall, William. "A Look at America's 'Hidden' Artist Colonies." *U.S. News & World Report*, May 3, 1976: 81–82.

Marcus, Adrianne. "A Letter From Ossabaw." *San Francisco Examiner*, June 6, 1976.

McGowan, John F. "Eleanor Torrey West." *Skidaway Scenes* 4, no. 3 (Summer 1988): 4.

Mitchell, Kent. "Sacrifice and Gift Earn GWF's Highest Honor." *The Atlanta Constitution*, April 23, 1978: 18D.

Montgomery, Diann. "They Call it Ossabaw Island." *The Periscope*, April 29, 1969.

Moore, W. Robert. "The Golden Isles of Guale." *The National Geographic Magazine* 65, no. 2 (February 1934): 235–64.

Morehead, Bill. "Deer Hunters In Paradise." *The Atlanta Constitution*, January 13, 1980: SM8.

Morrison, David. "Chimps As State Natives?" *The Atlanta Constitution*, September 12, 1973: 9D.

Nesmith, Jeff. "Ossabaw Isle Rights Going to 8 Colleges." *The Atlanta Constitution*, December 6, 1969.

———. "Project Genesis: A survival course on Ossabaw Island teaches 25 students to confront Nature and build a mini-society." *Atlanta*, September 1970: 24–30.

Nordheimer, Jon. "Ecologists Hope to Save Wild Islands Off Georgia." *The New York Times*, July 4, 1972.

Osier, David R. "Ossabaw Miracle." *Georgia Journal* (January/February 1997): 12–24.

"Ossabaw." *The Atlanta Constitution*, April 11, 1977: 4A.

"Ossabaw Adrift." *National Geographic* 200, no. 5 (November 2001).

"Ossabaw Purchase Completed by State." *Savannah Morning News*, May 12, 1978: 14C.

"Ossabaw Readies Retreat For Weary." *Savannah Morning News*, July 2, 1961.

Park, Hugh. "What a Georgia Jungle Offers You." *The Atlanta Constitution*, April 23, 1972: 23A.

Pearson, Charles E., and Fred C. Cook. "The Bead Maker's Midden: Evidence of Late Prehistoric Shell Bead Production on Ossabaw Island, Georgia." *Southeastern Archaeology* 31, no. 1 (2012): 87–102.

Penney, Veronica. "Eleanor Torrey West, Preserver of Her Inherited Island, Dies at 108." *The New York Times,* January 28, 2021.

Pennington, John. "Is Ossabaw on Death Row?" *The Atlanta Journal and Constitution Magazine*, July 16, 1972: 6–7, 18–20.

———. "A Plan to Save Some Special Places." *The Atlanta Constitution*, October 8, 1972: SM8.

———. "A Naturalist's View of the Golden Coast." *The Atlanta Constitution*, February 18, 1971: SM1.

Phillips, Patti. "The future of Ossabaw Island." *Savannah Morning News*, August 6, 1996: 2B.

———. "The Wild Life: Unique miniature donkeys flourish on Ossabaw Island." *Savannah Morning News*, August 6, 1996: 1B–2B.

Poles, Jim. "Georgia island will serve as mini-school this spring." *The Chronicle: Duke's Daily Newspaper*, January 17, 1974: 1.

Powledge, Fred. "Island Fever." *Esquire*, March 1977: 88–92; 114–120.

Press, Robert M. "Fantasy islands: Will crowds and hotels spoil the charm?" *The Christian Science Monitor*, August 2, 1982: 3.

Pringle, Laurena. "Mrs. Clifford West: She'll Answer to 'Sis' or 'Sandy.'" *Detroit Free Press*, March 12, 1967: 10-D.

Reetz, Jan. "Ossabaw's Jimbo: Caretaker for the Wilderness." *Savannah Morning News*, February 21, 1973.

Reetz, John. "Island of the Chimps." *The Atlanta Constitution*, February 2, 1975: 13B.

Rippin, Charles. "Ossabaw." *Coastal Quarterly* (Spring 1977): 34–38.

Robertson, Nan. "Artist Colonies Unite to Raise Funds." *The New York Times*, November 23, 1983: C13.

Seckinger, Julie Osteen. "Genesis Project." *Richmond Hill Reflections* 2, no. 4 (2010): 41–45.

———. "Sandy Footprints." *Richmond Hill Reflections* 3, no. 2 (2011): 57–62.

Shelton, Stacy. "Ossabaw's open door: Day visits may threaten fragile isle." *The Atlanta Journal-Constitution*, June 15, 2003: E1.

Smith, Phil. "Island Has Become Haven for the Distracted Artist." *Savannah Morning News*, March 31, 1963.

Sparks, Andrew. "Exploring Ossabaw." *The Atlanta Journal and Constitution Magazine*, May 18, 1969: 6–8, 40–42, 44, 47.

———. "Georgia's Wild Coast... Can It Be Saved?" *The Atlanta Journal and Constitution Magazine*, November 24, 1968: 8–11, 56–58, 60, 63.

Taylor, Robert. "Visual perception as subject." *Boston Evening Globe*, October 21, 1976.

"The Threatened Marshes of Glynn." *Life*, November 14, 1969.

"The Pigs Of Ossabaw Island." *The Hartford Courant*, July 15, 2001.

Tenenbaum, Samuel J. "Ossabaw in Retrospect." *Emory College Today* 1, no. 1 (June 1965): 9–11.

"Torrey To Make Ossabaw Island Residence Site." *The Atlanta Constitution*, April 12, 1924: 20.

"Torrey Paid $300,000 For Ossabow Holdings," *The Atlanta Constitution*, April 26, 1924: 17.

"Torry Will Build Home at Ossabaw at $400,000 Cost." *The Atlanta Constitution*, May 2, 1924: 15.

United Press International. "Ossabaw Island Still Private, DNR Explains." *The Atlanta Constitution*, April 21, 1977: 14A.

Wade, Allison and Kathryn Wade. "One More Ecosystem on Death Row?" *Catalyst For Environmental Equality* 2, no. 4 (1972): 16–19.

West, Eleanor Torrey. "Climate: For Contemplation, Communication and Work." *Dobbs Alumnae Bulletin*, November 1964: 16–17.

West, Eleanor Torrey. "Viewpoint: Ossabaw Island." *Research Reporter* 11, no.3 (1978): 9.

West, Justin, and Beryl Gilothwest. "House Bill 906 hurts all of Georgia." *Savannah Morning News*, June 20, 2020.

"Will Georgia Isle Be a Victim of Man?" *The Atlanta Constitution*, July 7, 1972: 29A.

Williams, Joy. "All glitter, but some are truly golden." *Sports Illustrated* 42, no. 18. (May 5, 1975): 64–65.

Wiltrout, Kate. "The lady and the island." *Savannah Morning News*, December 30, 2001.

————. "A willing captive." *Savannah Morning News*, December 31, 2001.

Winter, Don. "New Plan for Natural Areas Rises from Ossabaw Study." *The Atlanta Constitution*, September 26, 1971: 6A.

Wylie, Max. "Ossabaw Island: the Lab of Life." *Atlanta*, 1973: 88–91, 102–105.

Zaleski, Jean. "Getting Away From It All: Isolation as Inspiration." *Women Artists News* 7, no. 1 (April–May 1981): 5–6.

BOOKS AND EXHIBITION CATALOGUES

America 1976: A Bicentennial Exhibition. Washington, DC: Hereward Lester Cooke Foundation, 1976.

Bailey, Cornelia Walker, with Christena Bledsoe. *God, Dr. Buzzard, and the Bolito Man: A Saltwater Geechee Talks About Life on Sapelo Island, Georgia*. New York: Anchor Books, 2001.

Blauvelt, Andrew. *With Eyes Opened: Cranbrook Academy of Art Since 1932*. Bloomfield Hills, MI: Cranbrook Art Museum, 2023.

Brower, Kenneth, ed. *Guale, the Golden Coast of Georgia*. Washington DC: Friends of the Earth, 1974.

Burgard, Anna Marlis. *The Beachcomber's Companion*. San Francisco: Chronicle Books, 2018.

Burris Staton, Jennifer and Park McArthur. *Beverly Buchanan: 1978–1981*. Mexico City: Athénée Press, 2015.

Callahan, John F. and Marc C. Conner, eds. *The Selected Letters of Ralph Ellison*. New York: Random House, 2019.

Campbell, Emory S. *Gullah Cultural Legacies*. 3rd ed. Hilton Head Island, South Carolina: Gullah Heritage Consulting Services, 2008.

Cole, Henri. *The Marble Queen*. New York: Atheneum, 1986.

————. *Orphic Paris*. New York: New York Review of Books, 2018.

Collins, Lisa Gail. *The Art of History: African American Women Artists Engage the Past*. New Brunswick, NJ, and London: Rutgers University Press, 2002.

Danly, Susan. *Branching: The Art of Michael Mazur*. Amherst, MA: Mead Art Museum, Amherst College, 1997.

Dash, Julie. *Daughters of the Dust: The Making of an African American Woman's Film*. New York: The New Press, 1992.

Denes, Agnes. *The Book of Dust: The Beginning and the End of Thereafter*. Rochester, NY: Visual Studies Workshop Press, 1989.

Enderby, Emma, ed. *Agnes Denes: Absolutes and Intermediates*. New York: The Shed, 2019.

Fishman, Jane. *The Woman Who Saved An Island: The Story of Sandy West and Ossabaw Island*. Savannah: Real People Publishing, 2014.

Elman, Richard M. *The Man Who Ate New York (and Other Poems, Early And Late, Of Manhattan And Ossabaw Islands)*. New York: New Rivers Press, 1975.

Foskey, Ann. *Images of America: Ossabaw Island*. Charleston: Arcadia Publishing, 2001.

Greenberg, Alvin. *Delta q*. Columbia & London: University of Missouri Press, 1983.

Greenough, Sarah and Sarah Kennel. *Sally Mann: A Thousand Crossings*. Washington, DC: National Gallery of Art, 2018.

Gutierrez-Solana, Carlos. *By The Sea: 20th Century Americans By The Shore*. Flushing, NY: The Queens County Art and Cultural Center, Inc., 1979.

Hamilton, David. *Ossabaw*. Cambridge, MA: Salt Publishing, 2006.

Harlan, Will. *Untamed: The Wildest Woman in America and the Fight for Cumberland Island*. New York: Grove Press, 2014.

Harry Bertoia: Sculpting Mid-Century Modern Life. Dallas: Nasher Sculpture Center, 2022.

Hartridge, Walter Charlton. *Savannah: Etchings and Drawings by Christopher Murphy*. Columbia: Bostick & Thornley, 1947.

Hileman, Kristen. *Anne Truitt: Perception and Reflection*. Washington, DC: Hirshhorn Museum and Sculpture Garden, Smithsonian Institution, 2009.

Johnson, Ellen H. *Fragments: Recalled at Eighty: The Art Memoirs of Ellen H. Johnson*. North Vancouver, BC: Gallerie, 1993.

Kilgo, James, Jack Leigh, and Alan Campbell. *Ossabaw: Evocations of an Island*. Athens, GA: The University of Georgia Press, 2004.

Lafo, Rachel Rosenfield. *Belief in the Underground: The Art of Marcy Hermansader*. Lincoln, MA: DeCordova Museum and Sculpture Park, 1990.

Lax, Thomas (T.) Jean and Lilia Rocio Taboada, eds. *Just Above Midtown: Changing Spaces*. New York: The Museum of Modern Art, 2022.

Lazarus, Diane and Pauline Saliga, eds. *Ellen Lanyon*. Chicago: N.A.M.E. Gallery, 1983.

Leigh, Jack. *The Land I'm Bound To*. New York: W. W. Norton & Company, 2000.

Maney, David S., Frederick C. Marland and Clifford B. West, eds. *The Future of the Marshlands and Sea Islands of Georgia*. Sea Island, GA: Georgia Natural Areas Council and the Coastal Area Planning and Development Commission, 1968.

Mann, Sally. *Hold Still: A Memoir with Photographs*. New York: Back Bay Books, 2015.

————. *Mother Land: Recent Landscape of Virginia and Georgia*. New York: Edwynn Houk Gallery, 1997.

Marshall, Nancy. *Ossabaw*. Atlanta: Nexus Press, 1982.

Mayer, Musa. *Night Studio: A Memoir of Philip Guston*. 4th ed. Zürich: Hauser & Wirth Publishers, 2023.

McCullough, Holly Koons and Feay Shellman Coleman, eds. *Picturing Savannah: The Art of Christopher A.D. Murphy*. Savannah: Telfair Museum of Art, 2008.

McCullough, Holly Koons. *in situ: Betsy Cain*. Savannah: Telfair Museums, 2011.

McGee, Micki, ed. *Yaddo: Making American Culture*. New York: Columbia University Press, 2008.

McKittrick, Katherine. *Demonic Grounds: Black Women and the Cartography of Struggle*. Minneapolis: University of Minnesota Press, 2006.

Michelle, Trelani. *Krak Teet: A Catalogue of Black Savannah's Biographies*. Columbia: So Fundamental Publications, 2019.

Molesworth, Helen. *Leap Before You Look: Black Mountain College 1933–1957*. New Haven: Yale University Press, 2015.

Morgan, Phillip, ed. *African American Life in the Georgia Lowcountry: The Atlantic World and the Gullah Geechee*. Athens, GA: The University of Georgia Press, 2010.

Moutoussamy-Ashe, Jeanne. *Daufuskie Island, a Photographic Essay*. Columbia: University of South Carolina Press, 1982.

Nelson, June Kompass. *Harry Bertoia, Printmaker: Monotypes and Other Monographics*. Detroit: Wayne State University Press, 1988.

Older, Julia. *The Ossabaw Book of Hours*. Durham, NH: Oyster River Press, 2001.

Oliver, Valerie Cassel. *The Dirty South: Contemporary Art, Material Culture, and the Sonic Impulse*. Richmond: Virginia Museum of Fine Arts, 2021.

Pool, Elizabeth and Eleanor West. *The God of the Hinge: Sojourns in Cloud Cuckoo Land*. Augusta, GA: Harbor House, 2006.

Pressly, Paul M. *On the Rim of the Caribbean: Colonial Georgia and the British Atlantic World*. Athens, GA: The University of Georgia Press, 2013.

———. *A Southern Underground Railroad: Black Georgians and the Promise of Spanish Florida and Indian Country*. Athens, GA: The University of Georgia Press, 2024.

Reese, Rachel, ed. *Suzanne Jackson: Five Decades*. Savannah: Telfair Museums, 2019.

Savannah Unit, Georgia Writers' Project, Work Projects Administration. *Drums and Shadows: Survival Stories Among the Georgia Coastal Negroes*. Athens, GA: University of Georgia, 1940.

Stamford Museum and Nature Center. *Animals! Animals! Animals!* Stamford, CT: Stamford Museum and Nature Center, 1984.

Spear, Richard E. *The Art of Athena Tacha: A Complete Catalogue*. Pennsauken, NJ: Bookbaby, 2022.

Stuckey, Jill, Evan Kurtzler, and Jimmy Carter. *Ossabaw Island: A Sense of Place*. Macon, GA: Mercer University Press, 2016.

Sutter, Paul S. and Paul Pressly, eds. *Coastal Nature, Coastal Culture: Environmental Histories of the Georgia Coast*. Athens, GA: The University of Georgia Press, 2018.

Taylor, Francis Henry. *"Tex" Schiwetz: Sculpture in Bronze*. Worcester, MA: Worcester Art Museum, 1958.

Teish, Luisah. *Jambalaya: The Natural Woman's Book of Personal Charms and Practical Rituals*. New York: HarperCollins, 1985.

Torrey, Henry Norton. "The Story of Ossabaw." Self-published, 1926.

Truitt, Alexandra, ed. *Always Reaching: The Selected Writings of Anne Truitt*. New Haven and London: Yale University Press, 2023.

Truitt, Anne. *Daybook: The Journal of an Artist*. New York: Pantheon Books, 1982.

Turner, Lorenzo D. *Africanisms in the Gullah Dialect*. Chicago: The University of Chicago, 1949.

Vining, Elizabeth Gray. *Being Seventy: The Measure of a Year*. New York: The Viking Press, 1978.

West, Clifford B., ed. *The Sculpture of Berthold "Tex" Schiwetz*. Birmingham, MI: Birmingham Gallery, Inc., 1971.

West, Eleanor. *Maria Bosomworth and William Rodgers*. Savannah: The Beehive Press, 1976.

Wolfe, Melissa. *Simple Pleasures: The Art of Doris Lee*. Greensburg, PA: The Westmoreland Museum of Art, 2020.

Wright, Beryl J. *Tyrone Mitchell*. Newark: The Newark Museum, 1990.

DISSERTATIONS

Cole, Henri. "Off the coast of paradise." Thesis. Columbia University, 1982.

Keister, Margaret Ann. "The Ossabaw Island Project, a Program Fostering Creative Production and Experience." PhD diss. University of Georgia, 1992.

King, Linda O. "An Eccentric Place of Very High Quality: Ossabaw Island, Georgia as a Context for the Interpretation of Historical, Cultural, and Environmental Change on the Atlantic Coast." PhD diss. Georgia State University, 2015.

Roberts Thompson, Amanda. "People, Place, and Taskscapes of Enslavement: African American Life on the South End Plantation, Ossabaw Island, Georgia, 1849–1861." PhD diss. University of York, 2020.

FILMS

Collins, Sharon, writer. *Georgia Outdoors: Ossabaw*. Georgia Public Broadcasting, April 16, 2020. https://www.gpb.org/television/show/georgia-outdoors/season/2020/ossabaw.

Dash, Julie, dir. *Daughters of the Dust*. Kino International, 1991.

Finlay, Mark. *In The Beginning, Reflections on Year One: The Genesis Project on Ossabaw Island*. The Ossabaw Island Foundation, 2011. https://www.youtube.com/watch?v=_7lOz83qnW4.

Georgia Forestry Commission in cooperation with the Ossabaw Island Project Foundation. *Genesis: A Project of Human Ecology*. 1970. https://www.youtube.com/watch?v=QD_2fzMAlM8&t=140s.

Goode Bryant, Linda, dir. *The Presence of Black*. 2022.

Hamada, Helen. *2009 Meeting of Genesis and Ossabaw Island Project former directors and participants*. 2015.

McElwee, Ross, dir. *Sherman's March: An Improbable Search for Love*. First Run Features, 1986.

Ramming, Max, dir. *Island Vision*. 2021. https://vimeo.com/513580785 .

West, Clifford B., dir. *Berthold "Tex" Schiwetz, Sculptor*. OIP Film, 1962.

———, dir. *"Give and Take": A Story Of One Way To Preserve And Use This Diminishing Earth*. Radim Films, 1974.

———, dir. *Harry Bertoia's Sculpture*. OIP Films, 1965.

———, dir. *Ossabaw Island Project, Savannah, Georgia*. OIP Films, 1962.

———, dir. *Synthesis: Travis, Tiger, and Wild Boar*. OIP Films, 1962.

———, dir. *The Creative Journey: Arnold Blanch, Painter, Teacher*. OIP Films, 1965.

———, dir. *Untitled Film: A Search for Ecological Balance...* OIP Films, c. 1970.

West, Justin P., dir. *Ossabaw Island, Georgia*. The Ossabaw Foundation, 1990.

———, dir. *Ossabaw Island: Traces of Passage*. The Ossabaw Foundation, 1990.

PRIMARY/ARCHIVAL RESOURCES

Archives of American Art, Smithsonian Institution, Washington, DC

Oral history interview with Harry Bertoia, June 20, 1972.

Oral history interview with Ellen Lanyon, December 5, 1975–January 18, 1976.

Oral history interview with Marianne Strengell, January 8–December 16, 1982.

Oral history interview with Clifford West, February 26–28, 1975.

Harry Bertoia papers, 1917–1979.

Olav Hammarstrom papers, 1939–1980.

Ellen Hulda Johnson papers, 1872–2018, bulk 1921–1992.

Ellen Lanyon papers, circa 1880–2015, bulk 1926–2013.

Michael Mazur papers, circa 1936–2016.

Pete Schiwetz papers, 1939–1971.

Marianne Strengell papers, 1904–1980s.

Athena Tacha papers, 1959–2019.

Bryn Mawr College, Special Collections Department, Pennsylvania

Anne Truitt Papers.

Cranbrook Center for Collections and Research, Cranbrook Archives, Bloomfield Hills, Michigan

The Clifford B. West and Joy Griffin West Papers.

Georgia Historical Society, Savannah, Georgia

Ossabaw Island and Torrey family papers.

Library of Congress, Washington, DC

   Ralph Ellison papers, 1890–2007.

Massachusetts Institute of Technology
Libraries, Department of Distinctive
Collections Repository, Cambridge

   Roman Jakobson papers, 1908–1982.

The Ossabaw Island Foundation, Savannah,
Georgia

Rutgers University, New Brunswick Special
Collections Repository, New Jersey

   The Miriam Schapiro Papers, circa
   1891–2019; bulk 1940–2008.

Savannah College of Art and Design, Jen
Library Archives and Special Collections,
Georgia

   John Earl Collection of Photography.

UNC Charlotte, J. Murrey Atkins Library
Special Collections and University Archives,
Manuscript Collections

   T. J. Reddy papers.

University of California, Berkeley, The
Bancroft Library

   David Ross Brower Papers, 1924–2001.

University of Georgia, Hargrett Rare Book
and Manuscript Library, Athens

   Jack Leigh collection, 1911–2004.

   Eugene Odum collection, 1930–2002.

University of Pennsylvania, Kislak Center
for Special Collections, Rare Books and
Manuscripts, Philadelphia

   Carl Zigrosser papers, circa 1891–1971.

University of Pennsylvania, Weitzman
School of Design, Architectural Archives,
Philadelphia

   Venturi, Scott Brown Collection.

West family archives

INDEX

191

ACKNOWLEDGMENTS

Off the Coast of Paradise: Artists and Ossabaw Island, 1961–Now was first conceived more than five years ago as a way to share the work of the many incredible artists who participated in the Ossabaw Island Project. Savannah-based artist Betsy Cain first suggested the idea, asking the simple but provocative question, "Now wouldn't it be cool if there was an exhibition about *that*?" Our curatorial partnership, solidified in January 2024, has been an extremely supportive and fruitful collaboration. Although separated geographically, our near-daily emails and texts, and monthly, then bi-weekly video conference check-ins (along with a healthy dose of "this-can't-wait" phone calls) have been productive brainstorms, grounded in our sustained belief in this project and desire to see it come to fruition. We were consistently amazed by the stories of profound transformation that Ossabaw artists shared with us, demonstrating how the island maintains a powerful pull across time, space, and relationships. While hyper-localized in a certain sense, their stories and histories continue to reverberate across the country and around the world, emphasizing the enduring significance of the American South as a wellspring for the creative imagination. John Donne astutely noted that "No man is an island," and though our subject is an island, his enduring words have proved truthful in the collaborative efforts of the many people who have contributed to this project along the way. With this, we offer our sincere thanks to those who have assisted us, including those who have maintained long email threads, answered countless questions, grappled with seemingly endless logistics, hunted through their basements for photographs and documents, and generally supported us with words of encouragement.

We'd like to thank all of the living artists in this exhibition for trusting us with their work and for the studio visits, conversations, and email exchanges that helped us get to the heart of their practices and understand their unique relationships with Ossabaw Island. Thank you to Betsy Cain, Agnes Denes, Leslie Ferst, Helen Hamada, Marcy Hermansader, Suzanne Jackson, Sally Mann, Nancy Marshall, Ross McElwee, Tyrone Mitchell, Irene O'Garden, Athena Tacha, Rashod Taylor, and Betty Tompkins.

Many thanks to Allison Janae Hamilton (and her team, Phoebus Osborne, Laeticia Mello, and Arianna Adabachi) for embracing our idea for the exhibition and creating such a powerful film to represent the "Now" with *Venus of Ossabaw*. We are very grateful to First Team Films, LLC, especially the film's producer, Nora Clark, who made miracles happen, as well as Candice Hoyes, who contributed her beautiful song "Far Away Star," the brilliant actors Dami Adeyina and Alicia Sessions, and the talented director of photography Nikita Carpenter. Thank you to Mike Baierski, Ross Bartels, Gerrell Boone, Chad Darnell, Christina Fowler, Reva Grantham, Cori Graves, Naomi Graves, Todd Helms, Steve Lloyd, Hubert Mitchell, Mike Neal, Sarah Nelson, Anthony Peznola, Brian Phan, Critter Pierce, Trey Sorrow, Ryan Watterson, and Doug Westum. For assistance with the public presentation and projection of the film, we are indebted to the expertise of Matt Kaufman and Jeffrey Heinz of Kaufman-Heinz, LLC, and to Trinity United Methodist Church and Reverend Ben Godsen for the use of their facility.

Our deepest appreciation to Telfair Museums as the organizing institution of this ambitious exhibition, with recognition of previous curatorial support and inquiry of former Telfair staff members Shannon Browning-Mullis, Jessica Estes, Courtney McNeil, and Rachel Waldrop. We extend our gratitude to current Telfair colleagues including Executive Director/CEO Dr. David Brenneman, Executive Assistant Maria Sleight for assistance with the loan letters, Rights and Reproduction Assistant Curator Beth Moore, who tackled the challenge of sourcing images for the publication with aplomb, Chief Registrar Jen Levy for handling the complicated loan logistics, Associate Registrar Markecia Koulesser for her assistance with loans, Curator of Decorative Arts Dr. Elyse Gerstenecker for dividing and conquering, Assistant Curator of Historical

Interpretation Ahmauri Williams-Alford for her historical and preservationist perspective, Director of Education and Senior Curator Harry Delorme for programming, support, and knowledge, Chief Preparator Heath Ritch for technical know-how and exhibition design, Designer/Preparator Stephen Harmon for art handling assistance and design layout, Education Studio Programs Manager Kip Bradley and Outreach Coordinator Rachel Stayer for artistic programming, Controller & HR Manager Melissa Pollard, and Accounting Manager Samia Simshauser for budgetary assistance. As the curatorial intern in the summer and fall of 2021, Anna Robertson was instrumental in conducting initial interviews and research to jumpstart this exhibition and has remained invested in this project through her valuable contributions to the chronology and artist biographies in the publication. Additional thanks to Kylie De Jesus, Telfair's Melaver Family Curatorial Intern during the summer of 2024, who combed indexes of the *Savannah Morning News* at the Live Oak Public Library, compiled a bibliography, and performed other helpful tasks related to this exhibition. Profound thanks are due to former Director of Corporate and Foundation Relations Lauren Grant, who stewarded several successful grant applications and corporate funding for this project.

Many individuals graciously allowed us to interview them about their experiences at Ossabaw: Judy Barber, Al Bradford, Alan Campbell, Susan Earl, Dennis Elliott, Paula Eubanks, Rachel Garceau, Eunice Gross, Hanif Haynes, Lisa Irwin, Tim McClelland, Linda Reeves McIntyre, John McWilliams, Geoffrey Movius, Dr. Paul Pressly, Dr. Richard Spear, Justin West, and Wini Wood. We are grateful to the many people who helped facilitate our research into all aspects of this project. Thank you to our institutional colleagues Celia Bertoia, Harry Bertoia Foundation; Rosalie Bodkin, Juliana Sims, Nate Peek, and Caitlin Philippo, Georgia Historical Society; Mazie Bowen, Hargrett Rare Book and Manuscript Library, University of Georgia Libraries; Betty Boyd, Dettre Library and Research Center, National Museum of Women in the Arts; Linda Bridges, Cheri Lewis, and William Wood, Live Oak Public Library; Claudia Cannizzaro, Art OMI; Gabriela Chiu, Christina Lutz, Fernanda Perrone, Rutgers University Libraries; Mark Cole, Cleveland Museum of Art; Amber Esseiva, ICA VCU; Jenny Gheith, San Francisco Museum of Modern Art; Kathryn Goffnet, Cranbrook Art Museum; Alexa Griffith, Cooper Hewitt, Smithsonian Design Museum; Caitlin Haskell, Art Institute of Chicago; Sarah Heim, Kiask Center for Special Collections, Rare Books, and Manuscripts, University of Pennsylvania; Susan Laney and Sarah Cherry, Laney Contemporary; Kelly Long, Whitney Museum of American Art; Mark Meatto, Little Field Films; Orlando Montoya, Georgia Public Broadcasting; Nia Oke-Famakinde, Museum of Contemporary Art Chicago; Sheila Pleasants, Virginia Center for the Creative Arts; Michal Raz-Russo, Gordon Parks Foundation; Sally Radic and Musa Guston, Philip Guston Foundation; Deborah Rice, Cranbrook Center for Collections and Research; Jennifer Schlesinger, Obscura Gallery; Heather Isbell Schumacher, Stuart Weitzman School of Design, University of Pennsylvania; Laura Sievert, Arts Quincy; Alexandra Truitt, Anne Truitt Catalogue Raisonné; and Pavel Zoubok, Pavel Zoubok Fine Art. Thank you to Ann Bailey, Brad Bennett, Michael Billa, Roosevelt Brownlee, Julie Dash, Maura Jane Farrelly, Suki Fredericks, Pamela Nelson Harte, Elizabeth Hillbruner, Torrey Kingry, William Maier, Cooke Maroney, Katherine Orellano, Dr. Paul Pressly, Jamila Reddy, Winston Roeth, Stephen and Gloria Schoenholtz, Amy Sillman, Dr. Lowery Stokes Sims, Frank Stewart, Dr. Marin R. Sullivan, Terese Svoboda, Zelda Tenenbaum, Dr. Amanda Roberts Thompson, Anna West, John Williams, Dr. Wen Yao, and Dr. Lisa Jaye Young. The late Dr. Mark Finlay's extraordinary research for his incomplete book on Ossabaw Island was a fantastic resource. We are very grateful to Justin West for allowing us to access Sandy West's personal files.

This exhibition wouldn't be possible without the institutional and private lenders who so graciously agreed to part with their precious works. Sincere thanks are due to Elizabeth DuBose and Mark Frissell, the Earl family, Martin and Rebecca Eisenberg, Burdine and the late Lester Giese, Andrew Ginzel, Deborah Stroud, Justin P. West and Eileen McGowan, Lisa and Mason White, and to those who wish to remain anonymous. Thank you to our colleagues at galleries, including Beryl Bevilacque and Savannah Downs, Marianne Boesky Gallery; Ella Blanchon and Jennifer Brennan, P·P·O·W; Keri Cavanaugh, Chloe Lundgren, and Laura Stowell, GRAY; Eric Firestone, Maddy Henkin, and Jennifer Samet, Eric Firestone Gallery; halley k. harrisburg and Michael Rosenfeld, Michael Rosenfeld Gallery; Alitash Kebede and Jeffrey Landau, Alitash Kebede Arts; Sabrina Lefkowitz, Matthew Marks Gallery; Kenta Murakami, Macaella Gray, and Emily Huang, Ortuzar; Bryan Smith, Estate of Michael Mazur; Putri Tan, Gagosian; and Leslie Tonkonow, Leslie Tonkonow Artworks + Projects. And to lending institutional partners: Sofia Bakis, Claire McRee, Maria McWilliams and Max Weintraub, Allentown Art Museum; Selina Bartlett, Katherine Solendar, and Lucille Stiger, Allen Memorial Art Museum, Oberlin College; Adreonna Bennett, Katie Howell, and Andrew Pack, UNC Charlotte; Johanna Burton, Katherine Noland, and Tom Callas, The Museum of Contemporary Art, Los Angeles; Frances Francis, Gregory Harris, Maria Kelly, Randall Suffolk and Samantha Wright, High Museum of Art; Anne Helmreich and Susan M. Cary, Archives of American Art, Smithsonian Institution; Melissa Lindberg, Simonette N. dela Torre, and Rachel Waldron, Library of Congress; Jennifer Johns and Harry Philbrick, Pennsylvania Academy of the Fine Arts; and Benjamin Simons, Suzanne Fitzallen Jackson Foundation.

We owe our gratitude to everyone involved in making this publication a reality, especially Adam Squires and Jasmine Kan from CHIPS, who created a dynamic, thoughtful, and evocative design, our production coordinator Marc Sapir, who guided the ship and offered essential advice, our copyeditor Jessica Holmes, whose careful eye brought everything together, and Emily Bowles, who took on the considerable task of indexing the book. We want to thank our brilliant contributors Al Bradford, Henri Cole, Vaughnette Goode-Walker, Allison Janae Hamilton, Thomas Lax, Megan Mayhew Bergman, Justin West, and Wini Wood for their wisdom and insight. Much appreciation to our distributor, the University of Georgia Press, for helping to spread the word and get this publication out into the world.

Significant patrons, donors, and grant organizations have provided key financial support to make this exhibition and publication a reality. Thank you to VIA Art Fund for their support of Allison Janae Hamilton's *Venus of Ossabaw*; the Frances and Beverly DuBose Foundation, Inc., for their support of this publication; the Henry Luce Foundation, including Teresa A. Carbone; and the Teiger Foundation. We would also like to thank Lisa White for jumping in to support this project whenever we most needed it. Exhibition investment was also provided by the City of Savannah. Also vital were contributions to the major exhibition fund at Telfair Museums provided by Bob Faircloth and Linda McWhorter and Annual Exhibition Support provided by Director's Circle Council Members: Mrs. Cynthia Willett, Leslie and Angus Littlejohn, Mr. and Mrs. Steven J. Sayer, Mr. and Mrs. Alan Sheriff, Mrs. Inge A. Brasseler, Kerry and Lillian Breitbart, Mr. Robert F. Faircloth, Mr. and Mrs. Ronald J. Gantt, Ms. Lori Judge, Pamela and Marek Lewanda, Wilson Morris, Thomas V. and Susan G. Reilly, Cathy and Philip Solomons, Mr. and Mrs. Austin P. Sullivan Jr., Pamela L. and Peter S. Voss, Ms. Susan A. Willetts, and Mr. Alan K. Pritz.

Finally, we are very grateful to Elizabeth DuBose and Robin Gunn at The Ossabaw Island Foundation for their invaluable collaboration and support of this exhibition at every stage in the process through evolving timelines and manifestations. We were honored to present our research for the first time in "The Ossabaw Island Project, Genesis, and *Off the Coast of Paradise*," the keynote lecture at the Foundation's Ossabaw Night in Savannah on January 14, 2025.

Beryl: Ossabaw Island has played a monumental role in my life since my first visit at six months old, so this project holds great personal significance for me. My late grandmother, Sandy West, taught me about so many things, from animals to philosophy to magic to individuality, all through the lens of her beloved island. My work on this project is dedicated to her legacy. Thanks are due to so many of my family members, friends, and colleagues for their ongoing support of this exhibition and publication. For their thoughtful advice and assistance, I want to thank Eric Booker, Vic Brooks, Jennifer Burris, Susan Braeuer Dam, Elisa Eriksen, Austin Fenn, Parker Field, Jessica Holmes, Uchenna Itam, Karen Karp, Susan Laney, Melissa Lotery, Lily Lyons, Park McArthur, Serubiri Moses, Antonia Oliver, Andrea Schwan, and especially Thomas Lax, who pushed me to take my early ideas for this project seriously. A special thank you to Alexander S. C. Rower for offering me a master class in stewarding a family legacy over the last ten years. I am grateful for my Ossabaw community in Savannah, especially Louisa Abbot, Carmela Aliffi, Sherrie and Bobbie Black, Betsy Cain, Elizabeth DuBose, Emily Earl, Leigh Goff, Robin Gunn, Helen Hamada, Alan and Peggy Usher, Lisa White, and Jon Witzky. Thank you to my longtime friends Eve Andrews, Alejandro Calcaño, Riddhi Cidambi, Emily Hanno, Sarah Morrison, and Kento Spanos for their support. Many thanks to my family, especially my parents, Copper Giloth, John Dubach, and Eileen McGowan, as well as Emma Giloth, Christopher Hillbruner, Elizabeth Hillbruner, Torrey Kingry, Katherine Orellano, Bente Torjusen West, Anna West, and my late grandfather, Clifford West. I couldn't have done this project without the support of Kaitlyn A. Kramer, whose editorial (and life) advice is second to none, and Hannah La Follette Ryan, whose sharp eye and brilliant insights keep me on my toes. Finally, I am eternally grateful to my father, Justin West, for the endless wisdom, knowledge, advice, and love that he has bestowed on me throughout the process of working on this project and across a lifetime of shared experiences in the universe of Ossabaw. His knowledge and understanding of the island know no bounds.

Erin: Although I grew up in the Northwest Georgia mountains, I have lived in Savannah for over a decade, and this project has offered tangible and lasting connections to this place and landscape that I now call home. I owe gratitude to Courtney McNeil and Jessica Estes, who guided my career at Telfair Museums, and to Rachel Waldrop, whose mentorship and curatorial curiosity have long inspired me. This project has allowed me to dive deeper into the community I love, and I am grateful to many people here, but I will name a few particularly encouraging voices: Betsy Cain, Emily Earl, Susan Laney, Anna Robertson, Parker Stewart, and Jon Witzky. I am deeply grateful to my parents, David and Melanie Dunn, for their tireless support. And to my husband Ben Walke, with love.

We want to respectfully acknowledge the Guale, Muscogee, and other Indigenous peoples who have stewarded Ossabaw Island throughout the generations. We also acknowledge the descendants of enslaved West and Central Africans, whose forced labor transformed the landscape, and the Gullah Geechee people, whose communities still dwell along the coast. We honor the past and ongoing work to uncover and share the histories of Ossabaw to raise awareness of what has been given and taken.

Erin Dunn
Curator of Modern and Contemporary Art

Beryl Gilothwest
Guest Curator

CONTRIBUTORS

AL BRADFORD

Al Bradford grew up in Columbia, South Carolina, and graduated from Antioch College (BA in philosophy with minors in physics and music). Before coming to Ossabaw as an OIP member in 1974, Al was a newspaper reporter and civil rights worker, an assistant teacher to first-graders, a staff member at two museums, a professional musician, a music appreciation teacher, a Peace Corps Volunteer in the Philippines, a counselor at the national Peace Corps office, a community development worker, and a science writer. After his time at the OIP, Al was a Genesis member and sometimes director from 1974–1977 and co-director of the OIP from 1978–1982. Since leaving Ossabaw, Al has been a cartographer near Yosemite National Park, a waiter, a freelance writer, and a manuscript editor for *Academic Medicine*, a peer-reviewed journal in Washington, DC, near his present home in Silver Spring, Maryland.

HENRI COLE

Henri Cole was born in Fukuoka, Japan, and raised in Virginia. He has published many collections of poetry and received numerous awards for his work, including the Jackson Poetry Prize, the Kingsley Tufts Award, the Rome Prize, the Berlin Prize, the Ambassador Book Award, the Lenore Marshall Award, and the Medal in Poetry from the American Academy of Arts and Letters. His most recent books are *Orphic Paris*, a memoir (New York Review Books), *Gravity and Center: Selected Sonnets, 1994–2022* (Farrar, Straus and Giroux), and *The Other Love* (Farrar, Straus and Giroux). From 2010 to 2014, he was poetry editor of *The New Republic*. He teaches at Claremont McKenna College and lives in Boston.

ERIN DUNN

Erin Dunn is Curator of Modern and Contemporary Art at Telfair Museums in Savannah, Georgia, where she has been a member of the curatorial team since 2014. She has organized numerous exhibitions, including *Watershed: Contemporary Landscape Photography*, *Feels like Freedom: Phillip J. Hampton*, and *Frank Stewart's Nexus: An American Photographer's Journey, 1960s to the Present* in collaboration with The Phillips Collection, Washington, DC. Her writing has appeared in the exhibition catalogue for *Phillip J. Hampton, Late Night Polaroids: Photographs by Emily Earl*, and *Seven Rivers*, a monograph of photographer Ansley West Rivers. In addition, Dunn spearheads Telfair's #art912 initiative, which raises the visibility and promotes the vitality of artists living and working in Savannah. Dunn was the recipient of the Fall 2023 Margie E. West Distinguished Alumni Award from the University of Georgia's Lamar Dodd School of Art. She holds a BA from Emory University and an MA from the University of Georgia.

BERYL GILOTHWEST

Beryl Gilothwest is a curator and art historian based in New York. He is the grandson of Ossabaw Island Project and Genesis co-founders Clifford and Eleanor West, and he recently completed two terms on The Ossabaw Island Foundation's Board of Trustees. He is the Deputy Director of Research and Exhibitions at the Calder Foundation, which is dedicated to collecting, exhibiting, preserving, and interpreting the art and archives of Alexander Calder. He has collaborated with institutions all over the world on exhibitions of Calder's work, including The Museum of Modern Art, New York; Neue Nationalgalerie, Berlin; Musée national Picasso-Paris; The Museum of Fine Arts, Houston; and the Whitney Museum of American Art, New York, among many others. As a writer, he has contributed to exhibition catalogues and publications, including *Apartamento*, *The Brooklyn Rail*, *Art in America*, and *Degree Critical*. He holds a BA from Vassar College and is currently completing an MA at Hunter College, The City University of New York.

VAUGHNETTE GOODE-WALKER

Vaughnette Goode-Walker is Director of the Ralph Mark Gilbert Civil Rights Museum in Savannah, Georgia. Branding herself as a "historian who gives tours," she established the Footprints of Savannah Walking Tour Company in 2009 to educate visitors and local residents about the rich and diverse history of Savannah. Goode-Walker worked as a broadcast journalist in New York for ABC Radio and Television Networks and in Atlanta for CNN Radio and CNN International as a newswriter. She began her museum career at Telfair Museums and later worked at the King-Tisdell Cottage Foundation. Goode-Walker grew up in Savannah and graduated from St. Vincent's Academy, where she later taught history and now serves on the board. She holds a BA from Morris Brown College in Atlanta and an MA in history from Georgia Southern University.

THOMAS LAX

Thomas Lax is Curator of Media and Performance at The Museum of Modern Art, New York. They co-organized the exhibition *Just Above Midtown: Changing Spaces* (2022) with Lilia Rocio Taboada in collaboration with JAM's founder Linda Goode Bryant. They worked with colleagues across MoMA on a major rehang of its collection (2019) and co-organized the exhibition *Judson Dance Theater: The Work is Never Done* (2018) with Ana Janevski and Martha Joseph. Their other collaboratively-organized exhibitions include the Projects Series for emerging artists with Lanka Tattersall; *Unfinished Conversations*, inspired by the cultural theorist Stuart Hall; the contemporary art quinquennial, *Greater New York*; and commissions with artists including Neïl Beloufa, Maria Hassabi, and Steffani Jemison. Previously, they worked at the Studio Museum in Harlem for seven years, where they organized *When the Stars Begin to Fall: Imagination and the American South* and participated in the landmark "f show" contemporary art series.

MEGAN MAYHEW BERGMAN

Megan Mayhew Bergman is a fiction writer, filmmaker, and climate journalist. She is the author of three books, and her work has been featured in *The New Yorker*, *The New York Times*, *The Guardian*, *The Paris Review*, and *The Atlantic*. Megan is the Director of Creative Writing at Middlebury College and the Bread Loaf Environmental Writers' Conference. She serves on the boards of Hildene, the Conservation Law Foundation, and the Thoreau Prize, and has been a fellow at the American Library in Paris. Megan grew up in North Carolina and has worked closely with the coastal nonprofit organization 100 Miles over the last decade, spending significant time on the Georgia coast and falling in love with its islands and shorebirds. She is working on a documentary about Sandy West and Ossabaw.

JUSTIN WEST

Justin West was born on December 7, 1953, in Detroit, Michigan, to Eleanor and Clifford West, the co-founders of the Ossabaw Island Project and Genesis. He studied art at two experimental colleges and later received his MFA in media from the University of Massachusetts at Amherst. He taught for 30 years at the college level, founding the Electronic Media Program at Holyoke Community College in Massachusetts, where he is Professor Emeritus. West spent his childhood roaming Ossabaw and interacting with the members of both the OIP and Genesis: "What I learned in school was framed and often overshadowed by what I learned from the island and from the people who lived there. To a large extent, that is what has informed my teaching and professional work." West has produced several documentaries, including *Five Dimensions of Light* (2015), on the many ways we conceive of light, and *Robert Mallary: Pioneer in Computer Art* (1993), as well as several experimental works.

WINI WOOD

Wini Wood grew up in Illinois amongst fields of corn, transplanted herself to the Ossabaw Island marshes in 1980, and since 1982 has worked toward becoming a New Englander. She visited Ossabaw three times as a Genesis member, always in January (between semesters). On her third visit, she told then co-director Michael Billa that if ever a job as co-director came up, she'd like to be considered. Three months later, a letter arrived ("come on down"). She was working on her doctoral dissertation in linguistics at the time. Ossabaw took over until Genesis sadly closed its doors two years later. Wini taught at Wellesley College until her retirement in 2018, directing the Writing Program and later co-directing the Cinema and Media Studies Program. In 1994, she completed her doctorate at the University of Massachusetts at Amherst in Rhetoric and Composition, which focused on the rhetoric of electronic discourse.

This catalogue is published on the occasion of the exhibition *Off the Coast of Paradise: Artists and Ossabaw Island, 1961–Now*, organized by Telfair Museums and curated by Erin Dunn, Curator of Modern and Contemporary Art and Beryl Gilothwest, Guest Curator.

Telfair Museums' Jepson Center
March 13–September 6, 2026

Lead exhibition and catalogue support is provided by the Frances and Beverly DuBose Foundation, the Teiger Foundation, and the Henry Luce Foundation.

ISBN: 978-0-933075-25-2

Library of Congress Control Number:
2025907718

Editors:
Erin Dunn and Beryl Gilothwest

Design:
Adam Squires and Jasmine Kan, CHIPS

Production Manager:
Marc Sapir

Copyeditor:
Jessica Holmes

Printed by:
Brizzolis, SA, Madrid

Typefaces:
Hobeaux, ITC Souvenir Mono,
Times New Roman Seven

Paper:
Gardapat Kiara 135gsm
Fedrigoni Tintoretto Ceylon Wasabi 140 gsm

Printed in Spain

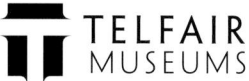

Telfair Museums
PO Box 10081
Savannah, GA 31412
telfair.org

ARTWORKS

IMAGE CREDITS